FOUNDATIONS IN BECOMING A PROFESSIONAL COUNSELOR

Ana Puig, PhD, LMHC-S, NCC, is a scholar and research director in the Office of Educational Research, College of Education at the University of Florida (UF) and affiliate faculty in the School of Human Development and Organizational Studies in Education, Counselor Education unit. Dr. Puig is a licensed mental health counselor and qualified supervisor in the state of Florida and a National Certified Counselor. She also holds a Spirituality and Health certificate from the Center for Spirituality and Health at UF. Her areas of specialization are multicultural spirituality and religion in counseling; complementary therapies and mental health; creativity in counseling and supervision; and group work. She has engaged in international research and education for over 16 years, predominantly focused on the Asia-Pacific region and in her native island of Puerto Rico. More recently, Dr. Puig has conducted research on impacts of hurricanes Maria and Irma on stakeholders in the K-20 school system in Puerto Rico. She has also led research on Streetlight at UF Health, a palliative care program providing psychosocial support to adolescents and young adults with chronic and terminal conditions. Dr. Puig is the author of over 40 articles, 8 chapters, and 65 invited or refereed presentations at the local, regional, national, and international levels. This is her second book. Dr. Puig is a fellow of the American Counseling Association.

Jacqueline M. Swank, PhD, LMHC, LCSW, RPT-S, is an associate teaching professor in mental health practices at the University of Missouri. She was formerly an associate professor of counselor education at the University of Florida. She has extensive experience working with children and adolescents and their families in various counseling settings, including outpatient, schools, day treatment, inpatient, and residential treatment facilities, and has worked clinically in both the United States and England. Her research interests focus on holistic growth and development of children and adolescents, counselor competency, assessment, nature and play-based interventions, and international counseling.

Dr. Swank is the author of over 80 articles and 16 book chapters, and this is her second book. She has been recognized for her scholarly work, receiving nine awards for specific research projects from professional organizations, including the American Counseling Association, Association for Assessment and Research in Counseling, Association for Counselor Education and Supervision, Association for Adult Development and Aging, American Horticultural Therapy Association, and Chi Sigma Iota. She has also received a University of Florida University Term Professorship. Furthermore, she has received nearly $1.2 million in federal funding.

She has a strong commitment to service, which has included serving as president of two national counseling organizations: the Association for Assessment and Research in Counseling and the Association for Creativity in Counseling. She has also served in several other leadership capacities at the local, state, and national levels. She was recognized for her service and contributions to the field of creativity in counseling in receiving the Association for Creativity in Counseling Professional Service Award and the Samuel T. Gladding Inspiration and Motivation Award, her contribution to the field of play therapy in receiving the Viola Brody Award, and her contribution to assessment and research in receiving the Association for Assessment and Research in Counseling Professional Level Exemplary Practice Award. She has a passion for international work, and has trained teachers and church leaders in using helping skills in Haiti. She enjoys teaching and mentoring students and has been recognized for her teaching in receiving the Diane E. Haines Teaching Excellence Award at the University of Florida.

Latoya Haynes-Thoby, PhD, LPC, NCC, CCTP, is an assistant professor of Counselor Education at the University of Connecticut. Her work explores the benefits of trauma prevention and trauma-responsive counseling that is culturally relevant and promotes resilience. As such, her research focuses on individual and community healing from trauma. Dr. Haynes-Thoby aims to broaden what we understand about human resilience, thriving, and well-being, especially related to the experiences of marginalized communities.

Derrick A. Paladino, PhD, LMHC, NCC, is a professor and department chair in the Department of Graduate Studies in Counseling at Rollins College in Winter Park, Florida. He also serves as a part-time counselor at Rollins College Counseling and Psychological Services. His clinical and scholarship interests fall within the areas of multiracial identity, college counseling and student development, and crisis assessment and intervention. He is the coauthor of the books *Counseling Multiple Heritage Individuals, Couples and Families* and *College Counseling and Student Development: Theory, Practice, and Campus Collaboration.*

FOUNDATIONS IN BECOMING A PROFESSIONAL COUNSELOR

Advocacy, Social Justice, and Intersectionality

Ana Puig, PhD, LMHC-S, NCC
Jacqueline M. Swank, PhD, LMHC, LCSW, RPT-S
Latoya Haynes-Thoby, PhD, LPC, NCC, CCTP
Derrick A. Paladino, PhD, LMHC, NCC

 SPRINGER PUBLISHING

Springer Publishing Company, LLC
11 West 42nd Street, New York, NY 10036
www.springerpub.com
connect.springerpub.com

Acquisitions Editor: Rhonda Dearborn
Compositor: Exeter Premedia Services Private Ltd.

ISBN: 978-0-8261-6385-1
ebook ISBN: 978-0-8261-6386-8
DOI: 10.1891/9780826163868

SUPPLEMENTS:

 A robust set of instructor resources designed to supplement this text is located at http://connect.springerpub.com/content/book/978-0-8261-6386-8. Qualifying instructors may request access by emailing **textbook@springerpub.com.**

Instructor's Manual ISBN: 978-0-8261-6387-5
Instructor's Test Bank ISBN: 978-0-8261-6388-2
Instructor's PowerPoints ISBN: 978-0-8261-6389-9
Podcasts ISBN: 978-0-8261-6393-6
Chapter podcasts may be accessed at http://connect.springerpub.com/content/book/978-0-8261-6386-8

22 23 24 25 / 5 4 3 2 1

Library of Congress Cataloging-in-Publication Data

Names: Puig, Ana, author. | Swank, Jacqueline M., author. | Haynes-Thoby,
  Latoya, author. | Paladino, Derrick A., author.
Title: Foundations in becoming a professional counselor : advocacy, social
  justice, and intersectionality / Ana Puig, PhD, LMHC-S, NCC, Jacqueline
  M. Swank, PhD, LMHC, LCSW, RPT-S, Latoya Haynes-Thoby, PhD, LPC, NCC,
  CCTP, Derrick A. Paladino, PhD, LMHC, NCC.
Description: New York, NY : Springer Publishing, [2023] | Includes
  bibliographical references and index.
Identifiers: LCCN 2022029017 (print) | LCCN 2022029018 (ebook) | ISBN
  9780826163851 (paperback) | ISBN 9780826163868 (ebook)
Subjects: LCSH: Counseling--Study and teaching (Graduate)--United States. |
  Counseling psychology--Study and teaching (Graduate)--United States. |
  Counselors--Training of--United States. | College teaching--United
  States. | Universities and colleges--United States--Graduate work.
Classification: LCC BF636.65 .P85 2023 (print) | LCC BF636.65 (ebook) |
  DDC 158.3071--dc23/eng/20220811
LC record available at https://lccn.loc.gov/2022029017
LC ebook record available at https://lccn.loc.gov/2022029018

Contact sales@springerpub.com to receive discount rates on bulk purchases.

Printed in the United States of America by Gasch Printing.

To future counselors who dedicate their careers to helping others and serve as advocates and seekers of social justice for their clients, the counseling profession, and themselves.

To our students, mentors, and colleagues who continuously teach us and challenge us to grow.

To our family and friends who provided ongoing encouragement and support during the process of writing this book while navigating the COVID-19 pandemic.

To G-d, however known, because now more than ever, we need to renew our faith in the collective Spirit of humanity that lives within each of us.

Contents

List of Podcast Contributors

Organized here by chapter, the Video Podcasts are available to support readers. Each chapter includes a podcast that helps place the chapter content into perspective and provides practitioner perspective and real-world application. Readers would benefit from listening to the podcast after reading each chapter. All podcasts are hosted by Ana Puig and can be accessed at http://connect.springerpub.com/content/book/978-0-8261-6386-8.

Chapter 1. The Counseling Profession, Advocacy, and Social Justice
Podcast Video 1. Counselor Identity Formation: A Call to Advocacy and Social Justice
Guest: Dr. Edil Torres-Rivera, American Counseling Association President Elect (2022–2023)

Chapter 2. Multiculturalism, Intersectionality, and Diversity in Counseling
Podcast Video 2. Applying the Multicultural and Social Justice Counseling Competencies
Guest: Dr. Kok-Mun Ng, Professor of Counseling

Chapter 3. Professional Counselor Identity
Podcast Video 3. Developing a Professional Counselor Identity
Guest: Dr. Kimberly Hart, Clinical Assistant Professor of Counseling

Chapter 4. Ethical and Legal Standards in Counseling
Podcast Video 4. Laws and Ethics in the Counseling Profession
Guest: Dr. Michael Kocet, Professor of Counseling

Chapter 5. Counseling Skills, Process, and Modalities
Podcast Video 5. Best Practices of Multicultural and Social Justice Counseling Competencies
Guest: Dr. Isaac Burt, Associate Professor of Counseling

Chapter 6. Orientations to Counseling and Theoretical Frameworks
Podcast Video 6. Relational Cultural Theory and Liberation Psychology Practice
Guest: Lucas Cole De Monte, Doctoral Student

FOREWORD

Becoming a counselor was one of the most transformative experiences in my life. It was the summer of 2000 that I began my master's program, and I was full of excitement, nervousness, hope, and determination. I learned new ways of communicating, especially the difference between listening to someone versus making them feel *heard*. I learned about the power of group work and how humans have sat in circles throughout all time and across all the continents in order to place both challenges and opportunities to heal right in the middle of the circle for connection and resolution. I learned about different approaches to counseling and theories of conceptualizing the presenting issues that clients bring to us. I learned about research methods and assessment. Every day was different and full of new learning whether I was in classes, working on projects with peers, sitting with my professors and practitioners, or spending late nights consuming everything I could about my new academic and professional "home" of counseling.

Except, as I look back on my earliest training as a counselor, I realize that—yes—I was learning new material and building the awareness, knowledge, and skills that would be the base of my counseling foundation—but I also remember some of the hardest moments in my classes where my transformation was about advocating for our professors to include more multicultural and social justice content across our classes. I remember how hard it was, as a queer and genderqueer femme person, to ask our faculty to bring in more 2SLGBTQ+ content. I remember how, as BIPOC (Black, Indigenous, people of color) students, we all would frequently have the "meeting" after our classes to process racial and other microaggressions that occurred or to plan the next email we were going to send to our faculty asking for more integration of multiculturalism, advocacy, and social justice across our courses. I remember how we banded together as students to start a yearly "Day of Learning" conference highlighting 2SLGBTQ+ and intersectional issues with presenters who ranged from faculty to 2SLGBTQ+ community organizers to clergy.

As I read the authors' new book, *Foundations in Becoming a Professional Counselor: Advocacy, Social Justice, and Intersectionality*, I was flooded with both these memories I shared above and realizations that this book you are holding in your hands or reading on your e-device is a marker of a transformation in our counseling profession. The authors have given you a gift with this book, one that centralizes intersectionality, advocacy, and social justice not as just one part of counseling, but as the entire point of our profession. As you move through the chapters, the foundation you receive will be remarkably different from the one that I received so many years ago where multiculturalism and social justice were things that *sometimes* got integrated into foundational training but were more often relegated to one multicultural class.

From the beginning of your learning how to be a counselor, the authors invite you to look at your own social identities and experiences of intersectional privilege and oppression in order to build your skills in being able to truly serve *all* of whom your clients are in terms of their own identities and experiences. With this ground underneath you, then you will learn the importance of professional identity, ethics, counseling approaches, theories, settings, research, and diagnosis and assessment. Latter chapters explore crisis and trauma counseling, as well as creativity and complementary and alternative approaches to counseling. These chapters truly make this textbook an innovative one, as you would typically first encounter these topics in a separate elective course.

So, I have to say that as I read the authors' book, not only was I able to remember those transformative experiences I had as a counselor, but I was also able to feel excitement about how *you*, the counselor-in-training, will have the solid multicultural and social justice ground underneath you as you embark on your counseling journey. I also want to share that I have been able to work with Dr. Ana Puig through our professional associations on various advocacy projects that sought to counter hate and increase empowerment, resilience, and thriving for communities. She is an absolute gem and the "real deal" when it comes to living authentically as a counselor–social change agent. I hope that you relish each sentence in this text and use this book as a springboard for dream building a world where racial justice and intersectional empowerment is the guiding light for our practice and our field.

In the spirit of community, solidarity, and liberation,

Anneliese Singh, PhD, LPC
Tulane University
Trans Resilience Project
Project AFFIRM
June 2, 2022

Preface

As counselor educators, we have taught classes in introduction to counseling, counseling theories, and multicultural counseling, among others. It always struck me that my students had to wait until the multicultural counseling class to learn about the principles of diversity, inclusion, social justice, and intersectionality. I wondered why the wait to broach these topics and not instill in emerging counselors a sense of duty and responsibility to embrace social justice and advocacy from the very beginning of their counselor education journey. Right before the COVID pandemic took hold of the world, I connected with Rhonda Dearborn at Springer and after several conversations this book idea found a home. My dear colleagues and friends, Jacqueline Swank, Latoya Haynes-Thoby, and Derrick Paladino, joined me. This book is an attempt to bring our vision to life in counselor education classrooms. Our hope is that students will be exposed and challenged to stretch themselves and lean into the sometimes difficult work of reckoning with the historical and deeply personal traumas of disenfranchised and marginalized peoples in our country and the world. The unpacking of privilege and at times accompanying complicit silence needs to be centered in counselor education. It is widely known that by the year 2040, the United States will be a majority minority country. Our students need to be ready to serve clients of diverse cultures and worldviews, spiritualities and religions, races, ethnicities, sexual and affectional orientations, and the various gender identities in a world that continues to evolve, change, and become ever connected in ways we could not have imagined.

Eldridge Cleaver is thought to have said: *"There is no more neutrality in the world. You either have to be part of the solution, or you're going to be part of the problem."* We wholeheartedly believe that all counselors and counselor educators of the world can and should be part of the solution. Our book is a small contribution to that end.

WHY THIS TEXTBOOK?

Our textbook approaches introductory counseling with an emphasis on advocacy, social justice, and intersectionality. We center the Multicultural and Social Justice Counseling Competencies (Ratts et al., 2015) as foundational to counselor training. We engage the student in exploration of the individual and collective impact of local, national, and global social issues on clients and the communities they inhabit. We provide a more robust social and cultural perspective on various issues salient to the profession than is typically found in many other textbooks. There are existing social justice and advocacy issues that have prevailed across generations and through historical changes in our society and the world. These will be introduced and discussed to further enhance student learning and contextualize the role of the counselor as advocate. This textbook will help students develop their sense of identity as advocates and seekers of social justice in the counseling profession.

WHAT WE OFFER

This textbook has key features to assist instructors to teach foundational material and help students to engage in reflection and dialogue about critical issues in counselor development. Noteworthy is our infusion of intersectionality, social justice, and advocacy for the client and the profession. We also stress the development of a professional counselor identity through self-actualization, reflection, and analysis activities that are engaging, innovative, and inherently challenging to counseling students. We begin every chapter with a reflection exercise, "Think About This," to prime students to think about the chapter content as it relates to their future as a counselor and to develop their own counselor identity. Goals and objectives are outlined at the start of chapters and set students up to achieve a set of outcomes. The latest Council for Accreditation of Counseling and Related Educational Programs (CACREP) Standards are mapped to each chapter to assist with accreditation requirements. In order to bring counseling to life for novice students, we feature "Voices From the Field" in every chapter. These reflective essays from seasoned experts and practitioners illuminate aspects of chapter concepts for the students. Underscoring our focus on social justice and advocacy, "A Call to Action" prompts, germane in each chapter, provide activities students can engage in to put learning into action that will help form their professional identity. "Case Studies" provide a vignette of a situation that will elicit critical thinking about the specific client issues/concerns relevant to the chapter content. All of these features can be used to prompt classroom discussions and invite critical thinking about real-life issues and concerns that clients may bring to the session. We developed a "Going Within" feature to provide reflection and practice exercises for students to explore their learning insights and challenges that they may be experiencing. The "Group Process" feature provides group prompts and process activities for students to share their "Going Within" reflections or to engage in small group discussions about the chapter topics.

Resources at the end of every chapter will invite further exploration of chapter topics outside the classroom. This text will be one of the first to map to the newest CACREP standards and offers a full suite of instructor ancillaries including an instructor manual, a test bank, PowerPoint slides, interviews, and syllabi for quarter- and semester-based programs.

In the conceptualization and development of this textbook, we approached the content intentionally and with an eye toward liberatory approaches and frameworks. Our aim was to integrate advocacy, social justice, and intersectionality wherever relevant and illuminate the ways in which beginning counselors can embrace the principles of emancipatory communitarianism (Prilleltensky, 1997) in the course of learning about the theoretical and practical foundations of counseling. In Chapter 1, The Counseling Profession, Intersectionality, Advocacy, and Social Justice, we introduce the student to the counseling profession and how it is different from the other helping professions. The chapter provides a guiding framework for social justice–focused counseling practice. We outline the history of the counseling profession's movement toward advocacy and social justice and discuss the new competencies that various professional organizations have developed to help guide ethical and transformational counseling practice. Students learn about the multicultural social justice counseling competencies and explore and unpack formative experiences that might influence their approach to counseling. After setting the stage for this unique focus, Chapter 2, Multiculturalism, Intersectionality, and Diversity in Counseling, highlights the topics of multiculturalism, intersectionality, and diversity. Here, we place special emphasis on student self-assessment of their own intersectional identities and facilitate student understanding of the ways in which these identities inform advocacy and social justice within the context of competent counseling practice. We invite deep reflection and exploration of issues central to counselor identity development. We also provide an overview of theories of racial and ethnic identity development, LGBTQ+ development, and marginalized populations to integrate our focus on otherness and the troubling of privileged identities in the context of counseling individuals from disadvantaged groups. Next, we discuss counselor professional identity development. In Chapter 3, Professional Counselor Identity, we address the developmental stages of counselor formation and growth, and provide an overview of common growing edges of beginning counselors (personal and interpersonal challenges), attend to a well-known occupational hazard (burnout and vicarious trauma) and how to prevent it, and introduce ways in which counselors can secure professional development and support (supervision and consultation). The concepts of wellness and self-care close this chapter. In Chapter 4, Ethical and Legal Standards in Counseling, we discuss the ethical standards that govern the practice of counseling and common ethical and legal dilemmas that counselors in practice contend with. CACREP and American Counseling Association (ACA) Standards are outlined and we end with the history and present state of accreditation bodies and licensure/certification across the United States.

The next two chapters delve into specific skills and theoretical frameworks that beginning counselors must learn in order to engage in multiculturally competent practice. In Chapter 5, Counseling Skills, Process, and Modalities, we introduce counseling microskills and techniques, the process of counseling, and various counseling modalities. The best evidence-based practices for each are reviewed in the context of advocacy, social justice, and intersectionality. The next chapter attends to the most commonly known counseling theories that guide counseling practice. Chapter 6, Orientations to Counseling and Theoretical Frameworks, provides a survey of counseling theories and how they are understood through the lens of social justice, advocacy, and intersectionality, a unique feature of this textbook. After introducing the framework of emancipatory communitarianism (EC) in Chapter 1, we propose its use as a lens to evaluate how all of the known theories of counseling and human development can be understood to highlight intrapsychic (individualistic) versus communitarian (collectivistic) values. We then move into exploring the various contexts whence we can counsel and provide client care. Chapter 7, An Introduction to Counseling Settings, reviews the types of counseling settings that counselors can practice in and the various populations and issues inherent in these contexts. Aspects of all previous chapters were integrated via practical exercises students can engage in, through "Going Within" and/or "Group Process" prompts. Social justice, intersectional, and advocacy considerations are also addressed.

Another important aspect of client care is the assessment and diagnosis of client presentations and the effective use of evidence-based (proved by research) practices. In Chapter 8, Research, Assessment, and Diagnosis in Counseling, we provide historical and contextual understanding of the way counselors have approached clients and determined appropriate courses of action. The problematic application of psychiatric diagnoses of clients from marginalized groups is explored. Practical aspects of service provision are discussed (e.g., selection of treatments, length and types of treatment, and the role of insurance companies). Importantly, the decolonization of the assessment, diagnosis, and research process is also addressed.

In Chapter 9, Substance-Related Disorders, Behavioral Addictions, and Counseling, we address the common models and approaches associated with substance use disorders and behavioral addiction treatment. Special emphasis is given to the historical social waves of various drug use and abuse epidemics and the most recent opioid addiction public health crisis in the United States. The political backdrop associated with these social problems is also addressed in the context of counselor advocacy, intersectionality, and social justice. A unique feature of our text is the in-depth exploration of crisis and trauma as distinct experiences clients bring into the session. In Chapter 10, Crisis Counseling, we cover basic crisis assessment and intervention skills, theories, populations, and types of crises. Current social and political issues influencing these situations are addressed therein. Next, in Chapter 11, Trauma Counseling, we highlight holistic impacts of traumatic events, human-made and natural, affecting individuals and communities nationally and globally. Trauma-informed care practices are discussed within these various contexts and populations, and current social and political issues influencing these situations are addressed.

The last three chapters of our text highlight counseling practices that have rapidly grown and continue to develop, providing counselors with unique and expansive approaches to client care. Chapter 12, Creativity in Counseling, covers the increasingly popular creative approaches in individual and group counseling. We discuss and provide in-depth examples and resources about specialized trainings, interventions, and techniques students can explore and consider adopting in their counseling practice with a variety of client populations. Next, in Chapter 13, Complementary and Alternative Approaches to Counseling, we attend to complementary and alternative therapies that can be used in individual and group counseling. Specialized trainings, interventions, and techniques are discussed. Finally, in Chapter 14, Current Trends in Counseling and the Future of Counseling, we provide an overview of emerging trends in the profession and potential impacts for the growth, development, and evolution of counseling and counselor education and how counseling will continue to be impacted by intersectionality, pursuit of social justice, and advocacy of clients.

In sum, *Foundations in Becoming a Professional Counselor: Advocacy, Social Justice, and Intersectionality* is an integrative and holistic textbook that introduces counseling students to the profession by centering the principles of advocacy, social justice, and intersectionality. The community psychology concept of emancipatory communitarianism serves as a lens for students to do a deep dive into the various foundational aspects of the formative mental health counselor journey. Our hope is that this introductory text will be beneficial to emerging counselors in their effort to become multiculturally competent and culturally humble learners and counseling practitioners.

Ana Puig
Jacqueline M. Swank
Latoya Haynes-Thoby
Derrick A. Paladino

REFERENCES

Prilleltensky, I. (1997). Values, assumptions, and practices: Assessing the moral implications of psychological discourse and action. *American Psychologist, 52*(5), 517–535. http://doi.org/10.1037/0003-066X.52.5.517.

Ratts, M. J., Singh, A. A., Nassar-McMillan, S., Butler, S. K., & McCullough, J. R. (2016). Multicultural and social justice counseling competencies: Guidelines for the counseling profession. *Journal of Multicultural Counseling and Development, 44*(1), 28–48. https://doi.org/10.1002/jmcd.12035

Acknowledgments

We acknowledge and honor our Black, Brown, Indigenous, LGBTQ+, immigrant, and refugee clients, counselors, and fellow humans and their multiple intersecting identities. We recognize the centuries of colonization, oppression, discrimination, disenfranchisement, marginalization, and erasure that you have endured. We affirm your right to be seen, heard, uplifted, and supported by all of us. You deserve to be free and to thrive and become the best version of yourself you have ever dreamed of. We value your strength, your beauty, and your contributions to humankind. Thank you for all that you are, all that you do, and all that you give, against all odds.

This textbook represents our commitment to engaging the process of decolonization of counseling pedagogy and practice.

INSTRUCTOR
RESOURCES

A robust set of resources designed to supplement this text is available. Qualifying instructors may request access by emailing textbook@springerpub.com.

Available resources include:

- Instructor's Manual
  - o Mapping of CACREP Standards by Chapter
  - o Exercises
  - o Additional Resources
  - o Example Syllabus
- Test Bank
- Chapter-Based PowerPoint Presentations
- Podcasts: Each chapter includes an in-depth interview that helps place the chapter content into perspective and provides practitioner perspective and real-world application.

CHAPTER 1

THE COUNSELING PROFESSION, ADVOCACY, SOCIAL JUSTICE, AND INTERSECTIONALITY

Ana Puig and Jacqueline M. Swank

Think about this...

When did you first think about professional counseling as a career path? What life events, experiences, or memories do you bring that inform your worldview and how you envision approaching your clients? What aspects of your personhood and identities might be helpful for you? What aspects might get in the way? How do you intend to take care of yourself as you navigate this journey of counselor education and practice?

LEARNING OBJECTIVES

After reading this chapter, you should be able to:

- Define the concepts of advocacy, social justice, intersectionality, emancipatory communitarianism, and multiculturalism and how they inform counseling practice
- Outline the historical and current trends that helped shape the counseling profession
- Demonstrate the principles of trauma-informed care in counseling
- Outline the stages of group work and its use as a therapeutic practice
- Identify counseling competencies and techniques and their applications in holistic and intentional ways during individual and group sessions
- Explain and unpack formative experiences that might influence your approach to counseling

INTRODUCTION

Ana's Story

This book was born of the lived experiences of the authors as counselors and counselor educators and a desire to introduce counseling students to the principles of advocacy, social justice, and intersectionality early in their counseling journey. *That means you!* The first author chose counseling as a career over a cup of coffee in her mother's kitchen. She grew up with the awareness that her mom provided couples' counseling to every married dyad filing for divorce in their small town's courthouse in Utuado, Puerto Rico. In her own words...

My mom is a social worker by training. I had no idea how she was able to do her therapeutic work in a township so small that some of the people she counseled attended the same social functions as my parents did. To this day, I think of her as "the vault." She navigated boundaries with great care; everyone trusted her. When I reflect upon this path, her light shines before me, a beacon leading the way. Unsure of my next steps after finishing a bachelor's degree in sociology, she planted the seed of this calling in my heart, on that day, at her kitchen table: "Have you ever thought about being a counselor...?" We invite you to reflect on the events that inspired you to undertake this journey, to enter this profession and become a counselor to people in need. What do you believe...?

I believe that counseling is a vocation. I think that counselors are first born, then made. We are inspired to be of service to others by providing psychological and emotional support. This desire is followed by pursuit of the necessary training to learn about theoretical frameworks, techniques, therapy modalities, and key ingredients that help people change and grow — the common factors of psychotherapy that create the fertile ground where seeds are planted and growth takes place. I see counseling as a profession of hope and equity, a labor of love, and commitment to justice. Professional counselors are advocates for individual and social change. Over the past 25 years as a professional counselor, 15 as a counselor educator, I have been very fortunate to experience human transformation very closely. This exposure to emotional and spiritual pain and growth left imprints I will not soon forget. It has always been my central wish to engage with other aspiring counselors and educators in the pursuit of individual, social, and global change. The notion of learning, researching, and exploring humanity is very exciting to me. Human beings, all of us, exhibit ideas, beliefs, and behaviors telling of our inner struggles. These manifestations of the spirit-self carry messages that when heeded can assist in our collective, personal, professional, and academic growth. Counseling and teaching are thresholds into new ways of thinking, feeling, and being. They are essential tools for healing the world and the people in it. I am proud to belong in the group of professionals helping to influence this process.

A good number of the students I have had the privilege of teaching and advising are members of disenfranchised, underrepresented minority groups. I feel honored to provide them with opportunities to learn, grow, and achieve in ways they never thought possible, perhaps because I see myself in them. My first year of college was memorable for its trials and tribulations. A stranger in a foreign land, I teetered on the edge of academic failure for what seemed like, back then, a very long time. Amid an alien culture, and what seemed initially as an incomprehensible language, I struggled to rise to the challenge and meet the goals before me, to hold on to the dream. As a 58-year-old Puerto Rican Jewish lesbian looking to enhance the quality of her own and others' lives, I am proud of my rich heritage, my spiritual life, and my sexuality. These intersections of identities color my vision of the world and its peoples. I believe we must approach counseling and education with keen awareness of how these intersections inform clients' positionality and the issues with which they wrestle. How we choose to live our lives, manifest our spirit, and relate to each other is critical to healthy functioning. The complexity, diversity, and uniqueness we all share cannot detract from our common humanity, that place of transcendence where skin color, gender, race, and sexuality meld and all we have left is the fire in the belly and our very own, still intangible, achievable dreams.

Counseling is the vehicle whereby individuals, families, and groups can learn to face their problems, embrace their shortcomings, and strive to overcome whatever challenges biology, family of origin, or dominant social structures have thrown at us. Effective counseling must be holistic, inclusive of the client's multiple identities, and aligned with each individual's value and belief systems. My goal as a counselor is to work myself out of a job. My job as a teacher is to guide my students to thrive, achieve their goals, and eventually become my colleagues. For having the opportunity to practice my work in these ways, I am forever grateful. We hope that the journey you are about to undertake in this course will help you to grow into the professional counselor you aspire to be. Let's get started!

HISTORY OF THE COUNSELING PROFESSION

The term *counseling* first appeared in writing in 1931; however, the origins of the counseling profession began much earlier (Leahy et al., 2016). Frank Parsons is the founder of the vocational guidance movement. He helped create principles and methods for providing vocational counseling, along with establishing the Vocation Bureau of Boston in 1908 that was dedicated to helping young people with the vocational decision-making process (Jones, 1994). Another early pioneer, Jesse Buttrick Davis, implemented the first systematic guidance program in a U.S. school; therefore, he is considered the first U.S. school counselor (Pope, 2009). A third counseling pioneer in the early 1900s was Clifford Whittingham Beers, who wrote *A Mind That Found Itself* in 1908 after being institutionalized from 1900 to 1903 and experiencing abuse while in the facility. Beers's book and advocacy work helped reduce stigma regarding mental illness and launch mental health reform, including the founding of the National Committee for Mental Hygiene in 1909 (Parry, 2010). The groundbreaking work related to vocational counseling led to the establishment of the National Vocational Guidance Association in 1913, which became the National Career Development Association in 1985, and the passage of the Smith-Hughes Act of 1917 that provided funding for vocational education in public schools. Other legislation passed in the early 1900s related to counseling included the Soldiers

Rehabilitation Act in 1918 that established vocational rehabilitation for veterans and the Smith-Fee Act in 1920 that required counseling for individuals with disabilities related to their service and assisted these individuals with obtaining employment. Furthermore, the first marriage and family counseling center was founded in New York City in 1929 (Leahy et al., 2016). In the 1930s, E. G. Williamson further advanced Parsons's work in the development of trait and factor theory, which is known as the first counseling theory (Neukrug, n.d.). Then, Carl Rogers published *Counseling and Psychotherapy* in 1942, which further contributed to the development of counseling, specifically humanistic counseling approaches (Leahy et al., 2016).

Legislation passed in the 1950s and 1960s advanced the counseling profession, including passage of the Vocational Rehabilitation Act Amendments of 1954 (fund college for rehabilitation counselors), National Defense Education Act of 1958 (fund schools to support students in science fields and to train counselors), and the Community Mental Health Centers Act of 1963 (fund counseling in community and health facilities) (Leahy et al., 2016). Additionally, in 1952, the American Personnel and Guidance Association was founded that became the American Association for Counseling and Development in 1983, and the American Counseling Association (ACA) in 1992, which is the largest counseling organization in the world (ACA, n.d). Accreditation standards for training programs also contributed to the advancement of the counseling profession, including the establishment of the Council on Rehabilitation Education (CORE) in 1972 that accredited rehabilitation counseling programs and the development of the Council for Accreditation of Counseling and Related Educational Programs (CACREP) in 1981 that accredited master's and doctoral level counselor education programs. CORE and CACREP merged in 2017, with CACREP also becoming responsible for accrediting rehabilitation counseling programs (CACREP, n.d). The credentialing of counselors that began with school counselor certification in the 1940s also contributed to the advancement of the counseling profession (Leahy et al., 2016). Virginia was the first state to license counselors in 1976 and California became the last state in 2009 (Shallcross, 2009).

From 2005 to 2013, the American Counseling Association and the American Association of State Counseling Boards sponsored the *20/20: A Vision for the Future of Counseling* initiative that involved 31 organizations. The goal of the initiative was to advance the counseling profession, which involved creating the *Principles for Unifying and Strengthening the Profession* (Kaplan & Gladding, 2011), and a consensus definition of counseling. The *Principles* included seven strategic areas for advancing the profession: (a) strengthening identity, (b) presenting ourselves as one profession, (c) improving public perception/recognition and advocating for professional issues, (d) creating licensure portability, (e) expanding and promoting the research base of professional counseling, (f) focusing on students and prospective students, and (g) promoting client welfare and advocacy (Kaplan & Gladding, 2011). The consensus definition is, "Professional counseling is a professional relationship that empowers diverse individuals, families, and groups to accomplish mental health, wellness, education, and career goals" (Kaplan et al., 2014, p. 366). Thus, the counseling profession has evolved, with a strong focus currently on unifying the profession to further advance and strengthen it. Table 1.1 provides an overview of the history of the counseling profession.

TABLE 1.1 HISTORY OF THE COUNSELING PROFESSION

1907: Jesse Buttrick Davis was the first school counselor in the United States
1908: Frank Parsons established the Vocation Bureau of Boston
1908: Cifford Whittingham Beers wrote *A Mind That Found Itself*
1909: National Committee for Mental Hygiene founded by Clifford W. Beers
1913: National Vocational Guidance Association established (renamed National Career Development Association in 1985)
1917: Smith-Hughes Act—funding for vocational education in public schools
1918: Soldiers Rehabilitation Act—vocational rehabilitation for veterans
1920: Smith Fee Act—provided counseling for individuals with disabilities related to service and assisted with employment
1929: First marriage and family counseling center in New York City
1931: Counseling used as a term in print
1930s: E. G. Williamson advanced Parsons's work to create Trait and Factory Theory, the first counseling theory
1942: Carl Rogers wrote *Counseling and Psychotherapy*, advancement of humanistic counseling approaches
1952: American Personnel and Guidance Association (later became the American Counseling Association)
1954: Vocational Rehabilitation Act Amendments—fund college for rehabilitation counselors
1958: National Defense Education Act—fund training for counselors
1963: Fund counseling in counseling and health facilities
1972: Council on Rehabilitation Education (CORE) established
1976: Virginia became the first state to license counselors
1981: Coucil for Accreditation of Counseling and Related Educational Programs (CACREP) established
2009: California becomes the last state to establish counselor licensure
2005–2013: 20/20: A Vision for the Future of Counseling initiative

Note: See citations for references in the section entitled History of the Counseling Profession in this chapter.

HOW COUNSELING DIFFERS FROM PSYCHOLOGY, PSYCHIATRY, AND SOCIAL WORK

The counseling, psychology, psychiatry, and social work professions have both similarities and differences. The major similarity between these professions is the focus on helping others. The psychiatry profession is the most different from the other three helping professions. Psychiatrists attend medical school, practice from a medical model, and prescribe medication to treat mental health diagnoses. Counselors, psychologists, and social workers may all provide counseling services, but their training, approach, specific services, and employment settings may differ. All three professions may have some similar courses in their academic training programs, but there are also differences in their training. Specifically, social workers practice at both the bachelor's level as case managers, and at the master's level as mental health clinicians, administrators, and in other positions. However, counselors must have at least a master's level degree, and psychologists typically have a doctoral degree.

All three professions have accreditation standards for training programs and licensure requirements, but these differ by profession. Regarding coursework and approaches, while clinicians in all three professions may administer and interpret tests and engage in the assessment process, a crucial component of clinical work, psychologists receive specialized training in administering, scoring, and interpreting specialized assessments (e.g., intelligence tests). Regarding approaches, counselors are typically trained in wellness, prevention, and developmental models, without a strong emphasis on the medical model. However, counselors receive training in mental health diagnosing and can work within a system that operates using a medical model. Additionally, counselor training typically focuses on the individual unit, while social workers are typically trained to have a broader perspective that focuses on systems and communities. Again, it is important to note that this does not mean that counselors cannot practice from a system perspective or work with systems, and that social workers cannot focus on the individual instead of a system.

There are also some similarities as well as differences in job positions. For example, in the schools, while counselors, social workers, and psychologists may all work in the schools, school counselors work predominantly with students and teachers and typically provide brief individual sessions, small group sessions, and classroom lessons, as well as other responsibilities. School-based mental health counselors provide more in-depth counseling services in the schools. While there are times when school social workers and school psychologists may also provide some of these in-depth counseling services, school social workers may also focus on connecting students and families with community resources. School psychologists typically focus on specialized testing, such as administering, scoring, and interpreting intelligence and achievement tests. Counselors, psychologists, and social workers may all work in private practice. It is also common for counselors and social workers to work in community agencies. Social workers may also work in government agencies or hospitals. Other settings where counselors may work include institutions of higher education, the legal system, inpatient and residential facilities, career centers, and rehabilitation centers, to name a few. Thus, counselors have some similarities as well as differences with other helping professionals and may work in a variety of settings. Next, we will discuss research related to counselors' perceptions of counseling.

Mellin et al. (2011) explored counselors' (n = 204) perceptions of the definition of counseling and identified three themes: (1) daily tasks and counseling services, (2) training and credentials, and (3) wellness and a developmental approach instead of a medical model. Additionally, the researchers found that most (97%) of the participants defined counseling generally, instead of related to specialty areas. This is an interesting finding as there is much debate in the counseling profession about counselors identifying as a counselor or by their specialty areas (e.g., school counselor, mental health counselor, marriage and family counselor), with Mellin et al. (2011) noting that the debate usually involves scholars, while their study focused on the perspectives of counselors. Participants also described how counseling was distinct from social work and psychology, with the researchers identifying five themes: (a) personal growth and wellness focus, (b) testing and assessment, (c) case management and community systems, (d) individual instead of a global focus, and (e) no differences. Regarding personal growth and wellness, participants commented that counselors focus on wellness, prevention, and developmental models, while the other two professions (i.e., psychology and social work) focus more on the medical model. Participants also shared that psychologists focused more on testing and assessment with a greater emphasis on pathology. Moreover, the participating counselors viewed social workers as trained to provide case management, including connecting clients to community resources. The participants also viewed counseling as focusing on the individual, whereas social work encompassed a more global perspective. Finally, 9% of participants viewed the three professions as similar, with no differences in practice (Mellin et al., 2011).

While these findings are interesting, it is important to note that they are based on counselors' perspectives about the counseling, social work, and psychology professions and may be based on assumptions. Specifically, while psychologists conduct several specialized tests, counselors are qualified to administer numerous tests and the assessment process is a crucial component of the counseling process. Additionally, while social workers at the bachelor's level are trained for case management, there are many clinical master's level social work programs that train social workers to provide counseling services to clients, similarly to counselors. Furthermore, while counselors may emphasize a focus on the individual, it is important that counselors also engage in a broader focus, such as engaging in advocacy for the profession, client groups, and counselors, in addition to an individual client (Mellin et al., 2011).

It is also important to consider the date of the study and what has occurred in counseling since the time of this study (e.g., consensus definition of counseling). However, it is unknown whether these perspectives remain among counselors. Nevertheless, with an increasing emphasis on interprofessional collaboration, it is important that counselors have a clear and accurate understanding of other helping professions and ways they can collaborate to best meet the needs of their clients. Having a clear understanding of counseling is also important to dispel myths, reduce stigma about counseling, and engage in advocacy at all levels. As you progress through this chapter, we invite you to think about your own perceptions and definition of counseling and how they might evolve over time.

THE ROLE OF ADVOCACY

Advocacy is crucial for promoting the welfare of clients, fighting stigma related to mental illness, and advancing the counseling profession. It has been a foundational component of the counseling profession since its origin with the work of Frank Parsons in vocational guidance and Clifford Beers in the mental health reform movement (Toporek & Daniels, 2018). Major advancements in advocacy within counseling occurred in the 1990s with the development of the multicultural counseling competencies (MCC; Sue et al., 1992), and then in 2003 with the adoption of the ACA Advocacy Competencies (Lewis et al., 2002), which were updated in 2018 (Toporek & Daniels, 2018). In 2015, the Association for Multicultural Counseling and Development (AMCD) and ACA endorsed the updated MCC (Multicultural Social Justice Counseling Competencies [MSJCC]; Ratts et al., 2016), which included an emphasis on social justice and advocacy Then, in 2018, ACA identified advocacy as one of the three pillars for their strategic initiatives. Thus, ACA has increasingly prioritized advocacy in the last few decades.

ACA Advocacy Competencies

The ACA Advocacy Competencies include two dimensions (extent of client involvement in advocacy, and level of advocacy intervention) and focus on addressing systemic barriers through the development and use of knowledge, skills, and behaviors (Toporek & Daniels, 2018). Regarding the first dimension, the extent of client involvement ranges from collaboration with clients and client groups to advocacy on behalf of clients and client groups. The second dimension includes three levels that range from the microlevel to the macrolevel: individual client/student level; community, organization, or school level (client groups); and the public arena (large scale). There are also six competency domains: (a) client/student empowerment, (b) client/student advocacy, (c) community collaboration, (d) systems advocacy, (e) collective action, and (f) social/political advocacy (Toporek & Daniels, 2018). In the following discussion, client is used to reference both clients and students.

Within the empowerment domain, the counselor works with the client using various strategies, including identifying strengths, helping the client identify external barriers, teaching the client self-advocacy skills, and supporting the client when engaging in self-advocacy. In the client advocacy domain, the counselor advocates on behalf of the client within either the organization where the counselor works or the broader system. In the community collaboration domain, the counselor works with a group to recognize and address barriers. The systems advocacy domain involves the counselor advocating on behalf of a group. Within the collective action domain, the counselor works with groups to address large-scale change, such as public policies and perceptions. Finally,

TABLE 1.2 ADVOCACY COMPETENCY DOMAINS AND EXAMPLES

DOMAIN	EXAMPLE
Client/Student Empowerment	Supporting an adult client in writing a letter to their boss or a student in writing a letter to their teacher to discuss a conflict.
Client/Student Advocacy	The counselor talks with the billing department within their agency about a client struggling with their insurance co-pay, suggesting setting up a payment plan to assist the client.
Community Collaboration	The counselor meets with a group focused on supporting people with severe mental illness in the community to help them advocate with the city council to have a space to hold meetings.
Systems Advocacy	A school counselor meets with the principal at their school to discuss strategies for supporting marginalized students within the school to address issues related to racial tension.
Collective Action	The counselor works with a group of community members to plan and implement a peaceful protest focused on addressing stigma related to mental illness. A school counselor works with interested high school students who want to organize a peaceful walkout to protest legislation that discriminates against LGBTQ+ students (e.g., see: https://www.wcjb.com/2022/03/03/buchholz-students-are-protesting-dont-say-gay-bill).
Social/Political Advocacy	A group of counseling students meets with legislators regarding support for funding mental health initiatives, conducts a letter writing campaign to political leaders, or appears on media platforms to raise awareness and obtain support for addressing systemic issues for marginalized clients.

at the social/political advocacy level, the counselor engages in advocacy generally independent of client groups. (Toporek & Daniels, 2018). Thus, counselors may engage in advocacy in multiple ways to support clients and the counseling profession. Table 1.2 outlines the advocacy domains and examples.

Ratts and Hutchins (2009) discuss multiple reasons why counselors need to infuse the advocacy competencies into practice. First, oppression is prevalent in our society and it negatively affects human development. Additionally, the need for change extends beyond the individual to include the system level. Furthermore, the competencies provide a framework for engaging in social justice advocacy, and help counselors determine the appropriate level of advocacy and when they should advocate with or on behalf of clients. Thus, advocacy is a crucial aspect of the counseling profession and, in many ways, a lifelong journey. Next, we discuss the principles of social justice and intersectionality, each a crucial aspect of client case conceptualization.

PRINCIPLES OF SOCIAL JUSTICE AND INTERSECTIONALITY IN COUNSELING

Our vision for counseling training centers on advocacy, social justice, and intersectionality. We aim to introduce you to multicultural issues in counseling early on in your educational journey. We believe this approach will better position you to provide competent, holistic, comprehensive, and empowering counseling services to your clients. Understanding and embracing the tenets of social justice form a critical step for beginning counselors. Social justice has been referred to as the fifth force in counseling and has increasingly had a role in the largest counseling organization in the world, ACA and its teaching and training division, the Association for Counselor Education and Supervision (ACES).

In 2008, Hugh C. Crethar and Manivong J. Ratts, representatives of the ACA division, Counselors for Social Justice (CSJ), wrote an open letter challenging the ACA presidential statement that ACA should adopt "a neutral and centrist" position in its approach to counseling. They contend that social justice in terms of counseling is

A multifaceted approach in which counselors strive to simultaneously promote human development and the common good through addressing challenges related to both individual and distributive justice. This approach includes empowerment of individuals and groups as well as active confrontation of injustice and inequality in society, both as they impact clientele and in their systemic contexts. In doing so, counselors direct attention to four critical principles that guide their work: equity, access, participation, and harmony.

In 2010, in an introduction to the special issue of the journal, *Counselor Education and Supervision*, Chang et al. (2010) challenged counselors and counselor educators to integrate social justice into their work. They contend that counselors "cannot separate counseling from social justice; both are necessary for helping clients achieve long-term optimal psychological health and well-being" (p. 83). Table 1.3 outlines the elements of social justice in counseling.

TRAUMA-INFORMED CARE

We believe it is important for you, as a beginning counselor, to develop and integrate trauma-informed care (TIC) into your practice. We see TIC as a critical aspect of counseling. We aim to introduce you to this increasingly prevalent concern and encourage you to delve deeper via other resources. As you develop your understanding of counseling skills, techniques, and approaches, you will also see how TIC will play a role in the work you do. The following is a brief overview of TIC.

TABLE 1.3 ELEMENTS OF SOCIAL JUSTICE

ELEMENT	DESCRIPTION
Equity	Attends to fair distribution of resources, rights, and responsibilities to all members of society
Access	Includes notions of fairness for both the individual and the common good based on the ability of all people to access the resources, services, power, information, and understanding crucial to realizing a standard of living that allows for self-determination and human development
Participation	Refers to the right of every person in society to partake in and be consulted on decisions that impact their lives as well as the lives of other people in their contexts and systems
Harmony	A principle of social adjustment wherein the actions revolving around the self-interests of any individual or group ultimately produce results that afford the best possible outcomes for the community as a whole

Source: Adapted from Crethar, H. C., & Ratts, M. J. (2008). *Why social justice is a counseling concern.* https://www.counseling.org/docs/default-source/Government-Affairs/why_social _justice_is_a_counseling_concern

The Substance Abuse and Mental Health Services Administration (Substance Abuse and Mental Health Services Administration [SAMHSA], 2014) Trauma and Justice Strategic Initiative, defines trauma thus:

The results from an event, series of events, or set of circumstances that is experienced by an individual as physically or emotionally harmful or threatening and that has lasting adverse effects on the individual's functioning and physical, social, emotional, or spiritual well-being. (p. 2)

Types of trauma include combat (e.g., Vietnam, Desert Storm), non-interpersonal experiences (e.g., suffering a disturbing event such as the COVID-19 pandemic), witnessing a violent event or death (e.g., the terrorist attacks of 9/11), surviving a life-threatening accident, and interpersonal experiences (e.g., being molested as a child; surviving rape or physical, emotional, or psychological abuse or neglect; or surviving a criminal act), among others (see Belik et al., 2007).

As a counselor, you are highly likely to encounter clients who are survivors of some form of trauma. The client's trauma may be recent or historical, and your approach to this work will depend, in part, on the traumatic events the client has experienced. Crisis response work is different from trauma work, though there is overlap. Our goal here is to provide a brief overview of TIC to encourage you to learn more about this type of approach. At a minimum, you should become aware of the basic principles that inform TIC. The Centers for Disease Control and Prevention's (CDC) Office of Public Health Preparedness and Response (OPHPR) worked together with SAMHSA's National Center for Trauma-Informed Care (NCTIC) to develop and deliver training to emergency responders so they can

TABLE 1.4 TRAUMA TREATMENT APPROACHES AND OUTCOMES

MODELS	OUTCOMES
ADULT MODELS	
Prolonged Exposure Therapy (PE Therapy)	Effective with veterans
Eye Movement Desensitization and Reprocessing Therapy (EMDR)	Similar to other techniques endorsed by World Health Organization and U.S. Department of Veterans Affairs
Seeking Safety	Supported by California Evidence-Based Clearinghouse and Society of Addiction Psychology (APA subdivision)
CHILD MODELS	
Child-Parent Psychotherapy	Supported by California Evidence-Based Clearinghouse
Attachment, Self-Regulation & Competency (ARC)	Research evidence for decreased PTSD symptoms and increased mental health, adaptive and social skills
Trauma-Focused Cognitive Behavioral Therapy (TF-CBT)	Highlighted as a model and promising program by California Evidence-Based Clearinghouse, SAMHSA, and National Child Traumatic Stress Network

APA, American Psychological Association; PTSD, posttraumatic stress disorder; SAMHSA, Substance Abuse and Mental Health Services Administration.
Source: Adapted from Menschner, C., & Maul, A. (2016), *Key ingredients for successful trauma-informed care implementation* (p. 8). https://www.samhsa.gov/sites/default/files/programs _campaigns/childrens_mental_health/atc-whitepaper-040616.pdf

recognize the ways in which trauma can affect individuals and communities. In the course of your training and work as a counselor, you may need to provide emergency mental health care to survivors of traumatic events. The CDC identified six principles that guide a trauma-informed approach: (a) safety; (b) trustworthiness and transparency; (c) peer support; (d) collaboration and mutuality; (e) empowerment voice and choice; and (f) cultural, historical, and gender issues.

Safety is central to providing TIC. The client must feel that you are a trustworthy, open, and honest provider. It is crucial that your focus in the moment be on what happened to the client, rather than what may be wrong with them (Menschner & Maul, 2016). Clients must learn about treatment options available to them and have a say in the counseling approach used. An overview of trauma-informed approaches to counseling and recorded outcomes is provided in Table 1.4.

Organizations that provide TIC must attend to safety practices to enhance the quality of the client's experience. Menschner and Maul (2016) caution about

TABLE 1.5 EXAMPLES OF CREATING A SAFE ENVIRONMENT

PHYSICAL ENVIRONMENT
Keeping parking lots, common areas, bathrooms, entrances, and exits well lit
Ensuring that people are not allowed to smoke, loiter, or congregate outside entrances and exits
Monitoring who is coming in and out of the building
Positioning security personnel inside and outside the building
Keeping noise levels in waiting rooms low
Using welcoming language on all signage
Making sure clients have clear access to the door in exam rooms and can easily exit if desired.
SOCIAL-EMOTIONAL ENVIRONMENT
Welcoming patients and ensuring that they feel respected and supported
Ensuring staff can maintain healthy interpersonal boundaries and can manage conflict appropriately
Keeping consistent schedules and procedures
Offering sufficient notice and preparation when changes are necessary
Maintaining communication that is consistent, open, respectful, and compassionate
Being aware of how an individual's culture affects how they perceive trauma, safety, and privacy

Source: Adapted from Menschner, C., & Maul, A. (2016), *Key ingredients for successful trauma-informed care implementation* (pp. 4–5). https://www.samhsa.gov/sites/default/files/programs_campaigns/childrens_mental_health/atc-whitepaper-040616.pdf

the possibility of retraumatization for clients being served if the context where you are providing services does not feel secure to the client. They outlined the safety factors that clients who have experienced trauma must feel in order for your work to be effective. These factors include the physical environment and the socioemotional environment. The authors add that the absence of safety for a trauma survivor can create heightened feelings of anxiety, potentially re-traumatizing them. Examples of safe environments are outlined in Table 1.5.

Counselors who work with traumatized clients need to seek and secure support from their peers and systems of care whence they practice. Key stakeholders must work in a spirit of collaboration and mutual care and assist the client to feel empowered to speak and be actively involved in their treatment planning and process. Counselors must also take into account the sociocultural factors (e.g., racial/ethnic, gender, socioeconomic), known to have a role in a client's experience of trauma. The trauma-informed approach is not singular or all-encompassing and practitioners must constantly attend to any changes at every level within the system (Menschner & Maul, 2016).

According to SAMHSA's (2014) Treatment Improvement Protocol, counselors must first be able to understand the prevalence and ubiquitous nature of trauma. Given the social and environmental factors and events (e.g., 9/11, wars in Iraq and Afghanistan, extreme weather, COVID-19 pandemic) that have transpired in the United States and across the world, it is no surprise that up to half of all clients who present for therapy report exposure to a traumatic event in their lifetime (SAMHSA, 2014). Finally, researchers suggest that individuals and communities who are exposed to racism, classism, or systemic forms of violence (e.g., police violence) are frequently members of minoritized or disenfranchised groups and experience trauma at a higher rate than those not belonging to these groups (SAMHSA, 2014). Thus, we contend that all counseling students should be trained in TIC that also attends to the individuals' salient identities. For a broader and more in-depth introduction to trauma counseling see Chapter 11.

INTRODUCTION TO GROUP WORK

The practice of counseling can take place through individual, couples, family, or group sessions, depending on the client's issues of concern. Brief definitions of each follow.

- Individual counseling is provided by a trained professional with a relevant master's or doctoral degree. Many are licensed professionals in their respective states and some have specializations in specific types of therapy. Individual therapy affords the most confidentiality and is also more expensive.
- Couples counseling is conducted with a dyad (traditional romantic partner configuration) or other romantic partnered relationship configuration (e.g., polyamory, or other types of open relationships; see https://www.choosingtherapy.com/polyamory).
- Family counseling involves family members as defined by the unit and there may be an identified client; however, the family unit is the focus of counseling. There are many types of approaches to family counseling and they focus on systemic dynamics rather than intrapersonal or intrapsychic dynamics.
- Group counseling involves one or two counselors conducting group work with a group of people, usually 6–12 clients gathered around a shared concern. There are many types of group counseling that address emotional or psychological issues (e.g., depression, anxiety, trauma) or substance-related disorders or behavioral addictions. Group counseling can be more cost-effective for clients.

In this section, we offer an overview of group work. In addition to individual sessions, while earning their master's or specialist degrees, many beginning counselors will experience group work during their practicum and internship experiences. Group work is a common intervention modality in community mental health settings and psychiatric hospitals, public and private. Groups can be task or work oriented (goal focused and short-term), psychoeducational (didactic and focused on a topic; e.g., stress management or anger management), or process oriented (group counseling or group psychotherapy). Group counseling is growth oriented and group therapy is geared toward more serious intrapersonal issues that require in-depth therapy. They can be open (anyone can join at any time) or closed (once members are established, no one else can join). The duration of groups varies broadly from short-term (4 weeks) to years. Facilitating a group may seem like a daunting experience at first and it is important that you have foundational training before you engage clients in a group setting. While providing comprehensive training in group counseling is beyond the scope of this chapter, we want to give you an introductory overview to get you started.

The ACA division that centers group counseling work is the Association for Specialists in Group Work (ASGW; asgw.org). This division has been in existence since 1973. Its mission is to empower group workers "with the knowledge, skills, and resources necessary to practice effective, socially just, and ethical group work in a diverse and global society" (https://asgw.org). An ASGW members' task force (McCarthy et al., 2021) outlined the guiding principles of group work into the following Parts: I. Opening Statement of Positionality and Process, II. Values in Group Work, III. Principles, Values, Ethics, and Diversity, and IV. Foundations for Training, Practice, Supervision, and Research in Group Work, which includes Section A: Definitions of the four types of group work, Section B: Education, Supervision, and Consultation, Section C: Guidelines for Pre-Group Planning, Section D: Facilitation of Group Work, Section E: Evaluation of Group Work, and Section F: Research on Group Work. Moreover, Singh et al. (2012) developed the Multicultural and Social Justice Competence Principles for Group Work. They are: I. Awareness of Self and Group Members, II. Strategies and Skills, which include (a) Group Worker Planning and (b) Group Worker Performing and Processing, and III. Social Justice Advocacy. Singh et al. also provide case examples to illustrate these principles as applied by group leaders. We encourage you to review these documents so that you can begin to understand how group work is conducted in an ethical manner with advocacy and social justice principles informing your approach.

Irvin Yalom, an existential psychotherapist and psychiatrist, has been the leading authority in group therapy for over 50 years. His seminal work, *The Theory and Practice of Group Psychotherapy* (now in its 6th edition) has been the most widely used text for group work. The stages of group progression were developed by Bruce Tuckman (1965) in the mid-1960s and they are:

- **Forming**: In this first stage group members are just meeting each other and discussing their goals for participating in group. The leader facilitates discussion about rules and individual roles and no actual work is done during this stage.
- **Storming**: This stage is characterized by conflict among group members as they begin to learn each other and react to each other's styles of communicating or relating to one another. The group leader's task is to facilitate conflict resolution and engage group members in this process in

productive ways. Groups can get stuck in this stage if unable to resolve the conflicts or impasses being experienced.

■ **Norming**: In this stage the group members move beyond conflict and begin to recognize and appreciate group leaders among them and learn to provide constructive feedback to each other. Some groups go back to the storming phase until resolution is achieved. Conflicts at this stage are easier to move through than before.

■ **Performing**: Members develop interdependence and begin to accomplish their goals by working well together. This is a highly fulfilling stage where group members are flexible and supportive of each other.

■ **Adjourning**: This one was added in 1977 and represents the beginning of the end for the group. Members feel closer to each other and may be sad about the impending end.

Yalom (1985) identified the following as therapeutic factors of group work: instillation of hope (clients believe that treatment will be effective), universality (clients feel they are not alone or abnormal), imparting of information (clients learn how to manage their issues or problems), altruism (clients share lived experiences and experience help from each other), corrective recapitulation of the primary family (reliving family conflicts through one another and solving them), development of socializing techniques (learning social skills with one another), imitative behavior (modeling positivity to each other), interpersonal learning (gaining insights about past experiences and learning to reframe them), group cohesiveness (bonding with each other), catharsis (ability to feel and express feelings), existential actors (clients accept responsibility for their lives and connect with each other, accept their own mortality and unpredictability of existence).

Effective group leaders have the following skills: engage and encourage members to participate, observe and identify group processes, pay attention to individual group members' behaviors, clarify and summarize for the group, open and close the session appropriately and in a timely manner, educate the group as needed, model good leadership, self-disclose as needed and in appropriate ways, give and receive feedback, ask questions that are open-ended, show empathic understanding, confront appropriately, respectfully, and with care, help members with making meaning of their experiences, help members integrate and apply what they are learning to their own lives, embody the ASGW ethical and professional standards, and keep the group focused and on task to help members accomplish their goals (Conyne & Diederich, 2013). We hope this brief introduction to group work will get you interested and excited about the possibilities of applying group counseling to your repertoire of counseling skills. Groups can be a powerful tool for client growth and transformation. Next, we introduce you to the Multicultural and Social Justice Counseling Competencies, a set of guidelines that will allow you to conduct counseling in an equitable and just manner.

FIGURE 1.1 MSJCC Conceptual Framework

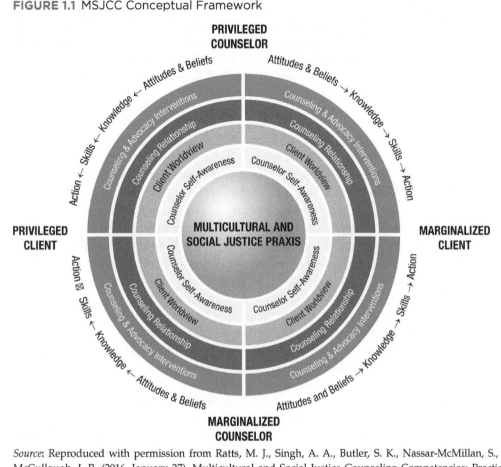

Source: Reproduced with permission from Ratts, M. J., Singh, A. A., Butler, S. K., Nassar-McMillan, S., & McCullough, J. R. (2016, January 27). Multicultural and Social Justice Counseling Competencies: Practical applications in counseling. *Counseling Today*. https://ct.counseling.org/2016/01/multicultural-and-social -justice-counseling-competencies-practical-applications-in-counseling

MULTICULTURAL AND SOCIAL JUSTICE COUNSELING COMPETENCIES

Ratts et al. (2016) developed the Multicultural and Social Justice Counseling Competencies (MCSJCC) and a conceptual framework to illustrate the relationships among its salient constructs: multicultural and social justice praxis, quadrants, domains, and competencies. We provide a summary of these concepts here and hope you will use the framework as a guidepost for your counseling education and practice moving forward.

The conceptual framework for the MCSJCC and main concepts associated with it are presented in Figure 1.1. At the heart of this framework is the notion that all counseling should be guided by multiculturalism and social justice.

Figure 1.1 includes new terms counselors should become familiar with, namely: quadrants, domains, and competencies. As described by Ratts et al. (2016):

Quadrants reflect the complex identities and the privileged and marginalized statuses that counselors and clients bring to the counseling relationship. Clients and counsel-

ors are both members of various racial, ethnic, gender, sexual orientation, economic, disability and religious groups, to list a few. These identities are categorized into privileged and marginalized statuses. A client or counselor may hold either status or both statuses simultaneously. These statuses are prevalent depending on how each individual is experiencing the current interaction. Being attentive of these statuses highlights how issues of power, privilege and oppression play out between counselors and clients.

There are four identity quadrants and combinations for counselors to consider: Quadrant I: Privileged Counselor–Marginalized Client; Quadrant II: Privileged Counselor–Privileged Client; Quadrant III: Marginalized Counselor–Privileged Client, and Quadrant IV: Marginalized Counselor–Marginalized Client. These combinations illustrate the multiple identities that you and your clients can bring into the therapy room. These in turn will inform how dynamics of power, privilege, and oppression will play out in the counseling relationship. Think about the salient visible and invisible identities that you hold and whether they carry power and privilege or marginalization and disadvantages: age, gender, race, ethnicity, socioeconomic status, sexual orientation, immigration status, occupation, religion, and ability. There may be others not listed here. Can you identify the places of privilege and marginalization for each? Can you think of how these may impact your counseling relationship if your client holds identities that are the same as or different from your own?

The domains presented are developmental and reflect your degree of multicultural and social justice competence. They are counselor self-awareness, client worldview, and the counseling relationship, and counseling and advocacy interventions. Your self-awareness will help you recognize your own cultural values, biases, and beliefs. Learning where you stand on challenging and contentious issues is important because they may get in the way of your ability to counsel clients. Learning about your client's worldview can in turn help you to better understand them. You need to become aware of where you stand vis-à-vis your clients and whether you share identities of privilege and/or marginalization. This awareness will help you better serve your client. The authors contend that counselors must learn about the systems the client inhabits and their impact on their well-being. Advocacy must occur at multiple levels within these systems. Counselors can be proactive in assisting clients to develop connections within their systems in order to receive support that could enhance the quality of their lives. Our emphasis on advocacy will assist you in developing these skills.

Ratts et al. offer multiple examples of the ways and multiple levels through which you can advocate and intervene on a client's behalf as you enter the counseling profession. In sum, the MCSJCC is a comprehensive framework that offers the counselor a lens through which we can see our own and our client's attitudes, beliefs, and values and examine how these inform worldviews and the dynamics of the counseling relationship. Most counseling interactions you will have will be with clients who are not like you. With the appropriate training and an open mind and heart, you can become an effective counselor and social justice advocate for the clients you will serve. We believe *emancipatory communitarianism* offers a similar opportunity for you to grow into the profession and we introduce this framework next.

EMANCIPATORY COMMUNITARIANISM AS A FRAMEWORK FOR COUNSELOR EDUCATION PEDAGOGY

In the course of completing foundational counseling training, as you have already begun to do, students such as yourself are tasked with examining your own attitudes, beliefs, and values so you may find a theoretical framework that resonates with you and is aligned with these attitudes, beliefs, and values. Kumar (2018) describes the relationship among attitudes, beliefs and values thus:

Attitudes arise out of core values and beliefs we hold internally. Beliefs are assumptions and convictions we hold to be true based on past experiences. Values are worthy ideas based on things, concepts and people. Behaviours are how these internalised systems (attitudes, beliefs and values) are expressed.

Kumar explains that these factors have a role in how we approach and integrate learning. He contends that understanding the differences among these concepts is critical to how we learn and perform any task; herein, the task is how you will approach counseling clients. Throughout this course, you will be encouraged and challenged to explore your attitudes, beliefs, and value system, and the various ways these areas have helped to shape who you are and how you will use your personhood as an instrument of counseling practice. As a professional counselor, you will be a catalyst for client change and growth. This training begins with yourself. We think learning about emancipatory communitarianism (EC) can serve as a lens whereby you will see the understanding of human beings more critically. We invite you to interrogate the ideas, concepts, and issues we will place before you, unpack their meaning and purpose, and explore the ways they can be foundational to your unfolding counselor identity. The idea of interrogating a theory or framework comes from the work of Critical Race Theorists (e.g., Kimberlé Crenshaw, Richard Delgado, Gloria Ladson-Billings) and invites the analytical questioning of assumptions about dominant paradigms and structures. Isaac Prilleltensky's work interrogates well-known theoretical frameworks through his proposed emancipatory psychology.

The most prevalent counseling theories do not offer an explanation of how some of these theories may actually serve to perpetuate social injustices that can harm clients already struggling with disenfranchisement, racism, and discrimination (Brubaker et al., 2010). In 1997, Prilleltensky advanced EC as a social justice framework to attend to the drawbacks of extant theories that he based on the theories' fundamental values. We contend that Prilleltensky's paradigm shift can be applied to the teaching of counseling theories in a way that invites troubling the dominant narratives commonly advanced in introductory counseling classes. We hereby invite you to learn more about EC so you can use this lens in your evaluation of approaches to counseling clients you will serve. Next, we provide an overview of this framework.

Prilleltensky classifies the prevalent theoretical approaches as traditional (e.g., cognitive-behavioral therapy, psychoanalytic), postmodern (e.g., narrative therapy, brief solution-focused therapy), empowerment (e.g., feminist therapy, liberation psychology), and EC (promotes balance between self-determination and distributive justice, maintains high degree of concern for well-being of individuals and communities, promotes grounded knowledge of the service of moral values, and believes the good life and the good society are based on mutuality, social obligations, and the removal of oppression).

Table 1.6 illustrates the ways in which EC conceptualizes four well-known psychological approaches. A close inspection of the table will help you see how the traditional theoretical frameworks that beginning students are introduced to, in practice, define client issues in asocial or disconnected, deficit-oriented terms and are reactive rather than proactive. EC, on the other hand, adopts a definition of problems that is interpersonal and attends to the client's experience of social oppression. A more detailed exploration of psychological approaches (i.e., counseling theories) vis-à-vis EC is provided in Chapter 6.

CONCLUSION

This chapter introduced the counseling profession, provided a history of the profession, and how it differs from psychology, psychiatry, and social work. We discussed advocacy in counseling practice, embracing social justice, intersectionality, trauma-informed care, and the basics of group work. Finally, we provided an overview of multicultural competencies and emancipatory communitarianism. The counselor development journey is lifelong. We encourage you to continue learning about these concepts as you grow into the professional counselor you aspire to be.

TABLE 1.6 SUMMARY OF VALUES, ASSUMPTIONS, AND PRACTICES IN FOUR PSYCHOLOGICAL APPROACHES

DOMAIN	TRADITIONAL APPROACHES	EMPOWERING APPROACHES	POSTMODERN APPROACHES	EMANCIPATORY COMUNITARIAN APPROACHES
Values	Promote caring and self-determination of individuals but neglect distributive justice. Major emphasis on helping individuals not communities.	Promote human diversity and self-determination of individuals and of marginalized groups.	Promote human diversity and self-determination of individuals. Also concerned with collaboration and participation but have equivocal stance with respect to distributive justice.	Promote balance between self-determination and distributive justice. High degree of concen for well-being of individuals and communities.
Assumptions	Based on scientistic assumptions about knowledge. Good life and good society are based on value-free liberalism, individualism, and meritocracy.	View knowledge as tool for action research. Good life is based on ideas of personal control. Good society is based on rights and entitlements.	Emphasize epistemological relativism and moral skepticism. Good life is associated with pursuit of identity. Assumptions informed by social constructionism.	Promote grounded knowledge at the service of moral values. Good life and good society are based on mutuality, social obligations, and the removal of oppression.

(continued)

TABLE 1.6 SUMMARY OF VALUES, ASSUMPTIONS, AND PRACTICES IN FOUR PSYCHOLOGICAL APPROACHES (*CONTINUED*)

DOMAIN	TRADITIONAL APPROACHES	EMPOWERING APPROACHES	POSTMODERN APPROACHES	EMANCIPATORY COMMUNITARIAN APPROACHES
Practices	Problems defined in asocial and deficit-oriented terms. Interventions are reactive.	Problems defined in terms of risk and disempowering condition. Interventions are reactive and proactive.	Problems defined in terms of clients' constructions of their own circumstancs. Clients encouraged to pursue their own identity.	Problems defined primarily in terms of interpersonal and social oppression. Interventions seek to change individuals as well as social systems.
Potential benefits	Preserve values of individuality and freedom.	Address sources of personal and collective disempowerment.	Value the importance of identity, context, and challenge dogmatic discourses.	Promote sense of community and emancipation of every member of society.
Potential risks	Victim-blaming and tacit support for unjust social structures.	Social fragmentation through pursuit of own.	Social and political retreatism. Skepticism and lack of moral vision.	Denial of individuality and sacrifice of personal uniqueness for good of the community.

Source: Reproduced with permission from Prilleltensky, I. (1997). Values, assumptions, and practices: Assessing the moral implications of psychological discourse and action. *American Psychologist, 52*(5), 517–535. http://dx.doi.org/10.1037/0003-066X.52.5.517

Summary

- The counseling profession continues to develop and evolve in its almost 100-year history.
- Counseling is similar and distinct from psychology and social work.
- Advocacy, social justice, and intersectionality are critical concepts in counseling.
- The MCSJCC and emancipatory communitarianism can help guide your counseling training and practice.
- Counselors should strive to provide trauma-informed care to clients of diverse identities individually and in group settings.

Voices From the Field

Jill Kanji, MEd, EdS, School Counselor, Alachua County Public Schools, Gainesville, Florida

Part of the role of a school counselor is recognizing needs and finding a way to address them. This is true when we look at academic data, needs assessments for social/emotional concerns, and basic needs (clothing, snacks, and school supplies). In the spring of 2015, a glaring need for advocacy and support hit me hard and prompted a need for action. For years, I had been working with students that identify as LGBTQ+ and hearing their struggles for acceptance, as well as their accounts of bullying in the schools. It was clear that a need existed for a way to better support these students and create a school culture that welcomes everyone. It was time to work on establishing a Gay-Straight Alliance Club (GSA; gsanetwork.org) at my middle school.

First, it is important to provide some historical background on GSAs in our school district. At the time, there were two high schools in the district that had established GSA clubs for students. A group of middle school students at my school had tried to start a "Tolerance Club" but it quickly fizzled out due to lack of interest or understanding what the club was about. I spent a great amount of time researching how to start a GSA, rules around starting a club at my school, and found an enthusiastic teacher to co-sponsor the club with me. We approached the skeptical principal for approval of our GSA plan and after some convincing, we were ready to offer our club to students for the 2016–2017 school year.

In a middle school, you never know who will be willing to take a chance at something new. Coming to a new club meeting after school takes a certain amount of bravery. My co-sponsor and I sat in a classroom on September 14, 2016, hoping that any student would walk through the door for our first GSA meeting. Twelve excited students attended the meeting that day and our GSA journey officially begun. During the years that would follow, the GSA would continue to grow and flourish in my middle school.

This student-led group can serve as a social club, a support club, or an activist club. Our GSA served at varying levels of all of these depending on the needs of the students and school culture at the time. We began by presenting information to the middle school faculty to raise awareness. The students shared accounts of bullying and harassment they have endured and talked about how they wanted to feel comfortable and be themselves at school. Over the years, we marched in Pride rallies to express support, affirmation, and acceptance of LGBTQ youth (youth.gov/feature-article/june-lgbt-pride-month), created t-shirts, made posters, removed graffiti from campus, collected money for the Trevor Project to support LGBTQ youth (www.thetrevorproject.org/strategic-plan) and to help educate students, teachers, and staff about high suicide rates (see Walls et al., 2008) among this group, curated a LGBTQ+ section in the school's library, and much more.

The joy that happened monthly at our GSA meetings is hard to put into words. The group that started as 12 eventually fluctuated up to almost 30. Each meeting was filled with support, friendship, and an energy that would keep me filled up for weeks. Watching the club welcome new members, grow together, and navigate the waters of advocating for LGBTQ+ issues was inspiring. Research shows all the positive outcomes of having a GSA in schools (e.g., see Goodenow et al., 2006; Kosciw et al., 2010), but hearing the laughter and sharing of stories at the meetings really drives home the importance of having this club available for all middle and high school students.

The GSA at my middle school had a positive and lasting effect on students and faculty, creating a safer and more welcoming environment for students to learn in. Throughout our school district, additional supports have been put in place for GSA sponsors and school counselors that directly affect LGBTQ+ students. We have had numerous professional development opportunities, created a district-wide support plan of best practices for schools, and GSA clubs are now active in most middle and high schools in our district. In 2020, I left the middle school where I started the GSA for a more rural middle school. I am proud to say that I have advocated for them to start a GSA and we are going strong in my new school.

A Call to Action

First, refer to Table 1.2 Advocacy Competency Domains and Examples. Think of a marginalized group in your community who would benefit from your individual or collective advocacy (e.g., LGBTQ+ youth, undocumented Latinx immigrants). Address the following: Who are the members of this group? What are the historical facts that inform their status as being disenfranchised and discriminated against? What are the salient issues that they face daily and affect their mental health and well-being? In the process of becoming an advocate for your clients, you may learn about extant civil rights groups in your community. Table 1.7. provides an overview of the top national nonprofit organizations dedicated to supporting a variety of groups. Some have regional or local branches you can contact for information. Choose an advocacy domain that you can act upon and develop a plan of action. Identify an organization that may provide knowledge and resources for you to better understand the group's situation (for examples, see Table 1.7.), reach out to them to obtain any resources you might need and strategize next steps, and seek supporting peers/allies to join you and to help implement your plan.

TABLE 1.7 TOP CIVIL RIGHTS NONPROFIT ORGANIZATIONS

ORGANIZATION	POPULATION OF FOCUS
American Association of People with Disabilities (AAPD)	To protect individuals with disabilities as defined by the Americans with Disabilities Act
American Civil Liberties Union (ACLU)	Protect the rights of all American citizens including "women, prisoners, those with disabilities, lesbians, and gay men."
Anti-Defamation League (ADL)	"Fighting hatred, discrimination and bias. The organization focuses on fighting anti-Semitism within the U.S. and around the world, as well as confronting all forms of discrimination and hate and securing justice and protection for those who have been impacted by such things. The group also provides educational services to help support respectful communities and schools."
Alliance for Justice (AFJ)	"Advocates to ensure that the U.S. justice system truly does provide equal justice for all people. Through its Justice Program, the organization focuses on the U.S. court system to ensure an independent judiciary, equitable access and fair treatment for all, and protection of constitutional rights and values."
Amnesty International	"Fight all kinds of abuses of civil rights throughout the world through seeking to change laws that are oppressive and bringing to justice those who abuse the rights of others."
Equal Justice Initiative (EJI)	"Protecting basic rights for vulnerable individuals and challenging economic and racial injustice. The civil rights group seeks to put a stop to mass incarceration, the death penalty, and other forms of excessive punishment."
National Association for the Advancement of Colored People (NAACP)	"Promotes the rights of African Americans and other racial minorities; to protect political, educational, and social rights of all people and to help banish hatred and discrimination."

(continued)

TABLE 1.7 TOP CIVIL RIGHTS NONPROFIT ORGANIZATIONS (*CONTINUED*)

ORGANIZATION	POPULATION OF FOCUS
National Gay and Lesbian Task Force (NGLTF)	"Promotes equal rights for same-sex couples and fights to end discrimination against people due to their gender identity. The organization is active in promoting social justice and equality while aiming for the goal of equal opportunities for all genders of people."
National Organization for Women (NOW)	"Aims to end discrimination based on gender; fight for issues such as workplace equality, right to abortion, birth control, and sexism. They want to eliminate harassment, violence, and racism."
Southern Poverty Law Center (SPLC)	"Aims to fight hate, teaching tolerance, and seeking justice for those who are victims of hate crimes."

Source: Adapted from White, M. G. (n.d.). *List of the top civil rights nonprofit organizations.* https://charity.lovetoknow.com/Leading_Civil_Rights_Nonprofit_Organizations

Case Study 1.1

Emmanuel is a 14-year-old Black Haitian cisgender male attending middle school in a rural county in the Southeast United States. His family moved to the United States after the earthquake of 2021 devastated their home in Port au Prince (see www.nytimes.com/live/2021/08/14/world/haiti-earthquake). He was referred to the school counselor by his English teacher after he submitted an autobiographical essay where he discussed his experiences of leaving home to arrive in a foreign land with his family and the struggles he has experienced with this process. He specifically described feeling angry, sad, and anxious about being bullied by older kids at the school and ridiculed for his French accent, limited English proficiency, and openly gay sexual orientation. He enters your office, sits down across from you, folds his arms and crosses his legs, and stares out the window.

RESPONSE QUESTIONS

Think about the concepts you have learned in this chapter and answer the following questions:

1. What are Emmanuel's apparent intersecting identities and how might they inform your conceptualization of his situation?

2. How would you broach discussing the reasons he was referred to you for counseling?

3. Who else might you involve in supporting Emmanuel during this difficult time?

4. When and why might you consider a referral?

5. Consider participating in a role play exercise where one of your class-mates plays the role of Emmanuel while you play the role of counselor. Discuss what you learned from this experience.

Going Within

The following Going Within personal values exercise and ensuing Group Process were adapted from the Choices program at Brown University (www .choices.edu/teaching-news-lesson/values-public-policy).

Tear a piece of paper into 10 pieces and write each of the following 10 values on a piece of paper until all are represented: (a) community, (b) cooperation, (c) democracy, (d) diversity, (e) equality, (f) freedom, (g) justice, (h) security, (i) self-reliance, and (j) stability. On the backside of each paper write a sentence or two that describes what this value means to you and how you interpret it. For example, one of you may think of community as your nuclear and extended family members. For someone else, community may represent the town where you grew up and all of the people that your family knows and socializes with. Someone else may think of community as a universal, all-encompassing con-cept, as in "We all belong in the global community." How you define commu-nity will also help you decide how important this value is to you.

Second, rank the order of these values according to a stepwise process of reflection and decision-making, as follows: randomly read two values and rank order them according to what you deem more important to less important. Remember, these are your personal values, there is no right or wrong way of doing this. Next, read a third value and place it where it belongs in the order of importance. Do this with all the remaining values until you have organized them to reflect your personal priorities today. Keep in mind that your values may change over time, depending on your lived experiences. Values are not necessarily static or permanent. Remember that the meaning of these words may differ for each of you. As a beginning counselor, you and your clients will encounter public policies that may align or conflict with these values in varying ways. Arguably, some or all of these values will inform the way you approach counseling advocacy and social justice for your clients, your community, and the counseling profession. When you are done, we will turn our attention to the Group Process.

Group Process 1.1

Once you are done ranking your values, split the class into small groups of 3–4 students to debrief the exercise. As a group, compare and contrast your rank-ings. How did you define each value? Share your understanding of each value with each other until everyone has a chance to speak. How are your definitions similar? How are they different? How are your rankings similar; how are they different? Was it easy or challenging for you to define, identify, and rank the values? Can you say where your understanding or appreciation of the value(s) come(s) from? In other words, who taught you about the value and its importance? When and where did you learn about each value? Once done, select a group member to report back to the class.

Group Process 1.2

Begin by reading the "Ten Strategies to Intentionally Use Group Work to Transform Hate, Facilitate Courageous Conversations, and Enhance Community Building" (Guth et al., 2019), listed under the Key References and available online. When you are finished, as a class, vote on one of the following topics for group discussion:

- LGBTQ+ student rights in K–12 schools
- Immigrants and refugees rights in detention centers in the United States
- Women's rights to choose terminating a pregnancy
- U.S. citizens' rights to free and affordable healthcare

Once the class agrees on a topic, keep in mind your value list and the order in which you placed them. Applying the information from the Ten Strategies document, engage in a class discussion to answer the following questions:

- What personal values do you hold that inform your opinion about the policies that exist currently regarding the topic?
- Where and how did you learn to hold said values? Who or what influenced your adoption of said values?
- How would you feel about helping a client who presents to you with issues that directly or indirectly relate to the policy in question?
- What would be your greatest challenge in your efforts to provide effective counseling and advocacy for your client?
- At what level would you feel most comfortable helping? What circumstance(s) would make you choose to refer the client to someone else if you think you are unable to provide support for the client?
- What ethical dilemmas do you anticipate experiencing in the process?

When you are finished discussing this issue as a class, write a one-page reflection about the experience. What happened and how did you feel? Were you surprised by any of the issues that were brought up? How did you handle the discussion? What was your degree of comfort/discomfort with the dynamics of the class? Were you able to articulate your position and opinion with ease or was it challenging for you? What aspects of your own identities were relevant to the discussion? Did anything about your identities and the topic being discussed surprise you? What would you like to learn more about based on what happened in class? When you think about the issues brought up by the exercise, what do you think is your biggest challenge going forward?

RESOURCES

ACA Advocacy Competencies: https://www.counseling.org/docs/default-source/competencies/acaadvocacy-competencies-updated-may-2020.pdf?sfvrsn=f410212c_4

Counselors for Social Justice: https://www.counseling.org/docs/default-source/Government-Affairs/why_social_justice_is_a_counseling_concern

Institute for Democracy and Electoral Assistance: https://www.idea.int/sites/default/files/publications/successful-strategies-facilitating-the-inclusion-of-marginalized-groups.pdf

Multicultural and Social Justice Counseling Competencies: https://www.counseling.org/docs/defaultsource/competencies/multicultural-and-social-justicecounseling-competencies.pdf?sfvrsn=14

Substance Abuse and Mental Health Services Administration TIP 57: Trauma-Informed Care in Behavioral Health Services: https://store.samhsa.gov/product/TIP-57-Trauma-Informed-Care-in-Behavioral-Health-Services/SMA144816

Stomp Out Bullying: How to Support Marginalized Groups: https://www.stompoutbullying.org/blog/support-Marginalized-Groups

The Trevor Project: https://www.thetrevorproject.org/volunteer

 Access this podcast at http://connect.springerpub.com/content/book/978-0-8261-6386-8/chapter/ch01.

KEY REFERENCES

Only key references appear in the print edition. The full reference list appears in the digital product found on https://connect.springerpub.com/content/book/978-0-8261-6386-8/chapter/ch01

Guth, L. J., Pollard, B. L., Nitza, A., Puig, A., Chan, C. D., Singh, A. A., & Bailey, H. (2019). Ten strategies to intentionally use group work to transform hate, facilitate courageous conversations, and enhance community building. *The Journal for Specialists in Group Work*, 44(1), 3–24. https://doi.org/10.1080/01933922.2018.1561778

Ratts, M. J., & Hutchins, A. M. (2009). ACA advocacy competencies: Social justice advocacy at the client/student level. *Journal of Counseling & Development*, 87(3), 269–275. https://doi.org/10.1002/j.1556-6678.2009.tb00106.x

Ratts, M. J., Singh, A. A., Nassar-McMillan, S., Butler, S. K., & McCullough, J. R. (2016). Multicultural and social justice counseling competencies: Guidelines for the counseling profession. *Journal of Multicultural Counseling and Development*, 44(1), 28–48. https://doi.org/10.1002/jmcd.12035

Toporek, R. L., & Daniels, J. (2018). *American counseling association advocacy competencies*. https://www.counseling.org/docs/default-source/competencies/aca-advocacy-competencies-updated-may-2020.pdf?sfvrsn=f410212c_4

CHAPTER 2

MULTICULTURALISM, INTERSECTIONALITY, AND DIVERSITY IN COUNSELING

Ana Puig and Latoya Haynes-Thoby

Think about this...

What are your most salient visible and invisible identities? Can you ascertain which afford you privileges and which bring marginalization? How might these identities inform how your counseling journey unfolds? What attitudes, beliefs, and values do you bring to this profession? How might these help or hinder your ability to serve and advocate for clients who are similar to or different from you? What types of client populations do you feel drawn to work with and why? What do you believe are the roles of advocacy and social justice in counseling practice with marginalized populations?

LEARNING OBJECTIVES

After reading this chapter, you should be able to:

- Name the Multicultural and Social Justice Counseling Competencies and their role in counseling practice and advocacy
- Explain main aspects of the human development theories and the multicultural orientation framework in the counseling field
- Identify the racial identity development theories and implications for counseling
- Discuss the generations name game and implications for client advocacy
- Assess LGBTQ+ development theories and applications to counseling

(continued)

- Discuss counseling people with disabilities across contexts, and implications for counseling
- Identify the most pressing issues for immigrants and refugees and their families and ways to advocate for these groups

INTRODUCTION

This textbook centers the Multicultural and Social Justice Counseling Competencies (MCSJCC; Ratts et al., 2015) as an aspirational guide for beginning counselors. The competencies underscore the importance of providing advocacy and embracing social justice as critical for efficacious client support. Counselors in training are encouraged to evaluate their own salient identities and their intersection with privilege or marginalization. These will in turn connect with the client's identities and invariably influence the client-counselor dynamics. The conceptualization of MCSJCC includes quadrants, domains, and competencies. You can read about the MCSJCC framework and the authors' explanation of its applications to counseling here: https://ct.counseling.org/2016/01/multicultural-and-social-justice-counseling-competencies-practical-applications-in-counseling. The MCSJCC is a broad framework whereby you can explore your attitudes, beliefs, and values vis-à-vis your client's. The juxtaposition of your and your client's ways of seeing the world will inform the nature and quality of your counseling relationship.

HUMAN DEVELOPMENT THEORIES OVERVIEW

As human beings develop, researchers have reported observable changes that occur across the lifespan (Arnett, 2015; Huitt & Hummel, 2003; Orenstein & Lewis, 2021). Counselors use developmental stage models as helpful tools that serve as guides in outlining the developmental processes that individuals complete at various points from infancy to the end of life, and multiculturally competent counselors also work to incorporate processes that reflect the cultural values of the clients that they serve. While individual models of development can be helpful, considerations of the unique needs of diverse client populations will be important to consider.

Theories of human development involve multiple dimensions (physical, cognitive, social, and emotional) and this process may be continuous or discontinuous throughout the lifespan. Development can occur in multiple directions whereby individuals make gains or advances, and experience losses or declines. Human beings are also malleable (also known as plasticity) and are influenced by the environments they inhabit. Human development can occur slowly and in stages or dramatically and suddenly. Environmental influences and events may account for the latter. Some theories posit that human beings are passive and shaped by environmental influences while others state that human development is active and individuals play a role in their own evolution. Finally, theories propose that development is dictated by genetics or nature and/or by the environment or nurture (Kuther, 2019). In the process of providing therapy to clients, you may encounter individuals coming to counseling to address unexpected life events that create opportunities for development (e.g., sudden loss, illness, accident, and change in employment status, among others). As a counselor in training, you can expect to explore these theories in greater depth through a dedicated course on human development across the lifespan. Next, we provide cursory overviews of these theories.

Psychoanalytic

Sigmund Freud is known as the father of psychoanalytic theory and psychoanalysis. He believed that most human development is driven by unconscious drives and proposed the psychosexual development theory comprising the oral stage, anal stage, phallic stage, latency stage, and genital stage. Table 2.1 illustrates the basic tenets of psychoanalytic theory.

Psychosocial

Erik Erikson's theory of psychosocial development (2021) builds on Freud's theory and presents eight stages of human development that are influenced by biological, psychological, and social changes in individuals as they progress from infancy to adulthood (Orenstein & Lewis, 2021). Jeffrey Arnett's (2015) theory of emerging adulthood posits that between Erikson's stages of adolescence and adulthood, human beings navigate a period of emerging adulthood from about 18 to 29 years of age. Relatedly, Piaget's theory presented four stages of cognitive development that are evidence of human beings' adaptation to the environment (Huitt & Hummel, 2003). Individuals must navigate and aim to resolve eight psychological crises. Erickson's Psychosocial Stages of Development are illustrated in Table 2.2.

Behaviorism and Social Learning

Behaviorist and social learning theories were developed in response to Freud's psychoanalytic theory. Proponents of behaviorism and social learning believe that only observable phenomena can account for human development. Specifically, these theorists studied observable behavior and contended that all behavior is the direct result of the social and physical environment. Moreover, the process of conditioning is thought to be responsible for these behaviors. Pavlov advanced classical conditioning while Skinner proposed operant conditioning. Bandura, on the other hand, developed the social learning theory, which states individuals and their innate dispositions interact with the environment and new behaviors are learned as a result. Bandura was responsible for coining the term *reciprocal determinism*.

Cognitive, Sociocultural, Systems and Attachment Theories

Piaget developed the cognitive developmental theory, which posits that thinking guides behavior. He believed human beings interact with the world to create schemas, or concepts and ideas about the world around them. Human beings are naturally driven to learn and this innate drive plus the ongoing exchanges with their physical and social environs influence development. Vygotsky proposed the sociocultural theory, which posits that human beings interact with others and their environment and this allows for the development of thoughts and behaviors. He believed culture, nurture, and nature all play a role in human development. Genetics, brain functioning, and individual maturation processes influence the person's capacities and development. Bronfenbrenner advanced the bioecological systems theory, which proposes that individuals are in constant relationship with the multiple systems and contexts they inhabit. He believed that individuals' innate traits interact with these systems and continually influence behavior and development. Finally, Bowlby's attachment theory proposed

TABLE 2.1 PSYCHOANALYTIC THEORY

STAGE (AGE)	BASIC DRIVE AREA	PLEASURES AND INFLUENCES	UNMET NEEDS- OUTCOME
Oral (0–18 mo)	Mouth, tongue, gums Weaning	Feeding and sucking	Overeating Overdrinking Nail biting
Anal (18 mo– 3 yr)	Anus	Passing or retaining Toilet training	Control issues (environmental order vs. chaos)
Phallic (3–6 yr)	Genitals	Opposite-sex parental attraction Fear or hostility for same-sex parent; child needs to push desires into unconscious mind and be close and learn from same-sex parent; resolving this conflict leads to embracing society's values and expectations	Guilt or lack of conscience
Latency (7 yr– puberty)	Dormant period	Child grows in skills, talents Focus on school, friends, sports	N/A
Genital (puberty through adulthood)	Genitals	Sexual relationships Sexual satisfaction	Concern with quality of relationships

Source: Adapted from Kuther, T. (2019). *Lifespan development in context: A topical approach.* Sage.

TABLE 2.2 ERIKSON'S PSYCHOSOCIAL STAGES

STAGE	CONFLICT	VIRTUE VS. MALDEVELOPMENT	DESCRIPTION
1. Infancy	Trust vs. Mistrust	Hope vs. Withdrawal	Parents or guardians provide food, shelter, stability, love
2. Early Childhood	Autonomy vs. Shame and Doubt	Will vs. Compulsion	Parents or guardians provide secure home environment while encouraging autonomy
3. Play Age	Initiative vs. Guilt	Purpose vs. Inhibition	Parents or guardians encourage child to explore, initiate their own interests and likes
4. School Age	Industry vs. Inferiority	Competence vs. Inertia or Passivity	Parents or guardians provide realistic expectations for school and home, compliments for their successes
5. Adolescence	Identity vs. Role Confusion	Fidelity vs. Repudiation	Individual weighing experiences, social expectations, desires, and personal values.
6. Young Adulthood	Intimacy vs. Isolation	Love vs. Distantiation	Individual developing close friendships and/or romantic relationships
7. Adulthood	Generativity vs. Stagnation	Care vs. Rejectivity	Engagement with younger generations via parenting, teaching, and/or coaching
8. Old Age	Integrity vs. Despair	Wisdom vs. Disdain	Reflecting on life accomplishments

Source: Adapted from Orenstein, G. A., & Lewis, L. (2021). Erikson's stages of psychosocial development. In *StatPearls*. StatPearls Publishing. https://www.ncbi.nlm.nih.gov/books/NBK556096

that children develop according to their relationship with primary caregivers. He believed that children seek closeness and safety and adults either provide these or fall short of doing so. There are attachment styles (secure, ambivalent, avoidant, disorganized) associated with the type of nurturing (met and unmet needs) the child received, creating potential relationship issues throughout the lifespan (Cherry, 2020).

There are multiple other theories we will not discuss here. We encourage you to explore these in greater depth throughout the course of your training. See the Resources section for additional information about human development theories. The theories mentioned here and main tenets are outlined in Table 2.3.

Multicultural Orientation Framework

Davis et al. (2018) state that the multicultural orientation (MCO) framework was developed to respond to trends in the counseling profession, specifically, the emergent multicultural counseling competencies. As we discussed earlier in this chapter, these competencies were revised and expanded to include social justice (Ratts et al., 2015). Multicultural competencies attend to the counselor's awareness, knowledge, and skills. Scholars were aiming to integrate these competencies into research about psychotherapy outcomes. The self of the therapist is a central focus of MCO. Salient constructs associated with this framework are cultural humility, cultural opportunities, and cultural comfort. The authors add:

MCO involves a way of understanding and relating to the cultural identities of clients. MCO language implies "a way of being with clients," particularly when one detects cultural dynamics that may require enhanced awareness, knowledge, and skills. The language of humility primes therapists to focus all resources within their grasp toward optimizing attentiveness and responsiveness to the client's needs (i.e., being other-oriented), including regulation of ego involvement that might enhance self-consciousness. (p. 91)

They assert that counselors who focus on their own goals may be more concerned with themselves than with whatever the client needs in the moment. Being hyperaware of yourself is not uncommon when you are just beginning to learn about being present for your client. Developing a multicultural orientation means working to become culturally humble and opening yourself to cultural opportunities, which will in turn enhance your comfort level when interacting with individuals whose culture is different from yours. Estrada et al. (2013) contend that new counseling students struggle with these concepts and may experience anxiety when exposed to exploration of their own privilege, a requirement for learning about cultural humility.

CULTURAL HUMILITY

Cultural humility requires that the therapist be other-oriented rather than self-focused, and express openness instead of interpersonal superiority (Davis et al., 2018). This may seem counter to the assumption that the therapeutic relationship is inherently hierarchical and the therapist holds the power in the relationship. This construct encompasses both inter- and intrapersonal aspects. Intrapersonal humility refers to the counselor's ability to see themselves accurately and

TABLE 2.3 HUMAN DEVELOPMENT THEORIES COMPARED

THEORY	PROCESS CONTINUOUS VS. DISCONTINUOUS	ACTIVE VS. PASSIVE	NURTURE VS. NATURE
Psychoanalytic (Freud)	Discontinuous	Passive—Humans have innate drives that motivate behavior	Nature emphasized; development is the result of whether drives are fulfilled
Psychosocial (Erikson)	Discontinuous	Active—Psychosocial tasks resolved by human interactions with their social environment	Nature and nurture play roles in helping individuals navigate stages successfully
Behaviorist (Watson, Skinner, Pavlov)	Continuous	Passive—Environment shapes the person	Nurture; behavior shaped by environment
Social Learning (Bandura)	Continuous	Active—Environment and individual traits and behaviors interact	Nature and nurture both influence behavior
Cognitive Developmental (Piaget)	Discontinuous, but need for equilibrium is a continuous process	Active—Individual schemas created through individual interaction with their world	Nature and nurture Brain development and drives interact with physical and social environment to influence development

(continued)

TABLE 2.3 HUMAN DEVELOPMENT THEORIES COMPARED (CONTINUED)

THEORY	PROCESS CONTINUOUS VS. DISCONTINUOUS	ACTIVE VS. PASSIVE	NURTURE VS. NATURE
Sociocultural (Vygotsky)	Continuous engagement with others supports increase in mental capabilities and skills	Active—Individuals and culture in constant interaction	Nature and nurture Humans interact with more advanced humans to learn new behaviors
Bioecological Systems (Bronfenbrenner)	Continuous Individual interaction with systems and contexts creates ongoing development and change	Active—Individuals interact with and are influenced by their contexts	Nature and nurture Individual innate characteristics interact with changing systems to influence behaviors and change
Attachment Theory (Bowlby)	Continuous However, traumatic events can create discontinuity and influence attachment style	Active—Individuals' innate need for closeness and security and interactions with caregivers influence attachment style	Nature and nurture Infants, children, and adolescents have innate needs for proximity and safety that are met or unmet by caregivers and these result in varied attachment styles that remain through life

Source: Data from Kuther, T. (2019). *Lifespan development in context: A topical approach.* Sage; Cherry, K. (2020, June). *Child development theories and examples.* https://www.verywellmind.com/child-development-theories-2795068; Cherry, K. (2020, June). *The different types of attachment styles.* https://www.verywellmind.com/attachment-styles-2795344

acknowledge their limitations. Interpersonal humility requires that the counselor possess an orientation toward otherness and a dearth of feelings of superiority. It is especially important for the counselor to put the client's worldview and values front and center rather than their own. A counselor's defensiveness or egoism would be counter to cultural humility. When you consider the array of counseling theories and interventions available to you, deciding which best align with your values and beliefs, while important, must be weighed against the presenting client and their issues. Davis et al. (2018) reminds us here that:

Theoretical perspectives in psychotherapy have developed within a cultural context that reflects Eurocentric, patriarchal, and middle- to upper-social-class values (to name a few privileged identities). Thus, clients belonging to marginalized groups may perceive misalignment in the values and culturally endorsed narratives about pathology and health often used by psychotherapists. (p. 91)

Furthermore, the traditional ways in which we conceptualize the process of therapy may also not align with a client's worldviews and expectations.

The process of therapy involves the following: intake, case conceptualization, treatment plan, strengthening and repairing the working alliance, growing through value conflicts when they emerge, and owning your limits as a counselor (Davis et al., 2018).

Davis et al. (2018) contend that the intake process as traditionally implemented represents majority culture encapsulation and centering; it assumes that the client should trust the therapist implicitly and without question simply because they showed up for the session. Moreover, the intake process is couched on a 1:1 engagement that only includes the client and takes place in a controlled environment such as the counselor's office. The intake process is an opportunity for the counselor to learn about the client's values, beliefs, experiences, and worldview and for the client to learn about their therapist. A culturally humble counselor challenges the normative intake process by allowing for the client's preferred methods of sharing information. It is also imperative that the counselor not make assumptions about the client but rather, check with the client to clarify or confirm aspects of their presentation that are relevant to the client's issues. Case conceptualization can also be carried out in a culturally competent fashion. This requires that the counselor understand the client's story and remain open to their point of view rather than creating a narrative that suits the counselor's views and opinions. The conceptualization of what the client brings to therapy must be a collaborative effort. Davis et al. (2018) go as far as stating that not following a collaborative approach is "tantamount to cultural arrogance" (p. 96).

The treatment plan should also be a collaboratively developed map of client goals and objectives, rather than a plan of action driven and led by the counselor. It is imperative for the counselor to attend to the client's wishes for therapy outcomes. Davis et al. (2018) add that in delivering treatment, "effective interventions may require consulting with family members or spiritual leaders in the client's life to negotiate a culturally acceptable way of addressing the client's presenting problem" (p. 97). Acknowledging the possibility of cultural ruptures occurring is also important. The process of strengthening or repairing ruptures in the therapeutic alliance will be ongoing throughout therapy. Finally, the counselor must acknowledge the limits of their competence and hold on to a spirit of curiosity and humility so they can learn from the client as much as the client might learn from them. In order to accomplish this, counselors may choose to engage in practices that highlight emphasis in the here and now and keep the ego in check (e.g., mindfulness, self-compassion).

CULTURAL COMFORT

Cultural comfort refers to the counselor's degree of comfort with the client's identities and the client's perception of that comfort. This is a necessary ingredient of the therapeutic alliance and the quality of the counselor-client relationship.

CULTURAL OPPORTUNITIES

Cultural opportunities refer to your ability to seize moments during therapy when you can learn more about the client's values, beliefs, worldview, and any other salient aspect of their identity. This has to occur organically and be born of your curiosity and genuine interest about the client's identities, visible or invisible, and their lived experiences.

Maintaining a multicultural orientation in your awareness as you develop a therapeutic relationship with your clients while applying the multicultural and social justice competencies will go a long way to help you become an effective counselor. Next, we provide a brief overview of the most prevalent racial identity development theories so that you may begin to understand the ways in which individuals from various racial/ethnic groups change, evolve, and become who they are. Keep in mind that theories are not immutable understandings of people; rather, they provide information that we may find useful in deepening our awareness of others. Always look at these through a critical and curious lens.

Racial Identity Development Theories

The Black Identity Development Model, developed by Dr. William Cross (1971, 1991, 1995; Cross et al., 2002), illustrates the process from race salience to sustained commitment and comfort in Black identity. Cross's original model was developed during the Civil Rights movement and highlighted Black American development toward acceptance (Cross, 1971). His model illustrated the process toward becoming Black, within the American context. It included five stages that highlighted movement from a framework that is largely influenced by White dominant culture to a framework that indicates a positive self-regard for Blackness. Cross (1971) theorized that Black development included (1) a pre-encounter stage, where identity is based on mainstream beliefs about what it means to be a Black person, with those beliefs being informed by White dominant cultural norms, and may include internalized anti-Blackness as an indicator of psychological unwellness; (2) an encounter stage, that is evidence of an awakening and questioning of a Black person's previously held negative beliefs about their own race and identity; (3) an immersion stage that involves the development of a new racial identity, a delving into Black culture, and an appreciation for Blackness; (4) an internalization stage that includes a movement toward viewing Blackness as one component of identity, among many; and (5) an internalization-commitment stage that is marked by action, higher activism, social change, and is evidence of psychological well-being. Over time, Cross, 1991 worked to continue to interrogate the evidence and his understandings of this process, resulting in an updated model with more nuanced processes within each stage. Cross (1991) most recent model of development continues to include five stages, but the stages include multiple processes that allow for differentiation among Black people's experiences of their own Black identity, including (1) the pre-encounter stage can include both positive or negative race salience, evidenced by either assimilation or internalized self-hate due to miseducation, (2) the encounter stage, (3) the immersion-emersion stage largely remained the same, but noted lowered emotionality regarding the development and delving into Black identity, followed by a collapsed fourth stage of internalization and the fifth stage, internalization-commitment, to (4) the internalization stage that is indicative of high positive race salience, self-acceptance, and sustained commitment.

The Asian American Identity Development Model, developed by Jean Kim (1981). Kim (2001) describes movement toward a psychologically healthy identity formation. Kim (1981) describes the process of Asian American identity development across six stages, including (1) ethnic awareness that occurs in early childhood, framed by family and significant adults that shape a person's attitudes about their ethnic identity; (2) White identification occurs in early education and, through prejudice, shapes a person's early sense of identity and self-concept, potentially leading toward a longing for Whiteness; (3) an awakening stage that includes heightened political awareness, and understanding of oppression; (4) a redirection that is evidenced by reconnection with Asian American ethnicity and culture, awareness of the role of oppression, and an increased ethnic pride; followed by (5) incorporation that includes heightened pride for Asian American culture, and a respect for other groups.

The Minority Identity Development Model (MID) was originally developed by Atkinson et al. (1998) to highlight common identity development features for minority populations. This model was renamed the Racial Cultural Identity Development Model (Sue & Sue, 2013). The Racial Cultural Identity Development Model (R/CID) was developed by Atkinson et al. (1998) and includes five stages that illustrate the process by which individuals who belong to minority groups move from conformity to integrative awareness. Atkinson and colleagues list the stages to include (1) conformity that is defined as a period in which a person of color believes what society has communicated to them about their place in society; they might hold low levels of racial salience for themselves, those within their own group, and other minorities, while having appreciation for majority culture; (2) a period of dissonance that is evidenced by a burgeoning conflict between previously held beliefs about one's own and other minority groups' inferiority, coupled with new considerations about nuanced appreciation for the majority culture; (3) resistance and immersion illustrates a process toward self and group appreciation; (4) introspection that includes introspection about the basis of feelings regarding self and group appreciation, as well as judgment or negative evaluation of other minority groups and majority culture; and (5) integrative awareness that highlighted more nuanced appreciation of self, cultural group, other minorities, and more selective evaluation of majority culture.

The Biracial Identity Development Model, developed by Poston (1990), addressed a gap in the literature regarding the developmental processes for people who held at least two racial identities. Poston posited that biracial people move from a place of personal identity to an appreciation for all of the identities that they hold. Poston posited that the developmental process occurs across five stages: (1) self-identity that occurs during early childhood, and is marked by a lack of awareness of the duality of identities that the person holds; (2) choice of group, or selection of one group over the other is described as being brought on by significant adults or members of the larger society; (3) enmeshment and denial that features guilt and denial about differences across cultural groups; (4) a stage of appreciation that is defined as a period of exploration and appreciation for both groups, including for biracial people who feel much more connected to one group; followed by (5) an integration stage that highlights an appreciation for both groups.

The White Racial Identity Development (WRID) Model, developed by Helms (1995), describes the process that White people navigate toward racial consciousness. Helms (1995) describes six stages: (1) contact, which includes a limited awareness of issues related to race and racism, and may include a denial of seeing racial differences; (2) a disintegration that often includes internal conflict about race and one's own racism; (3) reintegration that is evidenced by a movement back toward basic beliefs about racial inferiority for minoritized people and supremacy for White people; (4) a stage of pseudo-independence that includes work to understand the experiences of people of color, and this stage is usually brought on by a cathartic experience or event that strongly challenges the perspectives held in the reintegration stage; (5) an immersion/emersion stage that is evidenced by self-exploration of a White person, coupled with acknowledgment of White people having a race; followed by (6) autonomy that is includes an increasing awareness of Whiteness, acceptance of one's own role in the maintaining systems of oppression, including racism, and a willingness to continue to explore. These stages occur across two phases: (1) an abandonment of racism, and (2) a redefining of positive White identity.

The Latino Identity Orientations was developed by Drs. Bernardo Ferdman and Plácida I. Gallegos (2001), who described the variety of identity orientations for Latino people in the United States. The researchers describe six orientations: (a) an undifferential orientation that may include what appears to be a sense of denial about differences and a denial of seeing color, (b) a White-identified orientation that is marked by a dichotomous White or nonwhite alignment, (c) Latino as other, which includes movement away from self-description of being White, (d) subgroup identification that focuses on distinct cultures within their Latino heritage, and includes a positioning of Latino culture as being secondary to other cultural identities, (e) Latino-identified is described as including a clearer sense of pride in Latino cultural heritage, and (f) Latino-integrated that is marked by a greater awareness of the social construction of race, complex beliefs, and understandings of one's own identity as a Latino person (Ferdman & Gallegos, 2001; Gallegos & Ferdman, 2007).

Horse (Kiowa) (2005) developed an American Indian Identity Development model that highlights influences that impact the process by which Native American or Indian American people traverse toward greater consciousness.

FIGURE 2.1 Timeline of Racial Identity Development Models

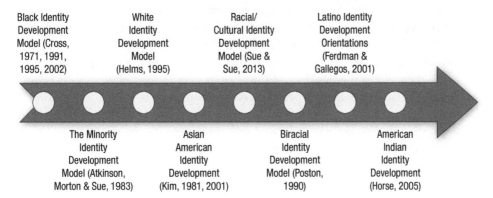

The influences include (a) Native American identity salience for a person, which is marked by the level of grounding in Native language and culture; (b) genealogy validity; (c) traditional Native worldview, as evidenced by the extent that a Native American holds a worldview that draws from Native American culture, ideology, and philosophy; (d) concept of self as a Native American; and (e) tribal enrollment or connection. Horse (Kiowa) (2005) notes the importance of considering the impact of societal influences that can frame or dismantle positive Native American identity and self-concept.

Counselors use the identity development models to explore both their own identity development, as well as the clients that they support. An understanding of the nonlinear process by which people journey through the identity development models will be important. Considerations for serving populations that fall within or outside a counselor's own personal experience should include challenging to address biases, assumptions, and the potential for harm in counseling. Figure 2.1 provides a timeline of the Racial Identity Development Models described above.

THE GENERATIONS NAME GAME AND IMPLICATIONS FOR CLIENT ADVOCACY

As counselors consider the components of cultural factors that influence people's worldview, the impact that the generation that a person has grown up with is often overlooked. A brief review of the most recent generations (i.e., Generation Z, Millennials, Generation X, and Baby Boomers) very easily brings to light societal influences that have impacted the perspectives of those who traversed a developmental timeline during shared time periods. Counselors know that generational groupings alone will not fully illuminate the experience of clients, but this information may shed light into shared practices and trends. Children born between early 2020 and now will have begun their early life and schooling experiences within the context of a global pandemic. Experiences that many adults view as unusual or outside the realm of normalcy are the only realities that many members of the emergent generation now know.

Generations span across a period of about 20 years, and often move from more generic names (e.g., Generation Z) to names that include components that might define the experience of individuals who have traversed toward adulthood during a shared time period (e.g., iGen or Zoomers). Shared experiences, trends, and realities shaped by societal level changes can largely influence both how the generations are defined and how they understand the world. As such, generational factors can be an important component to transgenerational work in the counseling relationship. While earlier generations have moved beyond more generic monikers, Generation Alpha has not yet traversed the first 20 years of their lives, yet they are representative of a cohort of human beings who largely began their primary educational experiences during the COVID-19 pandemic, a time of great loss, scarcity, and remote living.

Generations

Counselors utilize generational information in concert with other data about the clients that they support. As identities are not additive, but intersecting, generational identity is nuanced and will hold varying precedence for clients who hold multiple identities that may be privileged or marginalized. Holding space to learn about your clients' experiences and the identities that are most salient for them will be key. Considerations regarding the impact of generational groupings can be a helpful aid as counselors work to understand the factors that may have shaped the world that clients faced during key developmental stages.

GENERATION ALPHA

Individuals who are a part of the Generation Alpha cohort were born between the years 2012 through 2020. This generation is one of the most recent generational cohorts, and short of their experience-based moniker, they have been nicknamed Generation Alpha due to their ordering behind Generation Z. This generational cohort does not yet have a name that reflects their group identity, as generation naming is often a result of key cultural and social features that are made evident through the behaviors of that cohort as the members age (Twenge, 2018). Similar to the preceding generations, members of Generation Alpha were born at a time when technology would have been common and a very present part of their daily lives. Members of Generation Alpha are the most likely to have been exposed to technology for entertainment, socialization, and education during childhood. As a result of the COVID-19 pandemic, many members of this group, along with members of Generation Z, would have experienced at least one period of schooling through remote technology. Some members of Generation Alpha may have begun their preschool or kindergarten educational experiences through a remote learning format as a result of state, county, and countrywide shutdowns around the globe.

Based on resource access and various aspects of privilege, members of Generation Alpha's early educational experiences may have begun in the physical presence of caregivers, members of community level pods, or within more structured childcare settings designed to accommodate the health precautions enacted during the global pandemic. Many would have borne witness to a nationwide toilet paper supply panic, and widespread loss while navigating early life. While navigating the global pandemic, members of this cohort will have had knowledge of countless acts of race-based violence, acts of anti-Asian hate, international wars, the murder of the president of Haiti, the displacement of millions of people around the country due to government instability, and displacement of children and families at the southern border of the United States. Nearly 200,000 children in this cohort faced immediate loss by the end of summer 2021 (Hillis, Blankenship, et al., 2021; Wright, 2022). The National Institute of Health (NIH) reported that 1 in 500 children lost a significant caregiver as a result of COVID-19, and the rate of caregiver loss for children of color was nearly triple the rate of White children (Hillis, Unwin, et al., 2021). In addition to other sources of adversity, the COVID-19 global pandemic served as a source of adversity for many children, either through direct or indirect experiences of loss.

Individuals born within this cohort will have witnessed the impact of political change around the globe, and loss that may not have been coupled with grieving practices that were reflective of their own culture's traditional practices, due to pandemic-related risks, caution, and capacity limitations. These individuals would have also witnessed the process of their countries transitioning across various stages of the pandemic, and for many, this would include movement to in-person education for children whose families made the choice to return at varying stages of the pandemic. As this cohort ages, as with preceding cohorts, their moniker will likely reflect these shared experiences, challenges, and triumphs.

GENERATION Z

Individuals born from 1996 through the year 2012 are members of Generation Z, and their cohort immediately precedes Generation Alpha. People born within this cohort have often been described as being much more oriented toward socializing with peers through technology, and having had access to a smartphone for most of their lives, in comparison to previous generations (Twenge, 2018). The youngest members of this cohort would have experienced late elementary or middle school that may have included a time of remote learning due to the global pandemic. Older Gen Zers would have been entering early or emerging adulthood during the beginning of the global pandemic, they would have been toddlers during Y2K, and in early childhood when hijacked airplanes were flown into the World Trade Center in New York City on September 11, 2001. Younger members of this generational cohort would have navigated primary education via Zoom or other remote learning modalities during the early months of the COVID-19 pandemic, with many still having been enrolled in elementary school.

During pivotal times in their development, this cohort would have witnessed international periods of political unrest, wars, the kidnapping of nearly 300 Nigerian girls in Chibok, Nigeria, an economic recession that impacted several countries around the globe, and for many, some pivotal experiences of early adulthood were derailed due to the pandemic-related country-wide shutdowns. This cohort has witnessed what has been described as cataclysmic levels of societal trauma, including events that have resulted in recurring and ongoing death, loss, and heightened immediate health risks. While almost each generational cohort will have experienced shared loss, gains, and triumphs, members of Generation Z and the generations that have followed them will have been among the most recent that have shared large-scale levels of sustained societal trauma. This generation has borne witness to large-scale models of adversity, resilience, and growth. Late members of this cohort will have faced uncertainty, and a reemergence toward what many hope might represent some level of a "return to normal" as returns to in-person activity and masks mandates were modified. Members of this generational cohort, within the U.S. context, are described as having higher levels of diversity than any generation in the past (Parker & Igielnik, 2020), yet they continue to experience high levels of segregation during their K-12 schooling experiences (EdBuild, 2019).

MILLENNIALS

Individuals who were born in the years 1981 through 1996 are a part of the Millennial cohort. Millennials have been described as having the highest levels of diversity, in comparison to previous generations (Frey, 2016), with about 51% identifying as White. By the year 2019, more than 49% of adolescents in the United States identified as people of color (de Brey et al., 2019), in comparison to Generation X (Currier, 2018). This cohort also attained greater levels of postsecondary education than the previous generation (Frey, 2016), across racial and ethnic groups (Bialik & Fry, 2019), but the economic wealth gap continues to widen for Millennials of color in comparison to their White Millennial peers (Gale et al., 2020). Millennials are also much less likely to hold conservative views than previous generations (Fry & Parker, 2018).

Early Millennials would have been about 10 years old during the time of the Gulf War, with the conflicts holding the potential to shape their understanding of the world around them. Many late Millennials would have been 5-year-olds during the attacks of September 11, 2001, and this same subset of Millennials were entering early adulthood at the onset of the COVID-19 global pandemic. These conflicts were in tandem to military conflicts and unrest around the world. Many pivotal events that shaped Millennials are shared with members of other extant generations, such as the Columbine and Sandy Hook school shootings, the losses associated with Hurricane Katrina, the election of the first Black president of the United States, the passing of marital equality laws, the Boston marathon bombing, and the Great Recession of 2008. As with older generations that survived the Great Depression during key developmental stages, the losses associated with World War II and the Vietnam War, this generation's formative years will have occurred alongside times of global community trauma, and stressors that changed how they understood themselves in the world.

Unlike previous generations, many Millennials entered the job market during or right after the Great Recession of 2008, and the impact that this has had on lifetime earnings has been that Millennial household income is slightly lower than for members of Generation X, who would have entered the world of work in times of greater stability. Millennial household earnings continue to be higher than those of the Baby Boomer generation, but the value of that income is not the same, due to costs, inflation, and time context. Millennials have also been described as being much more focused on career fulfillment, and are much less likely to remain with one employer than Baby Boomers (Gallup, 2016). Their willingness to engage in career change in the search for fulfillment is girded by this group's attainment of higher levels of education than generations prior, with 39% of young adult Millennials holding at least an undergraduate degree, in comparison to 29% of Generation Xers, and 25% of Baby Boomers (Bialik & Fry, 2019).

Counselors can use this type of information in preparation for counseling Millennials, while keeping in mind that there are likely to be differential experiences among Millennials. Aspects of identity, coping, and available resources will largely shape how these experiences may have been integrated into how these events were navigated by any individual Millennial. It will also be important to note that individuals outside one specific generational cohort would have been impacted by these events as well, but in ways that may have been different based on where they were developmentally.

GENERATION X

Individuals born during the years 1965 through 1980 are largely described as Gen Xers, or members of Generation X. Younger members of Generation X would have been in elementary school when they witnessed news reports about the fall of the Berlin Wall and the U.S. Challenger space accident. Millennials were between adolescence and early adulthood when efforts toward marriage equality began to become more known. During this time, Millennials would have witnessed laws that aimed to identify marriage within a strict heterosexual paradigm. It would not be until 2015 when laws permitting marital equality were passed, with the *Obergefell v. Hodges* Supreme Court decision. In addition to being impacted by the attacks of September 11, 2001, Generation X had also witnessed the Oklahoma City bombing merely 6 years before. Younger Generation Xers navigated adolescence and entered early adulthood with these experiences at the forefront. Many members of this generation were reported to be less likely than preceding generations to enlist in the military (Schaeffer, 2021).

Early members of Generation X would have been preschool-aged children when birth control pills became more widely available in the early 1970s. They would have experienced societal shifts that resulted in greater openness to talk about sex than previous generations. This cohort was also among the first to be raised in homes that included two income earning parents, or single parents; and were much more likely to fit the moniker of "latchkey kids." In comparison to the Baby Boomers, Generation X children were much more likely to be home alone after school than children in previous generations. This early independence was quite different from their caregivers' own growing up experiences in many ways.

BABY BOOMERS

The world looked a bit different for individuals born during the time period between 1946 and 1964. World War II was beginning to subside in 1945, as the oldest members of the Baby Boomers were being born in 1946. The eldest Baby

Boomers would have been late adolescents, with the youngest nearing the end of elementary school, when John F. Kennedy was assassinated (1963), and as they bore witness to the passing of the Civil Rights Act in 1964. The early childhoods of the first groupings of Baby Boomers may have been impressed upon by the news of the U.S. landing on the moon in 1969, and the assassination of Dr. Martin Luther King, Jr., in 1968.

These cultural changes shaped and influenced how members of the Baby Boomer cohort understood the world, but their moniker is not necessarily telling of their lived experience. Twenge (2018) argues that the Baby Boomer's range includes individuals who may have been too young to have been influenced by the key features that are often used to define this cohort, such as the counterculture of the 1970s. Many Baby Boomers would have been too young to fully engage in the culture of the 70s, yet they received a moniker that was much more descriptive of the times that they were alive, as described by others. Baby Boomers' educational experiences were quite different from the groups that would arrive after, such as the cost of school, home purchasing, and the necessity for higher levels of education. Older members of the Baby Boomer cohort will have been very young when school desegregation Supreme Court decisions were passed in *Brown v. Board of Education* (1954). While school segregation is no longer legally protected, the fight to provide equal access for schools across the United States continues today (EdBuild, 2019).

TRADITIONALIST

Traditionalists represent a cohort of individuals who were born during the years 1928 through 1945 (Twenge, 2018). Many Traditionalists would have been small children during the Great Depression and World War II. Traditionalists have been described as being much quieter than their predecessors, so much so that they had been nicknamed the "silent generation," a term coined by *TIME* magazine in 1951. When comparing Traditionalists to their parents who navigated adulthood during the "Roaring Twenties," they were seen as much more likely to conform, and this is likely the result of the political dynamics during their early childhood experiences.

Younger Traditionalists would have lived through childhood and early adulthood while the Vietnam War (1955–1975) was taking place. Many older members of this cohort also enlisted in the wars, and would be shaped by either witnessing or direct experience, as military veterans, with the conflict (Schaeffer, 2021). Traditionalists would have witnessed the Vietnam War as an almost immediate follow-up from the Korean War (1950–1953). The United States' involvement in both wars, and the increased military activity, has been described as largely shaping this cohort's outlook on the world and their ways of living. The COVID-19 global pandemic presented immense laws across generations, but many older individuals were at heightened risk for harm (Yanez et al., 2020). While early reports highlighted the COVID-19-related risks for older adults, navigating the loss of this population reverberated across generations. This population represented a cohort of grandparents and great grandparents for Generation Alpha, Millennials, and Gen Xers. Counselors serving this population also consider the impact of uncertainty and grief as they witnessed their neighbors, friends, and loved ones from their own cohort die during the pandemic. Considerations for individuals at generational cusps, resulting in their straddling two generations should include discussions regarding how the client experiences themself within the context of the dual generations.

Considerations and Implications

Culturally appropriate counseling for individuals across generations will require considerations for the generational experiences and events that shaped the world around them (Hicks et al., 2018). These considerations will be especially important as counselors consider the impact of events that may have resulted in cultural or community shifts, such as trauma, access to education, liberation, and technological changes. Features that have resulted in shifts in cultural norms, such as the scarcity faced during the Great Depression, desegregation, women's rights, marriage equality, and the global pandemic have impacted individuals to such a degree that their monikers are often derived from those events. Despite the fact that clients across generations will vary, it will be important for counselors to consider the influences of each individual's experience in context. Working with clients in context will require that counselors consider their experiences as a part of the puzzle and not as the whole picture. Allowing for clearer understandings of clients in context will require counselors to understand the ways that identities intersect, and the multiple ways that those identities can shape clients' lived experiences, understandings of the world, and understandings of themselves. As counselors work to explore the impact of who clients are generationally, it will be important to ask questions, and to actively listen to learn more about how the events that may have shaped an entire generational cohort has influenced the client sitting in the counseling space with you.

LESBIAN, GAY, BISEXUAL, TRANSGENDER, QUEER+ DEVELOPMENT THEORIES

In the course of providing counseling, you will encounter individuals who identify as LGBTQ+. This fact in itself does not mean their sexual or gender identity is the issue that brought them to you. However, in our understanding of intersectionality, advocacy, and social justice, attending to the client's salient identities, while critical, is not sufficient. You need to ascertain, in collaboration with the client, how his, her, or their identity informs their presenting problem. Your client may be struggling with issues related to their sexual and/or gender identities.

Consider these questions:

■ When was the first time you became aware that LGBTQ+ people existed? In what context was this awareness born (i.e., positive or negative)?

■ What stereotypes do you have (positive or negative) about LGBTQ+ persons? How does your cultural or spiritual/religious background influence these stereotypes/perceptions?

■ What challenges or difficulties have you encountered or feel you may encounter in working with LGBTQ+ clients (children, adolescents, adults, or elders)?

The history of counseling includes the harmful practice of conversion or reparative therapy, an effort to "convert" LGBTQ+ individuals to heterosexuality. Multiple professional organizations (e.g., American Counseling Association, American Psychological Association, among many others) have issued statements against this practice and you should be aware it is considered unethical and has been shown to have deleterious effects, including increased suicidality (see www.hrc.org/resources/policy-and-position-statements-on-conversion -therapy).

In your work with LGBTQ+ clients, including minors, the following ethical considerations must inform your approach. Whenever working with children or adolescents, counselors must be aware of special circumstances surrounding the treatment of minors. Specifically, a counselor cannot guarantee complete confidentiality due to the parental right to know; however, you can play the role of advocate on behalf of a client (Corey et al., 1993). In the case of adult clients, counselors have an ethical and moral obligation to conduct LGBTQ+ therapy in affirmative ways (Buhrke & Douce, 1991). A therapist can guarantee complete confidentiality except in the following cases: imminent danger to self or another, instances of a medical emergency, when ordered to release information by a court of law, and when aware of reported abuse or neglect of children or the elderly.

Understanding the LGBTQ+ development theories could be helpful. These identity development theories were developed based on empirical research and we will provide a brief overview of each.

The Cass Identity Model

This model was intended to describe the coming out process for gay men and lesbians. The model is not bound by age or developmental stage and is applicable across the lifespan. According to Cass (1979), the potential for identity foreclosure is present at every stage. The individual may choose not to move further or continue through the stages. At the end of this process, the individual may have a positive, integrated gay or lesbian identity. The stages are as follows: Stage I: Identity Confusion—characterized by the feeling of being different and an awareness that a heterosexual identity does not feel right. The individual experiences dissonance and inner turmoil during this stage. Her or his feelings may include shame, fear, despair, hopelessness, and, in extreme cases, suicidal ideations. Stage II: Identity Comparison—characterized by feelings of difference; however, the person still attempts to show a public identity that passes as a heterosexual and keeps their lesbian or gay identity separate. The person may accept their gay or lesbian behavior, but reject displaying this identity in public. Stage III: Identity Tolerance—characterized by realizing one is probably lesbian or gay and separate from the heterosexual world; they have a longing to connect with other lesbian and gay individuals. Progress through this stage depends on their ability to make contact with the gay community (can be positive or negative). Stage IV: Identity Acceptance—the person has increasingly frequent contact with the gay community. The person begins to develop friend-ships and may choose to appear heterosexual, as needed, and avoid contact or relationships with people who are judgmental or unaccepting. The person may begin disclosing their identity to select significant others. Stage V: Identity Pride—the person immerses him, her, or themselves in the gay community, strongly identify with this community and when negative feelings are expe-rienced, they may be related to social oppression, prejudice, or discrimination. The person may embrace social activism and increase the level and frequency of disclosure of their identity to others. Finally, Stage VI: Identity Synthesis—here, the individual lets go of the "us vs. them" attitude and recognizes that some in the heterosexual community can be trusted. A sense of pride and identity inte-gration takes place.

Coleman Model and Troiden Model

Two other models are the Troiden (1989) and the Coleman (1987) Models. The Troiden Model's underlying assumptions are that identity development begins before puberty and stages follow a chronological order by the individ-ual's age. The stages are Sensitization (awareness of difference, possible mar-ginalization by peers and beginning internalization of negative self-concept), Identity Confusion (age 17–18, recognition of homosexuality, feeling excluded from belonging in the world), Identity Assumption (ages 19–22, managing stigma, less isolation, increase contact with the lesbian and gay community), and Commitment (age 23 and over, integration of homosexual identity). The Coleman (1987) Model contends identity development is marked by the way the individual creates romantic attachments and relationships and outlines five stages: Pre-Coming Out (suspicion that one is gay), Coming Out (thoughts of same-sex attraction and start telling others about it), Exploration (begin dat-ing), First Relationship (seeking intimacy), and Integration (personal and pro-fessional lives are integrated).

Dual Lesbian Identity Development Model

McCarn and Fassinger (1996) provided a survey of extant lesbian and gay identity formation models and proposed a new way of conceptualizing les-bian identity development that recognizes aspects of development that are relationship-oriented and more fluid. In the Dual Lesbian Identity Development Model, McCarn and Fassinger borrowed from the feminist literature the notion of sexual repression and the tendency of women to develop and come out in the context of a relationship. This model tracks personal identity development and relationship identity development as it relates to the reference group. Specifically, the model explores development from an Individual Development and a Group Identity Development through the following phases: Phase I: Awareness—beginning awareness of difference, same-sex attraction and feel-ings (individual level). Awareness of a lesbian/gay community and acknowl-edgment that heterosexism has kept this at bay, centering heterosexuality and ignoring the array of sexual orientations that do exist is abandoned and questioning of these assumptions begins (group level). Phase II: Exploration—acknowledgment of sexual attraction to women or a particular woman begins, not necessarily resulting in physical expression (individual level). Active pursuit of knowledge about lesbian lifestyle and groups with increased feelings of anger and guilt about having bought into heterosexist ideals. Search for group belongingness may begin (group level). Phase III: Deepening Commitment—deepening of knowledge about self and crystallization of lesbian attraction. Increased exploration of intimacy and identity, heterosexism, and homophobia emerge and are questioned when present (individual level). Deepening awareness of the oppression experienced by lesbians and also the value inherent in strong sisterhood. At this stage, group identity may become more salient and integrated (group level). Phase IV: Identity Integration—deeper acceptance of the desire for women and connection to self. Embracing a more public, open identity as a lesbian. Individual and group identities begin to merge and integrate (individual level). Synthesis of sexual identity, group social identity, and increased satisfaction with the self (group level).

Transgender Identity Development

Kuper et al. (2018) explored the transgender identity development experience using an intersectional approach. They delved into the dimensions of gender-related experience including gender identity, gender presentation, gender expression, and physical self-image. The authors conducted semi-structured interviews and analyzed data using inductive constructivistic grounded theory. Themes included intrapersonal processes (awareness, exploration, meaning making, and integration). The ability to express gender fully and for others to accurately reflect their sense of gender to them were both important aspects of self for participants. The authors reported great variability in gender-related experiences (i.e., individuals' description of internal sense of self, how the sense of self is expressed and communicated, and how this sense of self relates to others with similar and different gender expression). Researchers highlighted the complexity of understanding the intracategorical and intercategorical conceptualization of transgender identity. For additional information about transgender identity development, see Pardo and Devor (2017) under resources. There are many other models of sexual identity development and we invite you to further explore them so you may use them in your service to LGBTQ+ clients. Hall et al. (2021) conducted a systematic review and meta-analysis of sexual identity development you may find in the resources section.

COUNSELING CLIENTS WITH DISABILITIES

Counselors are very likely to work with a person who has a disability, including developmental, behavioral, sensory impairment, or a physical disability (Centers for Disease Control and Prevention [CDC], 2020). More than 25% of people, both incarcerated and not incarcerated individuals, in the United States report having a disability (CDC, 2020). This means that counselors work to be prepared to explore the role of disability on functioning and the impact of trauma on disability, along with strategies for advocacy (Council for Accreditation of Counseling and Related Educational Programs, 2015). More specifically, rehabilitation counselors work to provide counseling that aims to support the achievement of goals, across life domains, for people with disabilities (Commission on Rehabilitation Counselor Certification, 2016). It will be important for counselors to know that people with disabilities are whole human beings, with varying identities that intersect, and that the work that is done within the counseling relationship may be related to functioning with a disability, or it could be related to a wealth of other aspects of identity. While identities intersect, similar to working with individuals who hold other marginalized identities, it will be important for counselors to continue to challenge biases that might limit the view of the client before you, including patronizing perspectives.

While people with disabilities continue to face barriers that make it more difficult for them to receive adequate healthcare, related protections, safe and suitable housing, and economic resources (Chapin et al., 2018), people within this population live full lives that include love, families, career, and other components of everyday life. As such, counselors work to provide affirming services that both facilitate and expand existing resilience for this population (Hunter et al., 2020). Counselors who serve this population consider the intersecting identities that people with disabilities might hold, including other marginalized identities, and/or more privileged identities. It will be important for counselors not only to acknowledge the barriers that clients with disabilities might face, but also to work to employ approaches to counseling that acknowledge the intersecting identities of our clients as human beings (Hunter et al., 2020).

COUNSELING IMMIGRANTS AND REFUGEES

Mental health counselors are increasingly encountering clients who have immigrated and sought asylum in the United States due to civil unrest, violence, or persecution in their home countries or to seek improved financial opportunities (American Association for Marriage and Family Therapy, n.d.). Immigrant clients bring their own cultural, religious, and familial backgrounds into the session and counselors must be prepared to provide services that are multiculturally competent and trauma-informed (Goodman et al., 2017). Many immigrants and refugees may present with severe anxiety, depression, and posttraumatic stress as a result of traumatic experiences in their countries of origin (Goodman et al., 2017). Immigrants who had the opportunity and means to plan their arrival into the United States have a different experience from refugees, whose journeys are usually fraught with challenges and tribulations (Chung et al., 2011). Chung et al. (2011) remind us that there are multiple types of immigrant groups, including:

a) voluntary migrants (those who voluntarily migrant to the U.S. for more opportunities and a better life), b) undocumented people who entered the U.S. without legal papers, and c) those who are forced to migrate. The forced migration category is also comprised of a diverse group that includes survivors of human trafficking (Chung et al., 2008), refugees due to war or natural disasters, and also an increasing number of environmental refugees due to global warming and environmental racism. (p. 87)

The experiences of each of these groups vary greatly and so do their presenting issues when seeking therapy. Once resettled, immigrants may experience acculturation stressors, including language barriers, intolerance, prejudice, racism, xenophobia and discrimination, and financial instability and uncertainly, among others (American Association for Marriage and Family Therapy, n.d.; Chung et al., 2011).

Multiculturally competent counselors are aware of their own potential for experiencing political countertransference, defined as attitudes and beliefs against immigrant populations that are based on myths perpetuated by the media and fuel for intolerance and xenophobia (Chung et al., 2008). Rogers-Sirin et al. (2015) conducted a qualitative study exploring immigrant clients' perceptions of counselors' cultural competence and data were organized into competent and incompetent behaviors. Results indicated cultural incompetence manifested as (1) lack of clarity about what counseling entails, which led to client discomfort and confusion, (2) discrimination and microaggressions (Sue, 2010), exemplified by indirect or direct messages of discomfort or disapproval, and (3) assuming adequate cultural knowledge, for example, clustering groups of clients from different cultural background together as if they have a shared culture (e.g., Lebanese and Egyptian), and (4) pathologizing cultural differences, manifested through the counselor's expressing judgment about client's child rearing practices. On the other hand, clients reported cultural competence as follows: (1) counselor's openness to learn about the client's culture, manifested through curiosity and interest in the client, (2) using culture appropriately, for example, when the counselor explained the ways in which a client's culture may impact how they perceive therapy and what to focus on during sessions, (3) showing patience, and (4) showing empathy toward the client's process during therapy. The authors conclude that multiculturally competent therapists display transformative learning (Jun, 2010), which encompasses intellectual and emotional understanding of the client, emphasizing that conceptual learning about multicultural issues is insufficient. We want to invite you as a beginning counselor to learn as much as you can about cultures different from your own and always check with your client about your understanding of their particular cultural background. Finally, you can utilize your knowledge of multicultural and social justice competencies to advocate for immigrants, refugees and their families at the individual or systemic levels. Awareness of our implicit biases is critical to MCSJCC development and we discuss it next.

Understanding Implicit Bias

Implicit bias is an important concept to understand when aiming to develop multicultural competency. Payne et al. (2018) define implicit bias as an individual's propensity to confirm extant stereotypes that occur spontaneously in our thought processes. The tendency to stereotype leads to overgeneralization of ideas about certain topics or groups of people that may inadvertently lead to discriminatory behaviors and cause harm. Project Implicit (a.k.a., Harvard Implicit Association Test) is a study whereby the Implicit Attention Tests were developed. These tests assess individuals' implicit biases about various subject areas (e.g., age, skin tone, disabilities, among others) and groups of people known to experience prejudice and discrimination (e.g., Black, Asian, Latinx, Native Americans, among others). As a counselor in training, it is critical that you understand your own implicit biases. The Going Within section of this chapter will expose you to these tests and allow you to delve deeper into understanding the stereotypes and biases you may be holding. We invite you to explore these in greater depth throughout your counselor education journey.

CONCLUSION

In this chapter, we highlighted and discussed the topics of multiculturalism, intersectionality, and diversity. We anchored these topics on the Multicultural and Social Justice Counseling Competencies (MCSJCC; Ratts et al., 2015) and introduced you to the multicultural orientation framework. We provided an introduction to theories of human development, racial identity development, the generation name game, LGBTQ+ identity development, individuals with disabilities, counseling immigrants and refugees and their families, and other marginalized populations. We invited integration of your learning by focusing on your intersecting identities and how they inform your worldview, attending to otherness and critically evaluating your privileged and/or marginalized identities in the context of counseling clients from advantaged and marginalized groups. We engaged you in examining all of these concepts through a diversity, advocacy and social justice lens.

Summary

- The Multicultural and Social Justice Counseling Competencies (MCSJCC; Ratts et al., 2015) can serve as a lens to explore your development as a professional counselor.

- The multicultural orientation framework is a useful tool to approach work with clients.

- There are multiple theories of human development, racial identity development, and LGBTQ+ identity development that can inform your understanding of clients you will serve.

- Special considerations must be given to diverse groups of clients, including individuals from minoritized groups, individuals with disabilities, immigrants and refugees and their families, and other marginalized groups.

- Students must integrate learning by becoming culturally humble and critically evaluating their privileged and marginalized identities when counseling individuals from advantaged and disadvantaged groups.

- We encourage you to continue to examine all of these issues through a diversity, advocacy, liberatory, and social justice lens.

Voices From the Field

Christian Chan, PhD, Assistant Professor, Department of Counseling and Educational Development, The University of North Carolina at Greensboro

Intersectionality Still Teaches Me to Transform: A Reflection of Counseling Practice, Reflexivity, and Activism

Intersectionality continues to outline fundamental concepts guiding my personal and professional development. Drawing from reflections over the past decade in my personal and professional journey, intersectionality has been a central catalyst for how I began to make sense of the world as a person experiencing multiple overlapping forms of oppression and as a professional counselor connected to a calling for multiculturalism and social justice. Intersectionality, in this case, has been a life force integrated across my research, teaching, supervision, and practice. While the approach has invigorated my conceptualization of multiculturalism and social justice, it has led me to navigate the fullness of who I am as a brown queer person of color, a fat nondisabled cisgender male, a second-generation Asian American with multiple heritages, a child of two immigrants who experienced economic hardship and complicated migration histories, an individual with a middle-class upbringing with access to educational and career opportunities, and a pluralistic Catholic-centered in liberation theology.

However, intersectionality has still been a complex approach that is difficult for many practitioners to grasp. On occasion, it has been reduced to the common language of multiple identities and diverse identities. These definitions are inadequate for the rich movement that gave root to the ways we understand power relations and, more importantly, the genealogy of women of color and queer women of color responsible for shaping intersectionality (e.g., Combahee River Collective, Gloria Anzaldúa, Cherríe Moraga, bell hooks, Audre Lorde, Kimberlé Crenshaw, Patricia Hill Collins, Angela Davis). This discrepancy indicates several important areas for me and the counseling profession to examine. First, intersectionality led me to detect cultural, political, and structural messages around me and how I have reinforced these messages. For this reason, intersectionality illuminated my own challenges and gaps, especially when my experiences with racism, heterosexism, sizeism, and colonialism have blocked my attention to other forms of oppression (e.g., classism, genderism, ableism). Intersectionality also became the impetus to interrogate my own internalized biases as an iterative and ongoing process. I am not immune to internalizing messages about myself, community partners, and the communities I serve within these overlapping forms of oppression. As I reflect on my development, I can remember instances when I was challenged by colleagues for perpetuating a classist belief. These moments helped me to embrace the discomfort and emotions, recognize that these critical incidents changed my life, and further center myself within the praxis of intersectionality.

Intersectionality also reminds me that infusing its tenets requires an active process rather than a passive process. It has become even more important not only to detect biases, incidents of oppression, and the effects of inequity within my own counseling practices, but also to explicitly name and contextualize these issues with clients and students. Reinforcing my commitment to intersectionality continues to spark new ways of attending to cultural factors, privilege, and oppression and broaching these areas within professional counseling. Reflecting on these areas, intersectionality has led me to better grasp clients' and students' experiences of marginalization within their own communities, even in historically marginalized communities (e.g., Black, Indigenous, and people of color within LGBTQ+ communities). It has become crucial for me to honor experiences of both cultural capital and inequities to convey to historically marginalized and minoritized clients that they are valid, seen, and heard.

Moving beyond consciousness and interpersonal interactions, intersectionality still teaches me about my connection to community partnerships, outreach, community organizing, and activism that are vital to the wellness of communities we serve. In this capacity, intersectionality does not exist without its deeper relationship to the actionable opportunities for a social justice agenda (see Collins, 2019; Collins & Bilge, 2020). It is the reason why I revisit the power and privilege I hold, even if those experiences render me uncomfortable and vulnerable. It is the reminder for why intersectionality, multiculturalism, and social justice are no longer simply labels for me. It is a reminder to draw from opportunities to alter ingrained cultural messages, intervene in harmful policies, and dismantle multiple overlapping forms of oppression (Crenshaw, 1989). Additionally, intersectionality is a reminder that critical relationships are necessary for forms of group empowerment, community organizing, and engagement with mental health care.

I distinctly remember working with a client who shared her social identities with me as a Black, queer, and cisgender female youth. Central to her social identities was her cultivation and meaning of family. As I reflected on the application of intersectionality in counseling practice, I reflected on three major elements: (a) the counseling relationship; (b) cultural factors elucidating power; and (c) systemic and structural interventions. As the client and I navigated personal experiences with discrimination and microaggressions, it became apparent that we shared an overlap in our journeys with heterosexism. More pressing to her concerns, however, were the distinct notions of power within our counseling relationship and within her own family, given that every other family member is cisgender and heterosexual. Leveraging the application of intersectionality, I had to remind myself that in an effort to better support the client, I had to reflect on how my privileges could bias my own perspectives. Despite the overlap in our experiences with heterosexism, I could easily obscure the privilege and power that I carry within the counseling relationship, such that I inadvertently overlook specific discussions around race, gender identity, racism, and genderism. It was important for me to take ownership of the responsibility to broach cultural factors, such as how the client made meaning of her queerness within Black communities and how the broad categorization of LGBTQ+ communities might still produce a feeling of exclusion for Black LGBTQ+ individuals. Additionally, intersectionality became the lens in which I shifted our conversations to discuss how the client was navigating the confluence of racism, heterosexism, and genderism within her own family and network of friends, although not always simultaneously. At the interpersonal level of the counseling relationship and our ongoing weekly discussions, I walked through the possibilities of connecting the salient social identities of race, sexual identity, and gender identity and realize the profound meaning in integrating these social identities. The interconnectedness among social identities became a prime vehicle for self-love and agency.

Aside from interpersonal interactions within individual counseling, the premise of intersectionality played a key role in driving systemic and structural interventions within my practice. To intentionally empower and provide autonomy to the client, I discussed the possibility of meeting with family members to propose ways that they could be more affirming. In this approach, I provided an opportunity for the client to grant me permission to work collaboratively in a culturally responsive and affirming capacity. The intervention sparked further conversations about which areas she felt safe to discuss with her family and which areas could use further encouragement and support from me as the counselor. Drawing upon a larger systemic premise based on the services I provided to multiple clients, I distinctly highlighted opportunities for the community agency to produce a cultural audit of our interventions, engage in more ongoing discussions about culturally responsive practices in treatment team meetings, and curate more resources authored by Black queer practitioners, activists, and scholars within the work setting.

When I reflect again on the involvement of intersectionality in my own journey, I remember that heart and vulnerability are crucial factors for actively enacting multiculturalism and social justice. Intersectionality reminds me of my lifelong commitment to responsibility, accountability, and answerability as described in the *Multicultural and Social Justice Counseling Competencies* (Ratts et al., 2015). The approach teaches me that I still have opportunities to transform myself as a professional counselor and to transform the systems that marginalize specific communities of clients. Given the combination of these reflections,

I offer several questions and call professional counselors to use these questions as the impetus for their actions and practices:

- When we implement culturally responsive practices, for whom are these actions? Activism? Advocacy? Practices?
- In my practice, whose experiences have I recast or excluded?
- For what reasons have I recast and excluded the experiences of these groups? What biases or experiences growing up influenced these messages?
- What are my clients including and *excluding* from our discussions? What is said and unsaid?
- How have my own privileges or experiences with oppression contributed to the safety or *lack of safety* in my relationships with clients?
- What steps have I taken not only to reduce inequities, but also to reverse those inequities?

A Call to Action

In this section, we will ask you to identify resources for a population that you hope to work with. Using the MCSJCC model, consider your own marginalized and privileged identities. Think about what resources these clients may benefit from that are available in your geographical area. Create a brochure that highlights the resources that are currently available in the communities that you are in and you have added to the informational brochure. Develop a plan for dissemination, and share your brochure with the local counseling offices, agencies, and crisis organizations you highlighted.

Case Study 2.1

Manuel is a 46-year-old Mexican immigrant. He presents to your community mental health clinic for evaluation following a DUI (driving under the influence) arrest and court-ordered treatment for alcohol abuse. His 43-year-old wife, Elena and their 14-year-old daughter, Consuelo, accompany him. Consuelo tells you that her father and mother cannot speak English and she is there to translate for them. How would you approach the intake process? Whom would you engage in your agency for guidance about next steps? What are potential legal or ethical issues in your approach to counseling Manuel and supporting him and his family?

RESPONSE QUESTIONS:

1. How would you approach the intake process?
2. Whom would you engage in your agency for guidance about next steps?

3. What are potential legal or ethical issues in your approach to counseling Manuel and supporting him and his family?

4. Can you identify the multicultural and social justice considerations that would be important to consider in this case?

Going Within

This exercise will help you explore your implicit biases around a variety of topics (e.g., age, gender, race[s], disability, among others). Visit the Harvard Implicit Attention Project (Project Implicit) website listed under resources (implicit.harvard.edu/implicit). First, read the Frequently Asked Questions page. Then, visit the consent form page (implicit.harvard.edu/implicit/takeatest.html) before you go to the tests themselves (implicit.harvard.edu/implicit/selectatest.html). Select a test that represents a group of people or issues that you are not very familiar with (feel free to complete more than one test if you wish!). This will assist you in learning about yourself and going deeper into your unfolding self-awareness. After you complete the test and review your results, reflect on the following: Which test did you choose and why? What did you learn about yourself? How were the results similar or different from what you expected? What surprised you? Based on the results, what areas of growth and development can you identify? What concrete steps can you take to develop those areas?

Group Process

Divide the class into small groups of 6–8 students. Consider a time in your life that you encountered a person who might have appeared to be very similar to you. This person may have reminded you of your neighbor, a family member, or yourself. Think back to the process that took place for you to actually get to know that person beyond the initially assumed familiarity. Similarly, counselors will encounter clients who might feel very familiar. Remember what you learned about that person who may have been different from your initial assumptions about them. It will be important to work to be aware of your own reactions in your work to support clients, and for counselors to share their counseling experiences in supervision.

Discuss within your group: How might you work to hold space for a client to share who they are with you? How might this be challenging when the client appears to hold several identities that you also hold? How might shared identities be helpful in your work with clients? How might unexplored assumptions about shared experiences serve as a barrier for your client? What are some steps that you might be able to take in your work to acknowledge potentially shared assumptions about shared identities? How might you use the relationship and this type of discourse in counseling to facilitate a supportive counseling relationship with your client?

Finally, please take a look around your classroom, and consider who you see in this space. Take a moment to think: What assumptions are you making about the people in the room? What would you be missing without first working to really connect with the people you see? What assumptions do you make about classmates who you believe are more like you? What assumptions have you made about classmates who you believe are different from you? Consider the set of assumptions for both groups, and note your own emotional and physical reactions to the groups that are similar, or for those that appear different from you.

RESOURCES

Adams, M., Blumenfeld, W. J., Catalano, D. C. J., DeJong, K., Hackman, H. W., Hopkins, L. E., Love, B. J., Peters, M. L., Shlasko, D., & Zúñiga, X. (2018). Readings for diversity and social justice (4th ed.). Routledge.

Archer, D. (2021). Anti-racist psychotherapy: Confronting systemic racism and healing racial trauma. Each One Teach One Publications.

Bockting, W., Barucco, R., LeBlanc, A., Singh, A., Mellman, W., Dolezal, C., & Ehrhardt, A. (2019). Sociopolitical change and transgender people's perceptions of vulnerability and resilience among transgender individuals. Sexuality Research and Social Policy, 17(1), 162–174. https://doi.org/10.1007/s13178-019-00381-5

Bower, K. L., Lewis, D. C., Bermudez, J. M., & Singh, A. A. (2019). Adding grey to the rainbow: A narrative analysis of generational identity through stories and counter-stories of older gay men. Ageing and Society, 41, 957–979. https://doi.org/10.1017/S0144686X19001429

Bower, K. L., Lewis, D. C., Bermudez, J. M., & Singh, A. A. (2019) Narratives of generativity and resilience among LGBT older adults: Leaving positive legacies despite social stigma and collective trauma. Journal of Homosexuality, 68(2), 230–251. https://doi.org/10.1080/00918369.2019.1648082

Burgess, D., Prescod, D. J., Bryan, J., & Chatters, S. (2021). Raising youth critical consciousness: Exploring critical race pedagogy as a framework for anti-racist programming. Journal of School Counseling, 19(34), 1–37.

Capuzzi, D., & Stauffer, M. D. (2016). Counseling and psychotherapy: Theories and interventions (6th ed.). American Counseling Association.

Capuzzi, D., & Stauffer, M. D. (2016). Human growth and development across the lifespan: Applicationsfor counselors. Wiley.

Chang, S. C., Singh, A. A., & Dickey, L. M. (2019). Affirming mental health practice and treatment with gender diverse clients. New Harbinger.

Cherry, K. (2019, July). What is attachment theory? The importance of emotional bonds. Verywell Mind. https://www.verywellmind.com/what-is-attachment-theory-2795337

Cherry, K. (2020, June). The different types of attachment styles. Verywell Mind. https://www.verywellmind.com/attachment-styles-2795344

Collins, H. P., & Blige, S. (2018). Intersectionality. Polity Press.

Crenshaw, K. (1989). Demarginalizing the intersection of race and sex: Black feminist critique of antidiscrimination doctrine, feminist theory and antiracist politics. University of Chicago Legal Forum, 1989, 139–168. https://chicagounbound.uchicago.edu/cgi/viewcontent.cgi?article=1052&context=uclf

Crenshaw, K. (1991). Mapping the margins: Intersectionality, identity politics, and violence against women of color. Stanford Law Review, 43(6), 1241–1299. https://doi.org/10.2307/1229039

Crenshaw, K. (2015, September 24). Why insectionality can't wait. The Washington Post. https://www.washingtonpost.com/news/in-theory/wp/2015/09/24/why-intersectionality-cant-wait

DeBlaere, C., Singh, A. A., Wilcox, M. M., Cokley, K. O., Delgado-Romero, E. A., Scalise, D. A., & Shawahin, L. (2019). Social justice in counseling psychology: Then, now, and looking forward. The Counseling Psychologist, 47(16), 938–962. https://doi.org/10.1177/0011000019893283

Delgado-Romero, E. A., Singh, A. A., & De Los Santos, J. (2018). Cuentame: The promise of qualitative research with Latinx populations. Journal of Latina/o Psychology, 6(4), 318–328. https://doi.org/10.1037/lat0000123

Guth, L., Puig, A., Nitza, A., Chan, C. D., Pollard, B., Singh, A. A., & Bailey, H. M. (2019). Ten strategies to intentionally use group work to transform hate, facilitate courageous conversations, and enhance community building. Journal for Specialists in Group Work, 44(1), 3–24. https://doi.org/10.1080/01933922.2018.1561778

Hall, W. J., Dawes, H. C., & Plocek, N. (2021). Sexual orientation identity development milestones among lesbian, gay, bisexual, and queer people: A systematic review and meta-analysis. Frontiers in Psychology, 12, 753954. https://doi.org/10.3389/fpsyg.2021.753954

Hargons, C., Mosley, D., Falconer, J., Faloughi, R. Singh, A. A., Cokley, K., & Stevens-Watkins, D. (2017). Black lives matter: A call to action for counseling psychology leaders. The Counseling Psychologist, 45(6), 873–901. https://doi.org/10.1177/0011000017733048

Helms, J. (2019). A race is a nice thing to have: A guide to being a white person or understanding the white persons in your life. Cognella Academic Publishing.

Holcomb-McCoy, C. (2022). Antiracist counseling in schools and communities. American Counseling Association.

hooks, b. (1984). Feminist theory from margin to center. South End Press.

hooks, b. (1989). Talking back: Thinking feminist, thinking Black. South End Press.

hooks, b. (1992). Black looks: Race and representation. South End Press.

hooks, b. (1995). Killing rage: Ending racism. Henry Holt & Co.

hooks, b. (1996). Bone Black: Memories of girlhood. Henry Holt & Co.

hooks, b. (1996). Reel to real: Race, sex, and class at the movies. Routledge.

hooks, b. (1997). Wounds of passion: A writing life. Henry Holt & Co.

hooks, b. (1999). Remembered rapture: The writer at work. MacMillan.

hooks, b. (2000). Where we stand: Class matters. Routledge.

hooks, b. (2002). Communion: The female search for love. Perennial.

hooks, b. (2003). We real cool: Black men and masculinity. Routledge.

hooks, b. (2004). The will to change: Men, masculinity, and love. Atria Books.

hooks, b. (2012). Writing beyond race: Living theory and practice. Routledge.

Human Rights Campaign. (n.d.). Policy and position statements on conversion therapy. https://www.hrc.org/resources/policy-and-position-statements-on-conversion-therapy

Joffe-Walt, C. (2020, July 23). Introducing: Nice white parents. The New York Times. https://www.nytimes.com/2020/07/23/podcasts/nice-white-parents-serial.html

King, R. (2018). Mindful of race: Transforming racism from the inside out. Sounds True.

Love, B. L. (2019). We want to do more than survive: Abolitionist teaching and the pursuit of educational reform. Beacon Press

McIntosh, P. (1988). White privilege and male privilege: A personal account of coming to see correspondences through work in women's studies. https://www.collegeart.org/pdf/diversity/white-privilege-and-male-privilege.pdf

Menakem, R. (2017). My grandmother's hands: Racialized trauma and the pathway to mending our hearts and bodies. Central Recovery Press.

Oluo, I. (2019). So you want to talk about race. Seal Press

Project Implicit. https://implicit.harvard.edu/implicit

Saad, L. F. (2020). Me and white supremacy: Combat racism, change the world, and become a good ancestor. Sourcebook.

Singh, A. A. (2018). Queer and trans resilience workbook: Skills for navigating sexual orientation and gender identity. New Harbinger.

Singh, A. A. (2019). Racial healing: Practical activities to help you challenge privilege, confront systemic racism, and engage in collective healing. New Harbinger.

Singh, A. A., & Dickey, L. M. (2018). Psychotherapy with trans and gender diverse clients [Video]. American Psychological Association.

Sue, D. W., Sue, D., Neville, H., & Smith, L. (2022). Counseling the culturally diverse: Theory and practice (9th ed.). John Wiley & Sons.

Tuck, E., & Yang, K. W. (2012). Decolonization is not a metaphor. Decolonization: Indigeneity, Education & Society, 1(1), 1–40.

University of Florida College of Education EduGator Allyship website. https://education.ufl.edu/edugator-a

Yalom, I. (2017). The gift of therapy: An open letter to a new generation of therapists and their patients. Harper Collins.

Access this podcast at http://connect.springerpub.com/content/book/978-0-8261-6386-8/chapter/ch02.

KEY REFERENCES

Only key references appear in the print edition. The full reference list appears in the digital product found on https://connect.springerpub.com/content/book/978-0-8261-6386-8/chapter/ch02

American Association for Marriage and Family Therapy. (n.d.). *Immigrants and refugees.* https://www.aamft.org/Consumer_Updates/Immigrants_and_Refugees.aspx

Atkinson, D. R., Morten, G., & Sue, D. W. (1998). *Counseling American minorities: A cross cultural perspective* (5th ed.). McGraw-Hill.

Buhrke, R. A., & Douce, L. A. (1991). Training issues for counseling psychologists in working with lesbian and gay men. *The Counseling Psychologist, 19*(2), 216–234. https://doi.org/10.1177/0011000091192006 doi:10.1177/0011000091192006.

Chapin, M., McCarthy, H., Shaw, L., Braham-Cousar, M., Chapman, R., Nosek, M., Peterson, S., Yilmaz, Z., & Ysasi, N. (2018). *Disability-related counseling competencies*. https://www.counseling.org/docs/default-source/competencies/arca-disability-related-counseling-competencies-final-version-5-15-19.pdf?sfvrsn=c376562c_6

Chung, R. C.-Y., Bemak, F., & Grabosky, T. K. (2011). Multicultural-social justice leadership strategies: Counseling and advocacy with immigrants. *Journal for Social Action in Counseling and Psychology, 3*(1), 86–102. https://doi.org/10.33043/JSACP.3.1.86-102 doi:10.33043/JSACP.3.1.86-102.

Chung, R. C.-Y., Bemak, F., Ortiz, D. P., & Sandova-Perez, P. A. (2008). Promoting the mental health of migrants: A multicultural-social justice perspective. *Journal of Counseling and Development, Special Issue in Multicultural and Diversity Issues in Counseling, 86*(3), 310–317. https://doi.org/10.1002/J.1556-6678.2008.TB00514.X doi:10.1002/J.1556-6678.2008.TB00514.X.

Collins, P. H. (2019). *Intersectionality as critical social theory*. Duke University Press.

Collins, P. H., & Bilge, S. (2020). *Intersectionality* (2nd ed.). Polity Press.

Cross, W. E., Smith, L., & Payne, Y. (2002). Black identity. In P. B. Pederson, J. G. Draguns, W. J. Lonner, & J. E. Trimble (Eds.), *Counseling across cultures* (pp. 93–108). Sage.

Estrada, D., Poulsen, S., Cannon, E., & Wiggins, M. (2013). Orienting counseling students toward multiculturalism: Exploring privilege during a new student orientation. *Journal of Humanistic Counseling, 52*, 80–91. https://doi.org/ doi:10.1002/j.2161-1939.2013.00034.x.

Goodman, R. D., Vesely, C. K., Letiecq, B., & Cleaveland, C. L. (2017). Trauma and resilience among refugee and undocumented immigrant women. *Journal of Counseling & Development, 95*(3), 309–321. https://doi.org/10.1002/jcad.12145 doi:10.1002/jcad.12145.

Helms, J. E. (1995). An update of Helms's White and people of color racial identity models. In J. G. Ponterotto, J. M. Casas, L. A. Suzuki, & C. M. Alexander (Eds.), *Handbook of multicultural counseling* (pp. 181–198). Sage Publications.

Hicks, J., Reidy, C., & Waltz, M. (2018). Cross-generational counseling strategies: Understanding unique needs of each generation. *Journal of Counselor Practice, 9*(1), 6–23. https://doi.org/10.22229/yio309843 doi:10.22229/yio309843.

Horse (Kiowa), P. (2005). Native American identity. *New Directions for Student Services, 2005*(109), 61–68. https://doi.org/10.1002/ss.154 doi:10.1002/ss.154.

Hunter, T., Dispense, F., Huffstead, M., Suttles, M., & Bradley, Z. (2020). Queering disability: Exploring the resilience of sexual and gender minority persons living with disabilities. *Rehabilitation Counseling Bulletin, 64*(1), 31–41. https://doi.org/10.1177/0034355219895813 doi:10.1177/0034355219895813.

Kim, J. (2001). Asian American identity development theory. In C. L. Wijeyesinghe & B. W. Jackson, III (Eds.), *New perspectives on racial identity development: A theoretical and practical anthology* (pp. 67–90). NYU Press.

Poston, W. S. C. (1990). The biracial identity development model: A needed addition. *Journal of Counseling and Development, 69*(2), 152–155. https://doi.org/10.1002/j.1556-6676.1990.tb01477.x doi:10.1002/j.1556-6676.1990.tb01477.x.

Ratts, M. J., Singh, A. A., Nassar-McMillan, S., Butler, S. K., & McCullough, J. R. (2015). *Multicultural and social justice counseling competencies*. https://www.counseling.org/docs/default-source/competencies/multicultural-and-social-justice-counseling-competencies.pdf?sfvrsn=14

Rogers-Sirin, L., Melendez, F., Refano, C., & Zegarra, Y. (2015). Immigrant perceptions of therapists' cultural competence: A qualitative investigation. *Professional Psychology: Research and Practice, 46*(4), 258–269. https://doi.org/10.1037/pro0000033 doi:10.1037/pro0000033.

CHAPTER 3

PROFESSIONAL COUNSELOR IDENTITY

Jacqueline M. Swank and Ana Puig

Think about this...

What are important personal characteristics necessary to be an effective counselor? What qualities do you have that will help you be an effective counselor? What are some challenges you may experience in being an effective counselor?

LEARNING OBJECTIVES

After reading this chapter, you should be able to:

- Explain aspects of counselor identity development
- Identify the role of supervision and consultation
- Discuss the self of the counselor
- Recognize the importance of wellness and self-care practices
- Review areas of concerns for counselors, including burnout, compassion fatigue, secondary traumatic stress, vicarious trauma, and impairment

INTRODUCTION

Counseling leaders have emphasized the role of unifying the counseling profession to be able to advance it. The goal of unifying the profession was a key focus area within the *20/20: A Vision for the Future of Counseling Initiative*. The delegates involved in this initiative identified seven areas within the counseling profession that needed attention: (a) strengthening identity, (b) presenting ourselves as one profession, (c) improving public perception/recognition and advocating for professional issues, (d) creating licensure portability, (e) expanding and promoting the research base of professional counseling, (f) focusing on students and prospective students, and (g) promoting client welfare and advocacy

(Kaplan & Gladding, 2011). Specifically, within the strengthening identity area, the delegates outlined five components: (a) develop a paradigm that identifies the core commonalities of the profession, (b) identify the core knowledge and skills shared by all counselors, (c) reflect a philosophy among counselor education programs that unifies professional counselors that share core knowledge and skills, (d) reinforce to students that counseling is a unified profession composed of counselors with specialized training, and (e) reflect one identity in the accreditation of counseling programs (Kaplan & Gladding, 2011). Thus, having a unified counselor professional identity is of critical importance for advancing the counseling profession.

In the following sections, there are multiple areas discussed related to a counselor's professional identity. This includes a discussion of models related to counselor identity development, developing counseling competencies, and professional affiliations. Additionally, the author discusses professional and personal development and the importance of supervision and consultation. The chapter also includes a focus on the self of the counselor, counselor characteristics, burnout and related constructs, and wellness and self-care.

COUNSELOR DEVELOPMENT

Professional identity development focuses on three areas: (a) recognizing oneself as a professional, (b) encompassing professional skills and attitudes, and (c) focusing on the context of a professional community (Gibson et al., 2010). Scholars have proposed various models of professional identity development, including stage-wise development models and process development models. Stage-wise development models focus on identity development across stages. Scholars have often discussed various stage models in the context of supervision (e.g., Hogan, 1964; Loganbill et al., 1982; Stoltenberg, 1981).

Hogan (1964) proposed four stages of counselor development: (1) beginning counselors—lacking insight, insecure; (2) stage two counselors—struggling with autonomy versus dependency on a supervisor; (3) stage three counselors—demonstrating self-confidence; and (4) master counselors—demonstrating autonomy and assurance. Loganbill et al. (1982) discussed three stages of development: stagnation (lack awareness, simplistic linear thinking), confusion (fluctuate between feeling competent and incompetent), and integration (awareness, acceptance of self, stabilizing) that have some similarities to Hogan's stages. Loganbill and colleagues also identified eight issues that a counselor must resolve before they become master counselors, with counselors resolving these issues independently, meaning they might be at different stages with various issues. The issues include (a) awareness, (b) autonomy, (c) competence, (d) theoretical orientation, (e) ethics, (f) motivation, (g) purpose, and (h) respect for individual differences. Additionally, Stoltenberg (1981) proposed a four-stage model: (a) dependent on the supervisor, (b) dependency-autonomy conflict, (c) conditional dependency, and (d) master counselor. There are additional models of supervision that describe stages of counselor development with many having some similarities with these models.

Rønnestad and Skovholt (2003) also described counselor development, with their model beginning before the counselor enters their counselor preparation program. The model includes eight stages that were condensed into six phases: (a) lay helper, (b) beginning student, (c) advanced student, (d) novice professional, (e) experienced professional, and (f) senior professional. They also identified 14 themes related to counselor development. Among these themes was the integration of the personal self with the professional self, as well as a shift from an internal, conventional mode before the counselor preparation program to an external, more rigid focus during the program, and then a more flexible, internal mode following the program as the counselor obtains experience and confidence (Rønnestad & Skovholt, 2003). Other themes are discussed throughout this chapter. See Table 3.1 for the stage-wise development models.

A second type of professional identity development models is process development, which focuses on intrapersonal and interpersonal processes. The intrapersonal process pertains to the development of autonomy and self-evaluation, whereas the interpersonal process focuses on the role of the professional community in the counselor development process (Gibson et al., 2010). Gibson et al. (2010) interviewed counseling students at various stages in their

TABLE 3.1 PROFESSIONAL IDENTITY STAGE-WISE DEVELOPMENT MODELS

DEVELOPMENT MODEL	STAGES
Hogan (1964)	1. Beginning counselors (lacking insight, insecure) 2. Stage two counselors (struggling with autonomy versus dependency on a supervisor) 3. Stage three counselors (demonstrating self-confidence) 4. Master counselors (demonstrating autonomy and assurance)
Loganbill et al. (1982)	1. Stagnation (lack awareness, simplistic linear thinking) 2. Confusion (fluctuate between feeling competent and incompetent) 3. Integration (awareness, acceptance of self, stabilizing)
Stoltenberg (1981)	1. Dependent on the supervisor 2. Dependency-autonomy conflict 3. Conditional dependency 4. Master counselor
Rønnestad and Skovholt (2003)	1. Lay helper 2. Beginning student 3. Advanced student 4. Novice professional 5. Experienced professional 6. Senior professional

academic training program and developed a theory describing the transformation of counselor professional identity among counseling students. They identified three developmental tasks necessary to transform identity: (a) definition of counseling, (b) responsibility for professional growth, and (c) transformation to systemic identity. Across each of these tasks, there is movement across time and experience in three areas: (a) external validation; (b) coursework, experience, and commitment; and (c) self-validation. As students advance in their training, they move from external validation and references (e.g., textbooks, faculty) to more integration of oneself.

In applying the findings related to the developmental tasks to counselor training, Gibson et al. (2010) recommended students (a) develop their own definitions of counseling and compare them to expert definitions, (b) engage in self-directed learning early in counselor training, and (c) participate in early experience to practice skills with clients and engage with the professional community (e.g., conferences, collaboration with community partners). Regarding these recommendations, have you thought about how you define counseling (see the *Group Process* activity at the end of the chapter)? Reflecting on the definition of counseling can help with thinking about what you see your roles and responsibilities are as a counselor. This can be helpful for engaging in self-advocacy, such as a school counselor being asked to do tasks that are unrelated to counseling. It can also be helpful for engaging in legislative advocacy, in helping elected officials understand what counselors do and why it is important to fund counseling-related services.

Regarding the second recommendation, have you participated in self-directed learning? How might you do this to continue to enhance your growth and development as a counselor? Finally, have you attended any counseling trainings or conferences? While some conferences can be expensive, especially when they are not offered locally and require travel and lodging expenses, there are often local training opportunities that may be free or have a minimum cost, especially for students. In addition to viewing these trainings as learning opportunities, it is also important to view them as opportunities to connect with other professionals. Joining counseling organizations at the local and national levels is another way to connect with others in the counseling profession. You may also consider volunteering in the community to obtain experience with populations that you may want to work with in the future. While not all volunteer experiences may be related to counseling, they can still be valuable in learning more about various populations and connecting with other professionals. When engaging in community experiences, it is important that you communicate that you are a student and in the process of learning to be a counselor, but that you are not a practicing counselor yet, and ensure that you do not engage in activities that you are not qualified to do as a student.

Expanding upon the theory of transformational tasks of counseling students, Moss et al. (2014) explored the professional identity development of practicing counselors and found six influential areas: (a) adjusting to expectations, (b) confidence and freedom, (c) separation vs. integration, (d) experienced guide (external validation), (e) ongoing learning (experience and professional development), and (f) working with clients (self-validation). Participants discussed progression within the first three themes as they gained experience, and the last three areas facilitated movement. Moss et al. (2014) concluded that it is crucial for counselor educators to help counseling students develop realistic expectations for the counseling field. Furthermore, they emphasized the importance of counseling supervision to support continued counselor development.

Competency

Competency is an important aspect of counselor development. A competent individual is one who is "qualified, capable, and able to understand and do certain things in an appropriate and effective manner" (Rodolfa et al., 2005; p. 348). Swank et al. (2012) described counselor competency as focusing on multiple domains, including skills, knowledge, behaviors, and dispositions. Swank and colleagues developed the Counseling Competencies Scale (CCS) to comprehensively measure counseling competency. The CCS contains five factors: (a) professional behaviors, (b) counseling relationship, (c) counseling skills, (d) assessment and application, and (e) professional dispositions. In further examining the CCS, Lambie et al. (2018) identified a revised instrument (Counseling Competencies Scale Revised; CCS-R), which encompassed a two-factor model (counseling skills and therapeutic conditions, and counseling dispositions and behaviors) to replace the original instrument. The instruments are helpful for having a shared understanding of the components of counseling competency. Instructors and supervisors can use the instruments to evaluate students' and supervisees' competencies. Additionally, students and counselors can use them for self-evaluation to identify strengths and areas for growth. It is helpful for students to develop skills and practice in self-evaluation that they can use in their training program and throughout their careers.

Scholars have also developed competencies and best practices for counseling specific populations, as well as practicing in various counseling areas. These competencies and standards are helpful in identifying the skills, characteristics, and other aspects counselors need to work with diverse populations and in various settings. See the Resources section for links to various counseling competencies.

Professional Affiliation

Involvement in the counseling profession is an important component of having a professional counselor identity, which includes belonging to professional counseling organizations. These organizations advance the counseling profession in many ways, including providing opportunities for professional development (e.g., conferences, trainings, publications), engaging in advocacy (e.g., educating the public about mental health to reduce stigma and promote counseling, meet with political leaders), and offering opportunities for professional communities and networking, to name a few. Therefore, all counseling professionals, including counseling students, are strongly encouraged to become members of professional counseling organizations.

In addition to membership, it is important to consider ways to become actively involved in counseling organizations. This may include running for a leadership position in the organization, or serving in other ways, such as getting involved in a committee or task force. It is not too early in a person's career for a student to get involved in an organization. Thus, counseling students are encouraged to seek out opportunities to get involved. Many counseling organizations have a graduate student representative, as well as have student members serve on committees within the organization. After joining an organization, counseling students can reach out to the leaders of the organization to inquire about opportunities to become more involved in the organization.

The counseling profession has many professional organizations and due to membership costs, there are often limits to the number of organizations an individual can join. Therefore, it is important to carefully consider organizations to affiliate with as a counselor. As discussed in the introduction, having a unified counselor identity is important for advancing the counseling profession. Thus, this author encourages counseling professionals to strongly consider the umbrella organization for counselors, the American Counseling Association (ACA), when thinking about membership in professional counseling organizations. ACA is the largest organization for professional counselors. Joining ACA supports the advancement of a unified counseling profession.

In addition to having an identity as a professional counselor, individuals may also have areas of counseling specializations. ACA alone has 18 national divisions that focus on specialized areas of counseling (see Table 3.2), as well as two organizational affiliates (Association of Counseling Sexology and Sexual Wellness [ACSSW], International Association for Resilience and Trauma Counseling [IARTC]). There are also state branches, two international branches (Europe and Philippines), and four regions (Midwest, North Atlantic, Southern, and Western) of ACA. Two other professional counseling organizations that used to be divisions of ACA are the American Mental Health Counseling Association (AMHCA) and the American School Counselor Association (ASCA). There are many other professional organizations focused on counseling specialization areas that counseling professional may consider joining as well.

Are you a member of any professional counseling organizations? If not, after reading this section, have you thought about what counseling organization(s) might be a good professional home for you? If you are already a member of one or more professional counseling organizations, have you thought about how you might get more involved, if you are not already? Consider how you might use your talents to contribute to the organization, while also continuing your growth and development as a counselor.

Both the professional and personal development of counselors is important. Initial academic training for counselors (i.e., master's degree) provides a foundation for counselor development. However, the professional and personal development of counselors is a career-long process.

Professional Development

A key focus area of initial academic training is the development of basic counseling skills. While counseling students may also receive some specialized training during their counseling academic degree program, students should view their academic program as providing a foundation to build upon throughout their career. It is crucial that counselors continue to engage in professional development opportunities following graduation to develop expertise in working

TABLE 3.2 DIVISIONS OF THE AMERICAN COUNSELING ASSOCIATION

American College Counseling Association (ACCA)
American Rehabilitation Counseling Association (ARCA)
Association for Adult Development and Aging (AADA)
Association for Assessment and Research in Counseling (AARC)
Association for Child and Adolescent Counseling (ACAC)
Association for Creativity in Counseling (ACC)
Association for Counselor Education and Supervision (ACES)
Association for Humanistic Counseling (AHC)
Association for Multicultural Counseling and Development (AMCD)
Association for Spiritual, Ethical, and Religious Values in Counseling (ASERVIC)
Association for Specialists in Group Work (ASGW)
Counselors for Social Justice (CSJ)
International Association of Addictions and Offender Counselors (IAAOC)
International Association of Marriage and Family Counselors (IAMFC)
Military and Government Counseling Association (MGCA)
National Career Development Association (NCDA)
National Employment Counseling Association (NECA)
Society for Sexual, Affectional, Intersex, and Gender Expansive Identities (SAIGE)

with specific populations of interest, and in using specialized techniques and treatment models. Rønnestad and Skovholt (2003) found that a commitment to learn propels the counselor development process. Professional development is important in staying current on interventions supported by research and trends in the counseling field. The ACA (2014) *Code of Ethics* includes standards regarding practicing within the boundaries of a counselor's competence (C.2.a), and receiving training and supervision before engaging in new areas of practice (C.2.b.). Continuing education is also generally required for maintaining a counseling license, as well as certification in various counseling specialty areas.

Professional development for counseling students and counseling professionals may encompass a variety of learning opportunities. This includes conferences sponsored by professional counseling organizations, with many organizations offering yearly conferences that include educational sessions focused on various counseling topics. Counseling conferences may include in-depth training spanning multiple hours, or shorter training sessions that span 30 minutes or an hour. It is important to remember that, while not always the case, a short workshop (i.e., 1 hour) may provide an overview of a counseling strategy that the counselor will need additional training on before using the intervention with clients.

Professional development opportunities may also include workshops provided by professional organizations, training institutions, universities, and others with expertise in a specific counseling area. Workshops may span multiple hours, a full day, or multiple days and include a variety of learning strategies. With the evolution of technology, remote or virtual trainings are also becoming common practice. This may include live or recorded webinars/trainings, home-study programs whereby the individual reviews the materials at their own pace, or other technology-enhanced learning opportunities. Many counseling organizations also provide continued education for reading articles published in their journals and taking a brief quiz about the article to measure learning. ACA as well as the ACA divisions publish scholarly journal, with some also publishing newsletters or other publications. Some of the state branches, as well as other counseling organization also publish journals and other publications. See the Resources sections for a link to the *Journal of Counseling and Development*, ACA's journal, as well as information about the journals published by the divisions.

While learning opportunities are vast, it is important to ensure that the training is offered by a reputable organization and qualified presenters. Anyone can offer training in anything, with advancements in technology making this easier than ever. Therefore, it is important that counselors carefully review the quality of a training before participating in it. It is also important to note that counselors identified meaningful interactions with people (e.g., clients, supervisors, mentors, personal therapists, colleagues, friends, and family members) as a catalyst for growth (Rønnestad & Skovholt, 2003). Thus, it is important that counselors engage in opportunities to connect with other counseling professionals, in addition to attending trainings. This may include meeting with colleagues to share experiences, discuss ideas, and provide support, which could occur through a group consisting of practitioners that meets on a consistent basis. It may also occur at a counseling conference, as the networking opportunities provided at conferences and other training experiences provide a great opportunity to connect with others. While conferences and trainings provide rich opportunities to learn through educational sessions, the opportunity to engage with other professionals informally is also a powerful way to learn and grow professionally and personally. For counseling students, connecting with other counseling professionals may also include engaging in volunteer opportunities in the community, finding a counseling practitioner to serve as a mentor, or becoming involved in counseling organizations, as mentioned above. It may be challenging initially to take the first step in finding a way to connect with others, but the benefits are likely to far exceed the initial uncomfortableness in reaching out for networking.

While we discussed models focused on the development of professional identity earlier in the chapter, it is also important to consider ways counselors express their professional identity. Burkholder (2012) presents the Professional Identity Expression (PIE) model based on Boyer's (1990) work on scholarship. The PIE model is linear and begins with recognizing that professional identity involves both personal attributes and professional training (Nugent & Jones,

FIGURE 3.1 Burkholder's Professional Identity Expression (PIE) model.

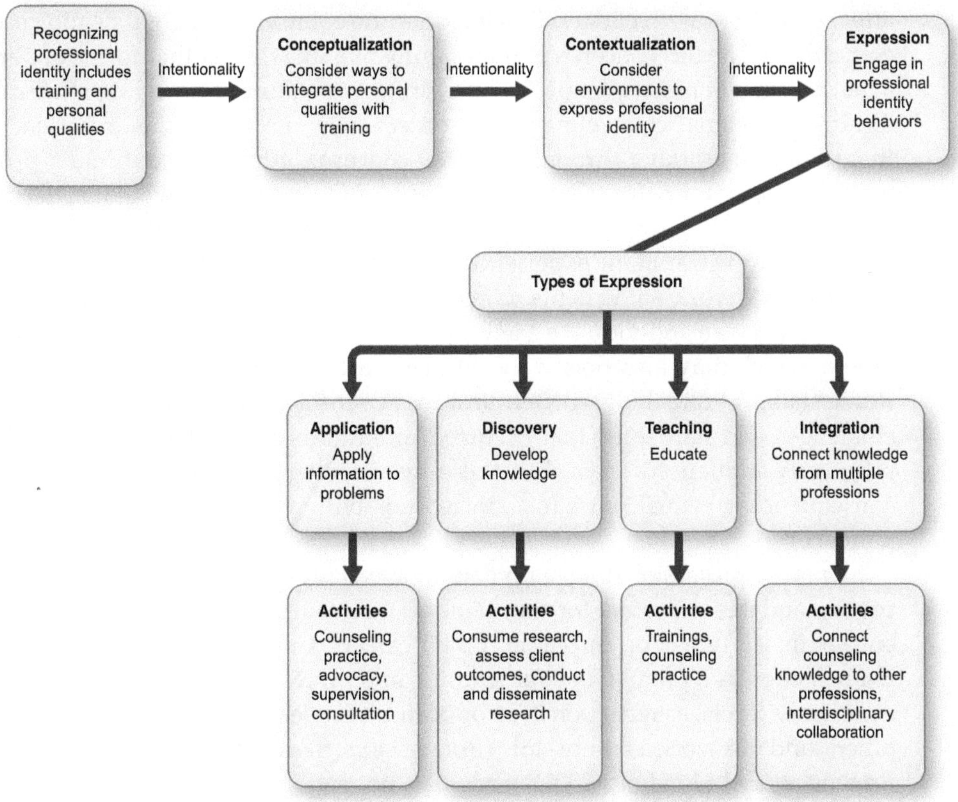

Source: Adapted from Burkholder, D. (2012). A model of professional identity expression for mental health counselors. *Journal of Mental Health Counseling, 34*(4), 295–307. https://doi.org/10.17744/mehc.34.4.u204038832qrq131

2009). With intentionality, the counseling professional moves to the conceptualization level, then the contextualization level, and finally the expression level. The expression level includes four components: (a) application, (b) discovery, (c) teaching, and (d) integration. See Figure 3.1 for a visual of this model, with sample activities included in each of the four components that were presented by Burkholder (2012).

Personal Development

Personal development is also a crucial area in the growth of counselors. The ACA (2014) *Code of Ethics* emphasizes the importance of counselors having awareness of their own beliefs and values and not imposing them on their clients (A.4.b.). Additionally, counselors monitor themselves, avoid providing counseling when impaired, and seek assistance for impairment (ACA, 2014, C.2.g.). A key aspect of personal development is self-awareness. Academic training programs typically emphasize self-awareness through self-reflection and other introspective activities throughout training.

In addition to exploring one's personal beliefs and values, it is important for counselors to explore and reflect on their own life experiences that may affect their work with clients. This includes the counselor's mental health concerns, mental health concerns of their family members, and other forms of personal trauma. Some academic training programs require counseling students to attend personal counseling, while others may encourage this experience. In addition to working through personal concerns, attending counseling provides an opportunity for the counseling student to experience what it is like to be a client. While counselors may have life experiences that negatively affected them, including traumatic experiences, not all life experiences negatively affect a counselor's work with clients. Life experiences help define who a person is, and influence an individual's view of the world and their interactions with others, which may also positively influence a counselor's work with clients. Rønnestad and Skovholt (2003) found that counselors reported that personal challenges and hardships that occurred in adulthood may have temporarily negatively influenced them, but these events often had positive long-term consequences for their work (e.g., increased ability to relate to clients, greater patience).

Similar to professional development, personal development is a career-long process and it is important for counselors to maintain strong self-awareness and engage in self-reflection throughout their careers. Counselors identified ongoing reflection as a prerequisite for learning and professional development at all experience levels, as reflection is an opportunity to learn more about ourselves, others, and our work as counselors (Rønnestad & Skovholt, 2003). Additionally, Rønnestad and Skovholt (2003) argue that not engaging in ongoing reflection may lead to stagnation or a deterioration process. It is also important that counselors seek counseling during their career, in addition to when they are in their training program, when they have personal concerns that may negatively affect their work with clients.

Self-awareness and reflection are also important in relation to the integration of new techniques in counseling. Counselors should explore and reflect on their reactions to a technique before integrating it with clients. This provides an opportunity to explore what may come up for the counselor that they might not be previously aware of prior to the experience. For example, a counselor interested in integrating mindfulness meditation to teach clients about ways to decrease stress and anxiety may choose to attend a retreat to learn more about mindfulness practice. Once undergoing the experience, the counselor may develop awareness of her own struggle with negative thoughts, rumination, and anxiety. This realization will serve to inform the counselor about her own growing edges or issues that need attention. Both counselor and client can benefit from this process. The counselor may choose to learn about this intervention in greater depth before recommending it to a client. Some interventions may be contraindicated for some clients for a variety of reasons. It is important that counselors have awareness of their own potential responses to particular interventions and issues of concern before offering an intervention to a client.

Supervision and Consultation

Supervision and consultation are crucial processes in the development of the counselor. A counseling supervisor is a skilled counselor who provides supervision to a more inexperienced counseling professional, such as counseling students and counselors working toward licensure. Supervision focuses both on the development of the counselor, and monitoring client services to ensure client welfare (Bernard & Goodyear, 2019). Counseling supervisors foster counseling competency by focusing on counseling skills, case conceptualization, and the self of the counseling supervisee, such as confidence (Bernard & Goodyear, 2019). This may involve discussing client cases, as well as reviewing client session recordings or observing sessions live. Supervisors may also integrate activities in supervision that focus on fostering self-awareness to help counselors recognize and address blind spots. Additionally, supervisors may help supervisees struggling with work-related concerns not specifically focused on clients, such as challenges with colleagues. Supervision helps ensure that counselors are practicing ethically and providing quality care for clients. It contributes to knowledge retention (Smith et al., 2007), as well as positive client outcomes (Callahan et al., 2009). Supervision is also an important self-care strategy, as supervisors can help process client cases, provide a different perspective, offer support, and help monitor a supervisee's wellness (Lawson & Venart, 2005).

Supervision is typically required for counseling students during their clinical experiences (practicum and internship), as well as mental health and marriage and family counselors working toward licensure following graduation. However, school counselors are credentialed by the state Department of Education upon graduation and are not typically required to receive supervision following graduation, unless they are also pursuing licensure. Nevertheless, all new counseling professionals should obtain supervision, when possible, to enhance their development as counselors. When it is not feasible to receive supervision, school counselors may consider consulting with others as needed.

Consultation differs from supervision in that the consultant and consultee can be at the same developmental level, instead of the hierarchy that exists in supervision, when the supervisor has greater expertise than the supervisee does. Supervision is also ongoing, while consultation may occur as needed. For example, a counselor may contact a colleague to consult about a specific client case. Consultation can be helpful for experienced counselors when they feel stuck with a client or they are experiencing an ethical dilemma that they are not sure how to address. It is important that counselors remain open to feedback regardless of their skill level and years of experience, as counselors in all stages of their careers can benefit from talking through an ethical dilemma and obtaining a different perspective. Thus, both supervision and consultation are helpful to promote counselor development and client welfare across a counselor's career.

THE SELF OF THE COUNSELOR

In addition to bringing the skills they learn in their academic training program to their sessions with clients, counselors also bring themselves to the session. While is it crucial to maintain boundaries with clients, the appropriate use of self is also important, as this may contribute to the therapeutic relationship. Use of self involves the integration of the counselor's experiences, personality, and thoughts and feelings in the counseling process, which may include self-disclosure, relationality, belief systems, attachment, and embodiment (Sleater & Scheiner, 2019). Self-disclosure involves the counselor sharing something personal about themself with the client, which may help build trust and enhance the therapeutic relationship when used purposefully. Relationality focuses on how the counselor and the client relate to each other, which may include relating on the subconscious level (Sleater & Scheiner, 2019). The counselor should also be aware of their belief systems and worldview and how this may influence their work with clients. Additionally, the counselor may tune in to the attachment style of the client and should be aware of this, such as becoming aware if they are taking on a parenting role with a client. Embodiment focuses on what the counselor is experiencing in their body during a session. Rogers (1961) also emphasized the importance of genuineness in counseling, which focuses on being transparent, real, and honest with the client. Being true to themselves will help counselors relate to their clients. Thus, it is important for counselors to not try to be some image of what they think counselors should be, but instead be true to themselves.

When engaging in self-disclosure or integrating other aspects of oneself, it is important for the counselor to be mindful of what they are doing, have good self-awareness, and make sure that they are intentional, so that they remain focused on the welfare of the client. Sessions with clients should not become focused on the counselor and their needs. Counselors should seek their own personal counseling to work through their personal concerns.

Counselor Characteristics/Dispositions

Scholars have examined the characteristics or dispositions that contribute to counselor effectiveness (e.g., Ackerman & Hilsenroth, 2003; Glenn et al., 2015; Pope & Kline, 1999; see Table 3.3.). The importance of these characteristics and gatekeeping related to them is emphasized in counselor training. Specifically, the Council for Accreditation of Counseling and Related Educational Programs (CACREP, 2015) requires CACREP-accredited counseling programs to identify and assess key dispositions of counseling students across multiple points in their training program, and then analyze and review the data (Standard 4G). However, while counselor educators in CACREP-accredited programs are required to evaluate counseling students' dispositions, faculty in individual programs have the freedom to decide what dispositions they will evaluate and the assessment strategies they will use to evaluate them.

While counselor educators may create their own assessments to measure counseling students' dispositions, scholars have also developed assessments to facilitate this process (see Table 3.4). Frame and Stevens-Smith (1995) developed

TABLE 3.3 COUNSELOR CHARACTERISTICS AND DISPOSITIONS

ACKERMAN AND HILSENROTH (2003)	GLENN ET AL. (2015)	POPE AND KLINE (1999)	FRAME AND STEVENS-SMITH (1995)	MCADAMS ET AL. (2007)	MULLEN (2021)
Open	Critical thinking-rationale, open-minded	Open	Open	Open	Open
Flexible	Flexible	Flexible	Flexibility	Flexibility	Flexibility and adaptability
Experienced	Strong philosophical or spiritual grounding	Cooperative	Cooperative	Cooperative	Cooperativeness with others
Respectful	Accepts and integrates feedback	Empathy	Willingness to accept and use feedback	Willingness to accept and use feedback	Willingness to accept and use feedback
Trustworthy	Authenticity and genuineness	Genuineness	Aware of impact on others	Awareness of impact on others	Awareness of own impact on others
Confident	Works with grace and humility	Acceptance	Able to deal with conflict	Ability to deal with conflict	Ability to deal with conflict
Interested	Creative, intuitive, and original thinking	Interest in people	Able to accept personal responsibility	Ability to accept personal responsibility	Ability to accept personal responsibility
Alert	Passion and purpose	Emotional stability	Able to express feelings effectively and appropriately	Ability to express feelings effectively and appropriately	Effective and appropriate expression of feelings
Friendly	Sense of humor	Friendliness	Positive	Attention to ethical and legal considerations	Attention to ethical and legal considerations

(continued)

TABLE 3.3 COUNSELOR CHARACTERISTICS AND DISPOSITIONS (CONTINUED)

ACKERMAN AND HILSENROTH (2003)	GLENN ET AL. (2015)	POPE AND KLINE (1999)	FRAME AND STEVENS-SMITH (1995)	MCADAMS ET AL. (2007)	MULLEN (2021)
Warm	Compassion and empathy	Warmth		Initiative and motivation	Initiative and motivation
Honest	Positive attitude	Fairness			Orientation to multiculturalism and social justice advocacy
	Consider multiple perspectives	Sensitivity			Professional wellness and self-care
	Gratitude and appreciation	Resourcefulness			Humility
		Sympathy			Professionalism
		Nonthreatening			Willingness to seek help
		Tolerance for ambiguity			
		Awareness of limitations			
		Capability			
		Patience			
		Sincerity			
		Confidence			
		Socialbility			

TABLE 3.4 INSTRUMENTS TO ASSESS PROFESSIONAL AND PERSONAL DEVELOPMENT

INSTRUMENT	AUTHORS	AREAS OF FOCUS
Counseling Competencies Scale Revised (CCS-R)	Lambie et al. (2018)	Counseling skills and therapeutic conditions, and counseling dispositions and behaviors
Assessment of Professional Counseling Dispositions	Mullen (2021)	Professional dispositions
Professional Performance Review Policy	McAdams et al. (2007)	Professional dispositions
Personal Characteristics Evaluation Form	Frame and Stevens-Smith (1995)	Professional dispositions
Professional Quality of Life Scale (ProQOL)	Hudnall Stamm (2009)	Compassion satisfaction and compassion fatigue (burnout and secondary traumatic stress)
Self-Compassion Scale-Short Form (SCS-SF)	Raes et al. (2011)	Self-compassion
Self-Care Assessment	Saakvitne and Pearlman (1996)	Wellness
Five Factor Wellness Inventory (FFWEL)	Myers and Sweeney (2004)	Wellness

the Personal Characteristic Evaluation Form, which evaluates nine essential functions using a five-point Likert scale. Additionally, McAdams et al. (2007) developed the Professional Performance Review Policy, which contains 10 dispositional areas. Most recently, Mullen (2021) developed the Assessment of Professional Dispositions, which includes a definition for each of the 15 dispositions and a rubric with a three-point rating scale. Thus, in addition to identifying counselor dispositions, scholars have developed assessments to measure dispositions. Table 3.3. contains a list of the dispositional areas for each of the assessments.

Advocacy

Being an advocate is an important role for counselors. This role involves advocating for the profession, advocating for clients, and advocating for oneself as a counselor. Advocating for the profession include activities that advance the counseling profession. Some example of this type of advocacy include educating the community about counseling and the stigma related to seeking counseling services for mental health, as well as meeting with legislators to encourage support for legislation to advance mental health initiatives. Client advocacy may involve advocating for individual clients or advocating for clients as a group. This may involve connecting clients with resources, as well as advocating for client resources for the community. This may also involve legislative advocacy for client groups, such as funding to support services for clients with severe mental illness. Additionally, counselors may help empower clients to advocate for themselves. Finally, counselor self-advocacy is also crucial. An example of self-advocacy is a counselor advocating within their agency for hiring additional mental health counselors, as well as lowering counselors' caseloads. In addition to promoting the mental health of the counselor, this example of advocacy also relates to the welfare of clients, as counselor well-being can affect client well-being, and more counselors can result in more clients being served.

Counselors may engage in advocacy through their use of self. This may involve telling a personal story to legislators or other decision-makers about why they became a counselor, or ways they have seen counseling change the lives of others. Counselors may also include their own personal story in writing letters to advocate for counseling and for their clients.

Common Growing Edges

Growing edges are the areas of counselor development that need to be honed and tended to by the counselor; they can be understood as areas where the counselor needs to grow. This type of self-awareness is critical to assist students in addressing their own issues and avoid having them spill into the therapy session. It is normal for counselors to struggle when they begin seeing clients in real life settings (versus role-playing in class). This is true for counseling students, as well as recent counseling graduates. Anxiety is a common experience for many beginning practitioners, but most master it with time and experience (Rønnestad & Skovholt, 2003). Factors contributing to anxiety for students beginning to see clients include the evaluation context of being a student, the achievement focus of academia, unrealistic expectations, and the fear of not knowing enough or being competent enough (Rønnestad & Skovholt, 2003). While this anxiety often continues to be present for novice counselors following graduation, it typically lessens as counselors become more experienced and develop greater confidence and competence.

Counselors may also struggle when they have a client with beliefs and values that conflict with their own belief system, or they disagree with a client's decisions. This may relate to religious beliefs, political views, or other values. It is important for counselors to remember that they do not need to have the same beliefs as their clients, or agree with their decisions, to work effectively with their clients. Counselors need to ensure that they stay focused on the client and do not attempt to impose their own beliefs on the client, as discussed above. This requires self-awareness, and may require supervision, consultation, and personal counseling, when needed.

Novice counselors may struggle with confidence, doubting their counseling abilities and thinking they do not know enough to work effectively with clients, sometimes referred to as imposter syndrome. It is important that counselors view the development of competence and learning as a career-long process, as there will always be things counselors do not know and areas for growth and further development. Researchers also found that counselors reported clients as being a source for learning, with client feedback contributing to counselor development (Rønnestad & Skovholt, 2003). Thus, counselors continue to learn beyond academic training in various ways.

Intentionality, or being purposeful in what you do in a counseling session, is important in counseling. New counselors may struggle with this if they are stuck in session and not sure what to do. It is important that counselors do not use a technique for the purpose of filling the space and passing the time in a session. When I was a new counselor, my supervisor told me that when, not if, I was stuck in session, to reflect. Thus, instead of searching for a cool technique or activity to fill the space, take a deep breath and remember to use your basic counseling skills.

Counselors may also be reluctant to be vulnerable with their clients, viewing this as a weakness. However, counselor vulnerability should not be viewed negatively. Counselors expect clients to be vulnerable in session; therefore, it is crucial for counselors to also be comfortable with vulnerability. Brown (2013) states that vulnerability is not weakness, it is an act of courage; it is the place where love, creativity, innovation, and belonging are born. She further contends that you cannot be empathic without being vulnerable (Brown, 2013). Thus, it is crucial that counselors are willing to be vulnerable when interacting with clients in session.

Burnout and Related Constructs

Serving as a helping professional can be taxing on one's own well-being and can present various concerns, including burnout. Maslach and Jackson (1981) identified three aspects of burnout: (a) emotional exhaustion, (b) negative, cynical attitudes and feelings related to clients, and (c) negative evaluation of one's work with clients and feeling dissatisfied with work. Additionally, in seeking to measure burnout specifically for counselors, Lee et al. (2007) developed the Counselor Burnout Inventory, which focused on five dimensions: (a) exhaustion, (b) incompetence, (c) negative work environment, (d) devaluing clients, and (e) personal life deterioration. While there are some differences among scholars in the conceptualization of burnout, there is agreement that burnout is a concern for counselors and other helping professionals. Compassion fatigue is another concern. While having some similarities with burnout, compassion fatigue focuses on "a response to stress related to interpersonal interactions" (Thompson et al., 2014, p. 59). Compassion fatigue originally related to interacting with individuals who had experienced trauma, burnout is more closely associated with the work environment. Compassion fatigue is similar to secondary traumatic stress, which mimics posttraumatic stress disorder, and may include hypervigilance, avoidance, numbing, and exhaustion. Compassion fatigue may be experienced from listening to individuals' stories of trauma (Baird & Kracen,

2006). Counselors may also experience vicarious trauma, affecting their views of the world, others, and themselves, from exposure to traumatic information (McCann & Pearlman, 1990). Vicarious trauma may affect schemas in five areas: safety, trust, control, esteem, and intimacy (Baird & Kracen, 2006). Finally, counselor impairment focuses on concerns with the functioning of a counselor that may negatively affect a client (Lawson & Venart, 2005).

In a content analysis study exploring burnout among novice counselors, Cook et al. (2021) identified 12 categories of burnout: (a) negative emotional experience, (b) fatigue and tiredness, (c) unfulfilled in counseling work, (d) unhealthy work environment, (e) physical symptoms, (f) negative impact on personal interest or self-care, (g) self-perceived ineffectiveness as a counselor, (h) cognitive impairment, (i) negative impact on personal relationships, (j) negative coping strategies, (k) questioning of one's career choice, and (l) psychological distress. Cook et al. concluded that it is important for novice counselors to be aware of symptoms of burnout they may be experiencing and to seek support from supervisors. Additionally, Skovholt et al. (2001) identified seven hazards that may provide challenges for counselors and contribute to burnout: (a) clients have an unresolved problem that must be solved; (b) clients are not always honor students—may not have the resources for success; (c) readiness gap between counselor and client; (d) counselor's inability to say no; (e) constant empathy, interpersonal sensitivity, and one-way caring; (f) elusive measures of success; and (g) normative failure. Researchers have also examined the relationship between various constructs to burnout, with Thompson et al. (2014) finding that as compassion satisfaction, mindfulness attitudes, and emotion-focused coping strategies (regulating emotional responses) increased, burnout decreased.

Self-assessment and self-awareness are crucial in monitoring for signs of burnout, impairment, and other concerns discussed here. Lawson and Venart (2005) recommend two assessments that counselors may use for this process. The Professional Quality of Life Scale (ProQOL; Hudnall Stamm, 2009) measures compassion satisfaction and two identified elements of compassion fatigue (burnout and secondary traumatic stress). The second assessment (Self-Care Assessment; Saakvitne & Pearlman, 1996) focuses on the domains of wellness. Thus, it is important for counseling professionals to be aware of the signs of burnout, engage in self-assessment to monitor themselves for the presence of these symptoms, and practice healthy coping strategies and self-care.

Wellness and Self-Care

Scholars describe self-care as having two areas of focus: (a) reduce negative outcomes, and (b) promote positive outcomes. Negative outcomes include stress and other factors that may be associated with an intensive, demanding work environment, while positive outcomes relate to healthy functioning and wellness (Butler et al., 2019). For counselors to be effective, they must ensure they are well, including emotionally and mentally healthy. Counselors cannot help others if they have not first focused on being well themselves. Myers and Sweeney (2004) proposed a model of wellness called the Indivisible Self, which originated as the Wheel of Wellness. The Indivisible Self model of wellness includes five factors. The first factor, essential self, encompasses spirituality, gender identity, culture, and self-care. The second one, creative self, includes emotions, thinking, positive humor, control, and work. The third factor, coping self, includes realistic beliefs, self-worth, stress management, and leisure. The next factor, social self, encompasses friendship and love. The final factor, physical self, includes exercise and nutrition. This model of wellness is applicable to working with clients, as well as relevant to the wellness of counselors and counseling students.

Maintaining counselor wellness involves engaging in self-care practices, which focus on the counselor caring for oneself. Self-care should be a priority throughout a counselor's career. The ACA (2014) *Code of Ethics* emphasizes the importance of self-care in maintaining a counselor's holistic well-being (physical, mental, emotional, and spiritual) to enable them to address their professional responsibilities (Section C Introduction). Additionally, CACREP (2015) has a standard related to counselor self-care strategies (Standard II.1.l).

Self-care is unique to the individual and may involve a variety of strategies and activities to promote holistic wellness and well-being within multiple domains. It is important that counselors develop self-care plans and continue to monitor their level of wellness and use of self-care practices. Reflection and journaling can be helpful in monitoring wellness and self-care (Bradley et al., 2013). Self-compassion is also an important self-care strategy (Coaston, 2017). Self-compassion involves three components: (a) self-kindness, (b) common humanity, (c) mindfulness (Neff, 2003). Coaston (2017) emphasizes treating oneself with the kindness and compassion that one would show toward their clients, instead of viewing a self-care or wellness plan as a remediation plan, list of New Year's resolutions, or focusing on areas of the counselor that need to be fixed. Self-compassion activities may include a self-compassion break designed to remind oneself of the three elements of compassion, engaging in soothing touch toward oneself (e.g., hug yourself, take deep breaths, stroke your own hand or arm), or writing a letter to oneself with compassion (Nelson et al., 2018). For more information about self-compassion, see the link for Neff's self-compassion website provided in the Resource list.

When thinking about developing a self-care plan, there are multiple self-care domains to consider. Butler et al. (2019) present six domains of self-care: (a) physical, (b) professional, (c) relational, (d) emotional, (e) psychological, and (f) spiritual. The physical domain focuses on caring for the physical body, which includes sleep, nutrition, exercise, and health maintenance and adherence (e.g., annual checkups, treatment regimens).Viewing physical self-care strategies metaphorically (e.g., care of a plant including sun and water; Bradley et al., 2013) can help a counselor have more self-compassion (Coaston, 2017). Additionally, planning activities for short durations may promote success when counselors have busy schedules (Coaston, 2017).

The professional domain focuses on addressing work-related stress, vicarious trauma, burnout, and other related constructs discussed in the previous section (Burnout and Related Constructs), and promoting job engagement. Self-care activities within this domain to cope with stress and prevent burnout include taking breaks throughout the day, taking vacations, developing coping skills, seeking personal counseling, and engaging in supervision and consultation.

Positive job engagement includes having a good job-person fit and maintaining work-life balance, instead of relying on work to meet all of one's needs (Butler et al., 2019). This includes counselors setting appropriate boundaries.

The relational domain focuses on connections with others. This includes relationships with different groups of individuals, including family, friends, and colleagues. Relationships with animals can also be valuable for providing social support. Butler et al. (2019) provide a reminder that it is important to have healthy relationships, letting go of destructive ones.

The emotional domain focuses on practices that address negative emotional experiences and foster positive ones (Butler et al., 2019). An important aspect of self-care within this domain is examining negative coping skills and developing healthy ones. Some strategies used to cope with negative emotional experiences may provide temporary relief, but they are not healthy or beneficial beyond the immediate moment, such as overeating, drinking, and excessively playing video games. Enhancing positive emotional experiences is also important in this domain, which involves identifying what makes you happy and doing it (Butler et al., 2019).

The next domain, psychological, focuses on activities that meet intellectual needs, as well as the overall needs of the mind. These are cognitive recreational activities that are pleasurable and stimulate the mind (e.g., puzzles, debate, the arts, playing games), as well as activities that provide opportunities for reflection and self-awareness (Butler et al., 2019). Coaston (2017) discussed several self-care strategies for the mind, such as mindfulness activities (e.g., mindful walking or eating), writing (e.g., journaling, creative writing), learning something new outside counseling (e.g., language, sport, game), and acknowledging efforts and successes. This may include sharing successes with colleagues to celebrate accomplishments and validate one's work (Bradley et al., 2013). On a difficult day, a counselor may need a reminder of why they are a counselor and of their client successes. This may include rereading letters from previous clients thanking the counselor or reflecting on client successes. The first author has experience counseling children. For years, she has had a heart posted on her bulletin board in her office that a former client gave her with the message, "The best therapist ever" (without the client's name visible), which reminds her, on tough days, of the many children she has worked with and why she became a counselor.

The final domain is spiritual and focuses on how we view our place in the world, what our purpose is, our source of hope, and what we find meaningful in life (Butler et al., 2019). Self-care activities in this domain may include interacting with a spiritual community, prayer, meditation, and interactions with nature and grounding activities (e.g., tai chi, gardening, massage). Counselors may also engage in a variety of creative interventions that promote holistic healing, including music, dance, and art (Coaston, 2017).

Now that we have discussed self-care, what is your assessment of your own self-care practices? Butler et al. (2019) report that reflecting on your current self-care practices is the first step in making a self-care plan. After reflecting on these practices, you can use Figure 3.2 to identify self-care practices that you can do within each domain and then develop a plan for when you will engage in the various activities. It is also important to set aside time to evaluate your self-care

FIGURE 3.2 Self-care domains presented by Butler et al. (2019).

plan and make revisions as needed. You are encouraged to begin this process right now using the Going Within exercise and Figure 3.2 to guide you. Butler et al. (2019) also discuss the importance of having an emergency self-care plan that you can use under extremely stressful circumstances that encompasses practices that you have found useful in the past, as well as a list of people who can provide support during these extreme circumstances. See the Resource list for the link for the emergency self-care worksheet created by Elaine Rinfrette, as well as the link for the full self-care starter kit developed by the University at Buffalo School of Social Work.

As a developing counselor, remember that you can only give of your overflow. You must dedicate time and energy to activities and practices that fill you up in order to be present for others. Consider what steps you can take right now to take care of you.

CONCLUSION

Counselor professional identity is crucial for unifying, strengthening, and advancing the counseling profession. While counselor training is crucial to the development of counselors, counselor growth is a career-long process. Thus, counselors should value and commit to personal and professional development, while also focusing on self-care throughout their career to grow as counselors and ensure they are healthy to provide the best quality of care to their clients.

Summary

- Scholars have developed multiple models to explain the professional identity development process.
- There are multiple sets of counselor competencies focused on different counseling specialty areas and working with various groups.
- Personal and professional growth and development is a career-long process.
- Supervision and consultation are crucial in the growth and development of counselors.
- Counselors are at risk for counselor burnout, compassion fatigue, secondary traumatic stress, vicarious trauma, and impairment.
- Wellness and self-care are important for preventing counselor burnout and other counseling concerns.

Voices From the Field

Christina McGrath Fair, PhD
Visiting Clinical Assistant Professor, Florida International University

As a beginning counselor, I worked at an outpatient community mental health clinic. It was not an uncommon experience to have 35–45 direct client hours per week. I do not mean to say that this is true of all mental health clinics. It was my experience, however. Having that many direct client hours each week was great for my paycheck and collecting hours for licensure, but not great for much else. I found that not only was I experiencing symptoms of burnout—getting sick, tired all the time, dreading the start of a new work week—but I was also not developing into the counselor I always thought I would be. I was not taking care of myself, and I was not providing clients with the level of therapeutic care that I knew I was capable of giving.

One of the truths about being a counselor is that we are in need of ongoing growth and development. This comes through additional training and continuing education, supervision, and consultation. It also comes from our experiences working with clients and what we learn about ourselves, counseling, and human beings when we engage in the counseling relationship. Throughout my time at the clinic, I found that I was not growing in the ways I had expected, and I frequently doubted my abilities as a counselor. I realized that it was not simply the large number of clients I was seeing or the hours that I was working that prevented the growth. The intentional practices that I was unable to find time for was leading the charge to burnout and just-barely-adequate client care. These intentional practices include increasing authenticity, reflection and increasing self-awareness, creating boundaries around my time and energy, and looking to professional peers for support. I will discuss these below.

In the introduction to counseling skills course, I emphasize to my students the importance of authenticity in the counseling relationship. As counselors, we are bringing ourselves and everything we are into the counseling relationship. Our own unique identities and experiences cannot be separated from who we are as individuals or who we are as counselors. Being a White cisgender female does not pause when I enter the counseling space. I cannot turn off my identity as an advocate for social justice or my stance as a feminist. Our professional identity is then borne out of our own biased beliefs about what a helping professional should be based on related to the ethics and values of our profession. Mine includes approaching work with clients from a feminist, cultural-relational framework, and broaching areas of identity and experiences within those identities with clients. This is what makes each counselor unique and what brings us together. When we are not given the time to engage in reflective practices in order to increase our self-awareness, we are not given the ability to be ethical and authentic practitioners.

Often when we think of engaging in self-care practices, we consider relaxation activities, self-indulgences, and fun. The less talked about self-care practices that are also needed include the ability to say "no," boundaries related to professional and personal time, and advocacy for oneself, one's clients, and one's profession. Novice counselors can sometimes struggle to say "no," especially when trying to complete hours for licensure and while receiving pre-licensure pay. It is important to remember that it can be difficult to get out of this level of overperforming once it starts. It is beneficial to set boundaries early in your career and be intentional about the use of your "downtime" by engaging in practices that are rejuvenating and refreshing for you. Community care, which involves us as counselors supporting one another and working together to promote the welfare of ourselves, our clients, and our profession is also needed. There is much to be gained by broadening your professional network and identifying a mentor(s).

My hope is that as you begin your journey in the profession, you are able to advocate for yourself so that you can be your personal best for your clients. In being able to care for yourself, you can better care for others. I hope that you can take the time to reflect and increase your self-awareness. This self-awareness will help you know how much you can give and when you need to rejuvenate. I hope that you will continue to grow into a counseling professional that is authentically you. You will then be able to engage in healthy therapeutic relationships with your clients, be intentional in your work as a counselor, and effect positive changes in your clients' well-being.

A Call to Action

Think about why you want to be a professional counselor. What brought you to this career path? What do you hope to accomplish in the process? Write a personal story that you could share with legislators to encourage their support for legislation expanding mental health services or with stakeholders to obtain their support for increased funding of mental health programs in the local community.

Case Study 3.1

Hector is a 25-year-old Puerto Rican male seeking counseling due to relationship issues. His boyfriend, Enrique, is openly gay and wants Hector to come out of the closet and introduce him to his family. Hector is terrified and feels guilty because he is just not ready to take this next step. His parents and two older sisters are devout Catholics and Hector knows they would disapprove of his sexual orientation.

RESPONSE QUESTIONS

Use the resources found in this chapter to inform your answers.

1. How competent would you feel to work with Hector and help him with this dilemma?
2. How would you approach this case?
3. What resources would you try to bring to your sessions to support Hector in his journey?
4. What strengths do you bring to this situation?
5. What growing edges would you anticipate?
6. How would you prepare yourself to be able to help Hector and Enrique?

Going Within

Think about your current level of wellness and use of self-care practices. Develop a self-care plan that you can use right now during graduate school, using Figure 3.2 to consider activities to incorporate within each domain. You may want to copy this figure and write activities you are currently doing/will do in each domain. Include in your plan specific self-care activities and days and times when you will practice these activities. Also, identify when you will review the plan to pinpoint what is working and what is not, and revise the plan as needed to promote wellness in your life.

Group Process

In small groups, discuss what counseling is and develop an agreed-upon definition. After your group develops your definition, look at definitions proposed by counseling experts. How is your group's definition similar and different from the experts' definitions? Is there anything you would change about your definition?

RESOURCES

Counseling Competencies

Addiction Counseling Competencies: https://store.samhsa.gov/product/TAP
-21-AddictionCounseling-Competencies/SMA15-4171

ALGBTIC (now known as SAIGE] Competencies for Counseling with Transgender Clients: https://secureservercdn.net/198.71.233.36/v8i.3d4.myft-
pupload.com/wp-content/uploads/2019/07/Competencies-for-Counsel-
ing-Transgender-Clients.pdf

American Counseling Association (ACA) Advocacy Competencies: https://
www.counseling.org/docs/default-source/competencies/aca-advocacy
-competencies-updated-may-2020.pdf?sfvrsn=f410212c_4

American Rehabilitation Counseling Association (ARCA) Disability-Related
Counseling Competencies: https://www.counseling.org/docs/default
-source/competencies/arca-disability-related-counseling-competencies-fi-
nal-version-5-15-19.pdf?sfvrsn=c376562c_6

American School Counselor Association (ASCA) School Counselor Professional Standards and Competencies: https://www.schoolcounselor.org/getme-
dia/a8d59c2c-51de-4ec3-a565-a3235f3b93c3/SC-Competencies.pdf

Association for Lesbian, Gay, Bisexual, and Transgender Issues in Counseling (AL-
GBTIC, now known as the Society for Sexual, Affectional, Intersex, and Gender Expansive Identities [SAIGE]) Competencies for Counseling with Lesbian,
Gay, Bisexual, Queer, Questioning, Intersex, and Ally (LGBQQIA) Individuals:
https://secureservercdn.net/198.71.233.36/v8i.3d4.myftpupload.com/wp
-content/uploads/2019/07/Competencies-for-Counseling-with-LGBQQIA
-Individuals.pdf

Association for Multicultural Counseling and Development (AMCD) Multicultural and Social Justice Counseling Competencies (MSJCC): https://www
.counseling.org/docs/default-source/competencies/multicultural-and-so-
cial-justice-counseling-competencies.pdf?sfvrsn=8573422c_20

Association for Spiritual, Ethical, and Religious Values in Counseling (ASER-
VIC) Competencies for Addressing Spiritual and Religious Issues in Counseling: https://www.counseling.org/docs/default-source/competencies/
competencies-for-addressing-spiritual-and-religious-issues-in-counseling
.pdf?sfvrsn=aad7c2c_8

Group Work Competencies and Best Practices: https://asgw.org/resources

Additional Resources

Counseling Journals: https://www.counseling.org/publications/counseling
-journals

Kristin Neff's Self-compassion website: https://self-compassion.org

Rinfrette, E. (n.d.). Emergency self-care worksheet. https://socialwork.buffalo
.edu/content/dam/socialwork/home/self-care-kit/emergency-self-care
-worksheet.pdf

The Counseling Roundtable Podcasts: The Counseling Roundtable

University of Buffalo School of Social Work Self-Care Starter Kit: https://social-
work.buffalo.edu/resources/self-care-starter-kit.html

Access this podcast at http://connect.springerpub.com/content/book/978-0-8261-6386-8/chapter/ch03.

KEY REFERENCES

Only key references appear in the print edition. The full reference list appears in the digital product found on https://connect.springerpub.com/content/book/978-0-8261-6386-8/chapter/ch03

Gibson, D. M., Dollarhide, C. T., & Moss, J. M. (2010). Professional identity development: A grounded theory of transformational tasks of new counselors. *Counselor Education and Supervision, 50*(1), 21–38. https://doi.org/10.1002/j.1556-6978.2010.tb00106.x

Hudnall Stamm, B. (2009). *Professional quality of life: Compassion satisfaction and fatigue version 5 (ProQOL).* https://proqol.org/proqol-measure

Kaplan, D. M., & Gladding, S. T. (2011). A vision for the future of counseling: The 20/20 principles for unifying and strengthening the profession. *Journal of Counseling & Development, 89*(3), 367–372. https://doi.org/10.1002/j.1556-6678.2011.tb00101.x

Nelson, J. R., Hall, B. S., Anderson, J. L., Birtles, C., & Hemming, L. (2018). Self-compassion as self-care: A simple and effective tool for counselor educators and counseling students. *Journal of Creativity in Mental Health, 13*(1), 121–133. https://doi.org/10.1080/15401383.2017.1328292

Rønnestad, M. H., & Skovholt, T. M. (2003). The journey of the counselor and therapist: Research findings and perspectives on professional development. *Journal of Career Development, 30*(1), 5–44. https://doi.org/10.1177/089484530303000102

CHAPTER 4

ETHICAL AND LEGAL STANDARDS IN COUNSELING

Jacqueline M. Swank

Think about this...

What is important to you? What do you value and believe and how might these areas influence your views about counseling? How do you make decisions and what factors influence your decision-making process?

LEARNING OBJECTIVES

After reading this chapter, you should be able to:

- Explain counseling certification, licensure, and accreditation standards
- Recognize various ethical and legal issues relevant to counseling
- Identify cultural considerations and social justice implications for the ethical decision-making process
- Employ an ethical decision-making model to determine a course of action for an ethical dilemma in counseling
- Outline personal beliefs and values that may influence ethical decision-making

INTRODUCTION

Laws and ethics are both important in the counseling profession; however, they are not the same thing. Laws are rules and regulations that a society agrees upon, and authorized bodies enforce, such as the government at the local, state, and national levels. In contrast, ethics focuses on what is considered right and how people should live (Remley & Herlihy, 2019). There are many laws and ethical standards for counselors to consider in counseling practice, with this chapter highlighting some key areas.

Have you thought about what ethical issues may be important in counseling? In examining ethical issues in counseling, Herlihy and Dufrene (2011) found the top issues focused on the ethical practice of counselors, counselor identity, counselor competence, and multicultural competence. Other important current issues included working with clients who are suicidal or homicidal, confidentiality, and multiple relationships and boundaries. In considering counseling issues that are important for the future, participants identified diversity and social justice as the most important. Other important issues included measuring counseling effectiveness, working with emerging populations and issues with medical advances, diagnoses, technology, professional growth, and licensure issues. Furthermore, Herlihy and Dufrene (2011) found important ethical issues for counselor training included ethical decision-making, gatekeeping, counselor identity, and boundaries and relationships. Thus, there are many ethical issues to consider in counseling; therefore, it is important to have ethical standards, as well as certification, licensure, and accreditation standards.

This chapter focuses on discussing accreditation standards, counselor competency, and licensure and certification standards. It also encompasses ethical standards, ethical decision-making models, and ethical and legal issues in counseling. Finally, the chapter addresses ethical advocacy as social justice practices.

ACCREDITATION STANDARDS

As a counseling student, do you know if your counselor preparation program is accredited? The purpose of accreditation for educational programs is to ensure that a program meets an identified level of quality in training students. While some programs may exceed the requirements established by an accreditation body, all accredited programs must meet the minimum requirements in order to maintain accreditation. Thus, by graduating from an accredited program, students should meet a standard level of competency. Within the counseling profession, there are currently two accreditation bodies: Council for Accreditation of Counseling and Related Educational Programs (CACREP) and Masters in Psychology and Counseling Accreditation Council (MPCAC).

CACREP

The process of accreditation began in the 1960s and 1970s when the Association for Counselor Education and Supervision (ACES) developed some preliminary standards and began accrediting some programs. Then, CACREP was established in 1981, and they used the standards developed by ACES, with revision, until CACREP published the first set of standards in 1988. The standards were then revised every 7 years (1994, 2001, 2009, 2016), except for a 1-year delay in publishing the 2009 standards to allow for the inclusion of disaster response aspects in the standards. The next revision will be in 2023.

In 2017, the Council on Rehabilitation Education (CORE) merged with CACREP; therefore, CACREP is now responsible for accrediting graduate level rehabilitation counselor education programs as well. CACREP is accredited by the Council for Higher Education Accreditation (CHEA). Programs can seek CACREP accreditation in eight master's level counseling specialty areas (addiction; career; clinical mental health; clinical rehabilitation; college counseling and student affairs; marriage, couple, and family; school counseling; and rehabilitation), as well as doctoral level accreditation in counselor education and supervision. Currently, there are over 870 accredited specialty areas in over 400 institutions (CACREP, 2020).

At the time this book was written, the most current published standards were the 2016 CACREP Standards. The 2016 standards have six sections. The first section, *The Learning Environment,* focuses on standards related to the institution, program, and faculty and staff. The second section, *Professional Counseling Identity,* contains the standards within the eight required core curriculum areas. The third section, *Professional Practice,* focuses on standards related to practicum and internship experiences. The next section, *Evaluation in the Program,* pertains to assessment and evaluation of students, faculty, site supervisors, and the overall program. The fifth section focuses on specialized content for each of the eight entry-level (master's level) specialty areas. The final section focuses on the specialized doctoral standards. There is also a glossary of terms following the doctoral standards section (CACREP, 2015).

MPCAC

MPCAC began as the Master's in Psychology Accreditation Council (MPAC) in 1995, and it initially only accredited master's level psychology programs. Then, in 2010, MPCAC was established to accredit both master's level psychology and counseling programs. As of 2020, there were 57 MPCAC-accredited programs (MPCAC, 2020). The MPCAC standards include seven major areas: (a) program mission and objectives, (b) program orientation and core curriculum (contains 11 curriculum areas), (c) research and clinical instruction, (d) institution, (e) faculty and staff, (f) program organization and administration, and (g) evaluations in the program (MPCAC, 2017).

In comparing the two accreditation bodies, CACREP has a history of being formed within the counseling profession, while MPCAC began in the field of psychology. CACREP accredits master's and doctoral level counseling programs, while MPCAC accredits both counseling and psychology programs, but only at the master's level. Regarding core curricula areas, CACREP has eight and MPCAC has 11. Additionally, CACREP has accreditation through CHEA, while MPCAC is working toward this accreditation. Finally, an important distinction between the accreditation bodies is that some state licensure boards align with CACREP.

COUNSELOR COMPETENCIES AND SCOPE OF PRACTICE

Scope of practice relates to areas of competency regarding knowledge and skills. It is important for counselors to be knowledgeable and to provide services within their scope of practice. Counselors should refer a client to another provider if they lack the competency to work with a client (American Counseling

Association [ACA], 2014, Standard A.11.a); however, they should base this decision on lack of skills, rather than their own values (Standard A.11.b). Additionally, counselors engage in ongoing professional development to continue to develop their competency, stay current on best practices for counseling (ACA, 2014; Standard C.2.f), and address values conflicts (Standard A.11.b). Counselors also engage in training and supervision before engaging in a new area of practice (ACA, 2014; Standard C.2.b). Professional development may focus on developing competency in working with a specific client population (e.g., children, college students, a specific marginalized population), area of concern (e.g., grief and loss, anxiety, addictions), or counseling modality (e.g., individual, group, family). With the increase in technology use, counselors may seek to provide counseling through online platforms (i.e., telemental health). Although counselors may interact with clients through video conference software in a similar manner to when the client is in the same room, it is important for the counselor to have training before offering telemental health services, as there are ethical and practice considerations that are unique to this counseling format.

There are many sets of competencies and best practices within the counseling profession. This includes, for example, competencies to guide practice in specialized areas (e.g., addiction counseling competencies; Substance Abuse and Mental Health Services Administration, 2006), as well as competencies regarding multicultural aspects of counseling. The ACA (2014) *Code of Ethics* also includes the importance of developing multicultural counseling competency related to awareness, dispositions, knowledge, and skills (Standard C.2.a). ACA provides a list of competencies related to counseling (www.counseling.org/knowledge-center/competencies), with other competencies and best practices also presented by other counseling organizations. See Table 4.1 for a list of some of the competencies and best practices for the counseling profession. Three examples of competencies related to multicultural aspects of counseling are the (a) Multicultural and Social Justice Counseling Competencies (MSJCC; Ratts et al., 2016), (b) Association for Lesbian, Gay, Bisexual, and Transgender Issues in Counseling (ALGBTIC; now the Society for Sexual, Affectional, Intersex, and Gender Expansive Identities [SAIGE]) Competencies for Counseling LGBQIQA (lesbian, gay, bisexual, queer, intersex, questioning, and ally) Individuals (Harper et al., 2009), and (c) Competencies for Addressing Spiritual and Religious Issues in Counseling (Association for Spiritual, Ethical, Religious Values in Counseling [ASERVIC], 2009).

The MSJCC (Ratts et al., 2016) focus on working with culturally diverse clients and addressing social justice concerns. The framework has four quadrants: (a) privileged counselor–marginalized client, (b) privileged counselor–privileged client, (c) marginalized counselor–privileged client, and (d) marginalized counselor–marginalized counselor. In each of the four areas there are developmental domains influencing multicultural and social justice practice: (a) counselor self-awareness, (b) client worldview, (c) counseling relationship, (d) counseling and advocacy interventions. Additionally, there are four competency areas (beliefs and attitudes, knowledge, skills, and actions) within the first three domains. The MSJCC provide a model for engaging in professional growth and development,

TABLE 4.1 COUNSELING COMPETENCIES

American Counseling Association (ACA) Advocacy Competencies
Association for Lesbian, Gay, Bisexual, and Transgender Issues in Counseling (ALGBTIC; now the Society for Sexual, Affectional, Intersex, and Gender Expansive Identities [SAIGE]) Competencies for Counseling LGBQIQA (lesbian, gay, bisexual, queer, intersex, questioning, and ally) Individuals
ALGBTIC Competencies for Counseling Transgender Clients
Animal Assisted Therapy Competencies
American Rehabilitation Counseling Association (ARCA) Disability-Related Counseling Competencies
Competencies for Addressing Spiritual and Religious Issues in Counseling
Competencies for Counseling the Multiracial Population
Exemplary Practices for Military Populations Group Work Competencies and Best Practices
Multicultural and Social Justice Counseling Competencies
Multicultural Career Counseling Competencies

Note: Links to competencies available at https://www.counseling.org/knowledge-center/competencies.

working with diverse clients, and engaging in social justice advocacy. Thus, it is crucial for counseling professionals to be familiar with these competencies and understand how they apply to their work with clients.

Harper et al. (2009) developed the ALGBTIC, now known as the SAIGE, Competencies for Counseling LGBQIQA. There are three competency areas: (a) working with lesbian, gay, bisexual, queer, and questioning individuals; (b) working with allies; and (c) working with intersex individuals; as well as an introduction; references and resources; and appendix. The first competency area has sections for each of the eight CACREP core curricula areas. The ally section has two areas: (a) framework for counselors identifying as allies, and (b) competencies for counseling allies. Finally, the intersex section discusses the concept of intersex and presents competencies in this area. Thus, counselors have competencies to guide their work with LGBQIQA.

Finally, an ASERVIC taskforce developed the Spiritual Competencies in 2009. These competencies focus on addressing spiritual and religious issues in counseling. Six areas guide the counselor in this practice area: (a) culture and worldview, (b) counselor self-awareness, (c) human and spiritual development, (d) communication, (e) assessment, and (f) diagnosis and treatment. Thus, through the development of competencies by various counseling organizations, counselors have a guide to providing quality, ethical care for diverse clients.

Counselor Impairment

A counselor needs to be professionally fuctional to be able to help someone else. Clients may come to counseling with intense emotions and have experienced traumatic situations. Counselors need to be in a place where they are emotionally, spiritually, mentally, and physically able to listen and be present for their clients. This highlights the importance of counseling professionals seeking their own counseling when needed, as well as engaging in self-care (ACA, 2014; Section C Introduction).

Counselors need to work through their own concerns to be available for their clients. Some counselor preparation programs require counseling students to receive counseling while they are in their academic program, while others do not require it, but strongly encourage it. Counseling preparation programs often require students to engage in ongoing self-reflection to develop self-awareness. Through this process, concerns may resurface from the past or arise that a counseling student did not have previous awareness of in their life. If this happens, it is crucial to work through these concerns so that they do not negatively affect future work with clients. Addressing personal concerns, and experiencing what it feels like to be a client, can be beneficial in becoming a counselor. Additionally, counselors may have personal concerns arise throughout their career at various points and enter counseling to address these concerns. It is important that counselors do not practice while they are impaired to avoid causing harm to their clients, and seek assistance in addressing personal concerns. Counseling professionals also have an obligation to help others (e.g., colleagues, students, supervisees) recognize their concerns and provide assistance to address impairment (ACA, 2014; Standard C.2.g, F.5.b).

Self-care and wellness are also important for counseling professionals to stay well. This may involve a variety of activities and practices to address multiple domains. Self-care activities will look different for various individuals, as it is necessary for people to engage in self-care practices that meet their needs, as self-care should not be forced or feel like a chore for the individual. However, it is essential for every counseling professional to engage in it to maintain their own well-being. Counseling professionals can begin to prioritize their own health and well-being while they are students by creating a self-care plan that involves ongoing engagement in self-care practices.

LICENSURE AND CERTIFICATION

Licensure

As with many professions, individual states oversee counselor licensure. The issue as it relates to the counseling professions is that there is inconsistency in licensure titles, scopes of practice, and education requirements across states. Kaplan (2012) reported there are over 45 different counseling licensure titles used throughout the United States. He also remarked that there are many different scopes of practice across states creating inconsistency in what counselors are able to do within their work as counselors. Furthermore, states differ in educational requirements, including graduate degree hours, supervised clinical practice hours, years allowed to obtain clinical hours, years of experience, and licensure exam (Kaplan, 2012). Regarding educational requirements, some states are now aligning with the CACREP standards, which could be one way to promote consistency in some educational requirements; however, only a few states are following this practice and not all counseling preparation programs are CACREP-accredited.

Inconsistencies create challenges for the profession, including confusion for the public and counseling professionals, as well as difficulty in offering care with lack of licensure portability across states. For example, a counselor who lives close to the state line may want to practice in two states, but experience challenges with the lack of licensure portability. Additionally, a client may move to another state and wish to continue counseling, but be confused in trying to find a counselor due to differences in titles and scopes of practice. This also becomes a challenge related to counseling conducted virtually (telemental health) because states have different regulations regarding seeing clients in their state when the counselor is not licensed in that state. Thus, there are many potential benefits to having consistency in licensure title, requirements, and scope of practice.

States typically require licensure or working toward licensure, through registration with the state, for mental health, as well as marriage, couple, and family counselors to be able to work as a counselor following graduation from an academic counselor preparation program. In some states, school counselors are also eligible for licensure, but in other states they must complete the requirement for mental health or marriage, couple, and family counseling to be licensure eligible. ACA compiles a list of licensure requirements, licensure titles, and other information. (See the resource list at the end of the chapter for more information.)

Communication is crucial in working toward the goal of license portability. The American Association of State Counseling Boards (AASCB), started in 1986, is an organization focused on facilitating communication between state counseling licensure boards. AASCB also works with other organizations representing counselors and the profession (AASCB, 2019). In 2005, ACA joined with AASCB to launch an initiative to focus on advancing the counseling profession known as *20/20: A vision for the future of counseling*. The initiative involved a group of 31 organizations, and although the intention was for it to last a few years, the initiative continued until 2013 (ACA, 2020). In 2006, the group identified seven principles for unifying and strengthening the profession (see Kaplan & Gladding, 2011), and all but one organization endorsed them. The principles focused on seven consensus issues for advancing the profession that included (a) enhancing counselor identity, (b) unifying the profession, (c) improving public understanding and advocacy for issues important to counseling, (d) developing licensure portability, (e) advancing research for the profession, (f) focusing on students and their development, and (g) promoting client welfare and advocacy (Kaplan & Gladding, 2011).

The group also sought to develop a unified definition of counseling, as well as a consensus licensure title, licensure scope of practice, and licensure education requirements. In 2010, following a Delphi study designed to identify the components of the definition, and discussion by the group, they reached consensus on a definition, and 29 of the 31 organizations endorsed it. The definition is: "Counseling is a professional relationship that empowers diverse individuals, families, and groups to accomplish mental health, wellness, education, and career goals" (Kaplan et al., 2014, p. 368). In addition, through Delphi methodology and discussions, the group worked to reach consensus about aspects of licensure to help move toward licensure portability. The consensus licensure title was Licensed Professional Counselor. The licensure scope of practice is available on the ACA 20/20 vision webpage (ACA, 2020). Twenty-eight of the 29 organizations endorsed the licensure title and 27 of the 29 organizations endorsed the scope of practice. Finally, the group developed a list of strategies to assist future groups with reaching the goals outlined in the *Principles for Unifying and Strengthening the Counseling Profession* (ACA, 2020). Although the work of the 20/20 group made progress in advancing the counseling profession, there is still a lot of work needed, including advocacy, to unify the profession; develop a consistent licensure title, scope of practice, and educational requirements; and obtain licensure portability. Efforts have continued in this area, including the Interstate Counseling Compact, which is a contract between states that allows counselors residing and licensed in a compact state to provide counseling in other compact states without requiring licensure in the other compact states. The legislature in multiple states has ratified the interstate counseling compact into law and advocacy continues in states that are not yet compact states. For more information about the Counseling Compact, see https://counselingcompact.org.

Certification

Some counseling certifications are required (e.g., school counselors), while others are optional. Certification means an individual has met standards in a designated area. In many states, school counselors are certified and not licensed, unless they meet the requirements for mental health or marriage and family license. The state oversees certification of school counselors. The name of this body is different depending on the state, with it called the Department of Education (DOE) in many states. Since this oversight is at the state level, similar to licensure boards, there are different requirements for states. States may require a few courses in teaching-related areas, but most do not require school counselors to have teaching experience. However, Texas requires 2 years of teaching experience. Refer to the ACA list of state school counselor credentialing/licensing agencies to find out more information about the requirements for specific states. (See the resource list at the end of the chapter for more information.)

The National Board for Certified Counselors (NBCC) oversees certification in multiple areas. NBCC certification signifies to the public that the individual has met standards required for the designation (NBCC, 2020), but it is not required to practice counseling, unlike mental health or marriage and family licensure or school counseling credentialing/licensing by the state. NBCC also has its own ethical code. The flagship credential offered by NBCC is National Certified Counseling (NCC). NBCC also offers three specialty credentials: Certified Clinical Mental Health Counselor (CCMHC), National Certified School Counselor (NCSC), and Masters Addictions Counselor (MAC) (NBCC,

2020). Because NBCC is a national credentialing body, the requirements for certification do not differ by state.

There are numerous other credentials offered within specialized areas of counseling. When considering whether to pursue earning a credential, it is important to think about your reasoning for wanting to obtain the credential. Is the credential for an area of practice you are interested in developing expertise in? You will also want to ensure that the credentialing body is credible. Is the credentialing organization a well-known, reputable entity within the counseling profession? Credentials are only as strong as the credibility of the organization overseeing them. Thus, counselors should research credentialing bodies and reflect on what will best help them reach their goals in providing counseling to specialized populations.

ETHICAL STANDARDS IN COUNSELING

There are many ethical codes within the counseling profession. This includes the ethical code for the largest organization in the world exclusively representing professional counselors, ACA, as well as ethical codes for counseling specialty organizations. Members of a professional organization follow the ethical guidelines for the organization. Organizations typically have an ethics committee that investigates ethical complaints for members of their organization. If the committee finds evidence to substantiate the ethical complaint, a professional organization may issue a variety of sanctions that range from acknowledgment of wrongdoing to termination of membership with the organization. It is important to remember that a professional counseling organization can only issue sanctions related to members of their organization. State licensure boards review ethical complaints made against counseling professionals licensed or in the licensure process and registered with the state.

In the sections below, we present the history and an overview of the ACA (2014) *Code of Ethics*, as well as an overview of a few additional codes for counseling specialty areas. The counseling specialty areas include the American Association for Marriage and Family Therapy (AAMFT), International Association of Marriage and Family Counselors (IAMFC), American Mental Health Counselors Association (AMHCA), and American School Counselor Association (ASCA). We are addressing both the AAMFT and the IAMFC ethical standards because counselors may align with one or both of these ethical codes. It is important to remember that counselors may be bound by other ethical codes or standards of care in addition to the codes described below, depending on their credentials and memberships in professional counseling organizations.

American Counseling Association Code of Ethics

As part of the leadership for the American Personnel and Guidance Association (APGA; now ACA), Donald Super developed the organization's first ethics committee in 1953 and the organization adopted their first *Code of Ethics* in 1961 (Allen, 1986). ACA has revised the code six times since development (1974,

TABLE 4.2 AMERICAN COUNSELING ASSOCIATION 2014 CODE OF ETHICS SECTIONS

Section A: The Counseling Relationship
Section B: Confidentiality and Privacy
Section C: Professional Responsibility
Section D: Relationships with Other Professionals
Section E: Evaluation, Assessment, and Interpretation
Section F: Supervision, Training, and Teaching
Section G: Research and Publication
Section H: Distance Counseling, Technology, and Social Media
Section I: Resolving Ethical Issues

Source: Data from American Counseling Association. (2014). *ACA code of ethics.*

1981, 1988, 1995, 2005, and 2014). It has evolved from being originally five pages to now being 21 pages. The code has also evolved across revisions to include a greater emphasis on cultural sensitivity (e.g., Standard A.10.f. that focuses on considering cultural consideration when a client offers a gift to a counselor). The 2014 version has nine sections (Table 4.2). This encompasses an additional section not included in the 2005 version focused on distance counseling, technology, and social media.

The ACA (2014) *Code of Ethics* begins with a preamble and purpose of the ethical code, and then it presents standards within each of the nine specified sections. The first section, *The Counseling Relationship,* focuses on the welfare and interest of the client. This includes standards related to client well-being, informed consent, and the relationship and role of the counselor. The second section, *Confidentiality and Privacy,* focuses on developing and maintaining trust with the client related to keeping information confidential and private when possible. This includes respect for the client's rights and privacy, limits of confidentiality, and client records. The third section, *Professional Responsibility,* focuses on the counselor's competency and behavior. This section includes the counselor's professional development and competency, and interactions with the public. The fourth section, *Relationships with Other Professionals,* pertains to working with colleagues and professionals in other disciplines. This area includes relationships with coworkers, employers, and employees, and being a consultant. The fifth section, *Evaluation, Assessment, and Interpretation,* focuses on the use of assessment. This domain includes competence in selecting, administering, scoring, and interpreting assessments, as well as use of assessment results. The sixth section, *Supervision, Training, and Teaching,* relates to the roles of a counselor educator and supervisor, as well as the roles of the student and supervisee. This includes standards related to the responsibilities of each role, including competency, welfare, evaluation, and gatekeeping. The seventh section, *Research and Publication,* focuses on the processes related to conducting and publishing research. This includes the researcher's responsibilities related to the entire research process (planning and conducting the study, and disseminating the results), and the rights of the participants. The eighth section, *Distance Counseling, Technology, and Social Media*, focuses on aspects of counseling that extend beyond the face-to-face in-person counseling setting. As stated earlier, this section is new to the 2014 version of the ethical code. It includes standards related to technology considerations with various aspects of the counseling process and the counselor's professional use of social media. The final section, *Resolving Ethical Issues,* focuses on addressing ethical dilemmas. This includes using an ethical decision-making model to address ethical concerns, and responsibility to report ethical violations. The final part of the ethical code is a glossary of terms. Thus, the ACA (2014) *Code of Ethics* is a detailed document to guide counseling professionals with engaging in professional ethical behavior.

American Association for Marriage and Family Therapy *Code of Ethics*

AAMFT revised their *Code of Ethics* most recently in 2015. The ethical code includes a preamble; statements about honoring public trust; a commitment to service, advocacy, and public participation; seeking consultation; ethical decision-making; binding expectation; and resolving complaints; as well as a section on aspirational core values (AAMFT, 2015). AAMFT then outlines ethical standards presented in nine areas. The ethical standard sections include responsibilities to clients, confidentiality, professional competence and integrity, responsibility to students and supervisees, research and publication, technology-assisted professional services, professional evaluations, financial arrangements, and advertising. Clearly, many of the areas are similar to sections of the ACA ethical code. However, the AAMFT standards focus specifically on counseling professionals who identify as marriage and family therapists.

International Association of Marriage and Family Counselors *Code of Ethics*

IAMFC is a division of ACA; therefore, its ethical code aligns with the ACA ethical code. The organization adopted their first ethical code in 2006. Then, they revised the code in 2011 and most recently in 2017. The IAMFC code contains a preamble and 10 sections. Although the IAMFC (2017) *Code of Ethics* aligns with the ACA (2014) *Code of Ethics,* it is distinct in that it focuses specifically on couple and family counselors. The code contains the following sections: the counseling relationship and client welfare, confidentiality and privacy, competence and professional responsibilities, collaboration and professional relationships, assessment and evaluation, counselor education and supervision, research and publication, ethical decision-making and resolution, technology-assisted couples and family counseling, and diversity and advocacy. Thus, many of the sections overlap with the ACA code, while some distinctions are also evident, such as a separate section for diversity and advocacy, which ACA infuses throughout their ethical code.

American Mental Health Counselors Association
Code of Ethics

AMHCA is a professional organization for clinical mental health counselors (CMHCs). The organization most recently revised the AMHCA *Code of Ethics* in 2020. The code includes a preamble and six sections. The sections include (a) commitment to clients; (b) commitment to other professionals; (c) commitment to students, supervisees, and employee relationships; (d) commitment to the profession; (e) commitment to the public; and (f) resolution of ethical problems (AMHCA, 2020).

American School Counselor Association
Ethical Standards

ASCA is the professional organization for school counselors. The organization adopted its first set of ethical standards in 1984, and since then, ASCA has revised the standards six times (1992, 1998, 2004, 2010, 2016, and 2022). The 2022 ASCA ethical standards include a preamble, purpose statement, six sections of standards, and a glossary of terms (ASCA, 2022). The first section, *Responsibility to Students,* is the longest section, containing 16 standards that include aspects of the counseling relationship, counselor roles and responsibilities, services, and virtual/distance school counseling. The next section, *Responsibilities to Parents/ Guardians, School, and Self,* has three subsections for focusing on responsibilities and roles in each of these areas. The third section, *School Counselor Directors/ Administrators/Supervisors,* focuses on the responsibilities of the director, administrator, and supervisor. The fourth section, *School Counseling Practicum/ Internship Site Supervisors,* focuses on the competencies, roles, and responsibilities of the site supervisors. The fifth section, *Maintenance of Standards,* pertains to procedures for school counselors to follow when concerned about the ethical behavior of another school counselor. The final section, *Ethical Decision-Making,* focuses on steps to take in resolving ethical dilemmas. Thus, the ASCA ethical standards provide some overlap with the ACA ethical code, while also containing additional ethical guidelines related specifically to the practice of school counselors.

ETHICAL DECISION-MAKING MODELS

The ethical codes are important to know and review in making ethical decisions. However, deciding what to do when experiencing an ethical dilemma in counseling includes multiple steps. There are six principles of professional ethical behaviors guiding the ethical decision-making process, described in the ACA (2014) *Code of Ethics*: autonomy, beneficence, nonmaleficence, fidelity, justice, and veracity. Autonomy focuses on an individual's right to make their own decisions based on their values and beliefs. Beneficence is promoting the well-being of others. Nonmaleficence is avoiding actions that would cause or create a risk of harm. Fidelity pertains to honoring commitments and obligations. Justice focuses on providing equitable and fair treatment. Finally, veracity pertains to being truthful. In addition to these principles, there are various ethical decision-making models. In the following sections, we provide an overview of three well-known models (social constructivist, value-based conflict, and transcultural integrative), as well as a fourth model that is predominately practice-based, while integrating components of other models, such as multicultural considerations. As you read the overview about these models, consider which one resonates most with you.

Social Constructivist Model

Cottone (2001) developed the social constructivist ethical decision-making process to include both the psychological and systemic-rational domains. Alignment with this model is the belief that interactions with others influence decisions. There are five steps in this model: (a) gather information from all parties, (b) examine the nature of the relationship, (c) consult with colleagues and examine the literature, (d) negotiate if there is disagreement, and (e) respond with consensus about what occurred and the course of action. The goal within this model is to reach consensus; however, if this is not possible, then the next step is interactive reflection. This step involves discussion with others to determine what needs to occur to reach consensus. If they do not reach consensus, then arbitration is the final step. Thus, although it has some similarities to other models, this approach emphasizes the decision-making process involving others, instead of being predominately one individual's process.

Value-Based Conflict Model

Some ethical dilemmas counseling professionals experience involve conflicts between their personal values and the values, behaviors, or lifestyle of their client, student, or supervisee. Kocet and Herlihy (2014) proposed the five-step Counselor Value-Based Conflict Model (CVCM) to be an adjunct to other ethical models when experiencing a value-based conflict. The first step focuses on determining the nature (personal or professional) of the value conflict. The next step involves exploring core issues and possible barriers to providing care. The third step includes seeking assistance or remediation for providing appropriate care. In addition to areas within this step that are consistent with other models (e.g., reviewing the literature, consulting with others), this step also involves ethical bracketing, which is intentionally separating or setting aside of the counselor's personal values to be able to provide ethical care (Kocet & Herlihy, 2014). The fourth step is determining and evaluating potential actions. The fifth and final step focuses on ensuring the proposed courses of action promote client welfare.

Transcultural Integrative Model

In developing the transcultural integrative model, Garcia et al. (2003) used Tarvydas's (1998) integrative model as a framework and integrated aspects of the social constructivist (Cottone, 2001) and collaborative (Davis, 1997) models. Garcia et al. maintain Tarvyda's four-step process, while including a focus on multicultural considerations within each step. The first step focuses on awareness and fact-finding. Within this step, Garcia et al. first emphasizes the importance of awareness related to cultural groups, counselor and client's cultural identities, counselor's knowledge of the client's culture, and counselor's awareness of their multicultural counseling competencies. Then, the counselor reflects on the dilemma related to their own and the client's worldview. Next, the counselor determines who to involve in gathering information based on the client's cultural, and in fact-finding, obtains relevant cultural information.

The second step focuses on the process of making a decision. This involves first considering cultural information while reviewing the situation. Then, the counselor considers a cultural perspective in exploring applicable ethical standards and institutional policies. Next, the counselor brainstorms possible courses of action, preferably with others, using a social constructivist approach to reach consensus, while remaining mindful of the cultural values of the client. Then, the counselor evaluates the consequences of each potential action while also remaining mindful of cultural considerations. The last two components of this second step involve consulting with others, including individuals with multicultural expertise, and deciding on a course of action using consensus if possible and in light of multicultural considerations.

The third step involves affirming the course of action. This involves considering potential areas of unawareness, such as how the counselor's values differ from the client's cultural values, as well as influences on various levels including collegial, institutional, and societal levels, in addition to the client's cultural level. The fourth and final step is planning and implementing the selected course of action. This involves developing a list of steps that include cultural resources. Then, the counselor considers barriers, including cultural barriers (e.g., discrimination), and actions that are culturally sensitive to address them. The final part of this last step is to implement, document, and evaluate the course of action, which includes using social constructivist techniques, and collecting and examining culturally relevant variables in the evaluation process. Thus, although many of the steps are similar to other models that mention cultural considerations (e.g., practice-based model), this model is unique in that it specifies cultural aspects to consider in each step of the decision-making process.

Practice-Based Model

Forester-Miller and Davis (2016) proposed a seven-step decision-making process that integrates components from several models. They encourage counselors to consider their worldview, as well as the worldview of their clients and other multicultural considerations when engaging in the decision-making process. The first step is to identify the problem by considering the facts and the various aspects of the dilemma. The second step is to apply the ACA *Code of Ethics*. Step three is to determine the nature and dimensions of the dilemma, which involves reviewing the principles for professional ethical behavior, examining literature related to the topic, consulting with colleagues and supervisors, and consulting with professional associations. The fourth step is to generate, through brainstorming, potential courses of action. The next step is to consider the potential consequences of all possible actions and decide on a course of action. Step six involves evaluating the course of action, which includes ensuring that it is appropriate through considering three tests

(Stadler, 1986): (a) justice (Would you treat other clients the same way in the same situation?), (b) publicity (Would it be okay if it was reported to the media?), and (c) universality (Would you recommend the course of action to other counselors?). The final step is implementing the course of action.

While this section did not present an exhaustive list of ethical decision-making models, it provides a few well-known examples that counselors may use when experiencing ethical dilemmas in their work as counselors. You are encouraged to continue to reflect on these models as you read about common legal and ethical issues presented in counseling.

LEGAL AND ETHICAL ISSUES IN COUNSELING

There are many state and federal laws related to counseling practice. Similar to ethical codes, it is crucial for counselors to follow these laws to provide quality care for their clients and avoid engaging in profession misconduct. Although there are too many areas of law and ethical considerations to discuss all of them in this chapter, we discuss some significant areas of focus and related legislation in this section, including (a) confidentiality, (b) privacy of information and records, (c) informed consent, (d) boundaries and relationships, (e) liability, and (f) ethical practice and religious beliefs.

Confidentiality

In the counseling process, counselors keep most client information confidential (client records and client conversations), meaning that they do not share this information with others without the consent of the client. However, there are some limits to confidentiality and it is crucial that counselors inform clients of these limitations through an informed consent process. Limits to confidentiality include risk of harm to the client or others. This includes suspected child abuse (physical, emotional, sexual) or neglect. In some states, it also includes suspected abuse or neglect of an elderly person, or a person with a disability. It is important to remember that the counselor does not need proof. They are required to make the report when they suspect abuse or neglect. Risk to the client may also include risk of self-harm (i.e., suicide). Furthermore, risk to others may include threats to harm others, or having a communicable disease that puts others at risk (ACA, 2014, Standard B.2.c).

Threat to others relates to the counselor's duty to warn and protect. In the landmark court case, Tarasoff v. Regents of the University of California (1976), a college student informed the psychologist that he intended to kill his girlfriend. The psychologist informed the police, but did not inform the client's girlfriend. The police investigated, and the client denied it and the police released him. The client stopped attending counseling and no one warned the girlfriend about the threat. The client killed his girlfriend a few months later, and her parents sued the university. The California Supreme Court ruled in their favor stating the psychologist has a duty to protect the public.

For minors, counselors are required to communicate information shared by a minor to legal guardians and obtain their consent to see a minor in counseling, except in a few situations noted in the discussion on minor consent law in the next section. At the beginning of counseling, it is important for counselors to discuss confidentiality with legal caregivers and their children to make sure everyone understands what this entails and to develop rapport with the child and the caregivers. When a child discloses information to the counselor that the counselor believes is important for the caregivers to know, the counselor can work with the child to discuss the information that they disclosed in session together with the caregivers. When facilitating group or family counseling, it is important for the counselor to discuss confidentiality with all clients and to emphasize the importance of them keeping confidential the information shared by others in session (what is said in the room stays in the room). However, the counselor should also inform clients that they cannot guarantee that group members or family members will maintain confidentiality. They can only guarantee that they (the counselor) will keep the information confidential within the limits of confidentiality.

A counselor may receive a subpoena for review of counseling records, appear for a deposition, or testify in court. Upon such receipt, a counselor should not ignore the subpoena, should seek legal consultation, and must maintain documentation in the client's file (CNA & Healthcare Providers Service Organization, 2019). When there is a subpoena for clinical records, it is important to review what information the court is requesting from the file, instead of submitting the entire client record. Additionally, when testifying, the counselor should stay focused and use care to answer only the questions asked in court. In some states, counselors have privileged communication, meaning they are not required to disclose the content of client conversations to the court.

Privacy of Information and Records

Privacy focuses on the client's decision to share personal information with others about themselves. This differs from confidentiality in that confidentiality relates to the counselor not sharing client information with others, or clients not sharing information with others that they hear during group or family sessions. To enact the Health Insurance Portability and Accountability Act (HIPAA) of 1996, the U.S. Department of Health and Human Services (DHHS) issued the Privacy Rule. The Rule protects all *individually identifiable health information*, including mental health data kept or transferred in any form. This information, called *protected health information*, refers to past, present, and future information (U.S. Department of Health and Human Services, 2013).

The Family Educational Rights and Privacy Act (FERPA) of 1974, also known as the Buckley Amendment, relates to students educational records. Parents/guardians have access to these records until the individual turns 18, and then the individual has the rights transferred to them. The educational institution may share the information with some other entities outlined in the law without the student's or parent's consent, such as school officials and accreditation bodies. Additionally, schools may disclose directory information (e.g., address, phone number) without consent, after notifying the student/guardian about the directory, unless the student/parent requests nondisclosure (FERPA, 1974).

In working with a client, a counselor may want to communicate with other professionals working with the client (ACA, 2014; Standard a.3) to ensure the professionals are working together for the optimal growth and development of the client. For example, when working with a child, a community counselor may want to talk with the child's teacher or the school counselor. Another example is talking with a client's psychiatrist or job coach. The counselor needs the client, or the client's parent/guardian if the client is younger than 18, to sign a release of information before they can share written or verbal information with other professionals outside the counselor's organization. It is important that the counselor only share information that is crucial for the other professional in working with the client. For example, the counselor may share with a child's teacher strategies to help the child cope with their anger in class that the counselor is working on with the client in counseling, as well as discussing how the child is doing in the classroom. The counselor would not share information about the family that is not relevant to the teacher working with the child. Sharing private or confidential information without client consent or legal request accounted for 4.4% of closed liability claims (CNA & Healthcare Providers Service Organization, 2019). Thus, it is crucial for counselors to understand laws and ethical considerations around privacy and confidentiality of client information. If counselors are unsure what to do regarding a situation related to privacy and confidentiality, they may seek supervision or consult with colleagues. While counselors may seek legal advice, professional counseling organizations typically offer consultation services for their members.

Informed Consent

Informed consent involves the sharing of information with clients, in verbal and written form, regarding both the counselor and client's roles and responsibilities and allowing the client to knowledgeably choose if they want to be in counseling. This process is ongoing throughout the counseling relationship (ACA, 2014; Standard A.2.a). Components of the informed consent document should include scope of treatment along with benefits and risks of the treatment, aspects and limits to confidentiality, roles and responsibilities of the counselor and the client, information about session time and frequency, and fees and payment. The counselor also provides clients information about the counselor's qualifications and experience (ACA, 2014; Standard A.2.b).

Some clients are not able to provide legal consent, such as minors (except for areas of minor consent law noted below), individuals in psychosis (break from reality), and other individuals who are unable to make their own decisions. These vulnerable populations need someone else to consent to treatment, as well as complete other paperwork (e.g., release of information form discussed in the previous section). When working with a minor, unless the child is court-ordered to treatment or the minor consent law applies, the counselor needs parent/guardian consent to see the child in counseling. However, the counselor should also discuss informed consent with the child or adolescent using language appropriate for their age and developmental level. The minor consent law relates to the minor being able to consent to treatment without parent/guardian consent related to substance abuse and confidentiality of records regarding this treatment (Confidentiality of Records Act, 2010). Minors may also seek some services regarding reproductive health without parent/guardian consent (Guttmacher Institute, 2020).

When parents are divorced, the counselor must have the consent of the parent(s) with custody of the child. It is also crucial for the counselor to determine what information they are required to share, as well as can share, with the noncustodial parent. The counselor may require the parent/guardian to bring in a court document showing proof of custody to ensure they have proper consent. This process can be helpful at the beginning of the counseling process to avoid any confusion, such as if the noncustodial parent contacts the counselor for information during the counseling process or requests to be included in the counseling process.

CULTURAL CONSIDERATION

The ACA (2014) *Code of Ethics* includes a focus on using culturally sensitive practices related to the informed consent process (Standard A.2.c). Additionally, Lasser and Gottlieb (2017) discuss several areas to consider, as well as recommendations in being culturally sensitive in the informed consent process, including (a) information shared, (b) people involved, and (c) response to authority figures. As stated above, informed consent involves informing the client about the scope of treatment, including benefits and risks of treatment so they have autonomy to make an informed decision about counseling. However, this approach may not be culturally sensitive for groups that do not prescribe to Western society beliefs and values; therefore, it may affect the therapeutic relationship and cause harm. For example, Navajos believe talking about risks may increase the possibility of them happening; thus, they may prefer to avoid discussing them. (Lasser & Gottlieb, 2017). At the client's request, counselors may decide to modify the informed consent process to be more culturally sensitive, which may involve gradually sharing information to allow the client to decide how much they want to know. The counselor must also document any modifications made to the consent process, as well as the rationale for such changes.

Western values also tend to be individualistic, while other cultures may value a more collective approach. Some clients may want to involve their family or community in making decisions about counseling. The counselor may be culturally sensitive by asking the client if they want to include others in the process of making decisions about counseling. Finally, the counselor should explore the client's views about authority figures, as some client cultures may follow whatever authority figures recommend, while in other contexts, people who have experienced oppression may be reluctant to trust individuals in authority (Lasser & Gottlieb, 2017).

Boundaries and Relationships

The ACA (2014) *Code of Ethics* has multiple standards that focus on boundaries and relationships. It is important for the counselor to discuss the counseling relationship and boundaries with the client at the beginning and throughout the counseling process as needed. There are times when the counselor may have multiple relationships with the client (interact with the client in other capacities in addition to counseling). An example of this would be a counselor seeing an individual for counseling who owns a company that the counselor has a business relationship with at the same time. In providing counseling to children, this may involve a counselor whose child has a relationship with a potential child client. Counselors should avoid multiple relationships when possible, which may involve the counselor referring a client, or potential client, to another provider. There are times when multiple relationship are not possible to avoid, such as a counselor working in a rural community where there are limited counselors. When unavoidable, it is crucial that the counselor and client discuss the dual relationship and establish clear boundaries. It is also important for counselors to consider behaviors that may blur boundaries (Standard A.6.b), and to ensure the counselor's behaviors are in the best interest of the client, instead of focusing on the counselor. Counselors should also be cautious about accepting clients with whom they have had a previous relationship, even when it was a casual or distant relationship (Standard A.6.a).

Regarding romantic/sexual relationships, counselors avoid these relationships with current clients or family members of a current client (Standard A.5.a). Additionally, counselors do not see a client with whom they had a previous romantic/sexual relationship (Standard A.5.b). Furthermore, counselors may not engage in romantic/sexual relations with a former client or one of their family members for at least 5 years after termination of counseling (Standard A.5.c). In examining liability insurance claims, CNA & Healthcare Providers Service Organization (2019) reported 55.2% of closed claims pertained to the counseling relationship, with 36.4% focusing specifically on romantic/sexual relationships, emphasizing concerns regarding this area of counseling and the need for clear boundaries.

Liability

In considering laws, it is important to discuss liability, which relates to being legally responsible for something (Cambridge University Press, n.d). When discussed within the context of counseling, liability usually focuses on whether the counselor's actions or lack of actions resulted in harm to the client, or negligence. A malpractice lawsuit may result from a counselor engaging in professional misconduct that is intentional or unintentional wrongdoing. Malpractice usually involves a civil lawsuit to determine if harm occurred (Remley & Herlihy, 2019). If the court determines harm, then the decision could result in the plaintiff receiving compensation. An example of a civil lawsuit in counseling may relate to a counselor's behavior that led to emotional harm of the client. A counselor may also experience criminal charges that pertain to illegal behavior that may result in probation, fines, and/or jail terms. Examples of criminal behavior in counseling is practicing outside one's scope of practice as outlined by state statutes, or a counselor having sex with a client who is a minor. Some acts may result in both criminal charges and a civil lawsuit.

Woody (2008) discussed seven reasons for increased liability and potential ethical and legal complaints related to providing counseling services to children and families. First, parents may use their children to lessen their own anxiety, which is particularly common related to child custody cases. Second, the government has increased their involvement in the provision of mental health services (e.g., insurance reimbursement, licensure standards). The third reason is the increase in mental health professionals involved in lawsuits. Additionally, reduced funding for mental health means clients seeking lower levels of care when they need intensive services. Society also has a lack of trust of healthcare workers, which leads to poor compliance with treatment, and affects the counseling relationship. The next reason is the requirements and restrictions from third-party payers, including limits to the level of care and the number of sessions. Finally, there are more practitioners trying to obtain clients and the competition may lead some practitioners to accept clients they do not have the skills to serve, use treatments they are not qualified to provide, and make errors due to trying to save money. Thus, multiple factors contribute to increased liability.

Although malpractice lawsuits are not as common against counselors as they are in other professions (e.g., medicine), they do occur in counseling, as well as ethical complaints to professional organizations and licensure boards. Wilkinson et al. (2019) examined ethical complaints made to state licensure boards in 49 states (all but Mississippi) and Washington, DC that resulted in disciplinary actions from 2010–2014, and found 936 total. The average number by state was 18.35, ranging from none in Kentucky to 75 in Illinois. The most common infraction (17%) was not obtaining the required number of continuing education (CE) hours, followed by nonsexual dual relationships (13%), sexual relationships with clients (9%), and misrepresentation to the public (7%). Together, infractions regarding relationships made up the largest category (22%). Thus, as discussed previously, it is crucial that counselors establish and maintain clear boundaries in the counseling relationship.

It is important that counselors know and follow state and federal statutes in providing counseling, as well as follow counseling ethical standards and use an ethical decision-making model. Additionally, we recommend that counselors have their own liability insurance. Employers may have liability insurance for their employees; however, counselors should consider also having their own liability insurance to protect themselves. Counseling students are often required to have liability insurance when they are in their clinical experiences (practicum and internship) and seeing clients. Some professional counseling organizations provide liability insurance free of charge during practicum and internship experiences for student members of the organization.

Ethical Practice and Religious Beliefs

Counselors' personal values are sometimes in conflict with the client's values and this poses an ethical dilemma regarding whether the counselor has the right to refer these clients to another provider. Herlihy et al. (2014) discussed four court cases (two focused on counselors and two on counselors-in-training) related to counseling professionals' religious values and counseling lesbian, gay, bisexual, and transgender (LGBT) clients. In the case of Bruff v. North Mississippi Health Services, Inc (2001), Bruff, an employee assistance program (EAP) counselor, told a client that she could not counsel her related to her relationship issues with her partner because lesbian relationships conflicted with her religious beliefs. The client complained, Bruff received administrative leave, and then her employment was terminated, with the employer stating that they were not able to reassign all clients that went against the counselor's religious beliefs. Bruff sued her employer and the appellate court found that although employers have the obligation to accommodate an employee's religious beliefs, this did not extend to Bruff's degree of inflexibility. The court based the decision on the legal issues, without taking a position on the ethical issues. The second case, *Walden v. Centers for Disease Control and Prevention* (2010), was similar to the *Bruff* case, where Walden, the EAP counselor, referred a client seeking counseling related to her same-sex relationship, stating it conflicted with her religious beliefs. The client filed a complaint stating they felt judged by the counselor. The employer asked Walden to refer clients without stating the referral was due to religious beliefs. Walden refused and filed suit after being laid off. The court ruled in favor of the employer, basing the decision on the way Walden addressed the situation, instead of basing the decision on her religious values. Thus, while employers are required to accommodate employees' religious beliefs, it appears courts require employee flexibility in working with their employers to make accommodations.

The other two court cases discussed by Herlihy et al. (2014) focus on lawsuits by counselors-in-training against universities after dismissal from their counselor preparation programs. In *Ward v. Wilbanks* (2010), Ward sued Eastern Michigan University (EMU) after they dismissed her from the program when she refused to comply with a remediation plan, established after refusing to counsel a client in her practicum that had previous counseling for a same-sex relationship. The court ruled in favor of the university, an appeal was filed, and the case was sent back to the district for a jury trial. The case was then resolved before trial, with Ward allowed to submit a withdrawal letter to EMU if she wanted to take this action (Dugger & Francis, 2014). The second student case was *Keaton v. Anderson-Wiley* (2010). Keaton had a remediation plan in her program at Augusta State University (ASU) due to concerns with separating her personal beliefs from her professional responsibilities after stating multiple times her beliefs against homosexuality. The faculty dismissed her from the program after she refused to complete the remediation plan. The district court denied the motion, it was appealed, and the federal court upheld the university's decision stating Keaton did not have the right to set her own training standards.

In both of the cases involving students, the court upheld the university's decision; however, Arizona has since passed legislation that an academic counseling program cannot discipline a student for refusing to counsel a client due to religious beliefs (Arizona HB 2565, 2011), and individuals have also presented legislation in other states. Additionally, Tennessee passed legislation in 2016 allowing counselors to refuse to work with clients based on personal beliefs (Tennessee SB 1556/HB 1840, 2016). These cases and legislation center on opposing views (counseling professionals' personal beliefs and values vs. counseling professionals' professional responsibilities to meet clients where they are and to help them work through the concerns they are experiencing in their lives). In the 2014 revision of the ACA *Code of Ethics*, ACA clearly specifies that counseling professionals should make referrals based on competence (Standard A.11.a), not based solely on the counselor's beliefs and values (Standard A.11.b). The

ACA ethical code also includes a standard about not engaging in discrimination (Standard C.5). As Kaplan (2014) stated, the *Ward v. Wilbanks* (2010) case also allowed ACA to clarify that (a) counselors cannot refuse to counsel groups of clients based on personal values or beliefs, (b) referral is a last option to avoid abandonment, and (c) ethical obligations begin with assignment of a case or first contact. Thus, counseling professionals prioritize the needs and the welfare of the client in making ethical decisions.

ETHICAL ADVOCACY AND SOCIAL JUSTICE PRACTICE

Justice is one of the six principles of ethical behavior discussed earlier that guide ethical decision-making. A counselor's beliefs about what is right and just affect their decision and engagement in social justice and advocacy (Crethar & Winterowd, 2012). Hailes et al. (2020) proposed seven ethical guidelines across three domains of justice for engaging in social justice work within psychology. The first domain, interactional justice, focuses on fairness in interpersonal interactions. It includes three guidelines: (a) reflecting on relational power dynamics, addressing these dynamics, and emphasizing empowerment and a focus on strengths-based interventions. The second domain, distributive justice, pertains to fairness in distribution of outcomes, such as pay and court decisions. This includes two guidelines: (a) committing resources to needs of marginalized groups, and (b) focusing time and money on prevention. The third and final domain is procedural justice, which focuses on fairness in the decision-making process. This includes two final guidelines: (a) interaction with social systems, and (b) increasing awareness about the effects of systems on the welfare of individuals and communities. Counselors may use these guidelines to emphasize the ethical principle of justice in all aspects of the counseling process, including decision-making.

In considering the decision-making process, it is also crucial that counselors do not assume that their clients' values and needs are the same as the counselor's need and perspectives, as this demonstrates lack of multicultural competence (Crethar & Winterowd, 2012). In discussing this concept, Crethar and Winterowd state the Golden Rule of social justice and advocacy within counseling is to "treat others as they would have counselors treat them," not treat others as you want to be treated. In further considering the client's needs and perspective, the counselor should consider the involvement of the client in the ethical decision-making process. There is a growing emphasis in counseling on social justice, advocacy, and multicultural competency on the client being a partner in the counseling process. However, Tarvydas et al. (2015) report that while some ethical decision-making models involve the client or consideration of their perspective, the counselor generally heavily influences the decision on the final course of action. Thus, Tarvydas et al. present a collaborative ethical decision-making process (Applied Participatory Ethics Model) that builds upon previous counseling and rehabilitation works. The model involves four phases that focus on (a) client-centered vs. professional-centered, (b) strength of therapeutic alliance, (c) level of client involvement, and (d) level of client empowerment. In using this model, counselors embrace a social justice focus by collaborating with the client, viewing them as a partner in ethical decision-making process, instead of the counselor being the sole decision-maker.

The ACA (2014) *Code of Ethics* also has standards addressing counselors' ethical responsibility to advocate at all levels (Standard A.7.a, A.7.b; Section C Introduction). In alignment with the ACA Advocacy Competencies (Toporek & Daniels, 2018), counselors may advocate on behalf of or in collaboration with clients at the individual level, community or organization level, and the public arena (Toporek & Daniels, 2018). Thus, counselors may engage in various advocacy activities to promote ethical standards that they uphold as counselors.

CONCLUSION

Ethical and legal issues are crucial for counseling professionals to be aware of and have knowledge and skills to address within counseling. This includes understanding applicable ethical standards and laws, and using an ethical decision-making model to address ethical dilemmas. Counselors need to have awareness of their personal beliefs and values, and engage in ethical bracketing to be able to prioritize the client's needs and well-being. It is also important for counselors to have awareness of professional development, research, and certifications to improve their counseling competency. Furthermore, counselors have an ethical responsibility to engage in social justice practices and advocacy to advance the profession and provide quality care for clients.

Summary

- Accreditation bodies provide standards for ensuring a level of quality in counselor preparation programs.
- Counselor licensure title, scope of practice, and education requirements are inconsistent across states, necessitating advocacy for consensus across states and licensure portability.
- Many counseling certifications are available for recognition of meeting standards in specialized counseling areas.
- Ethical standards and ethical decision-making models guide counselors in making ethical decision.
- Counselors have an ethical responsibility to engage in social justice and advocacy.
- Counselor have many ethical and legal issues to address in counseling, and are consistently aware of cultural considerations during this process.
- Counselors engage in professional development to enhance competency and engage in self-care and personal counseling to help prevent impairment.

Voices From the Field

Devika Dibya Choudhuri
Professor of Counseling, Eastern Michigan University

For the past two decades, I have maintained a practice where I work at low or no cost with clients who have experienced cross-cultural trauma, including sexual assault, abuse, and interpersonal violence for being female, trans, or LGB; refugees fleeing war and other disasters; and the multigenerational effects of trauma due to racism and colonization. I use a blend of neurocounseling approaches such as polyvagal, EMDR (eye movement desensitization and reprocessing), and somatic approaches together with insight-oriented therapies, for which I have received appropriate training and certification (Standard C2.a and b; ACA, 2014).

This past year doing virtual therapy (Standard H1.a, ACA, 2014) in the middle of the pandemic and being overwhelmed by the demand, I received a tentative message from a young cismale we can call Paul, who was the former client of a counselor I supervised a year ago. He (he/him pronouns) had lost his insurance after losing his job and had lost access to therapy. He stated that he was sure I was too busy, but he was feeling suicidal and his former counselor had told him about my work and might I have time to meet with him just once. I remembered the case, primarily because when I watched a part of the session, I asked my supervisee about the client's tribal affiliation. The supervisee didn't know he was Indigenous because the client hadn't mentioned it, and thought he was "just White." I asked him to tentatively raise the issue, and sure enough the client was deeply conflicted since his full Cherokee father abandoned the family when he was in his early teens with Paul being raised by his White Appalachian mother and grandmother.

I agreed to meet with Paul virtually after following up with the original counselor and checking that the client had terminated over a year ago (Standard A3, ACA, 2014). I was conscious that while I was familiar with Paul's story as a supervisor, he was not familiar with me. I addressed this openly sharing that I was familiar with elements that he had not told me himself (Standards A.2.c., B1.a, ACA, 2014) and Paul quickly seemed trusting of me, spilling out his story of being a first-generation graduate student in a helping field, extreme poverty of origin, little cultural capital in the elite school he was in, and a conflicted cultural identity filled with references to self-inadequacy, self-blaming, and a confusion about his experienced depression which he dismissed as "playing the victim" when "others had it so much worse." We reduced the severity of the emotional distress using several EMDR grounding and resourcing techniques (Standard A4.a; Shapiro, 2018), as well as the Flash technique (Manfield et al., 2017). The client appeared to also respond well to the Four elements exercise (Shapiro, 2018), which uses natural elements of earth, water, air, and fire to self-calm.

However, the key intervention appeared to be when I connected his difficulty with schoolwork and his depression with unresolved historical grief. As he said, "I can't believe how weak I am; I can't bring myself to do this even though it's the last assignment for the class!" I responded, "Well, it could kill you—seems to me to be a good reason to avoid." His eyes filled with tears, and he hedged, "I don't know what you mean." I said, "You and I both know the news has been filled with the hundreds of unmarked graves found at the residential school sites. These are children like you who were, quite literally, killed by education and false promises." There followed a couple of reprocessing sessions where he allowed himself to experience the anguish, guilt, and anger for those children, and counted himself as kin. He also allowed himself to mourn personally for his own abandonment. Paul was able then to envision himself as a future helper in a Native community assisting other youth with their struggles; a step that allowed him to gain greater motivation to complete his studies and shield himself from microaggressions that made his status as a Native man invisible. He created a visual project that depicted the deaths, mourning, and meaning and shared it in a course; and became visible to peers as a Native man. Finally, he was able to objectively see how many messages he had internalized from both his Native and Appalachian White families about education being bad and taking him away from his family. Advocating with Paul to reach out to university organizations and federal grants and sources of assistance (Standard A.7.a) was much easier after he realized how unworthy he felt and how much he saw such sources as not pertaining to him.

Cultural competency (Standard C2.a.) is an ethical requirement of counselors which includes assessing, recognizing and validating culturally presented aspects (Standard E.8), hypothesizing regarding cultural and sociopolitical sources of distress, and inviting clients to explore such sources, without appropriation. For instance, as a non-Indigenous person, it would be outside my brief to invite Paul to go on a vision quest, to participate in healing rituals, or to provide some other culturally sourced intervention that is within the cultural group. Connecting Paul with employers in Alaska who were looking for practitioners to work with Alaskan Natives and letting him find his own way is an important aspect of advocating without imposing personal values (Standard A4.b., ACA, 2014).

A Call to Action

Go to your state legislature website and identify a bill that has ethical implications for counseling (e.g., rights of a particular client group, counselor's rights or scope of practice). Alternatively, go to ACA's Government Affairs page to review identified federal and state issues. Write a letter, send an email, or schedule a meeting with your state or federal level legislators (depending on whether it is a state or federal level issue) asking them to support or refute the legislation depending on alignment with counseling ethical standards. You can find a letter template and other helpful information about the advocacy process in the ACA Advocacy Toolkit: https://www.counseling.org/docs/default-source/government-affairs/2020-advocacy-toolkit.pdf.

Case Study 4.1

Jacob is a 15-year-old African American male client. He expressed in the first session that it was not his idea to come to counseling and he was reluctant to share any information with you during the session. As the counselor, you have worked hard to build a relationship with him during your first few sessions and he has gradually shared more with you about what is happening in his life. During the third session, he shares that he has been sneaking out of the house at night to see his girlfriend. He says that if you tell his mom that he will never trust you again.

RESPONSE QUESTIONS

1. What do you do with the information that Jacob shared with you? Are you obligated to report it to his mom or others?
2. Use one of the ethical decision-making models presented in this chapter to determine a course of action.

Going Within

After reading the chapter, what areas can you identify that you may struggle with related to ethical decision-making in counseling. Do you have personal beliefs and values that conflict with counseling ethical standards? Consider how you would engage in ethical bracketing of your personal beliefs and values to be able to prioritize the needs and well-being of the client. Additionally, consider if there are areas in your personal life that you should receive your own personal counseling to work through to be prepared to work effectively with future clients.

Group Process

The instructor divides the class into small groups and gives each group one of the following situations. Students have the task of identifying what ACA (2014) *Code of Ethics* standards are relevant to the situation, and how the standards may help them in the decision-making process.

1. During the last session, the client hands the counselor a card and small wrapped box and says they want to thank the counselor.
2. A school counselor, who also has a private practice, is asked by a teacher in their school if they will see their child for counseling in their private practice.
3. A counselor notices one of his colleagues has becoming increasingly irritable lately and is often late or cancels sessions.
4. A client shares in the first session that they are coming to counseling to receive support in telling their family they are gay. This surprises the counselor and they are struggling, as the client's lifestyle is against their personal beliefs.

RESOURCES

Counseling Compact: https://counselingcompact.org/

State licensure information: https://www.counseling.org/knowledge-center/licensure-requirements

State school counselor certification/licensure agencies: https://www.counseling.org/knowledge-center/licensure-requirements/state-school-counselor-certification-licensure-agencies

 Access this podcast at http://connect.springerpub.com/content/book/978-0-8261-6386-8/chapter/ch04.

KEY REFERENCES

Only key references appear in the print edition. The full reference list appears in the digital product found on https://connect.springerpub.com/content/book/978-0-8261-6386-8/chapter/ch04

American Association for Marriage and Family Therapy. (2015). *AAMFT code of ethics*. Author.

American Counseling Association. (2014). *ACA code of ethics*. Author. https://www.counseling.org/resources/aca-code-of-ethics.pdf

American Counseling Association. (2020). *20/20: A vision for the future of counseling*. https://www.counseling.org/about-us/about-aca/20-20-a-vision-for-the-future-of-counseling#

American Mental Health Counselors Association. (2020). *AMHCA code of ethics*. Author.

Association for Spiritual, Ethical, Religious Values in Counseling. (2009). *Spiritual competencies: Competencies for addressing spiritual and religious issues in counseling*. Author.

CNA & Healthcare Providers Service Organization. (2019). *Counselor liability claim report: 2nd edition*. Author. http://www.hpso.com/Documents/Risk%20Education/individuals/Claim-Reports/Counselor/HPSO-CNA-Counselor-Claim-Report-2019.pdf

Council for Accreditation of Counseling and Related Educational Programs. (2015). *2016 CACREP standards*. https://www.cacrep.org/for-programs/2016-cacrep-standards

Harper, A., Finnerty, P., Martinez, M., Brace, A., Crethar, H., Loos, B., Harper, B., Graham, S., Singh, A., Kocet, M., Travis, L., & Lambert, S. (2009). *ALGBTIC competencies for counseling LGBQIQA*. ALGBTIC. https://www.counseling.org/docs/default-source/competencies/algbtic-competencies-for-counseling-lgbqiqa.pdf?sfvrsn=1c9c89e_14

International Association of Marriage and Family Counselors. (2017). *IAMFC code of ethics*. Author.

Masters in Psychology and Counseling Accreditation Council. (2017). *Accreditation manual*. Author. http://mpcacaccreditation.org/wpcontent/uploads/2020/05/MPCAC2017AccreditationManual050520.pdf

Ratts, M. J., Singh, A. A., Nassar-McMillan, S., Butler, S. K., & McCullough, J. R. (2016). Multicultural and social justice counseling competencies: Guidelines for the counseling profession. *Journal of Multicultural Counseling and Development, 44*(1), 28–48. https://doi.org/10.1002/jmcd.12035

CHAPTER 5

COUNSELING SKILLS, PROCESS, AND MODALITIES

Derrick A. Paladino

Think about this…

Attention is a powerful reinforcing agent in counseling and an everyday occurrence in our lives. Prior to reading this chapter, we would like you to consider your personal relational style. Answer the following questions:

1. *How do you positively attend to people in your life?*
2. *How do you negatively attend to people in your life?*
3. *Do you attend to certain people in your life in different ways? Why?*

In addition, think about:

1. *The last time you were fully heard.*
2. *The last time you were not fully heard.*

Sit with your answers to being heard. What comes up for you? How do you feel? What is on your mind? Did you have a somatic response? How did you feel with the individual(s) in your examples? The way we are with people is the core of our work as counselors. Hold these reflections in your heart and mind as you read this chapter.

LEARNING OBJECTIVES

After reading this chapter, you should be able to:

- Define and operationalize an effective counselor

(continued)

- Identify the conditions that create a strong therapeutic relationship
- Recognize the different basic counseling skills
- Recognize the process of counseling
- Summarize your role in aiding client change

INTRODUCTION

Think about the journey that led you to this moment and to the counseling profession. You might have been told by family and/or friends that you "have a great shoulder to rest" on or that you are "such a great listener." Maybe you have experienced the wonder that can happen in a counseling session and have a desire to give back and assist others. Perhaps your altruistic nature and passion for people guides you to want to help others. Maybe it is all of these. Regardless of the etiology of your journey, welcome. Counseling is a powerful medium that can facilitate hope for those in pain and struggling or simply in need of some guidance and direction.

To be a counselor takes courage. You are becoming a co-navigator different from anyone else in your client's life. A new type of relationship where the client feels understood, heard, and above all believed—a new type of relationship filled with genuineness, compassion, and transparency. With a holding environment such as this, clients can become brave inside the counseling relationship. Eventually that bravery enters the real world and with more performance in their lives.

"To master process, beginning counselors must develop a repertoire of helping skills as well as a theory of counseling that directs their application" (Meier & Davis, 2005, p. 1). In this chapter the rubber meets the road … or at least the onramp. You will have one to two semesters of counseling skills instruction in your program that will build and refine your talents. Here we offer you a preview of what this work looks like from the counseling chair. Effective counseling occurs when the counselor truly believes in their abilities and session work. Hopefully, this chapter feeds your fire for the field. This is an amazing profession that can touch so many lives.

THE EFFECTIVE COUNSELOR

"The ability of a therapist to instill confidence and trust within the therapeutic frame is essential to therapeutic success" (Ackerman & Hilsenroth, 2003, p. 1). During your counseling program, you will learn about basic skills, techniques, and theories, but there are some qualities that come up as essential to possess to be successful at this work. Scholars have pointed to different characteristics that set this foundation (Ackerman & Hilsenroth, 2003; Neukrug, 2016; Pope & Kline, 1999; Shaw, 2020, March 10). Ackerman and Hilsenroth (2003) analyzed studies reporting variables that positively contribute to a strong working alliance. The constructs were broken down into what personal attributes the counselor possesses and which techniques aid. Personal attributes include a counselor being flexible, experienced, honest, respectful, trustworthy, confident, interested, alert, friendly, warm, and open. Regarding what techniques and approaches positively add to a working alliance, the following emerged: exploration, depth, reflection, supportive, notes past therapy success(es), accurate interpretation, facilitates the expression of affect, active, affirming, understanding, and attends to the patient's experience (Ackerman & Hilsenroth, 2003).

Shaw, 2020, March 10 notes that presence, countertransference management, professional self-doubt, deliberate practice, and multicultural orientation are aspects of highly effective counselors. Two items of note are professional self-doubt and deliberate practice. These are important, as there should always be a balance between the counselor's confidence in their abilities, the direction of the session, and cultural humility that allows one to be a lifelong learner. In addition, successful psychotherapy outcomes have been found to be attributable to the helper and the client believing strongly in the effectiveness of the treatment (Roberts et al., 1993). Neukrug (2016) posits that an effective counselor should have nine characteristics. These are empathy, acceptance, genuineness, embracing the wellness perspective (i.e., one's ability to attend to their own wellness), cultural competence, having the "it" factor (i.e., the special quality that allows you to bond with the client), compatibility with and belief in theory, competence (e.g., including a thirst for knowledge and improvement), and cognitive complexity. Cognitive complexity suggests that "the best helpers believe in their theory and have a willingness to question it" (Neukrug, 2016, p. 26). They self-reflect, question truth, take on multiple perspectives, and evaluate systems in complex ways.

Finally, Pope and Kline (1999) assessed experts in the counseling field regarding the most important personal characteristics for developing counselors. Experts were also asked to rate how responsive to training each characteristic was. For example, they reported the possibility of each characteristic being taught in a 2-year program, in one semester of a master's program, or if it cannot be taught in a 2-year master's program. As seen in Table 5.1, the study suggested the most important personal characteristics include "empathy, acceptance, and warmth, while the least important include resourcefulness, sympathy and sociability" (p. 1339). In addition, warmth, capability, and patience skills were found to be responsive to training, whereas emotional stability, open-mindfulness, and interest in people were not receptive to development from training (Pope & Kline, 1999).

CARL ROGERS AND HIS CONDITIONS

Carl Rogers is one of the most prominent individuals in creating the humanistic approach. He founded person-centered therapy (PCT), also known as client-centered therapy. His work promotes individuals to become authentic and not a façade that conforms to others (Rogers, 1961). This occurs through the direction of PCT, a nondirective approach that places faith on the client's capacity to become aware of their struggles and develop the means to resolve them (Corey, 2017). Rogers felt passionate about the counseling relationship as a tool in creating a warm and trusting environment for the client. He states:

TABLE 5.1 COUNSELOR CHARACTERISTICS AS RANKED BY EXPERTS IN THE FIELD

	IMPORTANCE	RESPONSIVENESS TO TRAINING
Empathy	1	9
Acceptance	2	4
Warmth	3	20
Genuineness	4	8
Sensitivity	5	14
Flexibility	6	9
Open-mindedness	7	2
Emotional Stability	8	1
Capability	8	21
Confidence	10	9
Nonthreatening	11	17
Interest in People	12	3
Awareness of Limitations	12	17
Patience	12	19
Friendliness	15	9
Cooperative	16	21
Sincerity	17	14
Fairness	18	4
Tolerance for Ambiguity	19	9
Resourcefulness	20	4
Sympathy	21	4
Sociability	22	16

Note: Importance—the lower the number the more important the characteristic. Responsiveness—the lower number the less responsive to training it was judged to be.
Source: Pope, V. T., & Kline, W. B. (1999). The personal characteristics of effective counselors: What 10 experts think. *Psychological Reports, 84*(3 Pt. 2), 1339–1344. https://doi.org/10.2466/pr0.1999.84.3c.1339

To be of assistance to you I will put aside myself—the self of ordinary interaction—and enter into your world of perception as completely as I am able. I will become, in a sense, another self for you—a mirror held up to your own attitudes and feelings—an opportunity for you to discern yourself more clearly, to understand yourself more truly and deeply, to choose more satisfyingly. (Rogers, 1949, p. 89)

Though you will spend more time with PCT and other theories of counseling in Chapter 6: Orientations to Counseling and Theoretical Framework, we would like to introduce a few of Rogers's concepts as they create a foundation toward building intentional therapeutic relationships and effectively employing counseling skills.

Rogers (1957) created the necessary and sufficient conditions of change that assist with therapeutic personality change and are contained within the therapeutic relationship. They are:

1. Relationship: Two persons are in psychological contact.
2. Vulnerability: The first, whom we shall term the client, is in a state of incongruence, being vulnerable or anxious.
3. Genuineness: The second person, whom we shall term the therapist, is congruent or integrated in the relationship. (Therapist Responsibility)
4. Unconditional Positive Regard: The therapist experiences unconditional positive regard for the client. (Therapist Responsibility)
5. Accurate Empathy: The therapist experiences an empathic understanding of the client's internal frame of reference and endeavors to communicate this experience to the client. (Therapist Responsibility)
6. Perception of Genuineness: The communication to the client of the therapist's empathic understanding and unconditional positive regard is to a minimal degree achieved.

Let us sit with three conditions that fall on the responsibility of the counselor: Accurate empathy, unconditional positive regard, and genuineness/congruence. These three conditions allow for effective counseling skills.

Empathy is the ability to stand in the shoes of another and fully understand their world. Accurate empathy communicates a verbal or nonverbal understanding of the client's lived experience. It can be communicated both verbally and nonverbally. Verbally, the counselor speaks their understanding of the client's beliefs and emotions while adding in appropriate tone to convey compassion. Nonverbally, the counselor uses their body movements to communicate care and understanding. In traditional sessions this can look like leaning forward, appropriately putting your hand on a client's shoulder, nodding, and looking directly at the client. In telehealth sessions this can be more difficult but possible. Depending on how you are sitting, the client can still see you lean forward. In addition, if the counselor looks directly at the camera, the client will experience you looking right at them. At times, if we are looking at a client on the screen, that means our eyes may be a bit diverted from them.

For an empathy example, let us consider Navya, a client describing the pain of losing her father. The counselor would provide empathy by leaning forward, looking directly at the client (nonverbal empathy), and saying, "Navya, I can really see the hurt on your face as you talk about your father's death. You miss him so much." The counselor offers the client is accurate empathy to what she is experiencing—affect and belief. As you enter Navya's shoes imagine what it would feel like to receive these words. In addition, imagine how it would make you feel toward the counselor. Empathy is very powerful and can build a partnership with the counselor.

Rogers (1959) describes unconditional positive regard (UPR) as the following:

If an individual should experience only unconditional positive regard, then no conditions of worth would develop, self-regard would be unconditional, the needs for positive regard and self-regard would never be at variance with organismic evaluation, and the individual would continue to be psychologically adjusted and would be fully functioning. (p. 227)

The hope of UPR is that a client's "existing conditions of worth are weakened and replaced by a stronger positive self-regard" (Prochaska & Norcross, 2018, p. 109). That is, they will become free to accept themselves with love and compassion (Prochaska & Norcross, 2018).

For example, let us consider Liz who shares that she is "fed up" with her boss. Liz reported that her boss continues to place the blame on her for her coworkers' actions. A UPR response would hold no judgment for what has happened (i.e., that her boss is bad) but rather, provide empathy for Liz's state. A nonjudgmental response could be, "Liz, it must feel so exhausting and demeaning to always be blamed."

Genuineness and congruence refer to how a counselor enters the therapeutic relationship. What the counselor shares with the client should match their internal feelings and beliefs. That is, the counselor "should be, within the confines of this relationship, a congruent, genuine, integrated person" and "freely and deeply himself [they], with his actual experience accurately represented by his awareness of himself [they]" (Rogers, 1957, p. 97). One example comes to mind when thinking back on the 1965 Everett Shostrom films, featuring Carl Rogers, Frederick ("Fritz") Perls, and Albert Ellis (Shostrom, 1965). Each psychotherapist explained and then demonstrated their approach with the same client, Gloria Szymanski. In Carl Rogers's session, the following dialogue occurs (as provided by: Brodley & Lietaer, 2016):

Gloria:	"Yeah, and you know what else I was just thinking? I—I feel dumb saying it uh—that all of a sudden while I was talking to you, I thought, "Gee, how nice I can talk to you and I want you to approve of me and I respect you, but I miss that my father couldn't talk to me like you are." (Touches her chin.) I mean, I'd like to say, "Gee, I'd like you for my father." (Rogers: Mhm, Mhm, Mhm.) I don't even know why that came to me. (Smiles.)"
Carl Rogers:	"You look to me like a pretty nice daughter. (Pause) (Gloria: Looks down.) But you really do miss the fact that you—you couldn't be open with your own dad."

When Rogers says, "You look like a pretty nice daughter" he is offering a genuine statement to Gloria based on how he feels internally (i.e., congruence). If you get a chance to view this film, you will appreciate the impact of this statement on Gloria's face. It is one that speaks to Rogers's conditions in action. Below we provide Rogers's reflection on this moment.

I was genuinely moved, I probably showed it, by the fact that she told me near the end of the contact that, uh, she saw me as the father she would like to have. My reply was also a thoroughly spontaneous one that she seemed to me like a pretty nice daughter. I guess I feel that we're only playing with the real world of relationships when we talk about such an experience in terms of transference and countertransference. I feel quite deeply about that. I want to say, yes, we can put this experience into some such highly intellectualized framework, but when we do that, it completely misses the point of the very immediate "I-Thou" quality of the relationship at such moments. I felt that Gloria and I really encountered each other and that in some small but, I believe, lasting way, we were each of us enriched by the experience. (Brodley & Lietaer, 2016)

BASIC COUNSELING SKILLS

In this section, we use the foundation discussed earlier to consider basic counseling skills. As you read through this section, be mindful that everything that is offered from the counselor's chair should hold intention. Every concise reflection, every look, every question … everything. When we can have intention during an entire session, we are fully engaged with the client and the process. Even nondirective counseling theories have direction in how they are used.

A therapeutic relationship is required above all for skills to have an impact, and at the same time, basic counseling skills are required to build said relationship. As a counselor, your initial role is to use basic counseling skills to make personal contact with your client. "Making contact means being with the client, touching someone emotionally, and communicating" (Meier & Davis, 2005, p. 2). Basic counseling skills are universal, though there some scholars have shaped them into sequence and impact. Ivey et al. (2018) present the Microskills Hierarchy. The Microskills Hierarchy "summarizes the successive steps of intentional counseling and psychotherapy" (p. 11). The Microskills Hierarchy is a visual pyramid that contains basic listening skills, ethics, multicultural competence, influencing skills, stages of the counseling experience, and at the top of the pyramid, your ability for skill integration and transcendence. Table 5.2 displays this sequence in more detail. We also want to make a distinction between basic counseling skills and techniques. Basic counseling skills are what foster and create a therapeutic relationship. Techniques are found within theories of personality and counseling that assist with client issue process. Examples of techniques are role-playing, the miracle question, cognitive restructuring and reframing, early childhood recollections, and empty chair.

TABLE 5.2 MICROSKILLS HIERARCHY SEQUENCE

SEQUENCE	MICROSKILLS
13	Transcendence, determining personal style, skills integration
12	Applying skills to theory: crisis counseling and CBT
8–11	**Influencing Client Actions and Decisions**: focusing; empathic confrontation; reflection of meaning and interpretation/reframe; and stress management, self-disclosure, feedback, natural and logical consequences, directives, instruction, psychoeducation, and therapeutic lifestyle changes
7	**5 Stages of the Counseling Session:** (1) Empathic relationship, (2) Story and strength, (3) Goals, (4) Restory, and (5) Action
2–6	**Basic Listening Sequence:** attending and empathy skills; observation skills; questions; encouraging; paraphrasing; and summarizing, reflecting feelings
1	Ethics, multicultural competence, neuroscience, and positive psychology/resilience

Note: Number 1 in sequence is at the bottom of the pyramid.
Source: Adapted from Ivey, A. E., Ivey, M. B., & Zalaquett, C. P. (2018). *Intentional interviewing and counseling: Facilitating client development in a multicultural society*. Boston, MA: Cengage.

In this section, we introduce you to some basic listening and counseling skills. Below you will find the case of Martina. As you read through skills think about how you could use them to attend to Martina.

Case Study 5.1

Martina is a 36-year-old nontraditional college student embarking on her second career as a high school teacher. She is in her third semester of classes at a local state college. In the first session, she reported that even though this is something she really wants to be successful at, she is experiencing a fear being a failure. Martina stated, "This is a big undertaking for me in terms of a new life and career change." "I want to do something I actually care about."

In addition, she reported that her partner (Franco) believes that this is an added financial burden. On and off, he has passively-aggressively belittled her decision. His communication style with Martina has shut her down from sharing any aspect of her schooling

(continued)

(i.e., things that excite her; personal and academic struggles) with him. Martina reports that she has intentionally isolated herself from her peers. She reported that Franco, "just doesn't understand how much this means to me." Through her own report, Martina is having difficulty focusing on her coursework and at times has skipped classes to be with her family (partner and 2 children). She reports feeling sad and anxious.

The following basic counseling skills will be discussed: reflections, minimal encouragers, questions, summarization, confrontation, disclosure, and feedback. These will be placed into three main categories:

■ **Reflections:** Reflection of feeling, refection of content, refection of immediacy, summarization, and minimal encouragers
■ **Questions:** Open-ended questions, close-ended questions, and clarification
■ **Additive skills:** Confrontation, self-disclosure, and feedback

Reflections

Reflections are the vehicle of accurate empathy. They show a counselor's understanding of client feelings, beliefs, lived experience, and the immediacy of their experience. Reflection also allows the client to continue processing or reflecting on the topic they reveal. Within the scope of reflections, we will examine reflection of feeling, reflection of content, and refection of immediacy as well as summarization and minimal encouragers.

Reflection of feeling focuses on feeding back the client's affect. To provide this skill effectively, two things are of note: (1) the counselor must have a large capacity of feeling words to accurately match what the client is experiencing and (2) the more concise the refection the more effective. Before we get into the structure of a reflection of feeling let us discuss the preceding points. A strong feeling vocabulary will allow the client to be fully understood since it provides them with a mirror of what they are expressing to you as their counselor. Your client feels *seen* when you reflect their feelings accurately. Though saying the wrong feeling word or level of feeling word will not necessarily throw off the client, it is more effective to be accurate.

Meier and Davis (2005) suggest that beginning counselors can start with exploring the *Big Four* feeling word categories: (1) Anger, (2) Sadness, (3) Fear, and (4) Joy. Getting acquainted with these feelings in your own life can assist with providing accurate empathy to clients. These four feeling words are just the tip of the iceberg because they contain many other levels of feelings. For example, fear can also be described with the following words: scared, terrified, worried, spooked, horrified, concerned, petrified, shocked, startled, panicked, and frightened. Depending on the level of client's experienced fear we want to make sure that we use the feeling word that matches the most accurately. For example, if a client describes being in a bank while three armed robbers enter the building, you probably do not want to say, "that sounds off putting or startling." The word *terrifying* would fit better. Another poor choice would be saying, "you sound peeved" after learning that a stranger kicked their dog. Accuracy is important for trust and understanding in a therapeutic relationship. In addition, we want to make sure that (1) we are not using vague words that can have multiple definitions (i.e., depressed, upset) and (2) we are using words that are developmentally appropriate for our clients.

Finally, you want to make sure that you do not have a case of the *kind-ofs, a-littles, sort ofs, a-bits,* and *somewhats* (Paladino, 2005). These are known as minimizing phrases. To tell a client, "you feel kind of angry" is really telling them "you feel frustrated." Minimizers do have the potential to create a "barrier to building a strong working alliance" (p. 11). Paladino (2005) suggests that beginning counselors use minimizing phrases for several reasons:

1. We do not want to be incorrect (i.e., it is worth the risk to be *kind of* right than *absolutely wrong*).
2. Not wanting to reflect an emotion that the client is not ready to process (e.g., not shocking the client)
3. Fear of creating excess conflict in the world of the client (e.g., downplaying negative feelings can protect the client from feeling more hopeless)
4. Belief that we (the counselor) cannot fully relate to the client's experience
5. A safety guard for when the counselor has not been actively listening
6. A deficiency in the counselor's vocabulary level
7. It is just our vernacular.

Regardless of the reason, it is important for the beginning counselor to have awareness around this. Also, Paladino (2005) suggests that this is a two-way street in the counseling experience. Clients will also use these stems for a myriad of reasons. Sometimes it can be difficult for clients to allow themselves to fully accept a feeling for what that will mean. In this case, these types of phrases can be helpful: "Are you feeling a little angry or angry" and "I'm hearing you say that you were sort of scared, but I'm getting the sense from you that it was very scary."

Conciseness is the second area of note. You may find that as a beginning counselor you may not fully trust in yourself to say the *perfect* thing or that the client may not fully understand what you are reflecting. When this happens, there is a tendency to elongate your reflection to offer a rationale to your statement. It can turn a perfectly concise reflection like, "he betrayed you" into, "he betrayed you because you trusted him to watch over your best interests and when it came down to it he decided to turn his phone off and didn't respond to you until 2 days after and in text." Though the latter is accurate to the client's lived experience, it completely dilutes the strength of emotion.

In your practice, you will discover that concise reflections will always lead to richer and deeper client process. You will also find that the longer your reflection (not counting summarizations) the more likely the client will forget the first part of what you said.

The structure of a feeling reflection typically starts with "You sound …", "You feel …", and "I am hearing …" In addition, to provide accurate emotion reflections, one should not use the phrase "you feel like" because *feel like* is a belief,

TABLE 5.3 CONCISE REFLECTIONS OF FEELINGS

Example 1	Client: *Rikin is such an awful person! I can't believe that he let my cat run away!* Counselor: *You sound enraged.*
Example 2	Client: *Everyone was staring right at me. It was horrible.* Counselor: *You felt exposed.*
Example 3	Client: *I put in so many hours into studying that exam and I got the grade that allows me to keep my scholarship.* Counselor: *You feel very relieved.*

not a feeling. Table 5.3 includes some examples of concise reflections of feelings. Considering the case of Martina, think about which feeling words match her plight.

Reflection of content (also known as paraphrasing) is offering parts of the client's story back to them in order communicate our understanding. Though both reflection of feeling and reflection of content can be used together, using solely one or the other provides intentional direction for the client. A reflection of feeling will keep the client within the affective part of their experience and a reflection of content will allow the client to maintain focus on the event or notion of what happened. What you use depends on what you are looking for. For reflection of content, we are encouraging the client to share richer information. Two side notes: (1) paraphrasing is not parroting exactly what the client just said and (2) always try to use the client's name as it brings more attention and importance to what you are saying. Table 5.4 includes some examples of reflections of content. Considering the case of Martina, list reflections of content that would direct her to tell you more about her overall experience.

TABLE 5.4 EXAMPLES OF REFLECTIONS OF CONTENT

Example 1	Client: *I know I should be better at eating lunch and dinner, but when I feel pitiful, I always lose my appetite.* Counselor: *Fatima, I'm hearing you say that even though you know you shouldn't miss meals, a part of you finds that incredibly difficult. It's tough when your mind is somewhere else.*
Example 2	Client: *I won two 10ks in a row, got an "A" on a quiz, and solved a word jumble in under 10 minutes.* Counselor: *Nadia, you accomplished so much this month.*
Example 3	Client: *"Every time I visit my dad, I keep thinking back on my childhood. It was horrible. I feel shaky just thinking about walking up the driveway."* Counselor: *Kareem, going home brings back so many terrible memories.* Counselor combining reflection of feeling and content: *Kareem, it feels scary to imagine yourself returning to see you father.*

TABLE 5.5 EXAMPLES OF REFLECTIONS OF IMMEDIACY

Counselor reflections	■ *I noticed that while you were talking about Ryan, your hands started shaking.* ■ *Nicola, you're looking down and your eyes are becoming tearful.* ■ *I noticed that you don't look down anymore when we talk about Jorge.* ■ *You closed off when I began asking about your sister.* ■ *Your face is getting red and your fists are clenching.* ■ *You're quiet.*

Reflection of immediacy is when the counselor focuses on the client's verbal and nonverbal reactions in session. For example, a client may start to become tearful when talking about an experience or because of a reflection of feeling. A counselor's reflection of immediacy would bring that into the room by simply commenting on it. For example, something as simple as, "you're crying" brings the client's attention to emotions and thoughts connected to that behavior. Immediacy and working in the here-and-now can be quite powerful. The strategy is to reflect and then pause. Let the client process what you brought attention to and see where they take it. If the client is having difficulty sharing about their tears, you can use another reflection of immediacy stating, "I can tell that this is difficult to talk about." Table 5.5 includes some examples of reflections of immediacy. Considering the case of Martina, under what circumstance can you see yourself offering those reflections of immediacy in session?

Summarization brings together several concepts and emotions that a client has shared. Meier and Davis (2005) describe it as a "brief review of the major issues in counseling" (p. 35). It is used throughout a counseling experience to reflect on a previous session (at the beginning of a session), to tie together the learnings of an entire session (at the end of a session or counseling experience), or to bring together a theme or counselor understanding (after a client has shared a lot of information). The following list gives some examples of summarization sentence stems and an example of a counselor summary is given in Table 5.6.

- *A theme I am hearing in your descriptions is _____.*
- *It sounds like this whole event has brought you nothing but _____.*
- *You feel incredibly _____ that all of this has happened today.*

TABLE 5.6 EXAMPLE OF COUNSELOR SUMMARY

Midsession Summary	Client: *One of the reasons we split-up was because he always pushed me. I could never say no to him, and I always gave in. Now my mom will not leave me alone about it and is always in my face and making me go out.* Counselor: *Garrick, I am hearing that in a couple of relationships, in your life, it's difficult to put yourself and your wishes first.*

- *I want to stop you for a moment and make sure I am hearing you fully. You _____.*

- *Last session we talked about _____.*
- *Reflecting on your past 2 months in counseling I have seen _____.*

Considering the case of Martina, offer a summary to what you hear in her experience.

Minimal encouragers do what their name suggests. They offer verbal and nonverbal encouragement to the client for them to continue sharing emotions, context, and reactions. Examples of minimal encourages are saying "uh huh" and "mm hmm," restating certain keywords, and nodding one's head. Also, saying things like, "tell me more" or "keep going with that" qualify as minimal encouragers. We see these in everyday conversation and they are great to use to keep sessions moving along.

As you reflect on reflection, know that this is truly the foundation of basic counseling skills. We encourage you to attempt a 20-minute role-play where you only utilize reflections of content, feeling, immediacy, summarization, and minimal encouragers (i.e., no questions). We promise that you will feel depth and connection in your client work.

Questions

Questions allow us to dive deeper into the cognitive and emotional experience of the client as well assist to focus the session. For example, questions like "What was that like?" and "How did that make you feel?" bring more context to a client's experience. Regarding focusing a session, let us consider an example of a client sharing a story from between sessions as soon as the session starts. The story is detailed and offers a lot of information. It would be initially difficult to know what to do with this story if it is not directly connected to their presenting problem. In this case the counselor can ask, "As you think about _____ what feeling comes up for you?" or "What part of _____ do you think is the most important part for me to hear?" or "Which part of _____ sticks with you the most?" As you can see, questions are quite helpful in the counseling process. The caveat is that if a counselor relies on them too much or stacks questions, the client will be stuck in the story and never fully enter the process. In addition, "why" questions can put clients on the defense. It is preferred to phase all questions to use "what" over "why." Questions hold a lot of directive power and should always be used with great intention.

There are three main types of questions: open-ended questions, close-ended questions, and clarifying questions. Open-ended questions are deemed the most effective as they allow the client to guide their response as immediately connected to how they are feeling. Ivey et al. (2018), suggest that open-ended questions "help clients elaborate and enrich their story" (p. 114). Close-ended questions are used to discover facts about the client, their system, or their experience. They can also assist to focus the client and session theme. If you believe that you can ask a close-ended question in an open-ended style it is encouraged that you do so. Close-ended questions, when not retrieving facts, can foster a "yes"/"no" response from a client, thus stifling idea expansion and dialogue.

TABLE 5.7 EXAMPLES OF QUESTIONS

Open-ended Questions	■ *What are you experiencing as you sit here?* ■ *What is your plan for this semester?* ■ *How do you know she is the most supportive person in your life?* ■ *What led you to this decision?* ■ *What feels difficult about sharing this?*
Close-ended Questions	■ *What medication are you taking currently? Are you compliant?* ■ *What's your partner's name?* ■ *How far do you live from your family?* ■ *What do you do for a living?* ■ *Of these areas, what part feels most disturbing?*
Clarification Questions	■ *Can you clarify _____?* ■ *Can you describe _____?* ■ *Help me understand what you mean by _____?* ■ *Tell me what you mean by _____?*

Clarification questions allow the counselor to check in on their own understanding of the client's experience. Table 5.7 includes some examples of open-ended questions, close-ended questions, and clarification questions.

Bridging reflections are helpful when moving toward questions. They allow the client's last statement or idea to be acknowledged prior to moving to a question. It offers a better flow and transition and is especially useful when conducting intakes. For example:

Client: *I tried what we talked about, even though it was very difficult. I told Pilar that I feel hurt when she is dismissive.*

Counselor: *I can hear that it took strength to share your feelings with Pilar (bridging reflection). What was that like for you (open-ended question)?*

Considering the case of Martina, list any open-ended questions, close-ended questions, and clarification questions that would assist you to learn more about her experience.

Additive Skills: Confrontation, Self-Disclosure, and Feedback

Within additive skills, we find confrontation, self-disclosure, and feedback. The idea of confrontation always seems more intense than it is in counseling. Defined, confrontation is "the accurate pointing out of discrepancies in an individual" (Ivey et al., 1997, p. 47). If we look at confrontation on a continuum it can range from simply reflecting a feeling that a client has not shared yet (e.g., *I can imagine that you felt confused after he just showed up*) to something you notice in session that the client does not see (e.g., *I can't help but notice that every time I bring up your family, you change the subject*), to sharing information that is concerning (e.g., *I am concerned that if you continue taking that amount of heroine, you will die*). Essentially this is a challenge to the client, but it can be done with complete compassion and warmth.

In addition, one can see that confrontation is also an umbrella for self-disclosure and feedback skills. Self-disclosure is when a counselor "reveals a personal feeling or experience of his or her [their] own" (Meier & Davis, 2005, p. 32). This can be something that allows the client to feel normalization (e.g., *Mari, I've lost a pet before and I know how incredibly heartbreaking that can be. It makes sense that you are feeling so much struggle and sadness*) or the counselor's experience of the client in the moment (e.g., *Sheng, my experience of you sharing this experience is of a person who really cares about others and will always put their heart first*). This additive has the power to deepen the therapeutic relationship. As a warning, self-disclosure should always be done to move the session forward and should never be self-fulfilling.

Feedback offers clients supportive or challenging nonjudgmental information based on their past or present feelings, thoughts, and behaviors (Ivey et al., 2018). One example of feedback is a counselor's assessment of client growth. Positive feedback would include sharing a client's increased strength, assertiveness, self-esteem, and personal awareness. Challenging feedback would include sharing a client's decline in functioning, external locus of control, investment in counseling, and inability to say "no" in most circumstances. Considering the case of Martina, what additive skills might emerge in session? What examples come to mind?

THE COUNSELING PROCESS

The main goal of the counseling process is to move the client to attain goals associated with their presenting problem. In essence your job, is to put yourself out of a job. From the start of sessions, you should be working in a way that is transparent with the client to discover how they would like to feel, think, behave, and be at the conclusion of session. In fact, this is an important question to ask your client. Without direction, there no place to go toward. A large part of this process is maintaining a strong working alliance. Meier and Davis (2005) describe this as "the task of the counselor is to engage the client in such a way that both persons are working together to resolve the issue that brought the client to counseling" (p. 3).

Though the process is basically moving from initial contact to termination or launching, scholars offer different perspectives on the stages. Depending on what helping skills textbook your professor uses, you will learn different steps, but essentially, they follow similar progressions (see Table 5.8). Though many of these models are presented as stages, it is normal to have a flexible approach where stages can be coworkers. For example, all models have the creation of the client/counselor relationship at stage one. This stage should never have an end. Counselors should be vigilant in maintaining and fostering a constant strong therapeutic relationship. As sessions become deeper, more emotional, and the topic more untapped and scarier, what once allowed the client to feel safe may require additional work.

As you enter your counselor education, each course will build upon the last to teach each of the stages in depth. Your counseling skills course will focus on working alliance, therapeutic relationship, and basic counseling skills. The

TABLE 5.8 COUNSELING STAGE PROCESSES

AUTHOR	STEPS OR TASKS
Four primary stages (Gerig, 2007)	1. Establishing the relationship 2. Problem identification, assessment, and goal setting 3. Planning of strategy and its implementation 4. Evaluation and termination
Road map of the helping process (Young, 2017)	1. Relationship building 2. Assessment 3. Goal setting 4. Intervention and action 5. Evaluation and reflection
The five stages of the microskills session (Ivey et al., 2018)	1. Empathic relationship 2. Story and strengths 3. Goals 4. Restory 5. Action
Five-stage process (Hackney & Cormier, 2013)	1. Relationship building 2. Assessment 3. Goal setting 4. Interventions 5. Termination and follow-up

counseling assessment class will teach screening, informed consent, evaluation, and mental status exams. The diagnosis and treatment will teach diagnosis, treatment planning, long-term and short-term goal creation, and empirically based treatments and techniques. Your counseling theory course will teach major philosophy and theoretical models for working with clients.

CONCLUSION

In this chapter, you explored counseling skills and processes. You learned about general skills, how to use them, and what creates that bond with clients. How we intentional offer assistance will always be a hallmark of this work. Regardless, if you are providing individual counseling, group counseling, family counseling, couples counseling, or crisis assessment and intervention the basics will always need to be there as a foundation. Learn, reflect, and never stop practicing.

Summary

- While scholars have proposed different models of counseling processes, they all agree that the counseling relationship must be fostered for all else to occur.
- Personal attributes such as being honest, respectful, trustworthy, interested, alert, and warm consistently assist with a counselor's connection to clients.
- The working alliance is sustained through work that contains exploration, depth, reflection, support, and richness of process.
- Basic counseling skills are the foundation of all clinical work regardless of counseling theory.
- Within the many aspects of the counseling process, the main objective of the counseling process is to have a goal and move the client to attain desired change associated with their presenting problem.
- Intention behind using all skills offers better direction and focus within session work.

Voices From the Field

Shalini C. Roy, LMHC, Counselor and Training Coordinator
Counseling and Psychological Services (CAPS), Rollins Wellness Center –
Rollins College

One of my goals as a counselor is to invite a client to bring their whole self into the counseling room, to explore and share their various histories, identities, perspectives, and values. I also recognize that each space they find themselves in may have required them to edit this narrative, to shift what felt safe or "right" to show. Yet I am asking them to lay out their various beliefs and guidelines for living so that we can together take a look at how these play a part in their struggles and their joy, how to navigate these as we work collaboratively toward the outcome they desire. It's a big ask! Yet, not only is having a full picture important but the very vulnerable process of sharing this picture is a valuable experience for the client.

At the college counseling center within which I work one female client presented as seeking support for depressive symptoms and relationship struggles. She identified as a racial minority at a PWI (predominantly White institution), initially stating that this did not impact her in any way, sharing that it was no different from any other school she had attended. Hearing and then reflecting her truth was as important as asking the question as both gave her permission; permission to discuss race, permission to have and talk about her own personal experience, and permission to begin to recognize that she does not have to be amenable to what has always been.

She was open to the process of counseling, easily sharing stories about her family, friends, and romantic interests, but finding it difficult to identify emotions or personal needs. I would note this, she would laugh and agree. This consistent gentle challenge along with acceptance empowered her to eventually prioritize self-care on her own terms.

Over time her stories became more detailed and richer which allowed us to explore family dynamics and internal conflicts. She became more comfortable and willing to share "negative" thoughts and feelings as she explored and untangled her desire to be "accepted" and "acceptable" and reimagined what this meant. The insights and self-determination that she gained from the therapeutic process allowed her to begin to make choices based on her intuition and knowledge of self. She was able to facilitate difficult conversations at home and on campus.

Eventually she decided to change her major, a decision that she had not permitted herself to consider in the past but which ended up positively changing her college experience, increasing her self-confidence and expanding her possibilities. During our time together in the counseling room she had learned to trust and express herself, by being given the space to be herself.

How to create that safe space? What are the right questions, what is the right pace, what if I miss something, what if I say something wrong? It is so important to be aware of your own internal narrative and landscape as you sit with a client. I try to remind myself to slow down and be open, to listen carefully and respond intentionally. I can be a guide, I have the training and experience to assess, to consider possible connections and patterns, but I have no idea what the person sitting across from me has experienced or what they think about those experiences until they share that with me. I hope that the strong desire to listen and to understand, combined with the open acknowledgment that they know themselves best, creates a space, void of assumptions, within which trust can grow.

A Call to Action

Think about what it is like to be seen, heard, and believed. For many, this is something that is an afterthought because of privileges they hold. Privileges come in the form of gender, race, religion, age, dis/ability, culture, socioeconomic status, and sexual orientation. Explore community, national, world events to determine situations in which a nonprivileged population was not seen, heard, believed, and/or discriminated against. What is taken from them? How are they left feeling and experiencing their environment and how does that impact their worldview?

From this experience, write a letter or email to a mayor, senator, congressman, etc. that describes your feelings about the injustice connected to the event or experience you reflected on. Speak from empathy. Finally, share what you did with a peer, with a family member, on social media, or with your class.

Case Study 5.2

Eli, 51, has been in a relationship with his partner (Yasir) for 18 years. About 5 months ago, his partner passed away. Eli reported going through a difficult time, including constantly missing Yasir, feeling exhausted, withdrawing from friends and Yasir's family, "unpredictable tearfulness," and sporadic concentration issues at work (he is a dentist). Eli denied suicidal ideation. In addition, he reported that Yasir left him a large sum of money and he experiences anxiety when he thinks about using it and even acknowledging that there was a will. He is also concerned about Yasir's family regarding the money. Eli and Yasir's family did not see eye to eye on a lot. Eli has been estranged from his own family for as long as he has known Yasir.

RESPONSE QUESTIONS

Based on your reading, explore this case to determine the following:

1. What is Eli's presenting issue? Secondary concerns?
2. How would you create a safe working environment for Eli to feel brave sharing?
3. Placing yourself in the Eli's shoes, list three potential feelings the client may be experiencing.
4. Placing yourself in the Eli's shoes, identify two potential beliefs the client may have in relation to the presenting issue (i.e., about themselves related to the situation). Write this from the client's voice (e.g., "I ...").

Going Within

Imagine that you are graduated, licensed, and are embarking on opening your private practice. You must create (1) a business name and (2) a business tagline or motto, (3) your counseling philosophy, and (4) your therapeutic approach. You want these to communicate your counseling philosophy and your approach to therapy to clients. Your hope is that when clients read these that they will have a complete understanding of what it will be like to work with you and the counseling process. Create your business name and a one-line motto for your counseling practice. Hold on to these as you continue through the program to see if and how they evolve.

Group Process

The following are actual feedback excerpts from some students' first 20-minute counseling tape assignment. These statements focus on areas for growth. As a group, read through these to develop themes of significant areas in working with clients. How do you feel about your skills and your abilities in these areas at this point in your counselor education journey?

- If you know the answer to the question you are about to ask, then just reflect instead.
- Be mindful, too many questions will move the client to their head and away from their heart and affect.
- Your client's sigh is expressing a lot.
- You should never assume, because you and the client do not share a brain.
- Add in a summary to end the session.
- Focus on your client's experience over the action of others. "How does your partner doing that make *you* feel?"
- Reflect and then STOP. Your client needs time to process what you said. There might be something wonderful and deep that comes from it.
- "I'm just speaking out of experience." Be mindful of phrases like this. Keep the focus on the client.
- Be mindful of the multiple-choice question, i.e., asking a question and then offering answers. Allow the client to do this work and access what their true answer might be.
- Put in silence after your client looked down. They were in the middle of processing something. Then ask, "What's coming up for you?"
- Give a pause to get the client's reaction and then say, "Say more about that."
- Make sure to set up your camera in a way that the client sees you looking directly at them (telehealth session).
- To open your session, ask the client what they were thinking about as they were coming to the session today.
- Make sure that if you are taking notes the client knows this from the beginning. Your eyes go away from them when they are sharing and you are writing.
- Be mindful that there are about 3 minutes between the last two things you said. It is okay to jump in there with a few short/concise reflections of feeling and content.
- Think about how you can turn this into an open-ended question over a close-ended one.
- I might reflect "you really love your sister" to reinforce that support system.
- What you said landed great, but let the client finish their thought before sharing more.
- Your client will only think about, feel about, and respond to the end of a loooooooong reflection. Sometimes conciseness can bring about more.
- You had a smile as you reflected her fear.
- Trust yourself. The first thing you said was good.
- Be more intentional about the opening and closing of your session.
- That was a good shift in the session. Be sure to add in a summary refection to acknowledge what the client had just shared.
- How you welcome the client sets the tone for the session.

- Be mindful of stacking questions.
- This was a good reflection. Shorten it a bit because the beginning was very strong.
- Summarize what happened in the session before you end.
- Assessing if you were helpful during the 50 minutes and if your client was able to pull insight or awareness is important. This keeps you accountable and intentional during the session.

RESOURCES

American Counseling Association (self-care resources): https://www.counseling.org/knowledge-center/mental-health-resources/self-care-resources-for-counselors

Counseling Awareness Month: https://www.counseling.org/knowledge-center/mental-health-resources/counselingawarenessmonth

Therapist Aid: https://www.therapistaid.com

 Access this podcast at https://connect.springerpub.com/content/book/978-0-8261-6386-8/chapter/ch05.

KEY REFERENCES

Only key references appear in the print edition. The full reference list appears in the digital product found on https://connect.springerpub.com/content/book/978-0-8261-6386-8/chapter/ch05

Ackerman, S. J., & Hilsenroth, M. J. (2003). A review of therapist characteristics and techniques positively impacting the therapeutic alliance. *Clinical Psychology Review, 23*(1), 1–33. https://doi.org/10.1016/s0272-7358(02)00146-0

Brodley, B. T., & Lietaer, G. (2016). *Transcripts of Carl Rogers' therapy sessions.* https://anamartinspsicoterapiaacp.files.wordpress.com/2016/04/brodley-transcripts-of-carl-rogers-therapy-sessions.pdf

Corey, G. (2017). *Theory and practice of counseling and psychotherapy* (10th ed.). Cengage.

Ivey, A. E., Gluckstern, N. B., & Ivey, M. B. (1997). *Basic influencing skills.* Cengage.

Meier, S. T., & Davis, S. D. (2005). *The elements of counseling* (5th ed.). Brooks/Cole.

Pope, V. T., & Kline, W. B. (1999). The personal characteristics of effective counselors: What 10 experts think. *Psychological Reports, 84*(3), 1339–1344. https://doi.org/10.2466/pr0.1999.84.3c.1339

Rogers, C. R. (1949). The attitude and orientation of the counselor in client-centered therapy. *Journal of Consulting Psychology, 13*(2), 82–94. https://doi.org/10.1037/h0059730

Rogers, C. R. (1957). The necessary and sufficient conditions of therapeutic personality change. *Journal of Consulting Psychology, 21*(2), 95–103. https://doi.org/10.1037/h0045357

Rogers, C. R. (1961). *On becoming a person.* Houghton Mifflin.

Shostrom, E. L. (1965). *Three approaches to psychotherapy (part I)* [Film]. Psychological Films.

CHAPTER 6

ORIENTATIONS TO COUNSELING AND THEORETICAL FRAMEWORKS

Ana Puig

Think about this....

What are your views about human nature? What do you believe makes people behave in the ways they do? When you think about counseling a client, what aspects of the person do you think are most important to attend to: the mind (thoughts or cognitions), the heart (emotions or feelings), the body (the brain, neurology, and somatic responses), the spirit (the soul, meaning making, transcendental issues), all of them (holistic attention)? How do people change in the context of counseling? How have you experienced the process of counseling for yourself? How do you position yourself to make changes in your life, when needed? How do your own beliefs about what makes people think, feel, and behave as they do inform your approach to counseling practice?

LEARNING OBJECTIVES

After reading this chapter, you should be able to:

- Identify the schools of thought that each counseling theory falls under
- Describe the types of theoretical frameworks that can inform and guide counseling practice
- Outline the main principles or tenets of each counseling theory
- Evaluate and situate the theories using emancipatory communitarianism as a lens

(continued)

- Recognize the common factors of psychotherapy and how they influence counseling practice
- Describe the stages of change as experienced by clients seeking help

INTRODUCTION

This chapter introduces you to the most prevalent and well-known theories that counselors use in practice. We will outline the schools of thought that the theories are associated with and situate them within the emancipatory communitarianism framework. We will also introduce the stages of change that clients experience before and during the counseling process. As a beginning counselor, you will be tasked with developing your own theoretical orientation. Hundreds of theoretical frameworks are available to you (Archer & McCarthy, 2007; Prochaska & Norcross, 2003). Your adherence to one or more of these may change over time and even depend on the type of client and presenting issues that bring them to you for help.

SURVEY OF PREVALENT COUNSELING THEORIES

There are hundreds of counseling theories that guide practice (Archer & McCarthy, 2007; Prochaska & Norcross, 2003). In this chapter, we provide an overview of the following theories: psychodynamic, existential-humanistic, cognitive behavioral, constructivist postmodern, feminist, relational-cultural, integrative-eclectic, and the common factors of psychotherapy. We also discuss emancipatory communitarianism (Prilleltensky, 1997) as a community psychology framework to help evaluate and situate the theories within a set of values, assumptions, and practices that center on advocacy, social justice, and intersectionality. Table 6.1 provides a brief overview of these theories and the schools of thought with which they are associated. We will discuss the pros and cons of each approach to therapy at the end of the chapter (see Table 6.2.).

PSYCHODYNAMIC THEORIES

Psychodynamic theories are based on Sigmund Freud's original psychoanalytic postulations about the influence of psychosexual unconscious drives and other forces in humans that are shaped by early childhood experiences, and affect early adult human behavior. In our brief overview of these theories, we acknowledge there are other frameworks that broke away from Freud's original theoretical assumptions to develop their own understandings of individual personality development (e.g., Carl Jung's Analytic Therapy, Alfred Adler's Individual Psychology). These also include variations in subsequent theories proposed by Anna Freud and Erik Erikson (Vinney, 2021). Freud coined the term *psychodynamics*, basing his theory on observations he made while treating his patients. He surmised that the behaviors and symptoms he observed were due to unconscious drives because his patients seemed unable to stop them.

TABLE 6.1 SCHOOLS OF THOUGHT AND SELECT THEORETICAL
FRAMEWORKS

SCHOOL OF THOUGHT	THEORETICAL FRAMEWORK	DESCRIPTION
Psychoanalytic – Psychodynamic	First Force of Psychology Psychoanalysis (Freud) Attachment Therapy (Bowlby) Adlerian Therapy (Adler)	Client problems are due to unconscious drives or motivations and conflicting aspects of self that result from childhood experiences. The counselor is the expert.
Cognitive Behavioral	Second Force of Psychology Cognitive Therapy (Beck) Rational Emotive Behavioral Therapy (Ellis) Reality Therapy (Glasser, Wubbolding) Behavior Therapy	Counselor helps the client uncover irrational or negative beliefs and how to challenge and change them. Focus is on how thought change can lead to behavior and emotional change. Evidence-based therapy. The counselor is the expert.
Existential Humanistic	Third Force of Psychology Existential (Maslow) Person-centered (Rogers) Gestalt (Perls) Positive Psychology (Seligman, Csikszentmihalyi)	Clients have everything they need within them to live healthy and functional lives. Focus is on meaning-making and the purpose of life. Clients have unlimited potential. Counselors facilitate the client's reconnection or discovery of the resources they need to thrive. The counselor has empathy and unconditional positive regard for the client. The counselor is not directive or judgmental toward the client.

(continued)

TABLE 6.1 SCHOOLS OF THOUGHT AND SELECT THEORETICAL FRAMEWORKS (*CONTINUED*)

SCHOOL OF THOUGHT	THEORETICAL FRAMEWORK	DESCRIPTION
Multicultural Social Justice Contextual Systemic	Fourth Force of Psychology Feminist Multicultural Family Systems	The counselor strives to develop multicultural and social justice competencies, cultural humility, and advocacy dispositions. Also considered contextual and systemic Collaborative and empowering Client inhabits multiple systems that interact and inform their reality and presenting issues. Counselor collaborates with people involved within and across these systems to assist and advocate for the client. The counselor is a collaborator and advocate.
Transpersonal	Spiritual and Transcendental (Maslow, Jung, Grof)	Derived from humanistic psychology and the work of Abraham Maslow. Concerned with peak or mystical experiences, transcendence of the ego, and higher states of consciousness. The client is in charge and the counselor is a facilitator.
Constructivist	Solution-Focused Brief Therapy (SFBT, Kim Berg) Narrative Therapy (Epston & White)	Client co-creates their reality by interacting with cultural influences and ascribing meaning through interpretation of their world. Strong focus on language The client is in charge and the counselor is a collaborator guide.

Source: Adapted from Lonczak, H. S. (2022, July 7). *12 popular counseling approaches to consider.* PositivePsychology.com. https://positivepsychology.com/popular-counseling-approaches; Jennings, G. H. (2020, November 19). *Tag archives: Four forces in psychology.* https://passagesbeyondthegate.com/tag/four-forces-in-psychology

TABLE 6.2 OVERVIEW OF PROS AND CONS OF PSYCHOLOGICAL THERAPIES

THEORY/THERAPY	ADVANTAGES/ PROS	DISADVANTAGES/ CONS
Psychoanalytic/ Psychodynamic	Helps illuminate the effect of early childhood experiences on the development of personality and adult functioning Provides understanding of unconscious innate drives that help shape our behavior Attends to both nature and nurture in human development and behavior	Too deterministic and minimizes individual's ability to act freely and make choices Emphasis on the unconscious negates our ability to have control over our own lives Inability of researchers to study the unconscious mind; impossible to test its efficacy
Existential/Humanistic	Has something to offer all counselors Emphasizes self-determination and embracing of personal responsibility Helps the client increase appreciation for the value of anxiety and guilt, the role of death, and potential creative aspects of being alone and making choices for oneself	Does not provide a systematic foundation of principles and practices Proponents tend to use vague or abstract concepts Research on its efficacy or applicability is lacking Has limited application for clients who are lower-functioning, in extreme crisis, come from low socioeconomic status, or are nonverbal

(*continued*)

TABLE 6.2 OVERVIEW OF PROS AND CONS OF PSYCHOLOGICAL THERAPIES (*CONTINUED*)

THEORY/THERAPY	ADVANTAGES/ PROS	DISADVANTAGES/ CONS
Person-Centered	Helps clients with depression, anxiety, grief and loss, or stress Helps clients learn to trust self and others Helps clients to balance their ideal self and the actual self Helps clients become self-aware Helps clients have more fulfilling relationships Helps with self-reliance, self-esteem, and self-expression	May help some clients (verbal, intelligent, reflective) but not others (severe, complex issues, non-verbal) Uses the same strategies for everyone Limited research about its efficacy
Cognitive Behavioral	May serve as an ideal adjunct to psychotropic medication Fairly short term High degree of structure makes it adaptable for use individually, in groups, and with families Psychoeducation given is applicable to everyday life	Does not attend to root causes of underlying issues Not enough attention to other aspects of the client's issues (i.e., childhood trauma, interpersonal relationships) beyond cognitions and emotions May not be adequate for severe or complex issues Client must be highly motivated and willing to do the work. Homework can be time-consuming. Some techniques may create discomfort for clients before emotional overload improves.

(*continued*)

TABLE 6.2 OVERVIEW OF PROS AND CONS OF PSYCHOLOGICAL
THERAPIES (CONTINUED)

THEORY/THERAPY	ADVANTAGES/ PROS	DISADVANTAGES/ CONS
Constructivist/ Postmodern	Attention to contextual and cultural issues is a welcome change from individualistic perspectives Empowering for minoritized and disenfranchised communities	The notions that reality is subjective is considered controversial. May be at odds with how personality is understood by psychological theories
Contextual/Systemic	Attention to contextual, multicultural, and social justice issues is a welcome change from individualistic perspectives Empowering for minoritized and disenfranchised communities	Feminism originally considered monolithic or singular (women focused); inattentive to intersectional identities (LGBTQ+, Black and Brown peoples). This is changing in present-day feminist therapy. Some may not have a well-defined framework

Many of Freud's original ideas remain in today's psychodynamic theory and practice. Table 6.3 highlights examples of client issues and their root cause from a psychodynamic perspective.

Westen (1998) highlighted the main assumptions of psychoanalytic practice: (1) much of our mental life (thoughts, feelings, motivations, drives) resides in the unconscious and these are not known to us; (2) our conflicting mental responses to people or situations are independent of our awareness and warrant mental compromise; (3) our personality is heavily influenced by childhood experiences and these continue to affect how relationships develop in adulthood; (4) our interactions with others affect our own understanding of ourselves, people, and relationships; and (5) developing our personality includes regulation of sexual and impulsive drives, becoming independent, and being able to have healthy intimacy in relationships. Object relations theory is primarily credited for this new emphasis on relationships.

Object Relations Theory

Object relations theory posits that the nature and quality of early relationships, good or bad, invariably repeat themselves across time in other adult relationships. An individual must work through the dysfunctionality of these

TABLE 6.3 EXAMPLES OF ISSUES AND ROOT CAUSES FROM A PSYCHODYNAMIC PERSPECTIVE

ISSUE OF CONCERN	POTENTIAL ROOT CAUSE
Nail-biting	Early childhood event that elicited anxiety
Obsessive handwashing	Past childhood trauma
Skin picking and hair plucking compulsions	May be linked to developmental trauma
Pangs of nervousness	May be linked to a childhood memory after completing certain tasks
Agoraphobia (fear of open spaces)	Childhood experience that caused fear
Triskaidekaphobia (aversion to the number 13)	Commonly associated with childhood development, could be genetic or a learned behavior from parents

Source: Adapted from Masud, M. (n.d.). *Psychodynamic theory: Explanation with examples.* Advergize. https://www.advergize.com/psy/psychodynamic-theory-explanation-7-examples/ #Psychodynamic_Theory_Examples

primary relationships in order to break the cycle. People look at new relationships through the filter of old ones and this leads to transference, whereby we make inferences about the person we are interacting with, whether based on the actual current relationship or old ones (Vinney, 2021). Psychodynamic theory guides psychoanalytic therapy or psychoanalysis.

Psychoanalytic Therapy

The goals of psychoanalysis are to make unconscious thoughts or drives conscious, to strengthen the ego so that the client's behavior is grounded in reality rather than instinctual unconscious drives or cravings, and to encourage cathartic expression to release pent-up emotions that are tied to repressed memories. The function of therapy is to analyze behaviors and drives to develop the ability to become free to love, play, and work fully. The client needs to become aware, develop honest appraisal of the self, and learn to manage anxieties and fears. This work will help the client gain control of impulses and irrational behaviors, which in turn leads to satisfying interpersonal relationships (Archer & McCarthy, 2007). The process of therapy involves the development of *transference*, defined as the projection onto another person (e.g., the analyst) of feelings, past associations, or experiences. This is an important concept in psychoanalysis because it demonstrates that past experiences impact the present. Interpreting transference in the psychoanalytic setting can shed light on unresolved conflicts (American Psychoanalytic Association, n.d.).

Counselors, on the other hand, must remain watchful of the emergence of *countertransference* in which the counselor's own childhood experiences may trigger a reaction to the client. In psychodynamic counseling, the therapist is in charge of the session and the following processes take place: (a) exploration of unconscious material and defenses, believed to have originated in early childhood; (b) ongoing and repeated interpretations and exploration of client's resistance when it emerges; (c) facilitation and resolution of dysfunctional patterns; and (d) developing awareness of how core defense mechanisms and conflicts affect the client's daily life. The goal of therapy is also to help the client to achieve insight in the present moment (Archer & McCarthy, 2007). Some of the most common defense mechanisms, believed to assist individuals in coping with their fears or anxieties, are denial, displacement, projection, rationalization, reaction formation, regression, repression, and sublimation. Table 6.4 provides a brief description and example of each.

Psychodynamic theories have evolved considerably over time (Fulmer, 2018). Fulmer (2018) provides a succinct overview of the modern presuppositions of psychodynamic therapies and how they inform the goals of therapy. He highlights the new integration of multicultural considerations and concludes:

The cross-cultural implications of a modernized psychodynamic approach are immense. At the core of dynamic theory are ideas with universal appeal: that people have a persistent personality, that the past impacts the present, that childhood matters in later life, that psychological defenses are used to help people cope with the trials and tribulations of life, that people often feel conflicted and at odds within themselves, and that emotions have behavioral consequences. The dynamic system is inclusive not only of culture, but also of orientation in time and in psychology. (p. 5)

Fulmer contends, and we agree, that practicing counselors can avail themselves of aspects of multiple theories that may best serve their clients. He emphasizes that modern psychodynamic approaches are highly inclusive of the ever-changing world we live in and counselors need to adapt and respond accordingly. We elaborate upon this point in the Integrative-Eclectic and Common Factors of Psychotherapy section.

Existential-Humanistic Theories

Some proponents of existential counseling are Otto Rank, Victor Frankl, Frederick Perls, Rollo May, Paul Tillich, and Irvin Yalom. Existentialism is a philosophy concerned with meaning-making about the human experience. The aim of life is to ponder questions about love, death, and meaning. This framework focuses on the positive and active aspects of human growth and realization (Archer & McCarthy, 2007). The ultimate concerns of our existence are death, freedom, isolation, and meaninglessness (Yalom, 1980). Existential theory underscores the following aspects of being human: (a) capacity for self-awareness, (b) freedom and responsibility, and (c) search for meaning. A school of thought that followed existential-humanistic theories is transpersonal counseling. See Chapter 13 for a discussion about these approaches.

When clients develop deeper self-awareness, the possibility for experiencing greater freedom also increases. Having awareness entails the realization that (a) we are finite, we will all die one day, and we have limited time on this earth and in this life; (b) we all carry the potential and the choice to act or not to act in certain ways; (c) meaning must be sought, it is not automatic; and (d) we are all

TABLE 6.4 DEFENSE MECHANISMS

DEFENSE MECHANISM	DESCRIPTION	EXAMPLE
Denial	Blocking external stimuli from conscious awareness	An individual who uses alcohol excessively and refuses to recognize the negative consequences of their alcohol abuse
Displacement	Redirecting anger or other disturbing emotion to a safer and less threatening target	A person is mistreated by their superior at work and comes home and mistreats the family pet
Projection	Attributing our own unacceptable emotions to someone else	A person accuses another of mistreatment rather than acknowledge their own misbehavior
Rationalization	Using false or faulty logic to explain action or thoughts	A person blames their loss in a sports game to their opponent's cheating rather than their superior performance
Reaction Formation	Acting the opposite of our true emotions	A person is extremely nice to their in-laws whom they dislike greatly
Regression	Returning to an earlier stage of development and more immature behavior	A middle school child resorts to thumb sucking after having an upsetting interaction at school
Repression	Holding unpleasant or disturbing memories in the unconscious mind	A child who was sexually abused has no conscious memory of the events
Sublimation	Shifting antisocial or unacceptable impulses toward a more socially acceptable activity or behavior	A person who is sexually aroused and unable to fulfill their desire produces a beautiful work of art

subject to experiencing loneliness, meaninglessness, guilt, emptiness, and isolation (Archer & McCarthy, 2007). Individuals are free to make choices among whatever alternatives we are offered and the choices we make can shape our destiny. How we live, and who we become, are the outcome of the choices we make, and we must accept responsibility for being in charge of our own lives. We must pursue meaning in our daily existence by committing to work, create, and love fully.

Existentialists believe that anxiety, also referred to as existential anxiety, is a normal emotion that can be used constructively to address the existential dilemmas we encounter in daily living. Neurotic anxiety, on the other hand, emerges when we try to avoid existential anxiety. The former represents a loss of our sense of free will and our inability to assume responsibility for our lives. The goals of existential therapy are to address and eliminate neurotic anxiety, teach clients to manage their existential anxiety, and assist with achieving authentic living. The techniques used by existential counselors involve identifying instances when the client is shirking responsibility, and help clients to look at all the options available to make decisions. Also important is the exploration of grief and sadness about life milestones that may be associated with fear of isolation and death, all basic tenets of existentialism (we are all essentially alone and we will all die).

Existential therapists hold an open, honest, egalitarian, and authentic relationship with clients, Counselors aim to model authenticity, freedom of choice, and appropriate management of anxiety and anxiety-producing events. Central to existential anxiety is our need to face death squarely. This awareness of death as inevitable makes life more meaningful. The avoidance of this reality can render our lives meaningless. Existential counseling does not offer specific techniques; however, there are a number of well-known exercises that counselors can invite clients to do. A few examples are outlined in Table 6.5.

TABLE 6.5 EXISTENTIAL THERAPY EXERCISES

Invite Clients to Engage in Any the Following: ■ Write your eulogy. ■ Imagine your own death. ■ Focus on the loss of a person you love. ■ Outline milestones or major life events. ■ Engage in a silent retreat or a period of self-imposed isolation. ■ Write reflection essays about any of these experiences and process in the next counseling session.
Who Am I? ■ Write down 10 phrases that best describe who you are. ■ Order them in terms of priority and centrality to yourself. ■ Cross out each description, beginning with the least central one. ■ Write a reflection essay about this experience and process in the next counseling session.
Write Your Own Obituary ■ Write your own obituary during the next 48 hours. ■ Write a reflection essay on the exercise and process in the next counseling session.
It is imperative that you spend time preparing your client to engage in these activities and guide them in processing their experience. Uncomfortable feelings of sadness, anxiety, or anger may result and require your kind and compassionate witnessing.

Logotherapy

Frankl (1969), a survivor of the holocaust, developed the foundations and applications of logotherapy, an existential approach to counseling. In his book, *The Will to Meaning*, he outlined the techniques he used in his therapy practice. He asserted that life by itself is not meaningful; rather, our main goal in life is to find meaning. Frankl spoke of an existential vacuum fueled by feelings of boredom, meaninglessness, depression, addiction, and aggression. Humans have free will and agency; thus, we control our choices and are free to seek meaning and pleasure in life as part of our free will. Meaning-making is an experience we must discover and create intentionally and purposefully. Logotherapy invites clients to embrace tragic optimism, a feeling of positivity and hope in spite of the naturally occurring feelings of pain and guilt and the inevitability of death (Frankl, 1969).

Gestalt Therapy

Gestalt therapy was developed by Fritz Perls. His approach holds that individuals are much more than their inner drives (a criticism of Freud's psychoanalytic approach) and that behavior can only be understood through the exploration of the purpose and meaning we give to life. Perls believed that individuals could fulfill their potential by taking responsibility for themselves and cooperating with others. We are social beings and our ability to meet our own needs requires us to consider others in order to achieve psychological health and balance. Perls also believed that clients can be manipulative and avoid relying on themselves and taking personal responsibility. He contended clients must stand on their own, support themselves, and reintegrate disowned or fractured parts of themselves to become whole. Finally, he emphasized the importance of context and our position within it (Archer & McCarthy, 2007).

The core concepts of gestalt therapy follow. Counseling is focused on the client's present moment, the "here and now," and the initial goal is for the client to increase awareness of what they are feeling and doing in the moment. Gestalt is not interested in abstractions, rather, it encourages direct experiencing in the present. Instead of talking about past traumas, the therapy engages the client in the moment, to become the wounded child. Gestalt therapy helps the client explore their unmet needs and stay in the present moment to identify them and determine how they can be met. When a client has unfinished business and bottled up feelings about their past (could be in the form of memories or fantasies), they will experience challenges in relationships with others. The confluence of these factors results in preoccupation, compulsive behavior, and self-defeating behavior, among others. Contact in the moment is crucial during therapy. The first step toward increased awareness is recognizing that this moment is the only reality we know. Clients can develop healthy boundaries and connect with others, rather than develop defenses against this awareness. The most common ways clients avoid contact in the present is through introjection, projection, retroflection, deflection, and confluence. Table 6.6 outlines and defines these ways of avoidance and resistance.

TABLE 6.6 GESTALT AVOIDANCE BEHAVIORS (RESISTANCE TO THE HERE AND NOW) DEFINED

AVOIDANCE BEHAVIORS	DEFINITION
Introjection	Tendency to accept other people's beliefs and standards without considering congruence with who we are. Integrating what our environment provides without considering our own needs and wants.
Projection	This is the opposite of introjection, whereby a person disavows aspects of the self and places them on others or the environment. The person has difficulty discerning the inside from the outside world.
Retroflection	The person is not assuming responsibility for their feelings and directs energy inwardly instead of outwardly.
Deflection	This occurs when the person is avoiding contact or awareness. They use humor or abstractions, ask questions, or generalize to avoid emotional experiences of connection.
Confluence	The person is unaware of boundaries due to a high need for acceptance, and approval. The person does not see themselves as differentiated, merging identities with others important to them.

In gestalt counseling the goals and process of therapy include the exploration of client expectations, developing a hypothesis about what makes a client be who they are and do what they do, determining what the foreground or salient issue is, gaining understanding of incomplete gestalts, growing in self-awareness, exploring and practicing current struggles in session, reenacting issues in order to work through them, and spending time preparing the client for these reenactments. Gestalt therapy has a number of techniques counselors can use. For instance, the empty chair technique is commonly used to help the client confront an unresolved issue. The therapist asks the client to imagine the person or issue on the empty chair and talk to them. The client then sits on the empty chair and has a dialogue with themselves from the vantage point of the other person or issue they are working to resolve the conflict with. This process can lead to insights on the client's part to help resolve the conflict. See the Resources section for additional information about gestalt therapy.

Person-Centered Therapy

Carl Rogers created client-centered therapy, subsequently named person-centered therapy (Archer & McCarthy, 2007). This therapeutic approach is associated with humanistic and existential psychology and the human potential movement. Rogers was influenced by Otto Rank who emphasized the uniqueness of each individual client. Rogers believed that for a client to make progress, the counselor must hold unconditional positive regard, and the client must feel seen, heard, and understood. Unconditional positive regard means that the counselor shows absolute, unconditional support and acceptance for the client, regardless of what they say or do. The goals of therapy must be outlined by the client and no formal diagnosis is given. He outlined the necessary and sufficient conditions for change as (1) psychological contact (client and counselor can have an effect on each other); (2) a feeling of incongruence that drives the client to seek help (client is in a vulnerable state and their awareness of incongruence grows during therapy); (3) acceptance (unconditional positive regard); (4) counselor empathy; and (6) client perception of counselor empathy and acceptance.

Empathy is "a multifaceted construct used to account for the capacity to share and understand the thoughts and feelings of others" (Decety & Yoder, 2016, p. 2). Empathy requires that you fully understand how the client feels, and that you enter their world, while maintaining boundaries. It is imperative that the counselor is authentic and real and in touch with their own feelings during therapy. The therapist is open and attuned to the client's inner life, but does not necessarily self-disclose. Self-disclosure is defined as the counselor's ability to share about themselves with the client when their experiences, thoughts, and feelings are relevant to the client's own experiences, thoughts and feelings. The sharing underscores to the client that they are not alone and the counselor understands them fully. Self-disclosure is done whenever appropriate and needed to advance the client's progress or forward movement. The client-counselor congruence and genuineness of interaction is a critical component of therapy (Archer & McCarthy, 2007).

As a counselor, you must be nonjudgmental and accepting of the client. Being accepting of the client means that you see and understand them and hold space for them and their stories without judgment or expectations. Even if you disagree with them, do not impose conditions for the client to feel worthy. Your task is to work with the client to reframe and overcome their previous feelings of conditional worthiness. Sometimes, you will need to sense the meanings or feelings of which the client may be unaware, and process your understanding of the client through therapeutic dialogue. The client must perceive your empathy and understanding; having these qualities alone is not enough. As a person-centered counselor, you must be able to express your feelings of unconditional positive regard and empathic understanding to the client (Archer & McCarthy, 2007).

The client's involvement in the counseling process is also crucial. In accordance with person-centered counseling, the client sets the goals and direction of counseling and takes responsibility for change. They experience the counselor's empathy, unconditional positive regard, and genuineness, and in the process, learn to explore their feelings and themselves. According to Patterson (1985) genuineness means that counselors "are 'for real,' open, honest, sincere. They are involved in the relationship and not simply mirrors, sounding boards, or blank screens" (p. 63). The goal is for the client to learn self-acceptance, moving toward becoming their best authentic self and changing their behaviors and their life (Archer & McCarthy, 2007).

COGNITIVE BEHAVIORAL THEORIES

Cognitive behavioral theory (CBT) contends that an individual's perception of a situation determines their response rather than the situation itself. Essentially, what we think will influence how we feel (Archer & McCarthy, 2007). CBT is built on this premise and aims to help people change their cognitive distortions so that they can change the way the feel. CBTs include rational therapy (RT; later renamed rational emotive behavior therapy [REBT] by Albert Ellis) and cognitive therapy (CT, by Aaron Beck). Donald Meichenbaum (1977, 1985) developed cognitive behavior modification and the integrated cognitive-behavioral technique called stress inoculation. Finally, Francine Shapiro (2001) developed eye movement desensitization and reprocessing (EMDR) therapy to treat post-traumatic stress disorder (PTSD), anxiety, depression, complex grief reactions, phobias, somatic illnesses, and trauma. Her approach integrates aspects of CBT. A brief overview of each is provided next.

Rational Therapy and Rational Emotive Behavior Therapy

Cognitive approaches hold awareness that people have internal dialogues and that we are able to think about thinking, both uniquely human characteristics. The cognitive behavioral approaches emerged as a reaction to psychoanalytic theories and emphasize the role of thinking in human emotions and behaviors. Ellis was the first proponent of cognitive-based approaches in the form of RT (Ellis, 1962) and REBT (Ellis & Joffe Ellis, 2019). Assumptions of REBT are that human beings are rational and irrational, capable of growing (being reflective, creative, rational) and also capable of self-destruction, and that we are worthy of self-respect and worthwhile (Archer & McCarthy, 2007). This approach states that psychological disturbances are the result of unmet demands of the ego, which makes us believe we should be perfect in all ways, and that we should be liked by everyone. These irrational beliefs result in frustration when things do not go as we want or expect them to, and we tell ourselves this is awful and terrible. Ellis developed the ABCDE method to help clients challenge irrational beliefs. Table 6.7 outlines the ABCDE method and provides an examples.

As depicted in Table 6.7, the counselor assists the client to reframe the experience by working through the ABCDE method and find alternative ways of thinking about what happened and develop new behaviors that can help the client rethink their next steps. In this approach, the counselor is an active teacher, helping the client understand the REBT and ABCDE methods. The counselor is directive and persuasive. It is important that the counselor help identify the irrational thoughts quickly and help the client develop alternate thoughts in order to change their emotional and behavioral reactions. Types of irrational beliefs are (1) dogmatic demands (I must, you must, and they must... always!); (2) awfulising (this is horrible, terrible, and I will never get over it!); (3) low frustration tolerance (I can't stand this!); and (4) self- or other-downing (I am not good enough, you are not good enough!). In this therapeutic approach, the counselor-client relationship is not as important as in other approaches; however, it is still critical that the client and counselor have good rapport and connection. It is crucial, however, that the counselor help the client

TABLE 6.7 THE ABCDE METHOD

ACRONYM	DEFINITION	EXAMPLE
A—Activating Event	An event, thought, or feeling related to our personal goals or wishes and relating to the past, present, or future.	I asked my supervisor for a raise and was denied it.
B—Beliefs Held	Cognitions or thoughts we have about A that represent our normal assessment when encountering an event or internal motivation.	I should get a raise because I work hard and I deserve to make more money.
C—Consequences of AB Interaction	In the context of counseling, this is the resulting negative emotion or behavior from the interaction between A and B.	I am angry and upset because I did not get the raise I wanted.
D—Dispute Irrational Belief	I dispute the irrational belief (B) that caused my negative reaction.	There are many factors involved in getting a raise. The denial of my request is not the end of the world and I can make choices about what to do next.
E—Effective or Rational Philosophy	I develop a rational and effective way of handling what happened.	I am going to explore my options so I can figure out if there is opportunity for promotion where I work or if I need to look for other potential employment.

make the connection between their thinking patterns and the resulting feelings and behaviors.

In REBT, counselor interventions include cognitive, emotive, and behavioral techniques. Cognitive techniques involve having the client dispute irrational beliefs in session using the ABCDE method. Emotive strategies includes unconditional acceptance of the client, use of humor, telling stories or parables to help the client make connections, and exercises whereby the therapist has the client (a) reverse roles to experience the issue from a different perspective, (b) attach the feelings of shame that may emerge from the irrational thought, and (c) take risks in real time to practice behaviors they are struggling with (e.g., starting a conversation with a stranger to practice self-confidence). Behavioral techniques include homework assignments and in vivo desensitization (exposure), flooding (extreme exposure), antiprocrastination exercises, rewards and punishment, and skills training. REBT offers many opportunities for psychoeducation of clients and is a proactive approach to counseling.

Cognitive Therapy

Cognitive therapy (CT), proposed by Beck, focuses on the premise that humans actively construct their reality and that cognition (thoughts) mediates emotions and behavior. Thoughts are knowable and accessible to us, and in order to make changes, we must begin with changing our cognitions. Beck outlined a core concept called a linear path model, whereby schemas lead to automatic thoughts, which lead to negative interpretations that result in emotional and behavioral problems. A schema is a core belief that humans have developed throughout their life that influences how we interpret events. Automatic thoughts lead to automatic interpretation of events. CT focuses on changing schemas and thoughts that create negative interpretations. Beck called this a cognitive triad, which proposes that a negative view of the self leads to negative views of the world and the future. Beck further stated that the development of schemas and automatic thoughts are the result of early childhood experiences including critical incidents. The events we experienced helped create the schemas, beliefs, automatic thoughts, emotions, behaviors, and physiological responses we experience as adults (Beck, 1979). The following represents some of the most commonly held cognitive distortions that counselors can help client change:

- **Arbitrary inference:** arriving at an inappropriate conclusion, even though there is no evidence or contrary evidence for the conclusion
- **Selective abstraction:** focusing attention on a selective piece of information without considering the entire picture
- **Overgeneralization:** drawing a conclusion from limited data available
- **Magnification/minimization:** giving too much or too little importance to a specific event or situation
- **Personalization:** imagining that what happens is related to you or something you have done when there is no evidence to that effect
- **Dichotomous thinking:** holding on to all-or-nothing or black-and-white thinking (Archer & McCarthy, 2007)

The counselor's role in CT is to be flexible and have effective interpersonal skills to help the client. While the counselor uses direct challenges of irrational beliefs in REBT, in CT, the counselor uses the Socratic method (asks questions to uncover contradictions in a client's statements or thoughts). The Socratic method involves the counselor helping the client to define and clarify the problem; identify thoughts, images, and assumptions; examine the meaning of an event for the client; and evaluate the consequences of holding on to maladaptive thoughts and behaviors (see Table 6.8. for an example of homework involving a daily record of automatic or dysfunctional thoughts that may be affecting the client). Moreover, in CT, the therapist tends to have more of a leading than a

TABLE 6.8 DAILY RECORD OF AUTOMATIC THOUGHTS

DATE	EVENT (INTERNAL OR EXTERNAL)	AUTOMATIC THOUGHT	FEELINGS	BEHAVIOR	OUTCOME	RATIONAL ALTERNATIVE	NEW OUTCOME
8/20/22	External: I asked a new neighbor out on a date and she turned me down.	No one wants to date me. I am not attractive.	Disappointed and depressed	I withdraw and stay away from people.	Increased depression and loneliness	Just because someone does not want to go out with me does not make me unlovable. I deserve love.	Acceptance. Preservation of my self-esteem.

confronting approach. Finally the counselor-client relationship is collaborative and, while based on respect and trust, the counselor is considered the expert (Archer & McCarthy, 2007).

Some of the most common cognitive techniques are (1) question the evidence (Does being gay really mean you can't live a full and happy life?), (2) explore fantasized consequences (What will happen if he does break up with you?), (3) use of paradox and/or exaggeration (This week I want you to be three times as depressed as last week.), (4) use of scaling (On a scale of one to 10, how anxious were you?), (5) cognitive rehearsal (Let's talk through what you will be thinking next time.), and (6) replacement imagery (Can you imagine the interview going well?) CT also uses some behavioral techniques, including social skills training, assertiveness training, bibliotherapy, and relaxation training (Archer & McCarthy, 2007).

Behavior Therapy

Behavior therapy (BT) is "a form of psychotherapy that applies the principles of learning, operant conditioning, and classical conditioning to eliminate symptoms and modify ineffective or maladaptive patterns of behavior" (APA Dictionary of Psychology, n.d.). McLeod (2018) explained that Skinner advanced the concept of operant conditioning (a.k.a. instrumental conditioning), defined as a way of "learning where the consequences of a response determine the probability of it being repeated." McLeod added that "through operant conditioning behavior which is reinforced (rewarded) will likely be repeated, and behavior which is punished will occur less frequently." McLeod explained classical conditioning (a.k.a. pavlovian or respondent conditioning) as "learning through association.... In simple terms, two stimuli are linked together to produce a new learned response in a person or animal," also remarking that "John Watson subsequently proposed that the process of classical conditioning (based on Pavlov's observations) was able to explain all aspects of human psychology" (McLeod, 2021).

Behavior therapy techniques align with classical or operant conditioning principles. Classical conditioning techniques are aversion therapy, flooding, and systematic desensitization while operant conditioning uses contingency management, extinction, behavior modeling, and token economies (Cherry, 2021). Most of these are described in the following list:

■ **Aversion therapy:** involves pairing a behavior we want to stop with a negative (averse) stimulus to create an association that will eventually cause the undesirable behavior to stop.

■ **Flooding:** intense and fast exposure to negative object or event (i.e., source of a phobia) and preventing the client from getting away. This can be highly disturbing to the client.

■ **Systematic desensitization:** client makes a list of items or things that are fear-inducing and the therapist exposes the client to these stimuli in incrementally disturbing order while the client practices relaxation techniques. Used for severe phobias or anxieties.

- **Contingency management:** involves a formal contract or agreement between the client and therapist with a list of goals for behavior change. The document outlines the target changes, rewards, and punishment for completion or failure to complete the tasks outlined. The client cannot back down from the agreement.

- **Extinction:** involves stopping the reinforcement of undesirable behavior. Time-outs are a great example. Removing the child from the situation is expected to eventually extinguish the behavior (e.g., tantrums) (Cherry, 2021).

Stress Inoculation

Meichenbaum (1977, 1985) contributed to CBT by developing the stress inoculation technique and the cognitive behavior modification approach. We will highlight the former here. Stress inoculation (Meichenbaum, 1985) involves a stress rehearsal process comprising three phases: conceptual, skills acquisition, and application. The conceptual phase includes establishing the therapeutic relationship, discussing stress-related problems, gathering information, establishing goals, forming a treatment plan, educating the client about stress and coping and the roles of thinking and emotions in maintaining stress, and reconceptualizing stress by understanding how the stress process works, thinking about it differently, and laying the groundwork for positive change (Archer & McCarthy, 2007). During the skills acquisition phase, the therapist teaches the client coping skills to be used during stressful situations with the goal of lessening anxiety. The therapist then teaches the client to combine cue-controlled relaxation training with the development of positive coping statements. In the stress sequence, the therapist helps the client to prepare for the stressor, confront and cope with the stressor, cope with emergent feelings (e.g., being overwhelmed), evaluate their efforts, and provide self-rewards for their ability to withstand the stressor (Archer & McCarthy, 2007). Finally, during the application phase, the client practices the skills learned, and the counselor encourages the client to apply the new skills. The counselor can also suggest activities to continue improving, for example, role-playing, modeling behaviors, practice relapse prevention, and conducting follow-up sessions (also known as booster sessions), among others (Archer & McCarthy, 2007).

Eye Movement Desensitization Reprocessing

The last CBT-related approach we will feature is EMDR therapy. Shapiro (2001) developed this approach while working with individuals in distress due to traumatic memories. While walking in nature one day she noticed her own negative emotions lessened when her eyes darted from side to side during the walk. She later tried this bilateral stimulation (BLS) with clients, and the approach developed over time. EMDR treatment involves eight phases:

1. **History taking:** The counselor obtains a complete history and conducts an assessment of the client's presenting issues. The targets or focus of treatment are outlined (inventory of past memories, active triggers, and goals of therapy).

2. **Client preparation:** This involves the counselor describing EMDR to the client and introducing the steps they will follow during therapy (e.g., how eye movement or tapping is done). The counselor makes sure the client has tools to manage intense emotions, such as designating an image of a peaceful or calm space to go to when needed.

3. **Assessment:** In this phase, the memory to be triggered in session is identified and the counselor helps establish the image, thoughts, emotions, and body sensations associated with it. The counselor uses two measures to valuate changes in emotions and cognitions: Subjective Units of Disturbance (SUD) scale and Validity of Cognition (VOC) scale.

4. **Desensitization:** This involves the client focusing on the selected memory, while doing eye movements or tapping. The client reports thoughts that come up. The counselor decides which type of BLS to use (e.g., eye movement or tapping). This is done repeatedly until the client reports a lessening of the memory's level of distress.

5. **Installation:** The client's preferred positive thought or cognition is installed.

6. **Body scan:** This involves the client noticing their physical responses, while holding both the memory of distress and the positive cognition. Any remaining somatic distress is discussed and the BLS continues until symptoms lessen.

7. **Closure:** The end of the session is approaching. The counselor may give directives for the client to use between sessions if distressing feelings remain. Containing distress and enhancing safety are most important during this time.

8. **Reevaluation of treatment effect:** This phase marks the beginning of the next session when the counselor evaluates where the client is and how they are feeling. Assessment of improvement is done and any new memories explored. The focus of the current session is determined. (American Psychological Association, 2017)

Through EMDR, any negative or distressing memories associated with the traumatic event are unearthed and processed iteratively until resolution is achieved. The counselor teaches the client how to elicit positive cognitions to replace distressing feelings, thoughts, and body sensations. You can explore training in EMDR therapy via www.emdr.com.

CONSTRUCTIVIST AND POSTMODERN THEORIES

Constructivist postmodern therapies challenge the notion of knowable and absolute truths. They espouse the idea that truth is a subjective experience that each individual defines for themselves or co-constructs with others. Therapy involves deconstructing a client's notions of truth, and what they mean to them. Two postmodern approaches include narrative therapy and solution-focused therapy.

Narrative Therapy

White and Epston (1990) developed narrative therapy in the 1980s in New Zealand. Narrative therapy focuses on the premise that the ways we think and behave occur in the cultural and social contexts we inhabit. This approach holds that our view of the world emerges from complex and usually unconscious processes whereby we move through our memories of experiences and choose the ones that help us confirm the stories or narratives we hold about ourselves and others. Within this therapy approach, counselors view problems as separate from the person (outside the person). They teach the client to do the same. This approach provides a new perspective and way of viewing the issues. This allows the client to feel empowered to change the narratives (stories, patterns of behavior) that are affecting them. The process of therapy supports clients in rewriting their story so they can be more intentional and become more of who they really are (Psychology Today, n.d.).

Narrative therapy emphasizes the stories people tell themselves and carry through their lives. Individuals give meaning to these experiences and they, in turn, serve as lenses we view the world through. These stories relate to our sense of ourselves, our self-esteem, capabilities, interpersonal relationships, and the work we do. The aim of therapy is to empower clients and encourage self-acceptance, non-judgment, or non-blaming. The counselor and client collaborate to achieve the client's goals. A great resource for counselors is the seminal work of White and Epston (1990), *Narrative Means to Therapeutic Ends*. You can find this and other narrative therapy books in the Resources section.

Solution-Focused Brief Therapy

Solution-focused therapy (SFT), also known as solution-focused brief therapy (SFBT), was proposed by Steve De Shazer, Insoo Berg, Eve Lipchek, and Michele Weiner-Davis. It focuses more on the resolution of problems than their root cause. The approach is time-limited in nature and focuses on the premise that clients can solve their problems successfully by revisiting instances of success that they can replicate in their life (Archer & McCarthy, 2007).

The core tenets of SFBT are as follows: (1) solutions are not necessarily related to problems, (2) always maintain a future orientation, (3) focus on client strengths, (4) change is inevitable, (5) nothing is all negative, (6) there is no such thing as resistance, (7) simplicity is key (Archer & McCarthy, 2007). The counselor's role is to be a consultant to the client and help them reach their goals. Therapists believe the client is an expert in themselves and have everything they need to solve their problems. The counselor aims to create an environment where they can identify change and amplify it. SFBT is short-term, goal-focused, and evidence-based. According to the Institute for Solution-Focused Therapy: "In the most basic sense, SFBT is a hope friendly, positive emotion eliciting, future-oriented vehicle for formulating, motivating, achieving, and sustaining desired behavioral change" (Institute for Solution-Focused Therapy, 2022).

SFBT therapists recognize and acknowledge client distress, focus their attention on successes, use solution talk not problem talk, and apply a number of techniques aimed at maintaining a solution-oriented focus during the session. Some examples of these are the miracle question, scaling questions, coping questions, and reframing. The best-known technique is the miracle question. Here is an example of how counselors can go about applying it (Sutton, 2021):

Try out the following with your clients:

This may seem like a strange question to ask, but please bear with me. Imagine going about your life as normal and heading off to sleep at the usual time.

Unknown to you, during the night, something happens – a miracle. When you wake up the following day, something exciting has happened.

The very problem that brought you to see me today is no longer there.

What would be the very first difference you would notice in your life?

Helpful follow-ups:

The following questions offer valuable follow-ups and progress the dialogue. They help the client create and explore new possibilities. (Modified from Yu, 2019, p. 1931):

How will you know the miracle has happened?

What will others (parents, partner, children, work colleagues, etc.) notice about you that makes them aware things are different or better?

What would their reaction be? What would they do?

What would you do next?

What would we see (feelings, thoughts, and behavior) if we compared a before and after picture?

Have you ever seen elements of this happen before?

Another interesting technique used by SFBT counselors is intervention breaks. Breaks usually last a few minutes and allow the therapist to think about what is transpiring in the session or consult another therapist in real time about the interventions being used. The client also gets time to reflect on the session. The counselor can offer a compliment or an intervention to the client (e.g., an activity to move toward a desired goal). The type of activity is contingent on the client's level of motivation and readiness for change. SFBT is applicable to individual, group, couples, and children counseling modalities. It can also be used with clients who are being mandated to treatment (Archer & McCarthy, 2007).

CONTEXTUAL SYSTEMIC THEORIES

Feminist Theory

Feminist theory is rooted in the women's movement and the belief in equal rights and protections for all women and other disenfranchised groups. Many scholars have contributed to this emancipatory movement, aiming to challenge and disrupt the patriarchy and male hegemony in our political, cultural, and social life. Gilligan (1982) is a salient example. She conducted research that uncovered how adolescent girls define themselves in relational terms (i.e., the ways in which they give, nurture, care for others). Feminist therapists' view of human nature is paradoxical in that they hold a favorable and positive appraisal of women at the individual level, while in the larger context of society, they evaluate all forms of oppression, discrimination, and marginalization endured by women through a critical lens (Archer & McCarthy, 2007; Psychology Today, n.d.).

Feminist therapists are collaborators and aim to empower women to speak their truth and be their authentic selves. They help clients explore the cultural, social, and historical roots of oppression and ensuing distress. They are also critical of a society that stigmatizes people based on gender, race, body size, sexual orientation, or gender expression. The underlying tenets that inform feminist therapy are that the personal is political, and therapy is based on multiple categories of analysis, all of which are centered on the experiences of women. During therapy, the client's mental health issues are reframed to elicit a contextual understandings of the problem. The counseling relationship is egalitarian, and the counselor aims to decrease barriers to equality. Clients are viewed as unique, and counselors are facilitators of change. The goals of feminist therapy are co-constructed by the client and therapist, and aim to relieve or eliminate symptoms of distress. This can be done by exploring power dynamics and clarifying sources of stress. The counselor empowers the client to take action to improve their sense of themselves and the nature of their relationships. Counselors assist clients to get a bird's eye view of their life situation and contexts they live in, and they affirm and support diversity in all its forms. Some techniques of feminist therapy are: gender role analysis, power analysis, involvement in consciousness-raising groups, assertiveness training, assisting the client with reframing and relabeling their experiences or perceptions, and demystifying therapy (Archer & McCarthy, 2007). Finally, feminist therapy is applicable to women, men, couples and families, children and adolescents, and groups.

Multicultural and Social Justice Theories

In your exploration of multicultural social justice theories and cross-cultural and diversity issues in counseling, it is imperative that you prepare your heart and mind to receive, reflect upon, and process information that may be uncomfortable or upsetting, regardless of whether you are a member of the dominant culture or a marginalized and disenfranchised group. Sue and Sue (2013) provide the following suggestions for novice counselors to consider:

- Do not let your emotional reactions to deny or minimize the stories of the most disempowered in society.

- Try to acknowledge all of your biases openly so you can listen to your clients fully and in a nondefensive way.

- The more experiences you have with people of color (or people different from you), the more they will enhance your cultural competence.

- Explore yourself as a racial/cultural being with multiple visible and invisible salient identities.

- Try to understand what your intense emotions mean for you and what they are about, when they arise.

- Do not suppress dissent or disagreements. Lean into the tensions that arise so you may learn from them.

- Take an active role in exploring yourself and learning as much as you can about who you are as a human and who you want to become as a counselor.

Multicultural theories attend to issues of privilege, power, hegemony, diversity, equity, inclusion, cultural values, beliefs, and ethnic and racial differences. Within the multiplicity of our humanity, individuals and groups of people will encounter each other day-to-day; the counseling room is no exception. In fact, in the course of your practice you will, more likely than not, be tasked with counseling an individual or groups of individuals who are different from you. The need for multicultural competence cannot be overstated.

Vast numbers of theoretical frameworks attend to counseling individuals from diverse cultures, races, sexual and affectional orientations, religions, and spiritual traditions (see Davis et al., 2018; DeBord et al., 2016; Fuertes & Gretchen, 2001; Leong et al., 2014; Ponterotto et al., 2010; Rosmarin & Koenig, 2020; Sue & Sue, 2013). Multiculturally competent counselors prepare themselves to provide effective and culturally sensitive and responsive care to all people, regardless of background. For a comprehensive overview of multicultural social justice theories and applications, see Leong et al. (2014) in the Resources section.

Multicultural and social justice competencies have implications for counseling practice. You will be required to take a course in multicultural counseling as part of the CACREP accreditation guidelines. For our purposes, here is a list of some of the implications that have been advanced by researchers and practitioners in our field (adapted from Sue & Sue, 2013):

- People of color have biases and prejudice like everyone else.

- All oppression is detrimental. Avoid comparing oppressed groups to one another.

- Don't allow racial or ethnic or other identity conflicts break group cohesion.

- Not everything that affects people of color is due to racism. Blaming the victim is damaging and it is also counterproductive to assume all bad things that happen are about racism.

- Awareness and understanding of your own worldview and how it may conflict with the client's are very important.

- Communication styles are also important. Your style will have an impact on clients and you need to consider ways to modify how you present yourself so that you are congruent with your client's style.

- Your awareness and understanding of your own intersectional identities will help you relate with your clients' own identities.

- Develop comfort and ease in addressing issues of race, gender, sexual orientation, spirituality and religion, power, privilege, and equity.

- If you identify as White, you can be a great ally. White supremacy is the problem, not White people.

- Be attentive to the ways that people express offensive biases, prejudices, or discrimination. Do not be a silent observer. Speak up.

- Get to know people who have different visible and invisible identities.

You can find additional information about multicultural and social justice counseling concepts and applications in the resources section.

Relational-Cultural Theory

Relational-cultural theory (RCT) originated in the mid-1970s through the collective efforts of four counselors: Jean Baker Miller, Irene Stiver, Janet Surrey, and Judith Jordan. These clinicians wanted to develop a psychology of women to help inform therapy in a way that honored the lived experiences of women. Most known therapy proponents have been White, highly educated, heterosexual males, often at the exclusion of female voices. RCT proponents aimed to "understand the impact of race, culture, sexuality, and sociopolitical power issues" (Jordan, n.d.). RCT deconstructed the prevalent psychological theories, which traditionally focused on individualistic pursuits, to center the relational and cultural voices of women. This was not without criticism, as they initially presented the voice of women as a singular construct, rather than the multiplicity and complexity that are the voices of women from diverse backgrounds (Jordan, n.d.).

RCT was developed, in part, from a belief that people grow in connection across their lifespan, and relationships are essential for fruitful, thriving existence. Within RCT, isolation is viewed as destructive and detrimental. The goal of RCT therapists is to engage in deep relationship with clients so that clients may grow in deep connection to other significant people in their lives. The therapeutic process focuses on the client's images of their relationships, whether positive or negative, with the understanding that their expectations about these relationships inform and influence their future relationships. The goal is for the counselor to help the client lessen the effect of these relationships, while they try to connect with new ones. The therapy process focuses on growth-fostering connections, mutual empathy, and other cultural factors that are known to support, validate, and strengthen disenfranchised groups. RCT aspires to decrease the client's sources of isolation, and increase support when experiences of racism, homophobia, or classism create disconnection. RCT is essentially a feminist approach focused on social justice for all marginalized groups (Jordan, 2010).

INTEGRATIVE-ECLECTIC AND COMMON FACTORS OF PSYCHOTHERAPY

Most psychotherapy today is of an integrative and eclectic nature. Over time, experienced practitioners develop their own approach to therapy from the various theoretical frameworks they have used while practicing. Some call this systematic eclecticism.

Integrative psychotherapy can be seen as an art, and experienced therapists develop their own consistent, personal integrative approach over time. Personal integration often begins as a form of assimilation with a foundation in one theory and takes on a unique appearance as it is adapted to the personal strengths of different counselors and implemented with different clients (iResearchNet. com, n.d.).

Hubble et al. (1999) introduced the common factors of effective therapy. They conducted meta-analytic research on outcome studies of various types of therapy approaches. Meta-analytic research is a method that uses statistical analyses to explore and synthesize outcomes of multiple studies on a particular subject (Egger & Smith, 1997). Hubble and colleagues uncovered several common factors responsible for therapeutic change: the therapeutic relationship (responsible for 30% of the change), client factors (40%), theoretical framework or technique (15%), and expectancy or placebo (15%). Essentially, this means that whatever the client brings into therapy (their personhood, attributes, traits, dispositions) is the primary factor to effect positive change or improvement. The counselor-client alliance accounts for the next most important factor, and theory and techniques, as well as placebo effect (belief that the therapy works), represent the rest of the efficacy percentage. Who you are in relationship with the client is going to be more important and effective than what theory or technique you might choose to use. It is useful at this juncture to understand how clients approach the process of change.

PROCHASKA AND DICLEMENTE'S CYCLE OF CHANGE

Prochaska and DiClemente (1983) developed a model of client change that was adapted to understand a person's readiness to enter therapy. Later on, Prochaska and Norcross (2003) presented a transtheoretical model and in-depth analysis of the multiple systems of psychotherapy. You can find the latter work in the Resources section. This model of therapeutic change originated from studying individuals who were attempting to quit tobacco use. The stages of change are (1) precontemplation, (2) contemplation, (3) preparation, (4) action, (5) maintenance, and (6) relapse (or lapse). Table 6.9 provides a detailed explanation of these stages.

TABLE 6.9 CYCLE OF CHANGE

STAGE	DESCRIPTION	EXAMPLES AND FORWARD MOVEMENT
Precontemplation	The individual may be a long way from taking any action. When they weigh the pros and cons of changing, they will minimize the potential benefits of making any change.	You may have thought about giving up meat consumption to have better health or minimize your effect on the environment. When you think about the costs of a vegetarian diet and buying only plant-based products, you may not think it is worth the extra expense. The client at this stage needs to go inside and truthfully explore their motivations and the consequences of their actions or inaction. The counselor needs to be patient with the client's process, remind them they are in charge and they will move toward change when they are ready.
Contemplation	The individual begins to seriously consider the consequences of inaction. They begin to accept how their behavior is harmful to self and others. They may begin to imagine changing, but are still holding back.	Someone who binges on alcohol during the weekend may think about cutting back, but is not ready to give it serious effort because they want to feel loose and relaxed and they think alcohol can easily do that. The idea of stopping at two drinks is not appealing. The client needs to take a close look at the cons and the pros of changing habits. The counselor helps the client explore these pros and cons and begin to outline the positive consequences of change. The counselor helps the client identify blocks to overcome and feel more confident that change is possible.

(continued)

TABLE 6.9 CYCLE OF CHANGE (*CONTINUED*)

STAGE	DESCRIPTION	EXAMPLES AND FORWARD MOVEMENT
Preparation	The individual begins to decide that change may be possible and explore ways to accomplish this. This stage is characterized by small changes or baby steps. The individual understands the pros of change and begins moving in that direction at a faster rate.	A binge drinker may begin to keep track of the drinks they have during the weekend and apply some form of moderation management (moderation.org/getting-started-moderation-management/moderation-steps-of-change) to decrease alcohol consumption. A lot of work goes into preparing for actual change in anticipation of the action and maintenance stages. The client and counselor work collaboratively to develop goals and strategies for success. Planning and in-depth preparation are important here. Some clients will move forward drastically and others in more measured gradual steps.
Action	Stage marked by ongoing efforts and commitment to change.	The client seeks resources and support from others. Successes are celebrated. The client continues to move forward and acknowledges the newness of this process. The stage could last 3–6 months and obstacles may arise. Relapse or lapses are possible at this stage. The counselor reminds the client of their agency to continue navigating the change process and face challenges head on.

(*continued*)

TABLE 6.9 CYCLE OF CHANGE (*CONTINUED*)

STAGE	DESCRIPTION	EXAMPLES AND FORWARD MOVEMENT
Maintenance	After 6 months of successful work, maintenance begins. Confidence increases. Relapses are still possible. The process of remaining committed gets easier.	The client acknowledges temptation is still present and develops an action plan to avoid relapse. Honesty and openness are important and even if relapses happen, getting back on track is easier. The counselor continues to encourage, support, and empower the clients.
Relapse (or Lapse)	Individuals may relapse into old patterns of behavior. This is normal and can be expected.	The client looks at triggers that led to relapse or lapses and looks at these honestly and openly. The client recommits to change and starts where they are.

Source: Adapted from Practical Psychology. (2021). *Transtheoretical model and stages of change.* https://practicalpie.com/transtheoretical-model-stages-of-change-examples

EMANCIPATORY COMMUNITARIANISM

Emancipatory communitarianism (EC; Prilleltensky, 1996, 1997, 2001) is a theoretical framework that encourages a balance between an individual's autonomy or freedom and the idea of distributive justice. Distributive justice espouses concern for the well-being of people and the communities they inhabit (Kaufman, 2012). EC focuses on advocating for the individual's informed awareness of the goal of moral values, and promotes a belief in the good life and the good society, contending these are based on empathy, adherence to social obligations, and the elimination of oppression at all levels of society. We believe that EC is highly congruent with the counseling profession's centering of advocacy and social justice. In the course of counseling, advocating, and supporting clients, a culturally competent counselor also attends to the multiple intersecting identities they bring into the therapeutic alliance.

EC helps counselors to assess the morality of theoretical perspectives through embracing the following values: care and compassion, self-determination, human diversity, collaboration and democratic participation, and distributive justice. Prilleltensky outlined obstacles that psychologists and counselors face, may fail to address, and allow to get in the way of embracing a moral counseling practice. He described them as follows (we changed the term *psychologist* to *counselor*, which is more applicable here):

1. Counselors typically deal with the consequences and not with the roots of oppression.
2. Counselors typically frame problems of oppression and their solutions in individualistic terms and ignore their social dimension.
3. When counselors work with communities to promote emancipation, they do so in ameliorative, as opposed to transformative, ways.
4. There is a gap between counselors' knowledge about oppression and their hesitancy to address it.
5. Counselors are ill-equipped to deal with the oppressive actions of their clients. (Prilleltensky, 1996, pp. 309–310)

Prilleltensky admonishes counselors to find a way to balance the good life with the good society. As a future counselor, you will experience client issues that challenge you to navigate and negotiate the tensions between these sets of values. Western society values individualism, self-determinism, and freedom, at times to the expense of civic responsibility. Prilleltensky quotes Sandel's (1996) *Democracy's Discontent*: "the public philosophy by which we live cannot secure the liberty it promises, because it cannot inspire the sense of community and civic engagement that liberty requires" (p. 6).

Prilleltensky (1996) further explains the concept of moral principles and values conflicts using Kane's (1994) proposition of the Ends Principle, an extension of the Golden Rule (do unto others as you would have them do unto you). The Ends Principle contends we should treat others, in every interaction, as an End, never as a means to either ourselves or someone else. Kane admonishes us to always treat people with respect and allow them to live according to their own notions of what is a good life. Treating others as a mean purports we are trying to force our own views upon them without regard to their own will. Because there are instances when allowing a person to do harm is unacceptable (e.g., witnessing an attempted assault or a similarly abusive situation), Kane proposed the idea of moral sphere. A moral sphere means every person treats every other person as an End, an aspirational state that is not always tenable, but can guide our behavior. For example, we can stop a person attempting to assault another and intervene in their desire to cause harm (thus treating them as a means); however, in the process, we are restoring the moral sphere. Kane adds the caveat that we must treat every person as an end whenever possible; this way, the End Principle can be applied to all, and the moral sphere can be preserved for all of society. In times of conflicting values, we are admonished to apply this principle in our interactions with others, including our clients. Prilleltensky argues that counselors must also attend to our political values in order to give clarity to more subtle forms of value conflicts.

Political values exploration requires political literacy. Prilleltensky highlights instances where social policies have detrimental effects upon marginalized and disenfranchised groups. When a client arrives at our doorstep struggling with psychological and emotional distress, we must attend to the intrapersonal, interpersonal, and contextual factors in that person's life. A myopic approach would be detrimental to them and we would fall short of our efforts to help that client heal. Prilleltensky (1996) contends that

Political literacy helps [us] to see the connection between psychological stress and power structures. We should be able to see the breakdown of the moral sphere in unjust policies as much as in cases of rape. And we should strive to stop unjust policies as much as we should try to stop rapists. (p. 316)

Prilleltensky (2001) argues that counselors tend to emphasize and promote personal and interpersonal wellness to the detriment of our collective wellness. He asserts that embracing and practicing the tenets of social justice is the best way for counselors to balance our efforts and enhance our commitment to social action in the course of our work. Prilleltensky argues that the values we choose to live and work by should meet the following criteria: (1) our values should be congruent and align with what we believe to be a good society. Our ability to have agency over our lives should not infringe upon other people's ability to live their lives as they wish. (2) We should be neither too dogmatic, nor too relativistic; the former is inflexible and rigid and the latter too lax. (3) Values should work well together and complement rather than contradict each other, thus:

Caring should complement justice, collaboration should complement democratic participation, and human diversity should complement self-determination. Just like the value of health cannot be fulfilled without access to preventive and medical resources, self-determination cannot be promoted without justice and access to social resources. (pp. 752–753)

EC challenges us to delve deeper into our own contributions to inequities in society. This framework invites our reflection about the values we choose to embrace in our counseling and advocacy practice:

1. Are we breaking the moral sphere by favoring certain values and certain people at the expense of other values and other people?
2. Does our definition of moral sphere breakdown include both blatant and subtle abuses of power?
3. What can we do to restore the moral sphere, both at the interpersonal and social levels, if people are being treated as a means and not as ends?

We invite you to consider your own sense of what the End Principle and moral sphere mean to you. What might be the ways in which your counselor role contributes to your clients' lived experiences through the sociopolitical values that you hold? We will help you explore this further through the Going Within and Group Process sections of this chapter.

CONCLUSION

This chapter provided an overview of the most common counseling theories, and their schools of thought. We introduced you to the transtheoretical model of therapeutic practice and the cycles or stages of change that inform how clients experience readiness, and their movement or advances through therapy. Emancipatory communitarianism can serve as a lens we encourage you to use to choose a theoretical orientation to guide your practice. This process requires ongoing exploration of your value system and your worldview and consideration of the client populations you will serve. Keep in mind that values and perspectives about counseling practice may change over time as you grow and develop your counselor self.

Summary

- Counseling theories fall under different schools of thought, including psychodynamic-psychoanalytic, cognitive behavioral, existential humanistic, contextual systemic (including multicultural social justice), and constructivist postmodern.

- The transtheoretical model of therapeutic change outlines the cycle of change and client readiness to move through therapy efficiently and successfully.

- The common factors of psychotherapy are client factors, the therapeutic relationship, theoretical framework or techniques, and placebo, with each having a role in promoting client healing.

- Emancipatory communitarianism can be used as a lens to evaluate and situate the counseling theories and orientations you have learned about.

- Advocacy, social justice, and intersectionality can be applied regardless of the counseling theories and orientations you choose to guide your counseling practice.

Voices From the Field: Making Connections

Miguel A. Hernandez, LCPC, NCC
Department of Youth & Family Services, College Park, MD
Counseling Education and Supervision PhD Candidate, Capella University

The clinical training of a counselor involves initially being competent in one or two therapeutic approaches, proficient with some, and familiar with most of the mainstream ones. As is the case with many counselors, I have integrated the techniques from different approaches to fit the situations my clients have experienced. However, the most effective strategy that has helped me to develop the aforementioned integration was to be mindful to first focus on developing a therapeutic connection with the person in front of me.

I was fortunate to have learned this lesson before my clinical work began. I did an informational interview with a counselor who recommended the book *The Heart and Soul of Change* (Duncan et al., 2010). The book emphasizes the common factors of successful therapeutic outcomes; some of these included the importance of the therapeutic relationship, listening to the clients, and providing empathy for their experiences. The lessons proved useful in my work with veterans. In hindsight, it is easy to see why these techniques were valuable for challenging populations. I had a Marine friend who did not go past the first session with five therapists, before he found a therapist with whom he made a good connection and could receive the help he badly needed. The surprising part was that the therapist with whom he connected had not served in the military, which goes to show how important it is to connect with your clients.

Through the book, I also learned that in the same way situations outside the sessions derail any progress, there are opportunities where we can enhance what we do in the therapy session, with things we make happen beyond the 50-minute session. These activities are the ways we advocate for our clients. For example, after successful therapy, writing letters on behalf of the client so that they can be reunited with their children after child protective services involvement, ensuring that schools make interpreters available for parents during meetings, thus allowing their kids to be kids, rather than translators. It is always interesting to see mental health issues disappear when external factors contributing to them are resolved. It is often the case that the issues clients bring are expressions of needs, and that resolving these needs can lead to cessation of the problem. I will provide a specific example next.

Some years ago, I worked with a veteran who was experiencing serious hardships. My client was a White male in his late 20s, he was struggling with his transition out of the military, substance use, posttraumatic stress, and suicidality. My client was having difficulties making it to his mandated day-treatment program for substance use. As a result, he was close to being sent to jail. No regard was given to the hurdles he had to jump through to make it to the treatment center. To get to the treatment program, my client had to walk 10 miles to a commuter lot, so he could catch a ride for the other 40 miles of the trip, rain or shine. Besides the stress of his daily commute and missing appointments, my client did not have a job, his license was suspended, and he was couch surfing with a friend who found him on the streets. Last, he was also contending with the pain of leg wounds he received while serving in the military. I later learned of the invisible wounds he was also carrying on the inside.

As our initial 30-minute meeting passed the 2-hour mark, and in the same way you may one day experience with your clients, the veteran had saved the worst for last. When the time came for us to say our goodbyes, he remembered to mention that he should have died, as his brothers did back in the sandbox (military jargon meaning Iraq). My client was dealing with survivor's guilt. I suppose he saw the despair in my face and followed the comment by promising that he would not kill himself, at least not yet. While it can be daunting to discover that your client is suicidal, with training and practice you will learn, as I did, that it is by talking about the issue that solutions can be found. I had completed a training called Applied Suicide Intervention Skills Training, developed by a group called LivingWorks Education; the training is a 2-day experiential workshop that prepares you to have these types of conversations. One aim of the training is to get the other person to respond to the direct question "Are you thinking about killing yourself?" and then continue by following prescribed steps to come up with a plan to keep the person safe. Although I am an instructor of the course, I receive no financial benefit from LivingWorks as I teach the course on a voluntary basis to military veterans.

The reassuring part of learning of his wish to die was that he was the one who told me unprompted. He understood the implication of telling me he was suicidal. It is standard protocol for the Department of Veterans Affairs (VA) to ask if the patient is thinking about killing himself or herself, regardless of what the contact with the patient is about. My client was asking for help because the part of him that wanted to continue living was winning the battle. From that moment on, each time we met, I would check in with him about his suicidal thoughts and behaviors. Over the following weeks, my client completed the mandated substance use program; I connected him with the VA Post-9/11 Military to VA team (Post-9/11 M2VA Case Management Program), and he was able to secure a job.

The challenge when working with populations with multiple needs is how systemic barriers always pull them back to the hellhole they have been struggling to escape. Although my client was thriving in his new job, he was about to be fired because he could not get a security badge and ID for his job, and not for lack of agency or trying. The issue was that to get to the office where the badges were made, he needed to pass a security checkpoint that required identification. His identification documents were stolen when he was homeless.

To be an advocate for the people you work with does not mean you need to know all the answers, but that instead you are willing and ready to work with them to figure it out. When my client called in crisis the day before the deadline, I knew it was one of those times when we needed to quickly figure something out. I reached out to a colleague at the Department of Veterans Affairs who helped us expedite the process for the client to get a veteran ID. The only problem was that the "expedited" delivery of the document was going to arrive 2 weeks too late. Although we were not able to get an ID, the VA was able to provide my client with a memo, like the temporary IDs you get from the Division of Motor Vehicles while you wait for the real document. With the memo, my client was able to get through security, get his badge, and keep his job.

As you develop as counselors, I encourage you to be intentional about growing the therapeutic relationship, to be the advocate they know would support them as they navigate their issues, and while these systemic hurdles remain, to be an agent of change.

A Call to Action

While many clients will enter counseling with previous counseling experience, some clients will seek counseling for the first times in their lives. Some clients may be nervous about seeking help, as a result of not knowing what to expect. You can serve an important role in helping clients to learn more about what counseling is, what they can expect from counseling, and you can provide information that can help a client to know how to select a counselor.

Individually, or with a partner, create a flyer, poster, or pamphlet that includes information about what counseling is. Your knowledge about counseling can help clients to feel more confident and comfortable about entering counseling.

- List two to three questions that a client might want to ask a counselor before their first session.
- Based on what you have read so far about counseling theories and types of interventions, which one are you most drawn to? Write a brief summary of your philosophy of counseling, describe your theoretical orientation and potential areas of specialization. Remember, in this space, it is okay to speak from your future voice as a practicing counselor, either in practicum, internship, or post-graduation from your counseling program (i.e., summarize your approach to counseling, your theoretical orientation, and what you believe your areas of specialization will be after graduation. These may change over time and that is okay).

- List at least two mental health advocacy organizations in your area. It can be helpful to add two additional organizations that serve the client population that you hope to work with.
- List crisis response resource agencies (i.e., suicide prevention hotline/text line in your area or national, domestic violence helpline, housing crisis intake location, homeless youth hotline, or similar organizations).

Please remember to decorate and share your brochure or flyer (i.e., distributed as a printed resource, virtually to your social media channels, or within social spaces that you are a part of).

Case Study 6.1

Sam (they/them pronouns) is a 19-year-old, biracial, nonbinary client who identifies as pansexual and came to see you at the college counseling center where you are doing an advanced practicum. They report feelings of anxiety and depression, difficulty with academic tasks, and struggling with current classes. Their emotional issues and symptoms have been going on since high school. Sam saw a school counselor briefly during their senior year of high school and has not sought counseling since. During the intake process, they report a recent breakup from a 1-year long relationship. This breakup has made Sam feel "bummed out and irritable." Their primary coping mechanism is vaping cannabis and playing video games. Sam realizes they have been using cannabis more than usual in the past 3 months and this has resulted in lower academic performance and social withdrawal and isolation. Sam knows that something has to change but is not yet ready to give up vaping. They decided to come to the counseling center for help after their roommate encouraged them to seek support.

RESPONSE QUESTIONS

1. What questions would you want to ask Sam to better understand their presenting problem?
2. How would you help Sam determine what the goals of therapy could be?
3. What theoretical orientation would you choose to begin helping Sam with their issues?
4. What social or contextual issues would you want to explore with Sam to get a comprehensive picture of their concerns?
5. How would you approach counseling Sam about their relationship breakup and reported cannabis use? Would you want to explore anything else about their identities?

Going Within: The Fallout Shelter

This exercise will be completed individually and then in pairs. Each student will spend 15 minutes reviewing the instructions. After 15 minutes, the class will be divided in pairs and students will compare their selections and discuss the rationale for each. After 30 minutes, students will report back to the class and everyone will discuss their choices.

Instructions: The end of civilization as we know it is at hand. You are leading a special task force assigned to choose six (6) civilians to join a government-owned fallout shelter burrowed deeply in the earth, somewhere in a desert land. You have 15 minutes to decide who will be allowed entrance. All others will perish. Make your selections and prepare to discuss them with a colleague who has been tasked to do the same. After 15 minutes, you will both discuss your choices and rationale. You must have 100% consensus on your choices. The goal is to retain individuals who could assist in rebuilding the planet, 10 years thence.

The people:

- A 42-year-old male violinist. A drug pusher
- A 38-year-old trans woman. Former prostitute and IV drug user; sober for 5 years
- A 17-year-old pregnant high school dropout, low IQ
- A 22-year-old Black male militant, no special skills
- A 48-year-old female physician, cannot bear children
- A 69-year-old rabbi
- A 37-year-old ex-cop with a gun, thrown off the force for police brutality
- A 30-year-old law student, married
- A 29-year-old wife of the law student, recently discharged from a psychiatric hospital where she spent the last 6 months. She is heavily sedated. They refuse to be separated.
- A 45-year-old gay male architect

What did you learn about yourself and your values? What did you learn about the values of your peers? What was the most difficult decision you had to make and why? Did you change your mind at any point during the discussion? Why or why not? Can you determine one or more theoretical frameworks that may help explain the thoughts and feelings you had while reflecting and deciding your choices? In what ways do the tenets of the theories you chose apply to this exercise?

Group Process: Four Psychological Approaches
Class Exercise

Note: This exercise was conceptualized and designed by Brubaker et al. (2010) and is based on the four approaches conceptualized by Prilleltensky (1997). Used with permission.

You will need:

- Four pages labeled with the Families of Theories (A, P, Q, and C)
- Clear space in the classroom where students can align

- Every student will review the theory family and their descriptions
- Every student will then choose the theoretical family they think most closely aligns with their own beliefs and values

Family A

The main focus of these approaches is on personal adjustment. In these cases, there is a problem with the thoughts, feelings, or behavior of an individual. After diagnosing the problem, the therapist will use proven interventions to help the client adjust to troubling circumstances. These approaches largely assume that a good life consists primarily of self-enhancement, values caring and compassion, and promotes self-determination.

Family P

These approaches focus on vulnerable individuals and communities helping them to gain greater control over their lives, thereby reducing domination from oppressive forces. Problems are viewed within social systems and environmental influences, rather than within individuals. Focusing on personal power, the therapist will encourage clients to become experts in their own lives by gaining new knowledge and skills. These approaches assume that the good life is achieved through the attainment of personal and collective power.

Family Q

The main focus of these approaches is to question the dominant social discourse, which suggests a single "correct" answer, and allows clients the freedom to realize their own "truths." Problems are socially constructed and are not even necessarily related to the solution. A therapist may have a client use language to describe a problem on their own terms (e.g. "the crud" instead of "depression") or even ignore the need for naming a problem at all. Collaboratively, the client and counselor seek creative and innovative resolutions together. The good life is achieved through the development of one's own identity.

Family C

These approaches promote shared power and resources in society and suggest that all have responsibility toward one another as a part of a larger community. Problems are defined largely in terms of interpersonal and social oppression. Mental "illness" is primarily, but not solely, caused by forces external to the individual. Although the cause may be external, counselors encourage the oppressed individual and community to take responsibility to improve their own lives while respecting the rights of others. The good life is defined in terms of mutuality, social obligations, and the removal of oppression.

WHICH DO YOU MOST CLOSELY ALIGN WITH?

Clear out the floor space and position four stations to represent the approaches as follows:

-

-   -

Family P   Family C

-   -

-                  Family A   -

-   -

-                  -

Family Q

Have students line up with the family they most associate with. You may take positions between points to indicate multiple alignments.

Use the following discussion questions and integrate movement when possible:

1. What about these approaches appeal to you as a counselor? (Note distances toward and away from other approaches.)
2. How do these approaches relate to your personal values and beliefs?
3. What personal experiences have affected your values and beliefs? (You may have a person show how their theory would have been different at an earlier time.)
4. How might your experiences, values, and beliefs be similar to or different from your clients?
5. How might these differences or similarities impact your theory choice?

As you reflect on your choices during this exercise, keep in mind that you will continue to learn about counseling theories, approaches, and techniques throughout your educational journey. You will take required courses, continue to explore your beliefs and values, complete practicum and internship, and enter the world of professional counseling practice after you graduate. Keep an open mind and heart and remain flexible, curious, and culturally humble.

RESOURCES

Cognitive-Behavioral Therapy

Beck Institute: https://beckinstitute.org

CBT Techniques and Worksheets: https://positivepsychology.com/cbt-cognitive-behavioral-therapy-techniques-worksheets

CBT Worksheets and Resources: https://www.psychologytools.com/downloads/cbt-worksheets-and-therapy-resources

Ellis Institute: https://albertellis.org

The CBT Clinic (n.d.). Pros and cons of CBT. http://www.thecbtclinic.com/pros-cons-of-cbt-therapy

Constructivist

Good Therapy. (n.d.). Constructivism. https://www.goodtherapy.org/learn-about-therapy/types/constructivism

Granvold, D. K. (1996). Constructivist psychotherapy. Families in Society, 77(6), 345–359. https://doi.org/10.1606/1044-3894.932

Mahoney, M. J., & Granvold, D. K. (2005). Constructivism and psychotherapy. World Psychiatry,4(2), 74–77. http://www.ncbi.nlm.nih.gov/pmc/articles/PMC1414735

Neimeyer, R.A., & Bridges, S. (2004, February 15). Personal construct theory. In The internet encyclopaedia of personal construct psychology. http://www.pcp-net.org/encyclopaedia/pc-theory.html

Raskin, J. D. (2002). Constructivism in psychology: Personal construct psychology, radical constructivism, and social constructionism. American Communication Journal, 5(3), 1–26. https://faculty.newpaltz.edu/jonathanraskin/files/Raskin-2002-ACJ-reprint-updated-appendix.pdf

Feminist Therapy

Brown, L. S. (2018). Feminist therapy (2nd ed.). American Psychological Association.

Brown, L. S. (1994). Feminist therapy. American Psychological Association. Psychotherapy Video Series.

Pitts, C., & Kawahara, D. M. (2017). Radical visionaries—Feminist psychotherapists: 1970–1975. Women & Therapy, 40(3-4), 256–259. https://doi.org/10.1080/02703149.2017.1241558

Gestalt Therapy

Gestalt Therapy Books: https://www.goodreads.com/shelf/show/gestalt-therapy

Perls, F., Hefferline, R., & Goodman, P. (1951). Gestalt therapy: Excitement and growth in the human personality. Profile Books.

Integrative-Eclectic Therapy

Beutler, L. E., Consoli, A. J., & Lane, G. (2005). Systematic treatment selection and prescriptive psychotherapy: An integrative eclectic approach. In J. C.

Norcross & M. R. Goldfried (Eds.), Handbook of psychotherapy integration (2nd ed., pp. 121–143). Oxford University Press.

Brooks-Harris, J. E. (2008). Integrative multitheoretical psychotherapy. Houghton Mifflin.

Castonguay, L. G., Newman, M. G., Borkovec, T. D., Holtforth, M. G., & Maramba, G. G. (2005).Cognitive-behavioral assimilative integration. In J. C. Norcross & M. R. Goldfried (Eds.), Handbook of psychotherapy integration (2nd ed., pp. 241–260). Oxford University Press.

Frank, J. D., & Frank, J. B. (1991). Persuasion and healing: A comparative study of psychotherapy (3rd ed.). Johns Hopkins University.

Good, G. E., & Beitman, B. D. (2006). Counseling and psychotherapy essentials: Integrating theories, skills, and practices. W. W. Norton.

Moderation Management

Guide to moderation management steps of change: https://moderation.org/wp-content/uploads/2020/05/Guide-to-Moderation-Management-Steps-of-Change.pdf

Moderation management (2022). https://moderation.org/getting-started-moderation-management/moderation-steps-of-change

Multicultural Social Justice and Diversity Theories and Applications

Leong, T. L., Comas-Diaz, L., Nagayama Hall, G., McLoyd, V., & Trimble, J. (Eds.), The handbook of multicultural psychology, Vol. 1: Theory and research. American Psychological Association.

Leong, T. L., Comas-Diaz, L., Nagayama Hall, G., McLoyd, V., & Trimble J. (Eds.), The handbook of multicultural psychology, Vol. 2: Applications and Training. American Psychological Association.

Fukuyama, M. A., & Puig, A. (2016). Religion, spirituality and culture-oriented counseling. In P. B. Pedersen, W. J. Lonner, J. G. Draguns, J. E. Trimble, & M. R. Scharrón del Río (Eds.), Counseling across cultures: Toward inclusive cultural empathy (7th ed., pp. 477–498). Sage.

Fukuyama, M. A., Puig, A., Baggs, A., & Pence-Wolf, C. (2014). Exploring the intersections of religion and spirituality with race-ethnicity & gender in counseling. In M. L. Miville, & A. D. Ferguson (Eds.), Handbook of race-ethnicity and gender in psychology (pp. 23–44). Springer.

Fukuyama, M. A., Puig, A., Pence-Wolf, C., & Baggs, A. (2014). Religion and spirituality. In T. L. Leong, L. Comas-Diaz, G. Nagayama Hall, V. McLoyd, & J. Trimble (Eds.), The handbook of multicultural psychology, Vol. 1: Theory and research (pp. 519–534). American Psychological Association. https://doi.org/10.1037/14189-028

Lenes, E., Baggs, A., & Puig, A. (2016). Multicultural supervision training: A creative and mindful exploration of spiritual diversity. In M. Luke & K. M. Goodrich (Eds.), Group work experts share their favorite activities for supervision (Vol. 2, pp. 197–204). Association for Specialists in Group Work.

Parker, W. M. & Fukuyama, M. A. (2007). Consciousness raising: A primer for multicultural counseling (3rd ed.). Charles C Thomas Publisher.

Puig, A., & Adams, C. M. (2007). Introducing spirituality into multicultural counseling. In W. M. Parker & M. A. Fukuyama (Eds.), Consciousness raising: A primer for multicultural counseling (3rd ed., pp. 181–203). Charles C Thomas Publisher.

Sanabria, S., & Puig, A. (2012). Counseling Latin gays and lesbians. In S. H. Dworkin & M. Pope (Eds.), Case studies in lesbian, gay, bisexual and transgender counseling (pp. 185–195). American Counseling Association.

Narrative Therapy

Ackerman, C. E. (2022). 19 best narrative therapy techniques & worksheets. https://positivepsychology.com/narrative-therapy

Narrative Therapy Centre: https://narrativetherapycentre.com/about

Narrative therapy resources: http://www.narrativeapproaches.com/resources

White, M. & Epston, D. (1990). Narrative eans to therapeutic ends. W. W. Norton.

White, M. (2007). Maps of narrative practice. W. W. Norton.

Person-Centered

Course Hero. (n.d.). Humanistic and person-centered therapy. https://www.coursehero.com/study-guides/hvcc-abnormalpsychology/humanistic-and-person-centered-therapy

Lumen Learning (n.d.). Humanistic and Person-Centered Therapy. Retrieved from https://courses.lumenlearning.com/hvcc-abnormalpsychology/chapter/humanistic-and-person-centered-therapy

Smith, E. (2019). What are the advantages of Person-Centered Therapy? HealthyPlace. https://www.healthyplace.com/other-info/mental-illness-overview/what-are-the-advantages-of-person-centered-therapy

Positive Psychology

Snyder, C. R., Lopez, S. J., Edwards, L. M., & Marques, S. C. (2021). The Oxford handbook of positive psychology (3rd ed.). Oxford University Press.

Postmodern Therapy

Butler, C. (2002). Postmodernism: A very short introduction. Oxford University Press.

Institute for Solution-Focused Therapy: https://solutionfocused.net

Psychodynamic and Psychoanalytic Therapy

American Psychoanalytic Association: https://apsa.org/about-psychoanalysis

Relational-Cultural Therapy

Jean Baker Miller Training Institute: https://www.wcwonline.org/JBMTI-Site/relational-cultural-theory

Miller, J. B. (2012). Toward a new psychology of women (2nd ed.). Beacon Press.

Miller, J. B., & Stiver, I. P. (1997). The healing connection: How women form relationships in therapy and in life. Beacon Press.

Transtheoretical Approach

Prochaska, J. O., & Norcross, J. C. (2003) . Systems of psychotherapy: A transtheoretical analysis (5th ed.). Brooks/Cole.

Friedman, H. (2014). Finding meaning through transpersonal approaches in clinical psychology: Assessments and psychotherapies. *International Journal of Existential Psychology and Psychotherapy, 5*(1), 45–49.

 Access this podcast at https://connect.springerpub.com/content/book/978-0-8261-6386-8/chapter/ch06.

KEY REFERENCES

Only key references appear in the print edition. The full reference list appears in the digital product found on https://connect.springerpub.com/content/book/978-0-8261-6386-8/chapter/ch06

Beck, A. (1979). *Cognitive therapy and the emotional disorders*. Penguin.

Davis, D. E., DeBlaere, C., Owen, J., Hook, J. N., Rivera, D. P., Choe, E., Van Tongeren, D. R., Worthington, E. L., & Placeres, V. (2018). The multicultural orientation framework: A narrative review. *Psychotherapy, 55*(1), 89–100. https://doi.org/10.1037/pst0000160

DeBord, K. A., Fischer, A. R., Bieschke, K. J., & Perez, R. M. (2016). *Handbook of sexual orientation and gender diversity in counseling and psychotherapy*. American Counseling Association.

Ellis, A. (1962). *Reason and emotion in psychotherapy*. Lyle Stuart.

Frankl, V. E. (1969). *The will to meaning*. World Publishing Company.

Fuertes, J. N., & Gretchen, D. (2001). Emerging theories of multicultural counseling. In J. G. Ponterotto, J. M. Casas, L. A. Suzuki, & C. M. Alexander (Eds.), *Handbook of multicultural counseling* (pp. 509–541). Sage Publications.

Fulmer, R. (2018). The evolution of the psychodynamic approach and system. *International Journal of Psychological Studies, 10*(3), 1–6. https://doi.org/10.5539/ijps.v10n3p1

Gilligan, C. (1982). *In a different voice: Psychological theory and women's development*. Harvard University Press.

Jordan, J. (2010). *Relational-cultural theory*. American Psychological Association.

Kaufman, A. (2012). Theories of distributive justice. In R. Chadwick (Ed.), *Encyclopedia of applied ethics* (2nd ed., pp. 842–850). Academic Press. https://doi.org/org/10.1016/B978-0-12-373932-2.00227-1

Meichenbaum, D. (1977). *Cognitive behavior modification: An integrative approach*. Plenum Press.

Ponterotto, J. G., Casas, J. M., Suzuki, L. A., & Alexander, C. M. (Eds.). (2010). *Handbook of multicultural counseling*. Sage.

Prilleltensky, I. (1996). Human, moral, and political values for an emancipatory psychology. *Humanistic Psychologist, 24*(3), 307–324. https://doi.org/10.1080/08873267.1996.9986859

Prilleltensky, I. (1997). Values, assumptions, and practices: Assessing the moral implications of psychological discourse and action. *The American Psychologist, 52*(5), 517–535. https://doi.org/10.1037//0003-066x.52.5.517

Prilleltensky, I. (2001). Value-based praxis in community psychology: Moving toward social justice and social action. *American Journal of Community Psychology, 29*(5), 747–778. https://doi.org/10.1023/A:1010417201918

Prochaska, J. O., & Norcross, J. C. (2003). *Systems of psychotherapy: A transtheoretical analysis* (5th ed.). Brooks/Cole.

Shapiro, F. (2001). *Eye movement desensitization and reprocessing: Basic principles, protocols, and procedures* (2nd ed.). Guilford Press.

Sue, D. W., & Sue, D. (2013). *Counseling the culturally different: Theory and practice* (6th ed.). John Wiley and Sons.

Yalom, I. (1980). *Existential psychotherapy*. Basic Books.

CHAPTER 7

AN INTRODUCTION TO COUNSELING SETTINGS

Jacqueline M. Swank

Think about this...

Where do counselors work? How has counseling evolved in various settings? What type of setting do you see yourself working in as a future counselor? Why are you interested in working in this particular setting?

LEARNING OBJECTIVES

After reading this chapter, you should be able to:

- Outline the history and evolution of counseling within various settings
- Identify organizations that represent counselors and counseling practice areas
- Explain the aspects of counseling within various work environments
- Discuss social justice and advocacy considerations within various counseling settings

INTRODUCTION

Have you thought about what setting you want to work in as a future counselor? Counselors work with clients across the lifespan in a variety of settings. This chapter focuses on discussing many counseling settings. Although it is impossible to discuss every possible environment that counselors may work in, this chapter provides an overview of several settings. This includes private and public settings that provide varying levels of mental health services to clients. The continuum of care ranges from the least restrictive setting (i.e., outpatient) to the most intensive services that include inpatient and residential treatment. There are also other levels of care across the continuum, including intensive outpatient services and day treatment. In the sections that follow, the author discusses a variety of counseling settings. These settings include:

- Medical clinics and hospitals
- Correctional and forensic facilities
- Group homes, assisted living facilities, and nursing homes
- Community agencies
- Private practice
- Military and government
- Employee assistance programs (EAP)
- Religious institutions
- Rehabilitation facilities
- Colleges and universities
- Preschools and elementary, middle, and high schools
- Rural settings

For each setting, the author will provide an overview of the history, professional organizations for counselors working with the specialized population, and aspects of counseling provided within the various environments. The chapter will also include a focus on social justice and advocacy considerations for the various settings.

MEDICAL CLINICS AND HOSPITALS

The first psychiatric hospital, the Institute of the Pennsylvania Hospital, started in 1752 as part of a medical hospital. Other early facilities for individuals with mental illness included Bloomingdale Hospital in New York (1791) and McLean Hospital in Massachusetts (1818) (Geller, 2006). The first psychiatric hospitals were private facilities and had good intentions for the care and treatment of individuals with mental illness. This included moral therapy that involved tailored treatment for patients, including exercise and activities related to their interest. However, as the population increased, a need arose for large, state-funded facilities, which evolved into places that housed patients instead of treating them, due to overcrowding and lack of resources to meet patient needs. Conditions worsened and patients often resided long-term in these asylums (Tartakovsky, 2011, February 17). In 1843, Dorothea Dix wrote to the Massachusetts legislature about the inhumane conditions of the asylums. She reported hospital personnel kept patients in cages and closets, and the patients were naked, chained, and beaten. Her advocacy was the beginning of a movement to change the treatment of patients in asylums (Gollaher, 1993).

From the 1920s to the 1970s, there was a movement to deinstitutionalize mental health treatment by decreasing the number of patients in state-run inpatient psychiatric hospitals. The number of veterans' hospitals increased in the 1930s and 1940s and general hospitals took a greater role in providing mental health treatment in the 1960s through the presence of psychiatric units (Geller, 2006). Additionally, psychopharmacology became a focus of treatment in the 1950s (Geller, 2006). The number of patients within state-run inpatient facilities continued to decline from the 1970s to 2000, while the number of private facilities increased. There was also a trend for a shorter length of stay within hospitals (Geller, 2006).

In the 21st century, there remains a focus on short inpatient psychiatric hospitals stays as the cost for inpatient mental health treatment increases. Although legislation has supported deinstitutionalization, and the number of community mental health facilities has increased, the process of returning people with mental illness to the community has not been flawless. The need for community mental health is greater than available services at times, which leaves people without necessary treatment. Lack of adequate residential facilities has also led to increased homelessness of people with severe mental illness. Thus, a need exists for continued advocacy for expanding mental health services and addressing disparities in care. There also remains a need to address stigma related to mental illness by educating the general public.

Counselors working in a psychiatric hospital typically provide counseling within a medical model framework overseen by psychiatrists and driven by a mental health diagnosis. Within an inpatient crisis stabilization unit, clients typically stay 72 hours or less; however, clients may have a longer length of stay if needed for stabilization. Clients are in this level of care because they are suicidal, homicidal, or exhibiting psychosis and are a threat to themselves or others. Within this setting, counselors focus on crisis counseling and stabilization and they may meet with a client for multiple hours during a single day. Counselors work closely with the treatment team that typically includes a psychiatrist, psychiatric nurses, a case manager, recreational therapist possibly, and educational personnel for children and adolescents. The client and their family are also part of the treatment team. Counselors may provide individual, group, and family counseling and work with clients to contract for safety and develop discharge plans that involve less intensive mental health services at discharge, which may involve day treatment/partial hospitalization or outpatient therapy. The discharge planning process is crucial, as hospitalization may be traumatic for some clients, requiring trauma-sensitive follow-up care.

Counselors may also work within a long-term psychiatric hospital or residential treatment facility. Residential care provides an intensive level of treatment that is expensive. Although longer than 3 days that is typical of inpatient care, residential treatment is still usually time-limited, with an emphasis on transitioning to a less intensive and less expensive (from an insurance company's perspective) level of care (e.g., day treatment, outpatient) or alternative settings (e.g., group homes). Residential treatment may focus on a variety of mental health concerns (e.g., severe mental illness, eating disorders, alcohol or drug addictions). Some residential programs may follow a medical model, while others embrace other treatment approaches (e.g., wilderness therapy program). Residential treatment may follow inpatient hospitalization, but this is not always the case. Clients enter drug treatment facilities after they have undergone detox treatment, which involves ridding the body of the addictive substance. Detox generally involves medical staff to monitor individuals and provide care to manage withdrawal symptoms, as some withdrawal symptoms can be life threatening. Counselors working with clients in residential treatment

FIGURE 7.1 Continuum of care.

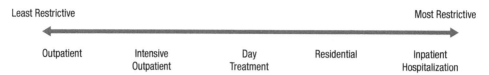

Least Restrictive   Most Restrictive

| Outpatient | Intensive Outpatient | Day Treatment | Residential | Inpatient Hospitalization |

settings may have sessions with clients daily or multiple times a week due to the intensive level of treatment.

Clients in a partial hospitalization or day treatment program receive intensive counseling services during the day, but they go home at night, instead of residing at the facility. They typically attend the program 5 days a week, with no attendance on the weekends. Partial hospitalization may serve as a step-down in treatment for clients who are in residential or inpatient crisis stabilization/hospitalization, or a step-up for clients in outpatient treatment to strive to prevent inpatient hospitalization or residential care. Clients in a partial hospitalization program typically receive daily group therapy, and individual and family therapy at least once a week if not more frequently. Children attending day treatment programs, as well as those in inpatient and residential treatment, receive educational services within the treatment facility. Figure 7.1 provides an illustration of the continuum of care, ranging from least restrictive to most restrictive treatment services.

Advocacy for social reform was crucial for instituting change to promote quality care and humane treatment of clients within psychiatric hospitals. Although significant changes have occurred across time, advocacy remains crucial today for clients in these settings, as well as counselors that work within them. Hospitalization is expensive; therefore, length of stays are short. However, each individual client has unique needs and concerns and counselors need to advocate for the services their clients need, as well as empower their clients and their families to advocate for themselves. Advocacy may involve talking with insurance companies to justify the need for continued treatment at the current or higher level of care. This can be a challenging and frustrating process; however, it is necessary to help ensure clients receive the appropriate level of care. Clients that are discharged from this level of care before they are ready may experience significant challenges that result in being hospitalized again within a short period after being discharged. This can be a traumatic experience for clients and create setbacks regarding progress in treatment, further emphasizing the importance of advocating for clients to receive the appropriate level of care.

CORRECTIONAL AND FORENSIC FACILITIES

In the 1960s, the deinstitutionalization of state psychiatric hospitals focused on returning individuals with mental illness to the community. However, due to lack of funding, there was insufficient community treatment to meet the needs of people with severe mental illness, leading to an increase in incarceration of this population (Kupers, 2015). Additionally, the War on Drugs, which began in the 1970s, imposed long sentences for drug-related crimes, including low-level offenses. Due to the comorbidity of substance use and mental illness, this movement to punish and curb drug use also led to the increase in incarcerations of individuals with mental illness (Kupers, 2015). Furthermore, the criteria for the criminal insanity plea changed, which also resulted in the incarceration of people with mental illness (Kupers, 2015). The increase in incarceration of this population is concerning because of the focus on punishment instead of treatment for mental illness. Incarcerated individuals with mental illness were often either isolated and warehoused, or integrated within the general prison population where they experienced abuse from other prisoners (Kupers, 2015). In both of these situations, there was a lack of treatment for this population.

The Supreme Court has heard cases related to alleged violations regarding the Eighth Amendment to the Constitution, which prohibits "cruel and unusual punishment." Specifically, the Supreme Court case of *Estelle v. Gamble* (1976) was important in the care of inmates, as the Court determined that prisoners must have access to medical care, which includes both physical and mental health care. Additionally, in 2011, the Supreme Court ruled in the case of *Brown v. Plata* (2011) that California had to release prisoners due to overcrowding that resulted in poor care, including mental health care. This led to the release of over 40,000 inmates. Thus, mental health services, in addition to physical healthcare, should be a priority within correctional facilities.

In the United States, the adult population incarcerated in 2018 was approximately 2.1 million, and there were nearly 4.4 million in community supervision (i.e., probation and parole; Maruschak & Minton, 2020). Specifically regarding mental health, 14% of adults incarcerated in prison and 26% in jails reported symptoms that met the criteria for serious psychological distress, and 37% and 44%, respectively, had been diagnosed with a mental health disorder in the past (Bronson & Berzofsky, 2017). Additionally, in 2017, there were 43,580 youth detained or committed in residential placements (Hockenberry, 2020). In examining mental health concerns of adjudicated youth, Shufelt and Cocozza (2006) found 70% met the criteria for one or more mental health diagnoses. Thus, a clear need exists for mental health services for individuals across the lifespan that are incarcerated, as well as those that are involved in the criminal justice system at other levels (i.e., probation and parole).

Correctional facilities may employ counselors directly, or contract with mental health agencies or counselors working in private practice. Counselors may provide a variety of services for incarcerated adults and youth. This includes initial screening and follow-up assessment as needed. Counselors may also provide individual, group, and sometimes family counseling. Furthermore, counselors may provide training for correctional officers and other personnel on a variety of mental health topics, including mental health concerns of individuals who are incarcerated, as well as self-care practices for staff. Understanding appropriate ways to respond to individuals with mental illness and those who have experienced trauma can be helpful for the staff in interacting with these individuals. This may include deescalation techniques that promote the safety of the individual who is escalated, other individuals who are incarcerated in the setting, and staff.

The International Association of Addictions and Offender Counselors (IAAOC), a division of the American Counseling Association (ACA), represents counselors working in criminal justice, as well as those working in addictions settings. They also advocate for best practices for treatment with these populations. The organization was formed in 1972 as the Public Offender Counselor Association (POCA). They changed the name to IAAOC in 1990 (IAAOC, n.d.). The journal for this organization is the *Journal of Addictions and Offender Counseling*.

In examining mental health treatment in correctional facilities, researchers identified 317 mental health units (MHUs) serving people with severe mental illness in a Google search, and 80% were located in prisons. Of these MHUs, 33% offered individual therapy, 53% group, and 23% both. Additionally, 53% had mental health staff and 24% provided correctional officers mental health training (Cohen et al., 2020). Regarding treatment outcomes for 5,180 inmates within 286 prisons, Nowotny (2015) found less than 50% of inmates with substance use concerns received treatment. Additionally, Latinos were less likely to receive treatment than White inmates were, but there was not a disparity found between White and Black inmates. The low level of treatment utilization is concerning because addiction is the most significant factor for recidivism and rearrests (Nowotny, 2015). Furthermore, researchers found that more than half of individuals receiving medication for mental health concerns did not receive medication during incarceration (Reingle Gonzalez & Connell, 2014). Low rates of treatment are also concerning because this may affect the safety and well-being of all inmates and facility personnel, as well as the rehabilitation of inmates with mental illness.

Researchers also examined the provision of mental health services for juveniles in correctional facilities through a national survey of clinical staff ($N = 94$) and found 50% of the 73 reporting respondents indicated mandatory individual counseling, 83% reported mandatory group counseling, and 29% reported mandatory family counseling (Swank & Gagnon, 2016). Additionally, regarding juvenile screenings and assessments, researchers found 98% reported their facilities conducted suicide screenings, and 97% conducted mental health screenings at admission. However, only 63% reported youth received an in-depth assessment and only 46% reported repeated youth screenings (Swank & Gagnon, 2017). Furthermore, within juvenile facilities, less than 60% of facilities reported training on various mental health topics, adolescent development, behavioral approaches, and self-care for facility staff who were not mental health personnel (nurses, administrators, correctional officers, and teachers), except for suicidality (approximately 70%) and physical/sexual abuse for nurses and administrators (about 62%; Gagnon & Swank, 2020). Thus, a need exists for trained clinical staff to provide mental health treatment in correctional facilities.

The prevalence of mental illness among individuals who are incarcerated demonstrates the importance of examining how we provide mental health care to individuals with severe mental illness in the United States. Kupers (2015) advocates for the integration of a community mental health model within correctional facilities that has 12 key components (see Table 7.1). In regard to these recommendations, it is crucial that screening involves assessing for suicide risk and that in-depth assessment follows screening when needed to guide treatment in correctional facilities. Additionally, screening and assessment need to be ongoing. Training topics may include recognizing mental health concerns

TABLE 7.1 COMPONENTS OF A COMMUNITY MENTAL HEALTH MODEL WITHIN CORRECTIONAL FACILITIES

Screening for mental health concerns
Access to treatment
Privacy and confidentiality
Sufficient personnel
Various levels of care (e.g., crisis intervention, inpatient, outpatient)
Documentation
Various therapeutic modalities
Communication between custodial, medical, and mental health staff
Staff training
Informed consent
Case management
Various rehabilitation programs

Source: Data from Kupers, T. A. (2015). A community mental health model in corrections. *Stanford Law & Policy Review*, *26*(1), 119–158.

and nonpunitive, therapeutic strategies for working with individuals with mental illness, including deescalating situations. Improving care within correctional facilities also involves reducing the incarceration rate of individuals with mental illness by emphasizing prevention through community-based care as well as diversion programs.

GROUP HOMES, ASSISTED LIVING FACILITIES, AND NURSING HOMES

A variety of housing options offer an alternative to institutionalization for people with severe mental illness, providing them support while affording housing in the community. A group home may include a house with multiple shared or private bedrooms, or shared or private apartments within a complex for residents. Staff assist individuals with living tasks (meals, cleaning) and treatment management, including help with medication, while promoting independence (Mental Health America [MHA], n.d.). Clients may receive counseling in the home or through outpatient services, as well as have access to crisis counseling. They may also receive job training. Clients are also able to provide peer support to each other. Availability of group homes may help clients maintain independence with support, and reduce the risk of homelessness, incarceration, and the need for more intensive mental health services.

Assisted living facilities and nursing homes provide another alternative to psychiatric hospitalization. However, in contrast to group homes, these facilities are more structured and often do not promote independence (MHA, n.d.). Staff are responsible for meeting many of the basic needs of clients in these facilities (e.g., preparing meals, washing and drying clothes), instead of assisting clients in completing these tasks. These facilities may not employ counselors, and instead, clients may receive counseling from counselors contracted through the facility, or offered by other outpatient counseling settings.

An important area of advocacy regarding group homes for people with mental illness is addressing the stigma of this population among the public. Community members may not want a group home for individuals with severe mental illness in their neighborhood. Additionally, residents in assisted living facilities and nursing homes who are not experiencing severe mental illness, and their family members, may also have negative views about this population living in these facilities. Stigma may relate to fears stemmed by misconceptions about people with mental illness. Providing education and opportunities to disprove myths can be valuable for advancing understanding and acceptance of this population. Atterbury and Rowe (2017) emphasize the importance of viewing people with mental illness living within the community as citizens of the United States with the rights and responsibilities of citizenship, instead of constantly perceiving them as clients or patients. This perspective focuses on social inclusion and engagement through integration of this population within the community (Atterbury & Rowe, 2017). By embracing this citizenship model, people with mental illness are empowered to perceive themselves as members of society and to advocate, along with counselors, for their rights as citizens, while advocating against segregation.

COMMUNITY AGENCIES

The Community Mental Health Act of 1963 focused on the development of community mental health centers. The deinstitutionalization plan began well, with this legislation providing federal funding to build facilities, as well as a focus on prevention and community partnerships. However, budget cuts led to difficulty sustaining these initiatives (Kupers, 2015), creating concerns regarding mental health treatment for people with mental illness. Funding has continued to ebb and flow over the years, creating challenges in providing quality mental health services for individuals experiencing mental health concerns.

Community mental health centers may include public and private agencies that serve clients across the lifespan or focus on a specific client population, such as children and adolescents or adults. Additionally, they may serve clients with a variety of mental health concerns or focus primarily on a specific area (e.g., substance use). Counselors providing outpatient counseling in an agency will typically have one session a week with clients, generally lasting 50 to 60 minutes; however, they may see some clients more or less frequently (intensive outpatient counseling) depending on the clients' needs. Regarding location, counselors may have sessions within the agency, see clients in their homes, or have sessions in other locations (e.g., schools or childcare centers for child

TABLE 7.2 ADVANTAGES AND DISADVANTAGES OF WORKING IN COMMUNITY AGENCIES

ADVANTAGES	CHALLENGES
■ Salary ■ Benefits—health insurance, retirement, paid vacation time ■ Not responsible for marketing or recruiting clients ■ Most work hours focus on counseling sessions and documentation ■ Paid professional leave time or pay for professional development ■ Complementary supervision for licensure and consultation networks for discussing cases ■ Staff responsible for billing insurance companies and collecting payments for services ■ May have staff to schedule sessions and answer the phone	■ Required minimum number of billable hours, which can be stressful to reach with client cancellations and no-shows ■ Established work hours ■ Clients assigned by supervisor ■ May share counseling or office space with other counselors ■ Established location ■ May be required to travel to other locations, such as clients' homes or schools

clients). Agencies may also have contracts with other organizations. For example, an agency may have a contract with a school district and counselors working at the agency may have offices and provides services at assigned schools, but the agency employs the counselor, not the school district. Counselors working in community agencies might choose to be members of the American Mental Health Counselors Association (AMHCA), an organization focused on advancing clinical mental health counseling. The organization was founded in 1976, and the organization started the *AMHCA Journal* in 1979, which is now the *Journal of Mental Health Counseling* (AMHCA, 2010).

As with any setting, there are advantages and disadvantages of working in a community agency (see Table 7.2). Regarding advocacy, counselors working in a community agency may need to advocate for the length of treatment with insurance companies, as insurance providers may only approve a specified number of counseling sessions. This may involve communicating directly with insurance providers to discuss client progress and the need for continued treatment. It is important that counselors are aware that insurance companies also employ mental health providers; therefore, they will have knowledge of mental health concerns and treatment approaches. Thus, counselors should be prepared to articulate the rationale for the level of care, treatment goals and objectives, and progress or lack of progress to advocate for additional treatment sessions when needed. Counselor may also need to engage in self-advocacy regarding work conditions, such as the minimum number of billable hours required by the agency and confounding factors (i.e., client cancellations and no-shows).

PRIVATE PRACTICE

Private practice is a diverse counseling area. Harrington (2013) reports that counselors working in private practice may work independently on their own, or work within a group practice with other clinicians. They may also have a practice situated within a different type of organization (e.g., physician's office, religious organization). Additionally, counselors may work full-time in private practice or work primarily in another setting (e.g., academia, schools, agencies) and see a few clients in private practice. Counselors may also contract with other organizations or companies (e.g., EAP, correctional facilities). Furthermore, they may provide consultation, coaching, and other specialized services within their practice. Due to the diversity of private practice, it is nearly impossible to get an accurate count of the number of counselors working in this type of setting.

There is not an organization known to this author that is dedicated specifically to counselors working in private practice. However, AMHCA focuses on the advancement of clinical mental health counseling. Therefore, counselors working in private practice may align with this organization. Counselors may also align with organizations that focus on their counseling specialty areas.

Counselors may choose to work in private practice for a variety of reasons. Advantages to working in this setting include the counselor's freedom and autonomy regarding making decisions about the practice. However, counselors in private practice also experience challenges, with one of the biggest challenges related to being responsible for the financial costs. In private practice, counselors must allocate time for running the business, or hire people to do various tasks related to it. Additionally, they may decide to apply to be a provider for insurance companies (i.e., managed care provider), or decide that they will not take insurance and only offer direct pay services. Similar to making decisions about other aspects of their practice, there are advantages and disadvantages to being a managed care provider. Although this may help with marketing and recruitment of clients, processing insurance claims takes time that may require hiring personnel or allocating the counselor's time to this task. Thus, counselors have several factors to consider in making a decision about having a private practice. See Table 7.3 for additional advantages and challenges of working in private practice.

The freedom and flexibility with private practice may seem desirable for many counselors. However, it is important to remember that professional freedom is associated with professional responsibilities (Brennan, 2013). Specifically, counselors working in private practice, especially sole practice, might be isolated from other practitioners. It is crucial that within this setting, counselors have a network that facilitates consultation (discussing client cases, ethical dilemmas) when necessary, as all counselors experience challenging cases that they need to consult with others about to provide quality, ethical counseling services for clients.

Counselors working in private practice may engage in social justice by offering some pro bono (free) counseling services or provide counseling to clients at a reduced rate, when clients are unable to afford services. This may present a challenge for counselors, as their private practice might be their sole income. Therefore, counselors want to consider the number of clients they can

TABLE 7.3 ADVANTAGES AND DISADVANTAGES OF WORKING IN PRIVATE PRACTICE

ADVANTAGES	CHALLENGES
▪ Be your own boss ▪ Decide days and hours for seeing clients ▪ Select location and freedom to personalize space ▪ Set fees ▪ Work with clients in a specialization area	▪ Overhead costs—purchase or rent space, utilities, furniture, insurance, equipment, cleaning, accounting services ▪ No employer benefits, such as health insurance and retirement ▪ Allocate time or hire personnel to process payment for services ▪ Marketing and recruitment responsibility and costs ▪ Isolated from other counselors if sole practice

Source: Data from Harrington, J. A. (2013). Contemporary issues in private practice: Spotlight on the self-employed mental health counselor. *Journal of Mental Health Counseling, 35*(3), 189–197. https://doi.org/10.17744/mehc.35.3.8742717176154187

realistically offer services to for free or at a reduced rate. Counselors may also establish partnerships with organizations or apply for grants to provide counseling for clients that are underserved. Thus, counselors manage multiple areas in starting and maintaining a private practice.

MILITARY AND GOVERNMENT

A critical need exists for providing mental health services for military personnel. The National Council for Behavioral Health (n.d.) reported that of the military personnel deployed in Iraq and Afghanistan, 30% (approximately 730,000) meet the criteria for a mental health concern necessitating treatment. Additionally, on average, 16.8 veterans die daily by suicide (U.S. Department of Veterans Affairs, 2019).

In the United States, the Veterans Health Administration is the largest employer of mental health providers (Pollack, 2019); however, counselors were not eligible for employment through the U.S. Department of Veterans Affairs (VA) until 2010 when Congress recognized them as a category of providers within the Veterans Benefits, Health Care, and Information Technology Act (2006). This recognition and eligibility became a reality after strong advocacy by counselors and counseling organizations; however, integration of counselors within the VA remained limited until April 2018 when the VA issued new qualifications standards that allowed counselors to fully practice within the VA, including employment in supervisor and coordinator positions (Pollack, 2019). This was a significant step for counselors, and it emphasizes the importance of advocacy for the profession. Advocacy for mental health care for veterans, as well as advocacy for counselors to serve this population remains important.

The Military and Government Counseling Association (MGCA) is the division of ACA focused on providing services to individuals in the military, as well as those employed by government agencies, and their families. The organization began as the Military Educators and Counselors Association (MECA) in 1978. They changed the name to the Association for Counselors and Educators in Government in 1994 to encompass counselors working with governmental employees. Then, in 2015, they changed the organization name to MGCA to encompass counselors working with the growing number of military personnel needing mental health services (MGCA, n.d.). The organization publishes the *Journal of Military and Government Counseling*.

Counselors working specifically in the VA have the title of licensed professional mental health counselors (LPMHCs). They may work in a variety of mental health programs within the VA, including primary care clinics, mental health clinics, substance abuse programs, programs for homeless veterans, employment programs, inpatient facilities, residential facilities, rehabilitation programs, recovery centers, posttraumatic stress disorder (PTSD) programs, readjustment centers, suicide prevention services, and case management services (Pollack, 2019). Additionally, they may provide individual, group, and family counseling within these various program services. Counselors may also work with individuals employed by governmental agencies. This may include an EAP, discussed in the next section.

In working with military service personnel and their families, it is crucial for counselors to understand the military cultural. Counselors working with military personnel and their families may engage in advocacy and social justice work to reduce the stigma among this population related to seeking mental health services and educate them about the confidentiality of receiving mental health services. Advocacy is particularly important for marginalized groups within the military, including women, and LGBTQ+ populations. In regard to working with LGBTQ individuals in the military, Johnson et al. (2013) provide four recommendations for mental health clinicians: (a) adopt an affirmative stance, (b) develop competency in working with LGBTQ populations, (c) respect and support clients' wishes regarding decisions about disclosure, and (d) work with military leaders to promote a positive culture. Thus, counselors are aware of treatment considerations in working with marginalized groups of military and government personnel.

EMPLOYEE ASSISTANCE PROGRAMS

People experience a variety of stressors and concerns that may affect their work performance. An employee assistance program (EAP) is a work-based initiative offering counseling and other services (e.g., screening, assessment, short-term counseling, referrals) to address work and personal concerns that may affect job performance (Employee Assistance Professionals Association [EAPA], 2011). Employees' families may also be eligible for services. EAPs also provide consultation for management in addressing workplace challenges (EAPA, 2011).

Masi (2020) described the history of EAPs, which began with the provision of employee outreach services within companies at the beginning of the 20th century. These services were rooted in welfare capitalism and occupational social work (e.g., housing, school, medical care) to promote employee satisfaction and retention. Alcoholics Anonymous (AA), which began in 1935, also contributed to the development of EAPs by leading to the creation of occupational alcoholism programs, which started as AA meetings held within company facilities. Occupational alcoholism programs evolved across time and led to EAPs in the 1970s offering counseling to address a variety of personal and work concerns (Masi, 2020).

The largest organization for employee assistance professionals is the EAPA, which began in 1971 as the Association of Labor and Management Administrators and Consultants on Alcoholism (ALMACA). It became EAPA in 1989. The organization publishes the *Journal of Employee Assistance* (Employee Assistance Professionals Association, 2019). There are also various other organizations representing employee assistance professionals, including the Employee Assistance Society of North American (EASNA) started in 1985, the Employee Assistance European Forum (EAEF) started in 2002, and the Asia Pacific Employee Assistance Roundtable (APEAR).

Today, EAPs are diverse and vary across companies. Regarding prevalence, 97% of companies employing over 5,000 workers, 80% employing 1,001 to 5,000, and 75% employing 251 to 1,000 have EAPs (EAPA, n.d.). EAP counselors may provide therapeutic services to address a variety of mental health concerns (e.g., depression, anxiety, alcohol abuse, trauma, stress). They may also help clients with family and relationship concerns. Additionally, EAP counselors may facilitate workshops on various topics related to mental health, including wellness and self-care. Furthermore, they may provide consultation services for management that include conflict resolution, as well as emergency response. EAP counselors may also seek certification through EAPA, called the certified employee assistance professional certification (CEAP).

With the adoption of the Individuals with Disabilities Education Act (IDEA), passed in 1990, EAPs work with employers to provide accommodations for employees with disabilities. Unfortunately, this does not address the intersectionality of a myriad of other identities (e.g., gender, race, sexual and affectional orientation) (Masi, 2020). Employees are diverse; therefore, it is crucial for EAP counselors to receive training and become skilled in working with diverse groups of clients. Clients should have access to EAP counselors who are skilled in working with diverse groups of clients, as well as have their request for counselor identity preferences considered in matching the client with a counselor. Professional organizations for employee assistance professionals have an important role in providing and advocating for training in working with diverse employee populations, as well as advocating for the employment of counselors from diverse groups and considering client preferences in counselors. Thus, through intentional efforts focused on training and advocacy, employees may have access to counseling services that are culturally sensitive.

RELIGIOUS INSTITUTIONS

Counselors may provide counseling within a religious framework, such as Christian counseling. It is difficult to define Christian counseling because Christianity is diverse and training of Christian counselors is also diverse (McMinn et al., 2010). When a client states they prefer to have a Christian counselor, or other religious counselor, it is important to clarify what this means. McMinn et al. (2010) reports that asking for a Christian counselor may mean the client wants a counselor who (a) is a Christian and will understand their worldview, (b) uses spiritually focused techniques while respecting Christian beliefs, (c) is both a Christian and someone who uses spiritually focused techniques, or (d) is a member of the Society of Christian Psychology (SCP), which is discussed below.

In discussing Christian counseling, McMinn et al. (2010) describe three approaches: (a) biblical counseling, (b) pastoral counseling, and (c) Christian psychology. Biblical counseling is a ministry of the church, with biblical counselors emphasizing the Bible as being superior to psychological theories and techniques. A second area of Christian counseling is pastoral counseling. This counseling approach may include religious leaders (e.g., pastors) who have limited training in counseling, or religious leaders with dual training in Christian ministry and counseling. Pastoral counseling differs from biblical counseling in that pastoral counselors typically embrace both biblical teachings and psychological techniques to help clients work through concerns and promote wellness. The pastoral counseling profession was formalized with the establishment of the American Foundation of Religion and Psychiatry in the 1930s and the American Association of Pastoral Counselors (AAPC) in 1963, as well as the integration of clinical training within educational programs. Pastoral counselors may provide services within the church or the community. They may also represent a variety of Christian denominations, as well as other religious faiths.

A third category is Christian psychology, or Christian counseling. One type of Christian psychology is integrationists who have training as mental health clinicians and value their faith. They seek to infuse both psychological skills and faith in their work with clients. The other group of Christian psychologists are members of the SCP. Individuals in this group have a theoretical base grounded in the Bible and other classical Christian writings. They differ from biblical counselors in that they believe in the integration of psychological theory with Christian writings. Additionally, they differ from integrationists in that they value Christian knowledge more than psychological theory and techniques.

In addition to Christian counselors who provide counseling services from a Christian perspective, there are also counselors who are Christian. Within this group, counselors may provide a Christian perspective when requested by the clients, but they do not facilitate their counseling sessions primarily from a Christian perspective. It is also important to remember that clients may receive support through church ministries provided by individuals who are not trained mental health professionals (e.g., lay counseling). These services may compliment or contradict counseling services.

The Association for Spiritual, Ethical, and Religious Values in Counseling (ASERVIC) is a division of ACA focused on spiritual and religious values as well as ethics in counseling. The organization, formally known as the National Catholic Guidance Conference (NCGC) became a division of ACA, formally APGA, in 1974. The organization changed the name to the Association for Religious and Values Issues in Counseling (ARVIC) in 1977, and then became ASERVIC in 1993 (Miranti, n.d.). The ASERVIC journal is *Counseling and Values*. There are also various other journals focused on integrating a religious perspective in counseling, including the *Journal of Psychology and Christianity* and the *Journal of Psychology and Theology*. An organization supporting Christian counselors is the American Association of Christian Counselors (AACC), which has membership consisting of licensed professionals, pastors, and church laypeople. Some mental health academic training programs also integrate a focus on infusing Christianity or other religions within counseling practice.

Counselors providing counseling from a religious perspective (e.g., Christian counselors) may provide counseling services for a variety of mental health concerns within private practice. They may also work in a counseling center established within a religious center (e.g., church, synagogue). State-funded counseling agencies may prohibit counselors from providing counseling strictly from a religious perspective. However, regardless of the counselor's personal religious beliefs, and the values of the organization, in alignment with the multicultural and social justice counseling competencies (MSJCC; Ratts et al., 2016), it is important for counselors to explore the religious/spiritual beliefs and values of the client, as this is part of the client's worldview.

Many religious affiliations value equity, access, and advocacy (Edwards, 2012). In aligning with the MSJCC, it is important for counselors to have self-awareness of their spiritual/religious values and challenge their biases (Ratts et al., 2016). When working in a religious institution, counselors should also consider the values of the institution, and ways these values may influence their work with clients. Additionally, it is crucial for the counselor to explore the client's worldview (Ratts et al., 2016). Counselors with strong religious beliefs may desire to work at a counseling organization that aligns with their values, and it is important to explore and reflection on how this may influence their work with clients.

Some people view particular religious affiliations (e.g., Christianity) as privileged today in Western society (Edwards, 2012). It is important to consider and acknowledge this privilege when engaging in social justice work. Additionally, regarding Christianity in particular, Brackette et al. (2015) report that Christian values and social justice align with each other. Jesus sought justice for people, and he called Christians to follow his example, and to "love your neighbor as yourself" (Matthew 22:39, *NIV Bible*). Therefore, God calls Christian counselors to serve people in need, and in doing so, to engage in social justice practices (Brackette et al., 2015). Thus, Christian counselors have a calling from both the counseling profession (Ratts et al., 2016) and God to have awareness of and acknowledge their privilege, and engage in social justice advocacy (Edwards, 2012).

REHABILITATION FACILITIES

Rehabilitation is a broad term, but for the purpose of this section, we will focus on physical rehabilitation that encompasses treatment following an injury or medical event (e.g., stroke). Rehabilitation programs originated early in the 20th century and became more common with soldiers returning from war (Sandel, 2019). Although counseling is important for individuals in rehabilitation programs, not all rehabilitation facilities employ counselors. Some may also contract with counselors in private practice or counseling agencies to provide services, or provide referrals for outsider counseling providers. Counselors working with clients in physical rehabilitation centers may focus on mental health concerns (e.g., posttraumatic stress disorder, depression), independent living goals, and vocational/career counseling.

Rehabilitation counselors have specialized skills and training in working with clients in rehabilitation programs; however, other counselors may also work with these clients. They help clients achieve their "personal, career, and independent living goals in the most integrated living setting possible" (American Rehabilitation Counseling Association [ARCA], n.d.). ARCA is the division of ACA that is dedicated to rehabilitation counseling. It publishes the journal *Rehabilitation Counseling Bulletin* (RCB).

In working with clients in physical rehabilitation facilities, counselors advocate for the least restrictive environment for their clients. Counselors also advocate for and with clients on obtaining employment that allows them to work toward reaching their full potential. This includes addressing ableist microaggressions and the intersectionality of this with other microaggressions experienced by people in marginalized groups that may arise within the work environment or other settings. Thus, counselors advocate for equitable experiences for people with disabilities.

COLLEGES AND UNIVERSITIES

Dr. Stewart Paton, a psychiatrist, started the first mental health counseling program on a college campus in 1910 at Princeton University, in response to students dropping out of school due to emotional concerns (Kraft, 2011). In 1920, the American Student Health Association, which later became the American College Health Association (ACHA), held their first meeting, which included a discussion of mental hygiene, and the need for mental health services on college campuses (Kraft, 2011). Mental health continued to be a focus in subsequent meetings and studies in the decades that followed; however, the focus remained on psychiatrists as college mental health providers. This presented a problem due to an insufficient number of psychiatrists to meet the need on college campuses.

By the 1950s, many colleges and universities were involving multidisciplinary teams that included additional mental health professionals to address the need for mental health services for college students (Kraft, 2011). College mental health services continued to evolve as more individuals enrolled in college in the 1960s with funding of the GI bill for veterans, as well as the increased need for services due to more drug and alcohol use by college students. Additionally, in 1961, the ACHA published the *Recommended Standards and Practices for a College Health Program*, which included a focus on mental health services (Kraft, 2011). Since then, mental health services on college campuses has continued to evolve to provide quality care for this population.

The American College Counseling Association (ACCA) is the division of ACA focused on college counseling. This organization began in 1991 after the American College Personnel Association (ACPA) disaffiliated with ACA, due to focusing more broadly on student affairs personnel. The origin of ACPA dates back to 1924 with the start of the National Association of Appointment Secretaries (ACPA, n.d.). The ACCA has a journal (*Journal of College Counseling* [JCC]), started in 1998, that focuses on advancing knowledge and informing college counseling practice. Additionally, the Association for University and College Counseling Center Directors (AUCCCD) promotes the management and facilitation of college counseling services in alignment with best practice standards.

With over 19 million individuals attending colleges and universities in the United States (National Center for Education Statistics, 2019), there is a crucial need for quality college counseling services for these individuals. College counselors work at various types of higher education institutions, providing mental health services for students pursing various degrees (e.g., associate, bachelor, master, doctoral). College counseling centers may employ diverse mental health professionals, including counselors, psychologists, psychiatrists, and social workers. Some college and university counseling centers may require a master's degree, along with being a licensed counselor, while others may require a doctoral degree in counseling or a related field.

College counselors may assess students for risk of self-harm or harm to others, offer crisis counseling, and provide individual, group, and marriage and family counseling to address a variety of concerns and promote wellness. Additionally, college counselors may provide outreach and psychoeducational services focused on various topics (e.g., transition to college, healthy dating, sexual assault, drugs and alcohol, wellness). They may also provide education and consultation services to faculty and other college and university personnel on recognizing students' mental health concerns and helping them access help. Furthermore, counselors may work within colleges and universities to provide career counseling, as well as counseling in conjunction with disability services. Thus, counselors working in colleges and universities may work in a variety of roles.

College counselors have a responsibility to engage in advocacy for students and the profession. This may involve advocating for the rights of marginalized groups of college students and helping them connect with resources, as well as advocating for inclusive institutional policies and procedures. Marginalized groups of college students may include racial minority groups; LGBTQ+ students; students with disabilities; nontraditional students (e.g., undergraduate students that are outside the traditional college student age of 18–21, college students who are married and/or have children); first-generation college students; and international students, as well as the intersection of these identities.

PRESCHOOLS, ELEMENTARY, MIDDLE, AND HIGH SCHOOLS

During the industrial revolution, a need arose to prepare students to enter the work force, as jobs expanded from focusing predominately on agriculture to include manufacturing jobs. However, in the early years, there were no dedicated school counseling positions; instead, teachers had some release time from teaching to provide counseling-related services to students (Gysbers, 2010). By the 1930s, schools were having various personnel providing counseling services, including hiring some social workers and school counselors, and there was a need for identifying the duties of a school counselor. This resulted in establishing an organizational framework that included guidance services within a larger group referred to as pupil personal services. The framework included five primary guidance services: (a) assessment, (b) information, (c) counseling, (d) placement, and (e) follow-up (Gysbers, 2010).

In 1946, the George Barden Act allocated funds for vocational guidance, and then in 1958, the National Defense Education Act included a section that focused on the development of training programs for school counselors (Gysbers, 2010). Elementary school counseling grew in the 1960s. Then, in the 1970s, there was a focus on unifying school counseling through consistent terminology. In the 1980s and 1990s educational reform continued, along with debate on the roles of school counselors. The American School Counselor Association (ASCA) published the first version of the *ASCA National Model* in 2003 solidifying the three foci of a comprehensive school counseling program to include academic, social/ emotional, and career development (Gysbers, 2010). ASCA has continued to revise the model as well as publish sets of standards and competencies in recent years. Thus, the school counseling profession continues to evolve across time.

ASCA started in 1952 as an organization to represent school counselors. The organization publishes a journal titled *Professional School Counseling* (ASCA, n.d.). They also advocate for the school counseling professional and have published a variety of resources for school counselors, including standards and competency documents. The Association for Child and Adolescent Counseling (ACAC), established in 2013, is a division of ACA that focuses on counseling related to children and adolescents, although it focuses on counseling within various settings, not only schools. The journal for ACAC is the *Journal of Child and Adolescent Counseling*, established in 2015 (ACAC, n.d.).

School counselors provide direct and indirect services to students within a school setting. Direct services involve interactions with students that include a variety of activities (e.g., classroom lessons, individual counseling, small group counseling, advisement). Indirect services involve the counselor engaging in activities on behalf of the student. This may include engaging in consultation, collaboration, and referrals that involve various stakeholders (e.g., other school personnel, parents/guardians, community providers).

Mental health counselors may also provide counseling for students within the school setting. This may involve counselors employed by community agencies having sessions with students in the schools, due to accessibility, with children and adolescents spending the majority of their time in schools. It may also include mental health counselors contracted by school districts to provide mental health counseling in the schools. The role of mental health counselors in the schools is not to replace school counselors, but instead to collaborate with school counselors to identify and provide intensive services to students needing them, since school counselors typically provide brief counseling interventions and refer students with higher levels of concerns and needs to mental health counselors. While children are accessible to counselors who provide mental health services with the schools, it can be difficult to get parents/guardians involved in treatment. This can present challenges, as parents/guardians can be important in the treatment process.

Violence in the schools and increased concerns about the mental health and well-being of children and adolescents has led to federal and state legislation to fund training of school professionals on mental health and to hire more mental health professionals to provide students counseling services. Additionally, some states are also requiring mandatory mental health education for children and adolescents. As mental health providers in the schools, school counselors and school-based mental health counselors have a crucial role in advocating for quality mental health education for students and quality mental health training for school personnel. It is also crucial that they engage in advocacy related to their role in the schools, as school counselors may be asked to take on various responsibilities that are not related to counseling (e.g., monitor the lunchroom, help with standardized testing). With large numbers of students in school settings, it is important that counselors have as much time as possible to provide mental health services to students. This requires educating school administrators and others about their role in the school, as well as using creativity to find unique ways to provide quality services to a large number of students.

Social justice is crucial in the school environment to identify and address achievement gaps for marginalized students (Griffin & Stern, 2011). It is important to note that in the last decade there has been a movement to replace *achievement gap* with *opportunity gap*, viewing societal decision (e.g., economic, political) as sharing responsibility for disparities, instead of blaming students and their families, communities, and teachers (Ladson-Billings, 2013). In being social change agents, Griffin and Stern (2011) emphasize the importance of collaborating with the family and the community, as well as the school, instead of working with students in isolation. They outline nine action strategies for school counselors (see Table 7.4).

School counselors may provide trainings to promote multicultural competency among school personnel (Storlie & Jach, 2012). This may involve providing education to personnel about challenges experienced by marginalized group, as well as strategies they can use to support them. Additionally, counselors can train personnel, as well as teach youth, about the use of inclusive language related to LGBTQ+ youth. Furthermore, counselors in the schools can provide both students and school personnel with resources. The resources for personnel may help further foster their knowledge and skills in working with marginalized students, as well as help them build acceptance and community within the classroom and larger school environment. Resources for students may offer further support, especially for marginalized students. Regarding undocumented Latino students specifically, Storlie and Jach (2012) provided

TABLE 7.4 ACTION STRATEGIES FOR SCHOOL COUNSELORS

Become culturally competent
Use data to demonstrate inequities
Obtain support from others
Voice concerns and perspective within the school (e.g., school administrators), and outside the school to other stakeholders (e.g., legislators)
Educate and empower families
Be involved politically
Don't be afraid to act
Be persistent
Engage in research

Source: Data from Griffen, D., & Stern, S. (2011) . A social justice approach to school counseling. *Journal for Social Action in Counseling and Psychology, 3*(1), 74-85. https://doi.org/10.33043/JSACP.3.1.74-85

additional strategies including (a) communication (written and oral) in the family's native language, (b) reduction of stigma and creation of culturally sensitive classrooms, (c) support groups and mentorship for undocumented students, and (d) legislative advocacy. School counselors and school-based mental health counselors have a crucial role to be social justice change agents.

COUNSELING IN RURAL SETTINGS

Counselors experience different opportunities and challenges when working in rural counseling settings. While multiple mental health resources may be available for clients in urban settings, clients in rural settings may experience difficulty accessing mental health resources due to limited mental health professionals (Wilson et al., 2018). This often requires counselors in rural settings to be generalists in providing services to diverse clients. Serving diverse clients also requires continuous engagement in professional development. While Oetinger et al. (2014) found counselors reported these factors as strengths and benefits to working in rural mental health, this may also contribute to burnout for some counselors.

Transportation can also be a concern when attempting to access mental health care. Urban areas may have public transportation available to address this concern; however, affordable transportation may not be available in rural settings, especially when clients need to travel a great distance to obtain mental health services. Counselors may have extensive travel time due to seeing clients in a large geographic area. Wilson et al. (2018) found counselors reported the importance of being creative in addressing challenges with distance (e.g., enjoying the scenic drive, scheduling clients in a specified area on the same day, using telemental health). Clients may also be reluctant to seek services in a rural area due to fear of others finding out within their small community that they are seeing a counselor. Counselors may also struggle with confidentiality and ethics related to navigating boundaries and multiple relationships within a small community when it is likely that they may interact with clients frequently in their personal life (e.g., place of worship, community events) (Oetinger et al., 2014).

Despite these challenges, Oetinger et al. (2014) found there were various personal and cultural reasons acknowledged by counselors for desiring to work in rural settings. Specifically, counselors acknowledged a need for counseling in rural settings and their desire to serve this population in need. They also shared enjoying the natural environment and having a slower pace in life, which Wilson et al. (2018) also identified related to the *way of life* expressed by counselors in rural communities. Additionally, in exploring the retention of counselors in rural areas, Wilson et al. (2018) found counselors reported connections with the community as a factor in working in rural settings, whether being raised in the community or moving to the area and developing these relationships. Thus, despite challenges to working in rural settings, counselors identified benefits to working in these communities.

The National Association for Rural Mental Health (NARMH) focuses on rural behavioral health. This organization serves various stakeholders within the rural mental health community, including service providers, as well as family members. NARMH has a journal titled *Journal of Rural Mental Health*.

In working with clients in rural settings, it is important that counselors do not assume that all rural communities are the same. Although there may be some similarities, communities have their own unique strengths and challenges. It is important for counselors to develop an understanding of particular communities, as well as their individual clients. Marginalized clients have unique challenges in rural communities where resources are already limited, as there may be few individuals with similar identities, resulting in limited support systems. In discussing recommendations for working with marginalized clients in rural communities, particularly lesbian clients, Hastings and Hoover-Thompson (2011) reported five broad areas. First, it is important for counselors to examine their own personal biases as well as consider if their marketing materials, forms, or décor in their office presents a biased view against marginalized groups. Second, counselors should attend to minority stress caused by the ongoing prejudice they experience for their marginalized identity. This includes providing a safe environment to discuss their experiences related to marginalization. The counselor can also help clients explore their own beliefs about their marginalized identities. Additionally, the counselor can help clients develop support networks, which includes providing information about support groups. Finally, counselors can provide education to colleagues and community members to promote support and understanding of people with marginalized identities (Hastings & Hoover-Thompson, 2011). Although these recommendations related to working with lesbian clients in particular, counselors can apply them to working with clients from various marginalized groups.

CONCLUSION

Mental health services have evolved within various systems across time, and counselors now serve clients through employment with a variety of public and private organizations, as well as being self-employed. As discussed in this chapter, counseling settings have unique advantages, as well as challenges. There are also counseling organizations that focus on counselors' unique needs in working with particular client populations. While the counseling settings may be unique in many ways, social justice and advocacy are important within all counseling settings and with all clients. Thus, all counseling professionals are responsible for embracing and applying social justice and advocacy principles in their work as counselors.

Summary

- Counselors serve clients across the lifespan with various presenting concerns within different counseling settings.
- The treatment of people with mental illness has evolved across time to shift from institutionalization to a community-based care movement.
- Various organizations exist to support counselors and promote counseling in diverse settings.
- A focus on social justice, advocacy, and intersectionality is important in diverse ways within counseling environments.

Voices From the Field

Mercedes Machado, PhD, LMHC, Clinical Assistant Professor, Counseling & Wellness Center,
University of Florida, Gainesville, FL

Most of my clinical work has been with communities of color in various settings, including community mental health agencies. Early on in my career as a mental health counselor, I realized the ethical and moral imperative we have as counselors to be social justice advocates. It was evident to me that many of the clinical concerns my clients presented with were exacerbated by unjust and oppressive systems and structures. Therefore, it feels most congruent for me to hold space for someone impacted by these systems and to work to dismantle and rebuild them. I believe that this is what it means to be a counselor and an advocate. These roles are interwoven and cannot be separated from one another.

Living and working as a person of color, specifically a Latina woman, in the counseling and counselor education fields, can be lonely at times. There aren't many folks who look like me, and I have certainly had to be the one to "show up" for clients of color in meaningful and helpful ways when they were overlooked. However, antiracist counseling and social justice advocacy is everyone's responsibility, and it can happen in counseling rooms and outside them. All counselors are tasked to educate and challenge ourselves about the many "isms" that profoundly affect our clients' lives. It is not enough to simply be tolerant. Our clients are counting on us to see their humanity, make space for them, validate their experiences, empower them, consider cultural contexts, honor their ancestral knowledge, and engage in dialogues about the barriers they overcome and the burdens they carry. These burdens undoubtedly exacerbate mental health conditions. I once had a client tell me that he felt like something was wrong with him simply because he was gay. He was experiencing symptoms of anxiety and depression as he grappled with his identity. After supporting him in processing his feelings, I shared that nothing was wrong with him, but that there was something wrong about the deeply rooted homophobia in our society. He seemed relieved by the idea that he was not deficient. Homophobia, White supremacy, xenophobia, sexism, and classism all do harm, and as counselors, it is vital that we acknowledge this harm as opposed to blaming a client for their pain or the ways they have managed to survive their oppression. My client and I ended up discussing the survival strategies he used to survive in a society that often "others" him and explored alternative survival skills that ensured safety and honored who he was. Perhaps it was the first time he felt like he was worthy. If we are to be true advocates, then we must acknowledge that our society and the world also need transformative and radical healing and that for many people, simply existing is truly an act of resistance.

In addition, when I think about social justice, I reflect on my first job after my master's degree as a counselor at a community agency in Fort Lauderdale, Florida. Community mental health work is "trench" work; it involves getting into the dark trenches with people in incomprehensible pain. Most of my clients were parents of color from low socioeconomic status suffering from mental health conditions, substance abuse, and trauma, which resulted in them being court-mandated to go to counseling. In their bodies and in their spirits, many of them carried racial, intergenerational trauma. Oppression made most of their lives particularly challenging. They suffered in silence due to limited access to financial resources, transportation, education, and healthcare. One of the women I worked with came to group counseling every Wednesday night after taking two buses to get there. By the time she got there, she was exhausted, but she always showed up. In group, I commended her on her efforts to get to group, acknowledged the systemic barriers she faced, and encouraged group members to support each other in getting to the agency through car-pooling or taking the bus together. I attempted to foster and build a safe community in group while also noticing the limitations I faced in making counseling more accessible. My clients were survivors of inequitable systems and structures that drastically changed the course of their lives and their children's lives. I am confident that I helped my clients during my time at this agency. However, I am also confident that the healthcare, housing, education, and criminal justice systems all need reform. This does not mean that I do not show up as a culturally aware, antiracist, ethical, open-minded counselor. It means I do the work that needs to be done, while envisioning and working toward a more equitable world.

As you become a counselor, consider how you can be a counselor who desires justice and fights for it not only when it's comfortable, but when it's risky and uncomfortable and hard. Counselors have the unique ability and privilege to enact change at both the micro and macro levels. This can include critically examining systems of oppression, centering the voices of people and clients of color, policy writing, organizing and marching around a cause, creating healing spaces, advocating for more resources for people at the margins, utilizing power and privilege for good, and so much more. Counselors are well positioned to be phenomenal advocates within and beyond the four walls of our offices.

A Call to Action

Identify a marginalized population that lacks mental health resources in your local community. Create a campaign to advocate for services for this group. Your campaign may be focused on the general public, or a specific group, such as city leaders or administrators in a specific community agency or school. The material you create should include information about the populations, including a description of who they are and their needs. Include statistics about the population if available. Create a list of recommendations for specific mental health resources to address the need in the community.

Case Study 7.1

Natasha is a 45-year-old Caucasian woman who presents as having mild depression. She works for a state agency and reports experiencing stress related to her job and difficulty trying to balance her work and home responsibilities. She reports that she has never received counseling and is unsure where she should go, but shares that she is a Christian and would like to have a counselor who shares her beliefs and values.

RESPONSE QUESTIONS

1. What are some factors to consider in thinking about the type of counseling that might be a good fit with Natasha?
2. What types of counseling settings would you recommend?
3. What additional information might be helpful in making recommendations of counselors?

Going Within

After reading the chapter, what counseling setting is most appealing to you and why? What aspects about the setting interest you? What challenges might you experience in working within the setting? What social justice and advocacy work seem particularly salient in this setting? What do you want to know more about related to providing counseling in the setting?

Group Process

The chapter includes a historical portrayal of the treatment of people with mental illness. In small groups, discuss what stands out to you about the shift from institutionalization to a community-based mental health model. Do you agree or disagree with community-based mental health care and why? In what ways has society accepted and/or rejected this model? What is the role of counselors in influencing the treatment of clients with mental illness now and in the future?

RESOURCES

American Association of Christian Counselors (AACC): https://www.aacc.net
American College Counseling Association (ACCA): http://www.college
counseling.org

American Rehabilitation Counseling Association (ARCA): http://www
.arcaweb.org

American School Counselor Association (ASCA): https://www.schoolcounselor
.org

Association for Child and Adolescent Counseling (ACAC): http://acachild.org

Association for Spiritual, Ethical, and Religious Values in Counseling (ASER-
VIC): www.aservic.org

Employee Assistance Professionals Association (EAPA): https://www.eapassn
.org

International Association of Addictions and Offender Counselors (IAAOC):
http://www.iaaocounselors.org/about

National Association for Rural Mental Health (NARMH): https://www.narmh
.org

U.S. Department of Veterans Affairs Veterans Health Administration: https://
www.vacareers.va.gov/Careers/MentalHealth

 Access this podcast at https://connect.springerpub.com/content/book/978-0-8261-6386-8/chapter/ch07.

KEY REFERENCES

Only key references appear in the print edition. The full reference list appears in the digital product found on https://connect.springerpub.com/content/book/978-0-8261-6386-8/chapter/ch07

Griffin, D., & Stern, S. (2011). A social justice approach to school counseling. *Journal for Social Action in Counseling & Psychology*, 3(1), 74–85. https://doi.org/10.33043/JSACP.3.1.74-85

Pollack, S. (2019). Interested in a VA career? *Counseling Today*, 62(1), 8–9. https://www.counseling.org/docs/default-source/default-document-library/ct_july_2019-au-va-employment2.pdf?sfvrsn=5361572c_2

Ratts, M. J., Singh, A. A., Nassar-McMillan, S., Butler, S. K., & McCullough, J. R. (2016). Multicul-tural and social justice counseling competencies: Guidelines for the counseling profession. *Journal of Multicultural Counseling and Development*, 44(1), 28–48. https://doi.org/10.1002/jmcd.12035

Swank, J. M., & Gagnon, J. C. (2016). Mental health services in juvenile correctional facilities: A national survey of clinical staff. *Journal of Child and Family Studies*, 25(9), 2862–2872. https://doi.org/10.1007/s10826-016-0436-3

Swank, J. M., & Gagnon, J. C. (2017). A national survey of mental health screening and assess-ment practices in juvenile correctional facilities. *Child & Youth Care Forum*, 46(3), 379–393. https://doi.org/10.1007/s10566-016-9379-5

RESEARCH, ASSESSMENT, AND DIAGNOSIS IN COUNSELING

Latoya Haynes-Thoby and Jacqueline M. Swank

Think about this...

How does research inform the decisions you make? What can we learn through the assessment process that may guide our work with clients? What is the role of a diagnosis in the counseling process? How do we engage in advocacy in our research and practice as counselors?

LEARNING OBJECTIVES

After reading this chapter, you should be able to:

- Describe the steps for critiquing research
- Recognize the importance of research in the counseling profession
- Define the counselor's role in the research process
- Identify ways to collect assessment data
- Explain the intake assessment process
- Outline the process of assessing progress and outcomes in counseling
- Discuss the history of the Diagnostic and Statistical Manual of Mental Disorders
- Distinguish between the treatment of a diagnosis versus the treatment of symptoms
- Analyze the use of evidence-based practice and the selection of treatment approaches
- Recognize multicultural considerations within the research, assessment, and diagnosis processes

INTRODUCTION

Counselors work to build and maintain strong helping relationships with clients to treat a variety of concerns, which begins with intentional efforts to understand clients' worldviews, cultural context, strengths, and needs. Throughout the assessment and diagnosis processes, counselors research client concerns and applicable treatment approaches. This involves reviewing the existing literature to examine best practices for specific clients and communities, symptom presentations, and client needs. This process also necessitates an understanding of clients' cultural contexts and worldviews. Counselors then collaborate with clients to develop treatment plans. In working with clients as they navigate needs that often exceed their current coping capacities, counselors engage in relationship building, psychoeducation, diagnosis, and advocacy.

RESEARCH AND PROGRAM EVALUATION IN COUNSELING

Research involves curiosity about a topic and a search for an answer, or having a problem and working to discover a solution. Scholars conduct research in counseling to inform practice through the discovery of knowledge about mental health concerns, to do no harm, and to provide effective treatments to serve clients better. Intervention and outcome-based research helps inform the counseling field about treatment approaches and counseling interventions that are effective.

Individuals working in institutions of higher education or at companies that employ researchers usually conduct the majority of research studies. Although counselors may conduct research either on their own or in collaboration with academicians, they more often engage in program evaluation to examine the effectiveness of a treatment approach or curriculum they are using in practice. Program evaluation may include outcome evaluation and process evaluation. For example, a counselor may engage in outcome evaluation to examine the effectiveness of an 8-week group curriculum in reducing depressive symptoms for clients. To measure the effectiveness of the group, the counselor may administer a pre/post-test assessment to group members. Additionally, the counselor may conduct a process evaluation by interviewing individuals or conducting focus groups with the participants to gather information about their experiences in the group, identifying strengths and areas for improvement within the group curriculum. Although this process takes time and effort, it is important because it provides useful information for the counselor in deciding whether to continue to use the curriculum as well as identifying ways to strengthen the curriculum. The program evaluation process also yields data that counselors may use to advocate for ongoing funding or new funding (e.g., grants) and employment of mental health personnel to facilitate mental health programs and services. Counselors may also seek to share their program evaluation results with the larger counseling community, which may include publishing the results in a counseling journal. Some journals have a practitioner focus or a dedicated section focused on practice.

TABLE 8.1 HOW TO BE A CONSUMER OF RESEARCH

Identify what you want to know.
Locate information and examine credibility of sources.
Critique the research methodology.
Examine the results while considering the limitation of the research.
Consider how the evidence applies to your work with clients.

It can be challenging for counselors to engage in research, as they may not have the extensive research knowledge or time to conduct research on a regular basis. However, counselors may be successful with embracing the role of a researcher and a practitioner when collaborating with others. For example, a counselor may work with a researcher to help conceptualize a study and make decisions about the research methodology. Then, the counselor may facilitate the intervention, while the researcher helps collect, analyze, and interpret the data. Then, the counselor and researcher work together to develop a manuscript based on the data and submit it for publication. They may also write a summary of the data to distribute to administrators in the counseling setting as well as other stakeholders (e.g., clients, funders, community members). Thus, both the counselor and researcher benefit, and contribute to the body of literature regarding the area of practice.

UNDERSTANDING WHAT WORKS: BEING A CONSUMER OF RESEARCH

Within counseling practice, it is important to be a consumer of research. This involves staying current with what is occurring in the field through reading literature relevant to the profession, including trends and best practices. This also involves searching for answers to questions and applying evidence to working with clients. For example, a counselor may research best practices in working with a particular client group. Additionally, they may search for empirically supported interventions to use with a specific client population. When engaging in this process, it is important to obtain credible evidence to answer the counselor's questions, and not accept what is read as facts without reviewing evidence to support an author's claims.

Technological advancements provide a wealth of information at one's fingertips; however, not all information is credible. Thus, counselors critically evaluate claims using a multistep process (see Table 8.1). First, counselors identify what they want to know and where they can find the answers to their questions. It is crucial that in this search for answers counselors use credible sources. Theoretical and research-based articles that are peer reviewed and published in credible journals are rigorous sources of information. Peer reviewed or refereed means that experts in the field have reviewed the content for accuracy and rigor and have determined that it meets standards for dissemination. The flagship peer-reviewed journal of the American Counseling

Association (ACA) is the *Journal of Counseling & Development*. The divisions of ACA also have peer-reviewed journals, as do other counseling associations (see Table 8.2 for a list of counseling journals). Counselors may also consider information that is not peer reviewed; however, they should examine whether the author provides empirical support for the claims. For example, many organizations and government agencies collect data or fund research to collect data through a rigorous process and publish the data and reports on their websites. Counselors would review the reputation of the sources and the content shared to determine the credibility of the information. Moreover, counselors may attend training or read textbooks grounded in theoretical and empirical support that provide references that the counselor may then access for additional information. In the process of reviewing information, counselors also consider whether it is factual or opinion-based, determining the evidence available to support the author's ideas or claims.

Not all evidence is credible or applicable to a specific client population. Reviewing a research study involves a critique of the methodology, including research design, participants, instruments, procedures, and data analysis. This is important in determining the rigor of the study and the relevance of the data for the counselor. For example, it is important to examine the representativeness of the sample in relation to the counselor's client population (e.g., age, gender, race). There may be empirical support for using an intervention with Caucasian adult females, but no, or limited, research on using the intervention with other racial groups. Thus, the counselor should consider how the intervention may affect Black adult females differently before using it with this client population.

When reviewing the results of a research study, the counselor also considers the limitations. This includes various factors that could influence the results (e.g., selection of instruments, research design, setting), as well as generalizability (applying the results from the study to the broader population). Finally, the counselor considers the implications, or relevance of the findings for their counseling practice (e.g., considerations when working with a client population, effectiveness of a treatment approach). Thus, the counselor engages in a rigorous process to obtain answers to their questions that will guide their counseling practice.

Being a consumer of research is important because the ACA (2014) *Code of Ethics* states that counselors use theory-driven and empirically supported treatments when working with clients (Standard C.7.a.), and do not use interventions that scholars suggest cause harm based on evidence (Standard C.7.c.). Additionally, counselors acknowledge the potential benefits and risks associated with innovative techniques (Standard C.7.b.). Through the consumption of research, counselors become aware of theoretically and empirically supported techniques, innovative treatments, and treatments that may cause harm. Counselors also learn about approaches that others use, and they are able to support these interventions as alternatives when supported by theory and research (Standard D.1.a.). Furthermore, counselors should have knowledge of current scientific evidence regarding their counseling area of practice (Standard C.2.f.). In addition to ethical mandates, being a consumer of research is also important due to the increasing emphasis on evidence-based practice, including pressure from insurance companies to use interventions with research support. Thus,

TABLE 8.2 COUNSELING JOURNALS

COUNSELING ORGANIZATION	JOURNAL
American Counseling Association	*Journal of Counseling & Development*
American College Counseling Association (ACCA)	*Journal of College Counseling* (JCC)
[a]American Mental Health Counseling Association (AMHCA)	*Journal of Mental Health Counseling* (JMHC)
American Rehabilitation Counseling Association (ARCA)	*Rehabilitation Counseling Bulletin* (RCB)
[a]American School Counselor Association (ASCA)	*Professional School Counseling* (PSC)
Association for Adult Development and Aging (AADA)	*Adultspan Journal*
Association for Assessment and Research in Counseling (AARC)	Two journals: *Counseling Outcome Research and Evaluation* (CORE) *Measurement and Evaluation in Counseling and Development* (MECD)
Association for Child and Adolescent Counseling (ACAC)	*Journal of Child and Adolescent Counseling* (JCAC)
Association for Counselor Education and Supervision (ACES)	*Counselor Education and Supervision* (CES)
Association for Creativity in Counseling (ACC)	*Journal of Creativity in Mental Health* (JCMH)
Association for Humanistic Counseling (AHC)	*Journal of Humanistic Counseling* (JHC)
Association for Multicultural Counseling and Development (AMCD)	*Journal of Multicultural Counseling and Development* (JMCD)
Association for Specialists in Group Work (ASGW)	*Journal for Specialists in Group Work* (JSGW)
Association for Spiritual, Ethical, and Religious Values in Counseling (ASERVIC)	*Counseling and Values*
Counselors for Social Justice (CSJ)	*Journal for Social Action in Counseling and Psychology* (JSACP)

(continued)

TABLE 8.2 COUNSELING JOURNALS (*CONTINUED*)

COUNSELING ORGANIZATION	JOURNAL
International Association of Addictions and Offender Counselors (IAAOC)	*Journal of Addictions & Offender Counseling* (JAOC)
International Association of Marriage and Family Counselors (IAMFC)	*The Family Journal* (TFJ)
Military and Government Counseling Association (MGCA)	*Journal of Military and Government Counseling* (JMGC)
National Career Development Association (NCDA)	*Career Development Quarterly* (CDQ)
National Employment Counseling Association (NECA)	*Journal of Employment Counseling* (JEC)
Society for Sexual, Affectional, Intersex, and Gender Expansive Identities (SAIGE)	*Journal of LGBT Issues in Counseling*

[a]Not divisions of the American Counseling Association (ACA).

counselors need to be good consumers of research and actively engage in consuming research on an ongoing basis.

Counselors may also help their clients be good consumers of research. This can be particularly important when clients bring up in session something they have read or heard about in the news or found on a website related to their presenting concerns or about an area of mental illness, or wellness and self-care. Counselors can be instrumental in helping clients learn how to distinguish what information is credible. Identifying credible information can be helpful for clients during the counseling process as well as beyond treatment.

Although it is important to be a consumer of research, it is not without challenges. Counselors may lack access to research articles. Joining professional counseling organizations helps address this because organizations typically offer members complimentary access to their journals. Although this is not access to all literature, it provides some resources. Counselors may also reach out to authors directly when they are interested in an article or other published work. Additionally, some journals are open access, offering anyone the opportunity to read articles without paying fees. Another challenge might relate to difficulty understanding the results in a research article. Reading the discussion section of a research article can help with understanding the results and the implications can help the reader consider how to apply the information to their work with clients. There are also free online videos and tutorials that counselors can use to obtain greater knowledge regarding interpreting statistics, as well as understanding other aspects of research.

SOCIAL JUSTICE AND ADVOCACY IN RESEARCH: DECOLONIZING THE RESEARCH PROCESS

Counselors' ethical codes encourage engagement in the research process in ways that reflect sensitivity and respect for diversity of the communities that counselors serve (ACA, 2014; American School Counselor Association, 2016; Association for Marriage and Family Therapists, 2015; Commission on Rehabilitation Counselor Certification, 2016; National Career Development Association, 2015). This requires counseling professionals to consider the potential effects of research outcomes on individuals and communities. As such, what we currently understand about a topic of inquiry may influence determinations related to research methodology, research design, sampling methods, the instruments used, and the procedures that are followed. These factors impact how we approach the actual research inquiry and effect the implications of the research, and the potential for outcomes that may benefit clients.

Research presents an opportunity for awareness about the effectiveness of working with clients and the potential for improved outcomes. Advocacy for clients, families, and communities is often reflected in the research conducted by counseling professionals, as many counseling research questions are developed with an intention to address a problem that clients and communities experience. In order to best answer a research question, researchers select an approach that corresponds to the inquiry. Counseling researchers use social justice frameworks in their research that may include qualitative (data consisting of words and meaning that is collected through methods such as interviews and focus groups), quantitative (data consisting of numbers), and mixed-methods (both qualitative and quantitative) research designs. Both qualitative and quantitative research inquires can help promote critical understanding of the challenges that clients and communities experience. Research frameworks and approaches that promote social justice often center the voices of participants, highlight the effect of the researcher's own perspectives in the interpretation of findings, and serve to challenge assumptions about research objectivity.

There are many research frameworks and approaches that focus on social justice including various community-engaged research approaches (e.g., participatory action research [PAR], community-based participatory research [CBPR], youth participatory action research [YPAR], photovoice) as well as counterstorytelling, critical approaches to quantitative research such as quantitative critical analyses (Johnson, 2021), and the use of reflexivity interviews (Pessoa et al., 2019). Using a community-engaged framework, researchers partner with members of the community in the research process at varying levels of engagement. Within PAR/CBPR, the participants become co-researchers and are fully engaged in identifying the problem, collecting data, analyzing the data, and developing potential solutions to the problem. Youth may also be involved in PAR referred to as YPAR. Photovoice is a PAR approach that involves the use of photographs to achieve three goals: (a) empower individuals to voice their perspectives about the needs and strengths of their community, (b) facilitate dialogue about important issues, and (c) reach policy makers to promote awareness and advocate for change (Wang & Burris, 1997). Researchers can use photovoice to highlight the realities of individuals who are marginalized and whose voices often go unheard by others. Mental health professionals and scholars have used photovoice with many populations including Black youth (Williams et al., 2020), LGBTQ college students (Bardhoshi et al., 2018), and survivors of loss by suicide (Mayton & Wester, 2019) to name a few. Photovoice can be used to illuminate often unheard perspectives or counterstories of marginalized populations (Goessling, 2018).

Counterstorytelling is also used to center the experiences of marginalized communities and to contextualize facets of a larger narrative that may vary from the stories and experiences of the majority culture (Solórzano & Yosso, 2002). Counterstories often challenge the narratives of majority stories through the inclusion of the voices of marginalized people, whose stories are often muted or completely omitted. Counterstorytelling is a methodology (Crenshaw, 1991; Crenshaw et al., 1995) that uses stories as a means to contextualize the realities of individuals, especially for those whose stories are often left unheard (Ladson-Billings, 1998; Solórzano & Yosso, 2002). Researchers have used counterstorytelling to explore the lived experiences of less privileged groups (Maxwell & Sonn, 2019), to highlight inequities for marginalized students (Gwathney, 2021), and to understand school inequities (Lechuga-Peña & Lechuga, 2018).

Researchers may focus on social justice within quantitative research by examining large datasets to highlight trends, patterns of inequity, and current needs (e.g., Bryan et al., 2017; Goodman-Scott et al., 2018). Additionally, critical race theory using a quantitative approach (QuantCrit) centers on reflecting and challenging assumptions about "unbiased" quantitative findings (Covarrubias & Vélez, 2013; Johnson, 2021). Through ongoing self-exploration, evaluation, and enlistment of deeper self-awareness, researchers consider the power structures that influence how people interpret the world around them, including social, political, and economic structures that influence understandings (Garcia et al., 2018). Instead of researchers illuminating truths, within critical research approaches, the participants are the experts and arbiters of knowledge (Brydon-Miller & Damons, 2019; Dillard, 2008). Using research approaches that highlight the voices of marginalized populations and aim to create a more socially just society are ways that counseling professionals can advocate while engaging in research.

ASSESSMENT PROCESS

The counseling assessment process is comprehensive and ongoing throughout a counselor's work with a client. Counselors obtain assessment data using three methods: (a) facilitating interviews, (b) engaging in observations, and (c) administering tests/instruments. The assessment process begins at the start of treatment when the counselor obtains information about various aspects of the client. As counseling continues, the client may share additional information across time. The counselor may also use one or more of the methods for obtaining assessment data to monitor the client's progress across sessions, as well as to assess counseling outcomes at the end of the counseling process.

The counselor may consider embracing a scientist-practitioner perspective when engaging in the assessment process in counseling through integrating research with counseling practice. The counselor considers all pieces of data and various explanations in regard to theory and research findings, while reflecting on their biases and the effects they have on clinical decisions. While considering research is important in this process, the counselor is also mindful of individual differences with clients, and thus values balancing research, individual client considerations, and cultural contexts in making decisions about treatment (Blair, 2010; Kirmayer, 2012).

The Association for Assessment and Research in Counseling (AARC) has collaborated with other divisions of the ACA to develop assessment standards and competencies. These standards are located on the AARC website, which is listed under the Resources (aarc-counseling.org/resources). Additionally, the ACA (2014) *Code of Ethics* includes a section on assessment. Within the introduction for the section, ACA emphasizes the importance of considering individual and cultural factors within the assessment process. These considerations are important within all three assessment methods (interviews, observations, and tests).

In the interview process, the counselor considers the content of the questions, as well as the approach used to ask them to ensure that these practices align with the client's culture. This includes wording and terminology the counselor uses to ensure it is understandable to the client and those who are culturally sensitive. Counselors should conduct the interview using the client's preferred language when possible, using an interpreter when needed. When observing a client, a counselor must ensure they do not classify behaviors as concerning or pathological, when they might be culturally appropriate for the client. For example, some clients may avoid eye contact because this is a sign of respect in their culture. In using tests, a counselor should select ones that are normed with the client population whenever possible. This means representation of the client group in the sample the researchers had in examining the psychometrics (reliability and validity) of the instrument. Although representation of the client group is preferred, it is challenging, at times, to identify instruments with inclusion of marginalized groups in the norming sample. When the counselor is unable to find a test normed for their client group, it is important that they carefully consider the construction of the test, including wording of items and response options (e.g., Likert scale), administration of the test, and interpretation of the results. Counselors may have colleagues and researchers help evaluate a test to determine cultural sensitivity. Although this may not include a rigorous research process, it provides some consideration in selecting culturally sensitive tests. Concern regarding representation within norming groups highlights a need for further development of tests normed for marginalized groups.

There are several resources available for identifying tests. The *Mental Measurements Yearbook*, published every 3 years, provides a review of numerous tests (Carlson et al., 2021). An individual can purchase a printed copy of the resource or pay for a copy of a review of a specific test. Universities may also subscribe to the *Mental Measurements Yearbook* database, thus providing it as a free resource for students and faculty. Counselors can also identify information about tests through test publishers. Also, many companies publish counseling related assessments (e.g., Pearson Assessments, Psychological Assessment Resources [PAR, Inc.], Western Psychological Services [WPS]).

Counseling professionals may also locate tests through searching scholarly articles. This may include articles focused on the development of instruments, which researchers develop for research but may not have formally published with publishing companies. A good journal for locating articles on instrument development within counseling is *Measurement and Evaluation in Counseling and Development*. After identifying an instrument of interest through an instrument development article, the counselor may contact the author and ask for permission to use the instrument. This can be advantageous for the counselor because the author may allow the counselor to use the instrument for noncommercial purposes free of charge. Additionally, counselors may identify an instrument through a research article about a topic of interest and then search the internet for the instrument.

Conducting a general search on the internet for instruments related to a specific topic may result in identifying instruments of interest; however, it is important to ensure that the instruments are well established and developed by a credible source. Additionally, counselors may develop their own instruments. However, it is important to recognize the limitations of this practice (e.g., unsure if the test measures what it is designed to measure) if the counselor does not engage in the rigorous process to examine the psychometric properties of the instrument (e.g., reliability and validity). Thus, there are several resources to examine and factors to consider when identifying and selecting tests.

In examining the use of multicultural assessment practices among psychologists (N = 239), Edwards et al. (2017) found 38% of participants reported not using a theory or framework, 17% used the *Diagnostic and Statistical Manual of Mental Disorders*, Fourth Edition (*DSM-IV*), and 11% reported using something else (e.g., clinical experience). The strategies most commonly used for multicultural assessment included exploring clients' backgrounds and examining their cultural belief systems. Additionally, the least common strategies included cultural related tests, professionals in the community, and interpreters. The researchers identified concern that although some clinicians were using researchsupported multicultural assessment strategies, many were not using them all the time, including integrating the strategies listed as most commonly used, exploring cultural considerations for presenting concerns, examining racial identity development and other psychocultural factors, and reviewing the literature on client groups. Although the participants were psychologists, and it is unknown if this is also true for counselors, the areas of multicultural assessment, identified in the article, are important for counselors to consider when engaging in the assessment process with clients.

Initial Assessment Process

At the beginning of the counseling process, it is crucial for the counselor to gather information in a comprehensive manner to help guide client treatment. Counselors use information gathered during the intake process for case conceptualization, diagnosis, and treatment planning. Relationship building is also crucial during the intake interview. The biopsychosocial-spiritual-cultural

TABLE 8.3 COMPONENTS OF THE BIOPSYCHOSOCIAL-SPIRITUAL-CULTURAL INTERVIEW

DOMAINS	AREAS OF CONSIDERATION
Biological	Medical conditions and illnesses, physical abilities, developmental milestones
Psychological	Psychological symptoms and illnesses, treatment, stressors, traumatic events including racial trauma, discrimination, and oppression
Social	Family background, living situation, sexuality, relationships (family and others), educational history, employment history, legal history, strengths, support systems
Spiritual	Religious and spiritual beliefs, values, and activities
Cultural	Cultural beliefs, norms, traditions, activities

interview enables the counselor to ask various questions to gather information within multiple domains: biological, psychological, social, spiritual, and cultural. This includes current functioning and conditions in these areas, as well as individual and family history. The biological domain focuses on medical conditions and illness, physical abilities, and developmental milestones. The psychological domain encompasses psychological symptoms and illness, treatment, stressors, and traumatic events. When considering traumatic events, it is important to include racial trauma, as well as discrimination and oppression, when working with a client from a marginalized group. The social area includes family background, living situation, sexuality, family and other personal relationships, educational history, employment history, legal history, strengths, and support systems. The spiritual domain focuses on religious and spiritual beliefs, values, and activities. Finally, the cultural domain encompasses information about the client's cultural beliefs, norms, traditions, and activities. Although integration of spiritual and cultural dimensions occurred to some degree within the *biopsychosocial* interview before adding spiritual and cultural domains to the name of the interview, this inclusion has further emphasized these areas as integral components of understanding an individual (Table 8.3). To understand the client holistically, it is important to consider the intersection of these domains and how they together tell the client's story.

During the intake assessment process, the counselor also observes the client's appearance, as well as verbal (e.g., tone of voice, speech clarity) and nonverbal (e.g., movements, facial expressions) behaviors. Furthermore, the counselor may administer tests to obtain additional data about specific areas. This may include administering a test to help gather further information to make an accurate diagnosis.

Multiple scholars have discussed cultural considerations related to the intake interview. Zalaquett et al. (2012) discussed the use of a diversity-sensitive developmental model during the intake interview and discussed several recommendations, including considering the language used to discuss the reason the client is entering counseling. Instead of referring to the reason as a *problem*, minoritized groups may prefer reframing the reason as a *challenge* or *concern*, as using problem language places the blame on the client. The counselor should also reflect on their beliefs and assumptions related to the client group before meeting with the client for the initial session. This helps the counselor have awareness of their biases and avoid making assumptions about clients before they get to know them. In relation to working with adolescents, Sommers-Flanagan and Bequette (2013) discussed formulating hypotheses and testing them during the initial interview instead of drawing conclusions about a client based on the counselor's views or experiences with adolescents. Additionally, counselors should have knowledge of the cultures of their clients. Finally, practitioners should have skills in working with the specific client group.

In conducting an intake interview with Asian American clients, Chang and O'Hara (2013) reported the importance of using a structured, directive approach; evaluating acculturation level; educating about the counseling process; understanding the client's reason for seeking counseling; using a scientific supported approach; developing multicultural competence; and considering the counselor and client's culture. Additionally, Gallardo (2013) explored relationship development during the intake assessment with Latinx clients specifically and found four major themes: (a) personalismo (prioritize the person first over the concern or task) and respeto (respect), (b) language and psychoeducation, (c) small talk, and (d) self-disclosure. Regarding conducting an intake interview with LGBTQI clients, Oh et al. (2019) discussed inclusion of the Cultural Formulation Interview (CFI) that is published in the *DSM-5* and recognition of five cultural domains: (a) client's cultural identity, (b) psychosocial stressors, (c) cultural conceptualization of distress, (d) culture related to resilience and vulnerability, and (e) cultural aspects of the counselor-client relationship. Furthermore, Heck et al. (2013) emphasized the importance of using affirmative language during the intake process with LGBTQ clients. Thus, it is crucial to be culturally sensitive during the intake interview process.

Measuring Treatment Progress and Outcomes

Throughout treatment, the counselor engages in the assessment process to continue to gather new information about the client as well as assess change in symptoms. The counselor may obtain data using any of the three assessment methods described earlier. Obtaining ongoing information about the client is crucial throughout the counseling process as clients' lives are dynamic, not static. For example, the client may experience an event that significantly affects their life (e.g., death of a loved one, loss of job). This information helps the counselor adjust treatment as needed and account for fluctuation in level of progress.

Ongoing assessment of progress is important for multiple levels of accountability. Specifically, the counselor can use data regarding progress for self-accountability by reflecting on their work with the client and determining where change might be needed to help the client to continue to progress in treatment. Additionally, when billing insurance companies for client services, the counselor may also be required to provide progress data to justify the continuation of treatment. The client may also want information about how they are progressing in treatment. For children and adolescents, the parents/guardians may also want to know their child's progress. Thus, the counselor may use progress data for various reasons to promote quality care for clients.

Measuring client outcomes, such as change in symptoms, is also a crucial aspect of the treatment process. This provides information about the success of treatment and completion of client goals. Similarly, to progress assessment data, this information is useful for the various stakeholders described previously. In addition to using individual outcome data, the counselor may also combine outcome data from various clients to assess the effectiveness of the program or intervention for multiple clients. This data can be helpful in presenting to administration for an organization to demonstrate the need and benefits of counseling.

As stated previously, it is crucial for the counselor to use appropriate assessment procedures for measuring client progress and outcomes. Assessment procedures that are not appropriate for the client (e.g., not normed with the client population) may present an inaccurate report of client progress and outcomes. Inaccurate information could have many consequences for the client, including harm to the client due to having a false perception of progress, as well as consequences for the counselor, other stakeholders, and the profession (e.g., present an intervention as being effective and encouraging use by other clinicians when there is not sufficient support for the intervention). Thus, the assessment process is an essential component of counseling, starting at the beginning of the counseling relationship through the intake session and continuing throughout the counseling process in obtaining new information and measuring progress and outcomes.

DIAGNOSING AND CASE CONCEPTUALIZATION

The diagnostic process is built upon a collaborative relationship between the counselor and the client. This process begins with information gathering that allows the counselor to better understand the client's experiences and presenting concerns. Counselors work to best conceptualize their client's experience using data gained through interviewing the client directly, as well as family members or parents, when appropriate. The interview process, known as the biopsychosocial-spiritual-cultural interview discussed in the initial assessment process earlier, includes information gathering related to mental health, ruling out physical health concerns, and gathering pertinent family history. Counselors work to understand client's cultural contexts, including their understanding of their presenting concerns, the cause of their current distress, and their cultural perspectives on the meaning of the presenting issue. The initial interview process may also include trauma screening, as many individuals seeking counseling have reported trauma histories, and this screening can allow for greater delineation between possible trauma symptoms and some mental health disorders. The counselor may also, with the client's permission, obtain information from other sources (e.g., primary care doctor, psychiatrist, school [when the client is a child]). Through gathering information, counselors work to understand the clients' experiences of distress, and its impact across life domains. This collaborative diagnostic process can serve as both a tool of affirmation and advocacy.

DSM: A HISTORY

The *Diagnostic and Statistical Manual of Mental Disorders* (*DSM*) was an outgrowth of early nosologies that served to classify mental disorders (Shorter, 2013, 2015). Current iterations of the DSM are in keeping with early European categorization of mental disorders based on symptoms. While earlier attempts at classifying psychological disorders grouped presenting ailments based on their underlying causes, those systems held less permanency because understanding symptoms led to addressing and resolving the disorders (Shorter, 2015). Disorders that have clearly understood underlying causes were found to be easy to resolve. The current symptom-based categorization used in the *DSM5* presents disorders that may hold etiologies that are less clear. As such, the *DSM* that professionals use today employs symptom-based criteria, along with specifiers, that can provide further clarity about a disorder and aid in treatment management (American Psychiatric Association, 2013). Tools to aid in the understanding and treatment of mental disorders have evolved over time. It was not until the beginning of World War II that the United States began to influence the development of the diagnostic manuals for the treatment of mental disorders.

Early development of diagnostic manuals in the United States included tools such as the *Statistical Manual for the Use of Institutions for the Insane* (SMUII), which was developed in 1942 by the U.S. Census Bureau to estimate the rate of mental disorders in the United States (Surís et al., 2016). Shortly after, in 1943, the U.S. War Department, led by William Minnenger, created the *Technical Medical Bulletin, Number 203*, known as the *Medical 203*, to provide discrete categories of mental disorders (Houts, 2000). *Medical 203* represented the growth of U.S. influence in the development of classification systems of mental disorders. It also predates the first *Diagnostic and Statistical Manual of Mental Health Disorders* (*DSM-I*). The *DSMI*, created in partnership with the American Psychiatric Association (Houts, 2000; Shorter, 2015), while heavily influenced by the *Medical 203*, was created with the intention of providing a unified system of diagnosis across mental health providers and treatment settings (Surís et al., 2016). To date, there have been seven iterations of the *DSM* (i.e., *DSMI*, *DSM-II*, *DSM-III*, *DSM-III-R*, *DSM-IV*, *DSM-IV-TR*, *and DSM-5*). Following the development of the *DSMI*, each successive publication of the *DSM* was designed with an intention to align closely with the International Classification of Diseases (ICD) codes. The ICD is a system developed in 1893, in Europe, that is now led by the World Health Organization (WHO) and is used in over 100 countries. This international system is used to evaluate, treat, research, and maintain international health and disease data. Alignment with the ICD codes can allow for the exchange and communication of disease and mortality prevalence data across countries, as well as the formulation of evidence-based treatments. In 1968, APA developed the *DSM-II* to largely align with the ICD-8 system. This version included criteria for child and adolescent mental disorders, as the previous version (*DSM-I*) only included symptom presentation of presumed adult disorders and did not include specific child or adolescent disorders. The *DSM-III* followed in 1980, which including a multiaxial system, and alignment with the ICD-9. The *DSM-III* marked the increasing recognition of the *DSM* (Shorter, 2013). Use of the *DSM-III* by hospital-based mental health providers and community counselors created a system of common language across mental health providers (Cooper, 2015; Kawa & Giordano, 2012). Over the expansive progression of the *DSM*, the list of diagnoses grew from about 50 at its inception to nearly 265 in the *DSM-III*, and nearly 292 disorders in the *DSM-III-R* (Shorter, 2013).

By 1994, the *DSM-IV* held 297 diagnoses, including an expansion of categories from the *DSM-III-R* that was published in 1984. The *DSM-IV* included seven additional sexual dysfunctions in comparison to the *DSM-III-R* (Kawa & Giordano, 2012), and removed homosexuality as a mental disorder (Drescher, 2015). The *DSM-IV* was also a shift toward a more medicalized and research-oriented model, with broader categorizations of disorders, as well as a movement toward a multiaxial diagnostic model (Kawa & Giordano, 2012). The *DSM-IV-TR*, in 2000, provided revisions to diagnostic criteria, such as the inclusion of autism spectrum disorders (ASD), including Asperger's disorder (First & Pincus, 2002). The publication of the *DSM5* in 2013 included several notable changes, including the removal of the multiaxial system and the Global Assessment of Function (GAF), a subjective scale that was used to rate clients' social, psychological, and occupational functioning. Additionally, Asperger's disorder was subsumed into the criteria for ASD. The *DSM5* also moved away from using Roman numerals as an indicator of the version of the current manual (i.e., *DSMIV* to *DSM-5*); which may also allow for greater ease of revisions (5.1, 5.2, etc.). Scholars also describe this change in numbering as evidence of a movement away from previous versions of the *DSM* (Surís et al., 2016). APA worked with WHO to align the *DSM5* with the ICD-9-CM and the ICD-10-CM codes (American Psychiatric Association, 2013).

The *DSM5-TR* (text revision) was published early in 2022. This version of the *DSM* includes updated text to multiple descriptive sections (e.g., prevalence, culture-related diagnostic features) based on the literature, updated codes and coding notes, and revisions to diagnostic criteria for multiple diagnoses (e.g., autism spectrum disorder, major depressive disorder, substance/medication-induced mental disorders). It also includes updated terminology and nomenclature (e.g., "desired gender" changed to "experienced gender," "natal male"/"natal female" changed to "individual assigned male/female at birth"), revised definitions, and renaming of disorders to be more current (e.g., "intellectual disability" changed to "intellectual developmental disorder"; APA, 2022). Additionally, the *DSM5-TR* includes a review of the effects of racism and discrimination on the development and diagnosis of mental disorders. It also includes a new diagnosis (prolonged grief disorder), symptom codes for indicating the history or presence of suicidal behavior and nonsuicidal self-injury, and restores the unspecified mood disorder category

(APA, 2022). Thus, the *DSM* continues to evolve to reflect current research and practice (Table 8.4) .

There continues to be controversy related to the expansion of behaviors and symptoms that might relate to a mental dysfunction, and the *DSM*'s continued use of categories (Cooper, 2015; Kawa & Giordano, 2012). Counselors continue to focus on best addressing the needs of clients' presenting concerns using the *DSM* as one of many sources of information to help guide the treatment process. As counselors begin to engage in decolonizing counseling approaches, less narrow methods of assessment, interpretation, and treatment will be required.

The limitations of the *DSM* and current systems of diagnosis have continued to be examined in clinical training programs. This includes recognition of the influence of pharmaceutical funding (Cosgrove et al., 2006) and the limitations of Eurocentric theories and approaches that continue to shape the discussion about mental disorders (Singh et al., 2019; Watkins & Shulman, 2008). Early development of categorical manuals used to establish our current system of diagnosis of mental disorders are rooted in very limited cultural frames. Without acknowledging the impact of social, cultural, historical, and spiritual systems of well-being, counselors continue to risk missing key components of clients' presenting concerns and needs (Singh et al., 2019; Wheeler et al., 2002; Watkins & Shulman, 2008). The need continues for recognition and deeper exploration of the historically and culturally rooted etiological considerations and approaches to treatment.

The Multicultural and Social Justice Counseling Competencies (MCSJCC; Ratts et al., 2015) emphasizes the importance of counselors continuously seeking to understand how their social positions, in relation to power and privilege across the dimensions of their identities, influence the way they see and understand the world (Ratts et al., 2015). In order to engage in this process, counselors must first work to gain awareness of themselves as they work to better understand how their worldviews are influenced by their own power and privilege (Ratts et al., 2015). Additionally, Singh et al. (2019) highlight the importance of recognizing the influences of oppressive and culturally limited foundations of current approaches to treatment. Ongoing efforts to gain self-awareness, awareness of our clients' worldviews, counseling relationships, as well as treatment will be required for counselors to adequately support clients (Ratts et al., 2015). Engaging in the work that is necessary to explore our own positionality, and the related privilege, power, and for some of us, marginalization, connects us to avenues that afford us the ability to comply with the ACA (2014) *Code of Ethics* regarding the promotion of autonomy, beneficence, fidelity, justice, nonmaleficence, and veracity.

TREATING THE DIAGNOSIS VERSUS TREATING SYMPTOMS

When clients seek counseling, they have often exhausted their available means to find relief from the pain they are experiencing. Counselors work to understand their clients' worldviews, lived experiences, and perception(s) of the sources of their presenting concerns. In seeking to understand a client's perceptions

TABLE 8.4 DIAGNOSTIC MANUAL CHANGES AND DEVELOPMENTS

VERSION	YEAR AND AUTHOR	# OF DISORDERS	SIGNIFICANT CHANGES
SMUII	U.S. Census Bureau, 1942	21	Prevalence of mental disorders
Medical 203	U.S. War Department, William Minnenger, 1943	52	Evidence of growing U.S. influence in mental disorder manual development
DSM-I	American Psychiatric Association (APA), 1952	106	More unified system of diagnosis
DSM-II	APA, 1968	182	Child & adolescent diagnosis; ICD-8 alignment
DSM-III	APA, 1980	265	Multiaxial system; ICD-9 alignment
DSM-III-R	APA, 1987	292	Clinician influence in the development of diagnostic criteria; removal of homosexuality as pathological
DSM-IV	APA, 1994	297	Seven sexual dysfunctions added; research-riented model; ICD-10 alignment
DSM-IV-TR	APA, 2000	363	Revisions to autism spectrum disorder; updated to reflect current research; reflected additional diagnostic features

(continued)

TABLE 8.4 DIAGNOSTIC MANUAL CHANGES AND DEVELOPMENTS (*CONTINUED*)

VERSION	YEAR AND AUTHOR	# OF DISORDERS	SIGNIFICANT CHANGES
DSM-5	American Psychiatric Association, 2013	157	Eliminated Asperger's disorder; removed multiaxial system and GAF scores; ICD-9-CM and ICD-10-CM alignment
DSM-5-TR	APA, 2022		One new diagnosis (prolonged grief disorder); updated terminology, codes, and literature; review of effects of racism and discrimination on manifestation and diagnosis of mental disorders

DSM, *Diagnostic and Statistical Manual of Mental Disorders*; ICD, International Classification of Diseases; SMUII, Statistical Manual for the Use of Institutions for the Insane.

of the root cause of a mental health challenge(s), counselors also invite their clients to share their understandings of the source of the concern, and an exploration of how the concern is understood within the client's familial or cultural contexts (ACA, 2014, Sections E.5.b., E.5.c.; American Psychiatric Association, 2013). Working with clients to obtain this information can be instrumental in co-developing culturally sensitive treatment plans with clients. This requires counselors to engage in self-reflection and maintain self-awareness, as they work to support their clients. Counselors' efforts to engage in this work promotes opportunities for clients to participate in counseling with lower risk of harm from the counselor. This can help to create a safer experience for marginalized clients (Cabral & Smith, 2011).

Throughout history, marginalized groups, including communities of color, have experienced discrimination across healthcare settings, including counseling. This maltreatment may be the result of a counselor's lack of awareness about a specific community, or the result of unaddressed bias (ACA, 2014; Perron et al., 2009; Schwartz & Blankenship, 2014). As such, counselors engaging in self-awareness, providing education, and addressing biases increase the opportunity for clients to have access to safe and appropriate mental health care. The counselor's willingness to engage in the necessary inner work to address biases allows for the development of healthy helping relationships.

Counselors work to build rapport and a therapeutic alliance with clients to provide a therapeutic space to address the client's presenting concern(s). Counselors gather data, and work with their clients to develop appropriate treatment plans. Counselors provide psychoeducation to clients about their diagnosis(es) and work to build collaboration in addressing presenting concerns. This work often includes affirming clients' experiences and partnering with the client to develop goals and objectives. A diagnosis can provide an opportunity for client advocacy and early collaboration in the larger work of treatment planning.

While counselors use the diagnosis process within treatment planning, treatment of a diagnosis alone can increase the risk of dehumanizing the treatment process. Diagnosis can represent another opportunity to connect with and support the needs of a client, another human being who is seeking support as they navigate challenges. Conceptualization of the client's concerns and the treatment plan should be related to the client's reported symptoms and best practices related to the treatment of the specific disorder. Effective treatment should reflect an understanding of the client's diagnosis, a collaborative treatment plan, and recognition of the client's experience. As such, a client's symptoms are often related to a potential diagnosis and should be considered in context when making decisions about treatment planning.

It is also important to acknowledge the effect of stigma regarding mental health diagnosis and treatment. Clients may have fears about receiving a diagnosis, or the potential effect that a diagnosis may have on their lives. Counselors can use the diagnostic process as a tool of advocacy, as they work to support clients in understanding what a diagnosis means, comprehending the diagnosis process, and discussing treatment options. Counselors work collaboratively with clients throughout treatment, and the diagnostic process should be collaborative as well. This collaboration should include psychoeducation about what a diagnosis means, support in helping a client to make meaning of the relevance of a diagnosis in their lives, and the utility of a potential diagnosis. It is also important to allow space for any questions that clients may have, as well as discussion related to culturally specific concerns about diagnosis in general.

Some clients may have concerns about the effect of a diagnosis on their career outcomes, perceptions of them by their loved ones, or their own perceptions of themselves. The use of person first language can be helpful as we describe a client's diagnosis. This means that we describe the client as having a diagnosis (i.e., "a person with bipolar disorder), instead of describing a person as the diagnosis (i.e., "a bipolar person"). A diagnosis should not take the place of a person's identity, and counselors work to be aware of the effect of how diagnoses are described in their work with clients. It is also important to allow space to process any concerns that a client might have and to support clients in their learning about what a particular diagnosis might mean. Additional avenues for support after receiving a diagnosis might include providing resources about supportive organizations, groups, or services, when appropriate. It can also be helpful to provide resources that a client can share with loved ones, as loved ones can be a helpful component of the client's network of support. Lastly, it is pertinent for counselors to continuously self-reflect and seek support regarding any personally or professionally held biases regarding diagnosis.

EVIDENCE-BASED PRACTICE: SELECTING TREATMENT APPROACHES

Counselors use evidence-based practices, which are approaches that have empirical evidence (research) supporting effectiveness in the treatment of a specific problem. There continues to be a need for additional data regarding minoritized populations; as such, it will be important to consider the populations that the evidence has been normed for when selecting approaches (Kirmayer, 2012). The client's context, including culture, identities, and needs, should be central in the process of treatment selection. Additionally, when selecting a treatment approach, counselors use interventions that they have expertise in and that reflects consideration of clients' values and expectations (Blair, 2010; Zalaquett & Haynes-Thoby, 2020). Expertise in a treatment approach includes having received adequate training in using it, as counselors are expected to practice within their areas of competence (ACA, 2014, Section C.2.a.). This may mean that a counselor who does not have expertise in an area will best support a client by providing a referral to a counselor who does have expertise in this area. Referrals are a part of the work that counselors do to support the needs of clients, as they aim to work within the scope of their expertise. When a client's treatment needs fall outside the scope of the counselor's competence, connecting the client to appropriate care through referral is also a means to provide appropriate care for clients. As such, counselors use a holistic approach to treatment by considering available evidence, the counselor's skills and expertise, and the client's wants and needs (Blair, 2010).

TYPES AND LENGTHS OF CARE

Selecting treatment approaches is guided by the clients' needs, including (a) severity of symptoms, (b) the client's overall health status, (c) recommendations for treatment, and (d) the client's contextual experience in relation to trauma history, marginalization, and access to resources. Counselors assess client's needs through working directly with clients to better understand their presenting concerns and their reasons for seeking treatment, coupled with shared knowledge of the client's values and beliefs. Clients are encouraged to share their understanding of their symptoms or presenting concerns, and counselors join with clients to design a treatment plan that reflects knowledge of appropriate treatments based on the clients' needs.

Counselors consider clients' presenting concerns and diagnosis(es) in formulating a comprehensive treatment plan that begins with the goals of treatment that are co-constructed with clients. Assessment processes assist counselors in exploring clients' experiences and symptoms, and recommending the most appropriate treatment type/setting, length of care, and adjunct services. Counselors consider clients' needs and severity level of concerns when determining treatment setting, which may range from outpatient services to residential treatment.

Brief therapies are often active and collaborative, and include key concepts of treatment in order to address pivotal client concerns within a limited timespan

(Lazarus & Watchel, 2010). Effective brief therapies include a clear plan to address presenting concerns within a specific timespan. As with many types of counseling, using brief therapies requires a counselor to have expertise and experience in the methods used, and the plan is constructed in collaboration with the client. Counselors partner with the client to develop an understanding of the client's presenting concerns, and identify primary areas to focus on in counseling, as well as assess the need for other services to meet the client's needs, such as medical care. Thus, counselors work with clients to determine the best course of treatment, using brief models of care, when appropriate, to focus on the clients' presenting concerns, while also addressing the challenges related to expectations of care within a specific timespan (Lazarus & Watchel, 2010).

CONCLUSION

This chapter focused on research, assessment, and diagnosis in counseling, with an emphasis on considering the unique, diverse needs of clients, families, and communities during these processes. During initial consultation and the intake process, and throughout treatment, counselors use evidence-based approaches and best practices to work with clients on addressing presenting concerns. The work counselors engage in to support their clients is often reflected in their advocacy activities, research consumption, and treatment selection. Counselors work with clients in ways that inspire hope, support development, and promote the use of new skills to navigate and broaden clients' outlook.

Summary

- Counselors should be consumers of research.
- The assessment process is ongoing throughout counseling to obtain initial information about a client, determine treatment, monitor progress, and evaluate outcomes.
- Treatment plans should be reflective of an understanding of clients' presenting needs, symptoms, and diagnosis.
- Counselors should consider clients' cultural contexts, and treatment approaches should reflect the integration of this knowledge.
- Counselors can use research as an opportunity for advocacy and to support the promotion of social justice.

Voices From the Field: QuantCrit in Counseling and Counselor Education Research

Kaprea F. Johnson, PhD
Professor, Department of Educational Studies, The Ohio State University

Quantitative critical analysis (QuantCrit) is an analytical framework that is utilized to address racism and center voices of persons and communities that have been systematically and historically marginalized by White dominant societal practices. This framework provides structure to interrogating systems that perpetuate economic, social, and emotional violence against marginalized ethnic and racial groups. The systems that carry the illusion of neutrality, such as education, healthcare, and criminal justice, and that often utilize statistics to tell their stories, are indeed the most important to critique and analyze using a QuantCrit framework. For counselors and counselor educators, our work and practice are influenced and influence those three major systems in American society, making it imperative for us to utilize a QuantCrit framework to reevaluate existing data-driven policies/practices and current research and program evaluation efforts. A foundational set of ideas to guide the utilization of QuantCrit was outlined by Gillborn et al. (2018) and included:

1. **Racism is multifaceted and its centrality within society is not readily quantifiable**. This means that the onus is "on us" to explore the social, political, and historical context because there is no "racism" question that will truly allow us to quantify the experience.

2. **Numbers are not neutral and can promote deficit analyses that serve White racial interests**. Data sources may be biased and are often used to disguise racism in our major systems (education, healthcare, and criminal justice). The responsibility is on the researcher ("us") to challenge claims of neutrality and objectivity.

3. **Categories are neither neutral nor given**. The units and forms of analysis must be critically evaluated.

4. **Data cannot "speak for itself."** Critical analyses should be informed by the experiential knowledge of marginalized groups.

5. **Statistical analyses have no inherent value but can play a role in struggles for social justice**. Statistics are socially constructed and are limited in the story they can tell; it is up to the researcher to apply the principles of Critical Race Theory to rearticulate and acknowledge the importance of race/racism in our practice and research.

These foundational ideas, self-reflectivity, and knowledge of the context in which you are engaging in research shape our awareness; it also allows us to apply Critical Race Theory (CRT) understandings and insights whenever quantitative data is encountered in policy, practice, program evaluation, and research. Utilizing QuantCrit, is a shift in intent, motivation, and focus on behalf of the researcher (Gillborn et al., 2018). The scope and purpose of the research is to uplift and support the liberation of marginalized and disenfranchised people and communities. The quantitative methods are the same, but the explanations and exploitations change. To start your journey with shifting your lens to a QuantCrit perspective, consider including a positionality statement in your research and reports that includes statistics. A positionality statement is a written self-reflection that can be included in a section on the "social location of the author(s)." This section can be used to advance your position within this area of research by identifying who you are, why you are engaging in this research, and your commitment to eradicating racism and oppression in your research endeavor. The reason it is not currently commonplace to have a positionality statement in quantitative research studies is because of the long-standing lie of neutrality and objectivity of "statistics" (i.e., numbers). A form of resistance from the dominant discourse of neutrality is your positionality statement. Your statement signals to the reader that you understand that numbers are not neutral; it counters the lie, provides the reader with context, and starts the process of counterstorytelling from a researcher perspective. Your positionality statement can also be utilized to start dialogue with coauthors/research team members about your internal wisdom on the topic or highlight that there is a need for experiential wisdom on the team from someone with whom the research will directly impact. Lastly, and most important, is ensuring space for participants to engage in counterstorytelling. This space elevates minority voices, experiences, and perspectives and places their experiential wisdom within the dominant culture research and literature.

An additional exercise to begin shifting your lens to a QuantCrit framework entails critically reengaging with published studies that you use to inform your research and practice decisions. I have drafted questions that can provide thoughts to reflect on as you critically review research studies or evaluation reports; additionally, this list can be used as a starting place to discuss the preparation of your next research or evaluation project. Points of reflection can engage the following:

1. Is context (social, historical, political, etc.) included within the introduction or literature review?
2. Is race/racism or intersectionality critiqued in the review of the literature?
3. If studies upheld White ideologies, liberalism, meritocracy, or claims of color blindness, was this called out as a critique (or condemned)?

4. Were deficit-based statements or statistics used about racial/ethnic groups within the literature review for justifying "the problem" (i.e., developing the problem statement)?
5. Does the theoretical framework help advance the stories of people of color; is it a critical framework that supports counterstorytelling?
6. Does the theoretical framework imply colorblindness, meritocracy, or uplift the dominant cultures discourse?
7. Does the theoretical framework help explain the research problem under investigation by centering race/racism?
8. In the methods section do the authors provide "context" for their research engagement with the topic?
9. Is there a positionality statement in the methods section that discusses the author's social location, connection to the work, and commitment to the community?
10. Do authors articulate their "intent" (i.e., dismantle systemic oppression; legitimatize a counternarrative; uplift the stories/voice of marginalized persons)?
11. How was experiential wisdom utilized (i.e., co-development of a scale; pilot study; inclusion of race-focused constructs; utilizing culturally appropriate scales/measures)?
12. Does the research question exclusively examine individual characteristics (e.g., differences between Black and White students' academic achievement) with no examination or acknowledgment of systemic racism?
13. Was race utilized in the study as a predictor (i.e., examining individual characteristics leading to a deficit approach)?
14. Were groups created that can potentially hide racism (i.e., White vs. non-White)
15. Was a counternarrative (i.e., counterstorytelling) included?
16. In the discussion, were people interrogated versus systems that cause oppression (i.e., conclusions that found an outcome based on a social location characteristic, such as race versus a discussion on racism)?
17. Was race/racism or intersectionality discussed in the discussion or implications?
18. Were the results connected to social justice?
19. Was a social justice action articulated in the discussion, implications, or concluding remarks?
20. Were tenets and/or CRT language included in the discussion or implication sections?
21. Does the implications section situate the results and what's added from a CRT perspective?
22. Do the concluding remarks reemphasize the action and next steps?
23. *Please add more reflections you use to critique research or evaluation reports.*

Voices From the Field: Diagnosis

Margaret "Peggy" Lorrah, Assistant Vice President of Student Affairs, Retired,
The Pennsylvania State University

As a recently retired licensed professional counselor and counselor educator specializing in trauma and addiction and a university administrator focusing on equity and inclusion for marginalized students, I am honored to share some of my perspectives and experiences with diagnosis. Having taught a Diagnosis for Counselors class for graduate students for approximately 15 years, I have been delighted to welcome students into the profession and to stress the importance of our being advocates for clients/consumers, beginning with the assessment and diagnosis process. I practiced as a feminist therapist with deep roots in person-centered and existential theory bases. Through this lens, assessment and diagnosis are part of a collaborative partnership between the client and me, and I understand and affirm that clients are the experts on their lived experiences. As I gather information about reasons an individual is seeking services, we talk about their concerns about the process, including what a diagnosis is and isn't. I am always clear to stress that diagnosis is simply a tool—a snapshot in time—that can assist in providing support and relief from distress; it *does not* define who the client is. When the client completes their initial sharing of issues and feelings, I tell them about the *DSM* and open it to the section that seems to best fit their description of what is currently happening. We then look at the list of symptoms and behaviors to see how they match the client's experience. As we narrow this, I discuss the pros and cons of the diagnostic category and address any questions or concerns. I focus particularly on long-term implications for any given diagnosis; for example, is this a diagnosis that could have an impact on one's schooling or employment; is it a diagnosis that could lead to current or future denial of insurance coverage; and is there stigma attached to this diagnosis that could be damaging in any fashion. Having this discussion allows the client to make an informed decision about the course of the work we might do together.

Within this framework, I would like to share what this has looked like over time for a particular marginalized population with whom I have had the opportunity to work clients who identify as transgender and who are seeking gender-affirming surgery. I will preface this by saying that the field has made tremendous strides in this area and that most of the credit for this goes to activists and advocates within the nonbinary, gender queer, LGBTQAA+ communities who insisted on their rights to have their lived experiences respected and honored. Along the way, there were many opportunities for medical and mental health professionals who heard and understood their concerns to provide support and advocacy within the field.

The community mental health agency where I worked in the late 1980s was situated an hour away from a large metropolitan medical center that provided both hormone therapy and what was then called "sex change surgery" to adult patients we now typically call transgender or gender queer. In order to be considered a candidate for this surgery, a patient would have to live for a year as "the other gender" and consistently work with a mental health professional for

2 years. Mental health professionals were called "gatekeepers" of this process, literally meaning that, no matter what else the circumstances were, if a practitioner decided that surgery was not indicated, it could not happen. At the end of the 2 years, the therapist was required to write a letter detailing the course of treatment and approving or disapproving the surgery. At that time, there was no diagnostic category pertaining to gender identity. It was not until 1994 and *DSM-IV* that gender identity disorder became a diagnostic category, with gender dysphoria taking its place with *DSM-5* in 2013.

From the time I began seeing clients referred by the medical center, I was clear that each person I met had made the choice to go forward after years of struggling with the knowledge that they were living as a member of a gender other than expected based on the sex or gender assigned at birth. Their descriptions of the process were typically pained and expressed as "My body doesn't match the gender I know myself to be." I had no doubts that this was true and that I did not have the right to override the clear decision a client had already made. I saw my therapeutic role as providing support, affirmation, and advocacy for these individuals, not making decisions for them. I have never used gender identity disorder as a diagnosis, and had I been seeing transgender clients after the category of gender dysphoria was added, I would not have used that as a diagnosis. I have always situated these diagnoses within the culture, not within the individuals with whom I have worked. Building from their lived experiences and in collaboration with clients, I have documented diagnoses such as generalized anxiety disorder and posttraumatic stress disorder with a qualifier such as "as a result of harassment and victimization occurring because of familial, community, or societal targeting and discrimination based on gender expression." I was clear about my rationale in my supportive recommendation letters that the "problem" was situated outside the client and that the requested surgery was the solution, and I found that the medical center was willing to honor the client's decision and proceed with the surgical intervention.

As the field has evolved to catch up with the lived experiences of transgender and gender queer individuals, many obstacles such as this have been lessened or removed, and the seventh edition "Standards of Care for the Health of Transsexual, Transgender, and Gender Nonconforming People" (Coleman et al., 2012) published by the World Professional Association for Transgender Health (WPATH) is clear to say that nonconforming gender expression or identity is not inherently disordered. In 2010, they issued a statement urging the "depsychopathogizing of gender non-conformity." I expect that we will continue to see an evolution of guidelines we use to assess affirming work with transgender, nonbinary, gender nonconforming, and gender queer individuals. My hope and expectations are that some folks reading this textbook will be at the forefront of advocacy and the continued striving for best practices as the field moves forward.

A Call to Action

Select a mental health diagnosis and research facts and myths/assumptions about the diagnosis, including multicultural considerations. Then, create a flyer/brochure/social media post to present this information to a population of your choice (e.g., general population, clients of a specific age group, family members, mental health professionals). Consider how you communicate that a diagnosis is not the client's identity, but can be a part of what explains a portion of their experience?

Case Study 8.1

Kam is a 17-year-old high school student in 12th grade. His mother reports that he has been spending less time interacting with his peers and more time alone in his room. Kam describes feeling depressed and reports struggling to feel hopeful over the past few weeks. He previously played sports and participated in the school band. Kam described himself as being very successful in soccer, graphic design, and playing the trombone in the past. Recently, Kam has begun to disengage, and has struggled with discussing life after graduation. Kam reports wanting to feel excited again, but states that he just feels "out of it."

RESPONSE QUESTIONS

1. How might you approach your work with Kam?
2. What additional information might you need to know about Kam in order to best understand and partner with him in navigating his presenting concerns (cultural context, familial relationships, symptom presentation, etc.)?
3. How might understanding Kam's cultural contexts aid in your selection of treatment and interventions?

Going Within

Think about the components of the biopsychosocial-spiritual-cultural interview discussed in the assessment section in this chapter. What area(s) might be difficult/uncomfortable for you to discuss with clients? What steps can you take to address this difficulty/uncomfortableness so that it does not negatively affect your future work with clients?

Group Process

In small groups, discuss your thoughts about mental health diagnoses, creating a list of advantages and disadvantages. Explore whether the pros and cons differ for specific populations and marginalized groups. Consider if there are actions counselors can take to prevent or reduce the disadvantages. Have a spokesperson from each small group present the information to the class for a classroom discussion.

RESOURCES

Association for Assessment and Research in Counseling: https://aarc-counseling
.org/resources
Buros Center for Testing. (n.d.). Mental Measurements Yearbook: https://buros
.org/mental-measurements-yearbook
Pearson Assessments: https://www.pearsonassessments.com
Psychological Assessment Resources (PAR, Inc): https://www.parinc.com
Western Psychological Services (WPS): https://www.wpspublish.com

Access this podcast at https://connect.springerpub.com/content/book/978-0-8261-6386-8/chapter/ch08.

KEY REFERENCES

Only key references appear in the print edition. The full reference list appears in the digital product found on https://connect.springerpub.com/content/book/978-0-8261-6386-8/chapter/ch08

American Psychiatric Association. (2013). *Diagnostic and statistical manual of mental disorders* (5th ed.). American Psychiatric Publishing.

American Psychiatric Association. (2022). *Diagnostic and statistical manual of mental disorders, text revision DSM-5-TR (5th ed.).* American Psychiatric Publishing. https://www.appi.org/dsm

Johnson, K. (2021). *Introduction to QuantCrit for counseling researchers.* ACES Diversity and Inclusion. https://www.youtube.com/watch?v=KkMB7EKQaUo

Kawa, S., & Giordano, J. (2012). A brief historicity of the diagnostic and statistical manual of mental disorders: Issues and implications for the future of psychiatric canon and practice. *Philosophy, Ethics, and Humanities in Medicine, 7*(2), 1–9. https://doi.org/10.1186/1747-5341-7-2

Kirmayer, L. J. (2012). Cultural competence and evidence-based practice in mental health: Epistemic communities and the politics of pluralism. *Social Science & Medicine (1982), 75*(2), 249–256. https://doi.org/10.1016/j.socscimed.2012.03.018

Ratts, M. J., Singh, A. A., Nassar-McMillan, S., Butler, S. K., & McCullough, J. R. (2015). *Multicultural and Social Justice Counseling Competencies.* https://www.counseling.org/docs/default-source/competencies/multicultural-and-social-justice-counseling-competencies.pdf?sfvrsn=14

Singh, A. A., Appling, B., & Trepal, H. (2019). Using the multicultural and social justice counseling competencies to decolonize counseling practice: The important roles of theory, power, and action. *Journal of Counseling & Development, 98*(3), 261–271. https://doi.org/10.1002/jcad.12321

Zalaquett, C. P., Chatters, S. J., & Ivey, A. E. (2012). Psychotherapy integration: Using a diversity-sensitive developmental model in the initial interview. *Journal of Contemporary Psychotherapy, 43*(1), 53–62. https://doi.org/10.1007/s10879-012-9224-6

SUBSTANCE-RELATED DISORDERS, BEHAVIORAL ADDICTIONS, AND COUNSELING

Jacqueline M. Swank

Think about this...

What are some substances that are misused? What are some behavioral addictions? What is the etiology of addictions and what are effective ways to treat addictions?

LEARNING OBJECTIVES

After reading this chapter, you should be able to:

- Review the history of drug use in the United States
- Outline the prevalence of problematic drug use and disorders/addictions in the United States
- Explain the etiology of addictions
- Identify three systems to classify drugs
- Discuss common behavioral addictions
- Identify addiction treatment settings
- Describe the continuum of care for addictions
- Recognize stigma related to addictions

INTRODUCTION

Substance-related disorders and behavioral concerns and addictions are prevalent in the United States. Therefore, across their careers, counselors will likely work with many clients who have these concerns, disorders, and addictions, or have family members experiencing them. Thus, it is important that counselors have knowledge about various substances misused, problematic behaviors, and skills in working with clients with these concerns and their family members. This chapter focuses on a review of the history of drug use and prevalence rates in the United States. Additionally, the author discusses the etiology of addiction, classification of drugs, types of drugs, and different types of behavioral addictions. The chapter also includes a discussion of the treatment process, treatment settings, and evidence-based practices for treating addictions. Finally, the author discusses stigma related to addictions and outlines strategies for addressing it.

HISTORY OF DRUG USE IN THE UNITED STATES

People have used drugs for recreational and medical purposes in the United States since the country began (History.com, 2019). In describing the history of drug use, Buchanan (1992) reports two movements: (a) drug use increasing throughout history following a major national crisis, and (b) efforts against drug use. Buchanan discusses three periods of increased drug use in U.S. history that are highlighted below: (a) following the Revolutionary War, (b) after the Civil War, and (c) in the 1960s. Alcohol consumption has been woven into the social fabric of U.S. society since the founding of the country; however, there was a dramatic increase following the Revolutionary War. Many people in the United States became concerned with the increase in alcohol consumption as the crime rate increased. This led to support for the temperance movement, which began in the 1830s and focused on moderation of alcohol, often emphasizing abstinence (Buchanan, 1992).

According to Buchanan (1992), alcohol use rose again after the Civil War in the 1860s and 1870s, and the use of cigarettes, opium, and morphine also became popular. Cigarette use increased with Northern soldiers exposed to tobacco plantations in the South during the Civil War. The invention of the hypodermic needle in 1850 increased the use of narcotics. While some soldiers became addicted to morphine after receiving it when wounded, during the war, the biggest percentage of individuals experiencing addiction were White upper and middle class women. This may have resulted from restricting their access to alcohol, and thus, they substituted other substances (e.g., opium, heroin). Additionally, opioids were commonly used in various medicines, including cough syrup (Woody, 2014). According to History.com (2019), cocaine was available for purchase in the Sears and Roebuck catalogue in the 1890s.

The Progressive Era was characterized by many reforms, including another wave of prohibition (Buchanan, 1992). The first laws regarding the use and distribution of opiates and cocaine were passed in the late 1800s and early 1900s, including the Harrison Narcotics Tax Act of 1914, which required people to be registered and taxed for producing and distributing cocaine and opioids (Woody, 2014). Alcohol prohibition (18th Amendment) was passed in 1919 and not overturned until 1933 with the 21st Amendment. During WWI, American soldiers were given free cigarettes, and there was limited action to address smoking until the Surgeon General's report in 1964 related to the health effects of smoking (Buchanan, 1992).

A third wave of increased drug use occurred in the 1960s and 1970s, with a surge in use of marijuana and psychedelics (e.g., LSD, psilocybin; Buchanan, 1992). In 1970, the government passed the Controlled Substances Act that regulated certain substances (see the five schedules of drugs presented in the "Classification of Drugs" section and Table 9.1). Then, in 1971, President Richard Nixon launched an initiative called the War on Drugs, which focused on stopping illegal drug use by increasing prison sentences for users and dealers (History.com, 2019). When Ronald Reagan became president in 1981, he reprioritized the War on Drugs, and in 1984, his wife, Nancy Reagan, started the "Just Say No" to drugs campaign (History.com, 2019). However, antidrug legislation was criticized for the emphasis on imprisonment instead of treatment programs, the increase in incarceration rates for nonviolent drug offenses, and for targeting people of color (POC), who were arrested at higher rates than White people (History.com, 2019). In 2014, approximately half of all incarcerations were for drug-related offenses (History.com, 2019).

Another key event occurred in the late 1990s related to opioid use. Pharmaceutical companies convinced physicians that prescriptions for opioid pain relievers would not lead to an addiction to opioids. This led to an increase in opioid prescriptions, misuse of prescriptions and nonprescription opioids, opioid overdoses, and babies having opioid withdrawal symptoms due to their mother's use during pregnancy (U.S. Department of Health and HumanServices [DHHS], n.d.). Tragically, in 2016, more than 42,000 people died from an opioid overdose, with an estimated 40% involving a prescription opioid (DHHS, n.d.). Then, the DHHS announced a public health emergency to address the opioid crisis in 2017. Thus, drug use continues to be a significant health crisis in the United States (see Table 9.2).

PREVALENCE OF DRUG USE IN THE UNITED STATES

The National Center for Drug Abuse Statistics (National Center for Drug Abuse Statistics, 2022) provides a wealth of information regarding the prevalence of problematic drug use and the consequences of misuse in the United States. According to the survey, there were 53 million people age 12 and over (19%) who misused prescription drugs or used illegal drugs in the last year. Additionally, 14.8 million (11%) of those who drank alcohol had an alcohol use disorder. There are also differences in the types of drugs used and the pattern of drug use across populations. Specifically, males are more likely to be affected by substance use disorders and drug use, and drug use is highest (39%) among people ages 18–25 years. Moreover, club drugs (i.e., ecstasy, cocaine, LSD, methamphetamine) are most common in high-income places, while inhalants (i.e., gasoline, paint thinner, glue) are most common among low-income users. Also, veterans are more

TABLE 9.1 DRUG CLASSIFICATION SYSTEMS

DRUG CLASSIFICATION SYSTEM	CATEGORIES
LEGAL DEFINITION	**Schedule I**—highest potential risk and no acceptance for medical use Examples: heroin, ecstasy, LSD, marijuana
	Schedule II—high potential risk Examples: cocaine, Vicodin, methamphetamine, oxycodone, Ritalin, Adderall, fentanyl
	Schedule III—moderate to low potential risk Examples: Tylenol with codeine, anabolic steroids, testosterone
	Schedule IV—low risk Examples: Valium, Xanax, Ativan, Ambien, Tramadol
	Schedule V—lowest risk Examples: Robitussin AC, Lomotil, Lyrica, Motofen
EFFECT ON MIND AND BODY	**Stimulants**—uppers Examples: cocaine, Adderall, methamphetamine
	Depressants—downers Examples: alcohol, barbiturates, opiates
	Hallucinogens—alter perception of reality Examples: LSD, PCP
	Inhalants—huffing Examples: paint thinner, gasoline, glue

(continued)

TABLE 9.1 DRUG CLASSIFICATION SYSTEMS (*CONTINUED*)

DRUG CLASSIFICATION SYSTEM	CATEGORIES
CHEMICAL COMPOSITION	**Alcohol**—suppress CNS Examples: beer, wine
	Barbiturates—slow down CNS Examples: Amytal, Luminal
	Benzodiazepines—interact with neurotransmitter Examples: Ativan, Valium, Xanax
	Cannabinoids—create a high Examples: marijuana, hashish
	Opioids—serve as painkillers Examples: heroine, fentanyl, oxycodone

CNS, central nervous system; LSD, lysergic acid diethylamide; PCP, phencyclidine.
Source: Information from Juergens, J. (2022, May 23). Drug classifications. Addiction Center. https://www.addictioncenter.com/drugs/drug-classifications

likely to struggle with illegal drug use and misuse of prescription pain medication than the general U.S. population. Regarding the consequence of problematic substance use, over 70,000 people die each year from a drug overdose, and over 95,000 people die each year due to alcohol abuse. Substance use disorders (SUDs) affect over 20 million people in the United States who are age 12 and older, with marijuana and prescription pain medication being the most common substances misused. Thus, substance-related concerns and disorders are significant issues in the United States, with some groups being at a higher risk.

ADDICTION ETIOLOGY AND PROCESS

A substance is "a psychoactive compound with the potential to cause health and social problems" (DHHS, 2016, p. 1–6). The DHHS (2016) defines addiction as "the most severe form of substance use disorder, associated with compulsive or uncontrolled use of one or more substances. Addiction to drugs is a chronic brain disease that has the potential for both recurrence (relapse) and recovery" (p.1–6). Viewing an addiction as a chronic disease is a medical model perspective, with changes in the brain and genetic predispositions serving as etiological factors (SAMHSA, 2019). Addiction involves three stages: (a) binge/intoxication, (b) withdrawal/negative affect, and (c) preoccupation/anticipation (DHHS, 2016)). In the binge stage, the individual takes the substance and experiences a pleasurable effect, referred to as a high, through activation of the brain reward system. In the second stage, the individual experiences a negative effect associated with not having the substance (i.e., withdrawal). The third stage involves seeking the substance. The pleasurable experience resulting from

TABLE 9.2 HISTORY OF DRUG USE IN THE UNITED STATES

DATE	EVENT
1800–1830	Increase in alcohol consumption following the Revolutionary War
1830s	Temperance Movement to moderate alcohol consumption and promote abstinence
1860s–1870s	Popularity of cigarettes, opium, and morphine
1850	Invention of hypodermic needle
1890s	Cocaine for sale in Sears and Roebuck catalogue
Late 1890s	Progressive Era with another wave of prohibition
1914	Harrison Narcotics Tax Act passed
1917	United States enters WWI and soldiers are given free cigarettes
1919	18th Amendment passed: alcohol prohibition
1933	21st Amendment passed: overturns 18th Amendment
1964	Surgeon General's report on the health effects of smoking
1960s–1970s	Third wave of drug use: marijuana and psychedelics (e.g., LSD, psilocybin)
1970	Controlled Substances Act passed
1971	Nixon's War on Drugs initiative launched
1984	"Just Say No" to drugs campaign launched
Late 1990s	Increase in prescriptions for opioid pain relievers
2017	U.S. Department of Health and Human Services announces public health emergency to address the opioid crisis

Source: Data from Buchanan, D. R. (1992). A social history of American drug use. *The Journal of Drug Issues, 22*(1), 31–52; Woody, G. E. (2014). Progress in addiction treatment: From one-size-fits-all to medications and treatment matching. *Substance Abuse, 35,* 110–113; History.com. (2019). *War on drugs.* https://www.history.com/topics/crime/the-war-on-drugs#section_1

consuming the substance increases the likelihood of repeated use (DHHS, 2016; Ouzir & Errami, 2016).

In addition to the medical model, SAMHSA (2019) described five other models: moral/legal, psychological, spiritual, sociocultural, and integrated. Within the moral/legal model, addiction involves behaviors that violate moral codes and laws. Treatment focuses on abstinence and external control through incarceration and hospitalization. In considering addiction from a psychological perspective, the causes consist of emotional dysregulation, psychopathology, and learning impairment, with treatment focusing on therapies that address these areas, including behavioral, cognitive, and psychodynamic approaches. In the spiritual model, addiction is a spiritual disease, with a need to recognize self-limitations. Treatment focuses on using 12-step models or other faith-based recovery programs. Within the sociocultural model, addiction is rooted in social and cultural factors, including cultural and family beliefs and values, socio-economic status (SES), substance availability, family and cultural norms and expectations, and laws and consequences. Treatment focuses on considering cultural factors, while focusing on developing healthy relationships and social skills (SAMHSA, 2019).

The final model of addiction, discussed by SAMHSA (2019), is the integrated treatment model, which is more widely embraced as an optimal approach. Within this model, the etiology of addiction involves multiple factors rooted in the various models previously presented. This may include a genetic predisposition, personality traits (e.g., impulsivity, desire for risk taking), environmental factors (e.g., socialization, cultural factors, early life experiences such as abuse and trauma), and the presence of a psychiatric disorder (Ouzir & Errami, 2016). Treatment involves embracing a biopsychosocial-cultural-spiritual approach (SAMHSA, 2019).

CLASSIFICATION OF DRUGS

There are many systems to classify the thousands of drugs available. The Addiction Center (Juergens, 2022a) describes three common classification types: (a) legal definition, (b) effects on the mind and body, and (c) chemical makeup (see Table 9.1). The federal government established the five drug schedules or classifications in 1970 with the passage of the Controlled Substances Act. This system is based on the potential for problematic use and physical and psychological dependency, and level of acceptance for medical purposes. Schedule I (e.g., heroin, LSD, marijuana) has the greatest potential risk for problematic use and dependency and no acceptance for medical use, and schedule V (e.g., Robitussin AC) has the lowest level of potential risk. The second drug classification system is based on the effects of the drugs on the mind and the body. The Addiction Center (Juergens (2022a) discusses four categories within this system: (a) stimulants, (b) depressants, (c) hallucinogens, and (d) inhalants. A third classification system involves grouping drugs by chemical composition. The Addiction Center (Juergens, 2022a) describes five categories in this system: (a) alcohol, (b) barbiturates, (c) benzodiazepines, (d) cannabinoids, and (e) opioids. While there are many drugs that may be addictive, there are also other types of addictions.

SUBSTANCE-RELATED DISORDERS

There are 10 classes of drugs within the substance-related and addictive disorder section of the *Diagnostic and Statistical Manual of Mental Disorders* (DSM-5).

However, the *DSM-5-TR* (text revision) was published early in 2022. Some changes to the substance-related and addictive disorders section include change in diagnostic criteria to the substance/medication-induced mental disorders, and updates to codes and coding notes (American Psychiatric Association [APA], 2022). The 10 classes of drugs, listed in the *DSM-5-TR*, are as follows:

- Alcohol
- Caffeine
- Cannabis
- Hallucinogens (with separate categories for phencyclidine and other hallucinogens)
- Inhalants
- Opioids
- Sedatives, hypnotics, and anxiolytics
- Stimulants (amphetamine-type substances, cocaine, and other stimulants)
- Tobacco
- Other or unknown

This section of the *DSM-5* also includes gambling disorder (discussed in the behavioral addictions section below). There are no other behavioral addictions included in the *DSM-5* because according to the American Psychiatric Association (APA, 2013), there is not enough evidence to identify them as mental disorders.

There are two groupings of substance-related disorders in the *DSM-5*: (a) substance use disorders and (b) substance-induced disorders that includes intoxication, withdrawal, and other substance/medication-induced mental disorders (anxiety disorders, bipolar and related disorders, delirium, depressive disorders, neurocognitive disorders, obsessive-compulsive and related disorders, psychotic disorders, sexual dysfunctions, and sleep disorders). Nine of the 10 classes of drugs listed above have a substance use disorder, with caffeine being the only exception (APA, 2013). Nine of the classes have a substance intoxication disorder (all except tobacco), and eight have a substance withdrawal disorder (all except both hallucinogen categories [phencyclidine, and other hallucinogens] and inhalants). Discussing the criteria for each of the disorders included in the substance-related and addictive disorders section of the *DSM-5/DSM-5-TR* (APA, 2013, APA, 2022) is beyond the scope of this chapter, but you can read more about this directly in the *DSM-5/DSM-5-TR*. However, a brief description of each of the 10 classes of drugs follows.

Alcohol

Alcohol depresses the central nervous system (CNS) and impairs judgment. It can also damage the body, including the liver, which may result in cirrhosis. It is the most commonly misused drug (Juergens, 2022a), and 261 Americans die a day as a result of excessive alcohol use (National Center for Drug Abuse Statistics, 2022). Examples of alcohol include beer, wine, and liquors.

Caffeine

Caffeine stimulates the CNS and can increase concentration and improve a person's mood (Hilliard, 2021). Many people consume caffeine to increase alertness, especially in the morning (e.g., drinking coffee). People who consume too much caffeine may experience a variety of symptoms including restlessness, nervousness, and irritability (APA, 2013). Additionally, individuals who regularly consume caffeine may experience headaches and fatigue if they try to stop consuming it (APA, 2013). Sources of caffeine include soft drinks/soda, coffee, tea, and energy drinks.

Cannabis

Cannabis is material that comes from the cannabis plant or similar synthetic compounds. It is referred to by many names, including weed, pot, grass, hash, mary jane, etc. It is typically smoked, but may also be ingested. It creates a high and is the second most commonly misused drug, following alcohol (Juergens, 2022a). In addition to being used recreationally, cannabis is also used for medical purposes.

Hallucinogens

Hallucinogens can be taken orally (most common), smoked, snorted, or injected (APA, 2013). Hallucinogens alter the state of reality and may cause visual and auditory hallucinations, known as tripping (Juergens, 2022a). Phencyclidine is also known as PCP or angel dust, and two examples of phencyclidine-like substances are ketamine and cyclohexamine. Examples of other hallucinogens include ecstasy, DMT, and MDMA (APA, 2013).

Inhalants

Inhalants involve inhaling (huffing) volatile hydrocarbons (toxic gases). Individuals can inhale these toxic gases from many common products, including paint, fuel, and glue (APA, 2013). Inhaling the gases can result in feeling high (Juergens, 2022a).

Opioids

According to the Addiction Center (Juergens, 2022c) opioids are synthetically manufactured, while opiates come from opium that is in poppy plants. They produce similar effects; therefore, they are usually grouped together. These substances activate the brain receptors and depress the CNS (Juergens, 2022c). An addiction to these substances may begin by receiving a prescription for pain medication from a doctor. They serve as painkillers, while also creating pleasure. They are the most addictive substances (Juergens, 2022c). Examples of opioids and opiates include codeine, oxycodone, heroin, morphine, fentanyl, demerol, and methadone (Juergens, 2022c).

Sedatives, Hypnotics, and Anxiolytics

Sedatives, hypnotics, and anxiolytics include barbiturates, barbiturate-like hypnotics, benzodiazepines, and benzodiazepine-like drugs. Barbiturates cause the CNS to slow down and are used for anesthesia and to treat various conditions including epilepsy. Benzodiazepines (benzos) interact with gamma-aminobutyric acid-A (GABA-A), a neurotransmitter. They are used to treat sleep disorders and psychiatric conditions, including anxiety (Juergens, 2022a). Examples of drugs in this category include sleeping pills, Ativan, Valium, and Xanax.

Stimulants

Stimulants (uppers) produce dopamine in the brain, causing the individual to experience pleasure. They increase concentration and energy, and increase productivity (Juergens, 2022a). They are taken orally, injected, or snorted. Stimulants include both prescription drugs and illegal drugs. Examples of prescription drugs include Adderall, Ritalin, and Concerta. Examples of illegal stimulants include cocaine, crack, and crystal meth.

Tobacco

Tobacco contains nicotine, which is a stimulant, but it affects the body differently than some other stimulants. Instead of producing a high like cocaine, it causes an increase in breathing and blood pressure due to stimulating the adrenal glands (Juergens, 2022b). Examples of tobacco include cigarettes, cigars, and chewing tobacco. There are 58.8 million people who use tobacco (National Center for Drug Abuse Statistics, 2022).

BEHAVIORAL ADDICTIONS

When people think of an addiction, they may think of alcohol or a variety of drugs; however, an individual may also have an addiction related to a compulsive behavior, which are known as behavioral or process addictions. A behavioral/process addiction is "any compulsive-like behavior that interferes with normal living and causes significant negative consequences in a person's family, work, and social life" (Wilson & Johnson, 2013). Behavioral addictions affect the brain similarly to addictions to substances (Wilson & Johnson, 2013). While the only behavioral addiction included in the *DSM-5* is gambling disorder, other behavioral addictions were considered with the internet gaming disorder listed as a condition for further study (Konkolÿ Thege et al., 2015). Additionally, people with symptoms of various behavioral addictions may be diagnosed with impulse control disorders, not otherwise specified.

There is controversy about whether more behavioral addictions should be included in the *DSM*. Specifically, some clinicians are concerned that classifying more behaviors as addictions, thus medicalizing them, will result in the public not taking psychiatric disorders seriously, due to increasing numbers of people that will have some type of *DSM* diagnosis (Konkolÿ Thege et al., 2015). Another potential concern is that if more people are diagnosed with some addictions, the public may start viewing these addictions as a feature of life instead of as psychopathology (Konkolÿ Thege et al., 2015; Sussman et al., 2011). A third concern is that medicalizing these addictions shifts the focus away from the systems that may increase a person's risk for these behaviors by putting the focus instead on the person (Konkolÿ Thege et al., 2015; Lee & Mysyk, 2004). Thus, there are areas to consider when thinking about adding more behavioral addictions to the *DSM*. We discuss eight common behavioral addictions next: food/eating, exercise, gambling, gaming, internet, sex, shopping, and working.

Food Addictions

Food addictions or eating addictions may include binge eating and compulsive overeating. Palatable foods in particular (e.g., rich in sugar, salt, and fat) may trigger the reward and pleasure center of the brain (increase dopamine transmission) that is also activated by drug addictions (Goodman, 2020). In a review of 25 studies, the weighted mean prevalence of food addictions was 19.9% among adults, with the rate being double among individuals who were overweight (24.9%) compared to those with a healthy body mass index (BMI; 11.1%) (Pursey et al., 2014). To assess for addictive eating behaviors, scholars developed the Yale Food Addiction Scale Version 2.0 (YFAS 2.0; Gearhardt et al., 2016). Additionally, the Dimensional Yale Food Addiction Scale for Children 2.0 (dYFAS-C 2.0; Schiestl & Gearhardt, 2018) is designed for children. Food addictions may be more difficult to recover from than other substances because people need to consume food to sustain life; however, people in recovery from food addictions may choose to avoid certain foods, such as highly palatable foods (Goodman, 2020). In addition to counseling, treatment may also include working with a nutritionist. There is also a 12-step program for individuals with food addictions called Food Addicts Anonymous (FAA), which believes that food addiction is a biochemical disorder and can be managed by not consuming addictive foods and having a nutrition plan (FAA, 2021).

Exercise Addiction

Engaging in frequent exercise does not necessarily mean that someone has an exercise addiction, as athletes train intensively, and this alone does not mean they have an addiction. Having an exercise addiction or engaging in compulsive exercise means that one's life revolves around exercise, with exercise becoming a priority above everything else. Individuals with an exercise addiction may also exercise even when they have an injury (Freimuth et al., 2011). The prevalence of exercise addiction is approximately 3% among the general population (Sussman et al., 2011). Common co-occurring disorders with exercise addiction are eating disorders and body image disorders (Freimuth et al., 2011). Instruments used to assess for exercise addiction include the Exercise Dependence Scale-Revised (EDS-R; Downs et al., 2004) and the Exercise Addiction Inventory (EAI; Terry et al., 2020). A treatment goal may be to return to moderate exercise, instead of eliminating exercise completely (Freimuth et al., 2011). There are also support groups for people with an exercise addiction.

Gambling Addiction

Gambling has increased with the legalization and acceptance of it. Gambling disorder is the only condition in the "non-substance-related disorders" subsection of the "substance-related and addictive disorders" category in the *DSM-5*. The prevalence of problem gambling ranges from 0.1 to 6.0% (Abbott, 2017). Individuals at risk for a gambling addiction include young adults, males, Indigenous people and some ethnic minority groups, individuals with low socioeconomic status (SES), and those who are not married (Abbott, 2017). Gambling may occur with other disorders, such as substance use disorders (Abbott, 2017). An assessment used to evaluate problematic gambling is the Brief Problem Gambling Screen (BPGS; Volberg & Williams, 2011). There are various treatment options for individuals with a gambling addiction, as well as support groups (Gamblers Anonymous), and a gambling addiction hotline run by the National Council on Problem Gambling.

Computer and Internet Addictions

The Addiction Center (Hoeg, 2021) lists five types of computer and internet addictions, including (a) cybersex addiction, (b) net compulsion (e.g., online gambling, compulsive online shopping), (c) cyber relationship addiction, (d) compulsive information seeking, and (e) computer or gaming addiction. In a systematic review and meta-analysis, Pan et al. (2020) found the weighted average prevalence for generalized internet addiction was 7.02%. An assessment to measure problematic internet behavior is the Internet Addiction Test-Revised (IAT-R; Mak & Young, 2020). While included within this section, gaming addiction is distinguished separately from internet addiction, as it does not necessarily include games played on the internet. Gaming disorder was included in the 11th edition of the *International Classification of Diseases* (*ICD-11*), and researchers estimate the gaming addiction prevalence rate to be 3.05% worldwide (Stevens et al., 2021). There are multiple screening and assessment instruments for gaming disorder, with a systematic review of instruments published by King et al. (2020). In addition to various treatment options, there are support groups for internet and technology addictions and gaming addiction.

Sex Addiction

A sex addiction, or hypersexual disorder, has two types of symptoms: behavioral and cognitive and emotional (Karila et al., 2014). The prevalence of sex addiction-related disorders is 3% to 6% (Karila et al., 2014). In addition to the consequences of other addictions, a sex addiction also creates a risk for sexually transmitted infections (STIs) and pregnancy, and it may co-occur with other addictions. Karila et al. (2014) present a review of instruments for screening and assessing for sexual addiction. There are various treatment options for sexual addiction and there are also support groups (Sex Addicts Anonymous; SAA).

Shopping Addiction

There are a variety of terms used for shopping addiction, including compulsive or excessive shopping, shopaholism, spendaholism, and excessive buying (Lee & Mysyk, 2004). This addiction may be particularly associated with legal and financial concerns, including large debt, which may lead to bankruptcy. In examining compulsive buying, Maraz et al. (2016) found a pooled prevalence rate of 4.9%, with females and individuals who are young being at increased risk. Excessive shopping exists among people in all socioeconomic statuses (Lee & Mysyk, 2004). Other factors related to compulsive buying include predisposition, credit accessibility, and influence of the media (Lee & Mysyk, 2004). There are multiple instruments reviewed by Maraz et al. (2016) to use in assessing for shopping addiction. Support groups for individuals with a shopping addiction include Debtors Anonymous and Spenders Anonymous.

Work Addiction

Work addiction is characterized by working long hours without enjoying it, as well as having a work-life imbalance. The etiology is similar to other addictions, including how it affects the reward center of the brain, personality traits, and social and environmental factors (Sussman, 2012). The estimated prevalence rate for work addiction is 10% (Sussman et al., 2011), and people with higher education levels and overachievers may be at greater risk for this addiction (Sussman, 2012). A consequence specifically related to work addiction is burnout, which is characterized by emotional exhaustion and a negative attitude about work (Maslach & Jackson, 1981). Sussman (2012) describes a variety of instruments used to assess for work addiction. Work addiction may be addressed at the societal, organizational, and individual levels (Sussman, 2012). Workaholics Anonymous (WA) is a support group for people with work addiction.

SUBSTANCE USE CARE

Transtheoretical Model of Change

To begin our discussion about treatment for substance-related concerns and disorders, it is important to start with describing the Transtheoretical Model of Health Behavior Change, sometimes referred to as the Stages of Change Model, that was developed by Prochaska and DiClemente (1983). It is called the transtheoretical model because it involves components from multiple theories to provide a comprehensive theory. The model originally included five stages, but it now has six stages. It can be applied to any behavior that an individual wants to change, including substance-related concerns and disorders. Progression through the stages is a process and individuals may cycle back through various stages during their process of change.

The first stage is precontemplation. A person in this stage is not ready to take action to make a change. This may include being in denial that they have a behavior that necessitates changing or they may not have experienced negative consequences of their behavior that create awareness of a need for change.

Contemplation is the second stage that focuses on getting ready for change. In this stage, people are thinking about changing, but they are also experiencing ambivalence about it. They may see some negative consequences of their behavior and think about goals, but they are not ready for action. The third stage is the preparation stage, when a person is ready to act and they have prepared for it. This may include identifying what needs to be changed, creating a plan for how to make the change, and obtaining resources to help make the plan a success. The fourth stage is the action stage when individuals engage in steps to change their behavior. Maintenance is the fifth stage, which focuses on continuing to make progress started in the action stage (Prochaska & DiClemente, 1983). The sixth stage, which was added later, is the relapse stage. This stage encompasses times when the individual has returned to using or participating in the problematic behavior. For many individuals, progression through the stages is circular, not linear, as individuals may relapse and recycle through various stages. In the subsections below, the discussion focuses on the care continuum. The continuum, as reported by DHHS (2016) includes five areas: enhancing health, primary prevention, early intervention, treatment, and recovery support.

Enhancing Health and Prevention

Enhancing health focuses on promoting holistic growth and development through wellness and primary care. Prevention is the next level of the care continuum. Regarding substance-related concerns and disorders, there are many evidence-based interventions for people across the lifespan, ranging from children under 10 years old to older adults. Examples of programs for children 10 and younger include the Nurse-Family Partnership (focuses on children younger than 5), the Good Behavior Game (school-based intervention), Raising Healthy Children (school and parent involvement), and the Fast Track Program (school and home components). Programs for children aged 10 to 18 years include both school and family programs as well as internet-based programs. Researchers have also examined programs for college students, working adults, and older adults. See DHHS (2016) for a description of these programs. When considering the use of prevention programs, it is important that they are designed for diverse communities. The programs highlighted by DHHS have support for use with communities of diverse backgrounds. As research continues to advance in this area, it is important to continue to focus on the inclusion of diverse communities and explore cultural adaptations.

Another strategy focuses on prevention policies. This includes policies such as taxing substances and activities, regulating access, addressing drinking and driving, and reducing underage use (DHHS, 2016). It is crucial that effort is focused on implementing and enforcing policies after developing them.

Early Intervention

Screening, Brief Intervention, and Referral to Treatment (SBIRT) is an evidence-based approach used with individuals who show early signs of substance-related concerns and disorders. The approach is comprehensive, brief, universal, and appropriate for adults and youth. It targets specific behaviors; is appropriate for various settings including hospitals, primary care, and schools; and has strong

TABLE 9.3 SUBSTANCE USE ASSESSMENTS FOR ADULTS AND ADOLESCENTS

ASSESSMENT	AREA OF ASSESSMENT	POPULATION
AUDIT (Alcohol Use Disorders Identification Test; World Health Organization, 1982)	Alcohol	Adults
DAST-10 (Drug Abuse Screen Test; Skinner, 1982)	Drugs	Adults and older adolescents (16 and above)
DAST-A (Adolescent version; Martino et al., 2000)	Drugs	Adolescents
ASSIST (Alcohol, Smoking, Substance Involvement Screening Test; World Health Organization, 1997)	Alcohol, drugs	Adults
CAGE (Cut Down, Annoyed, Guilty, Eye-Opener; Ewing, 1970)	Alcohol	Adults and adolescents
CAGE-AID (CAGE Adapted to Include Drugs; Brown & Sanders, n.d.)	Alcohol, drugs	Adults and adolescents
ASSIST-Y (Alcohol, Smoking, Substance Involvement Screening Test for Youth; World Health Organization, 1997)	Alcohol, drugs	Adolescents
CRAFFT (Car, Relax, Along, Forget, Family/Friends, Trouble; Knight, 1999)	Alcohol, drugs	Adolescents

research support (SAMHSA, 2011). The screening process is an important first step in identifying the severity level of the concern and determining the appropriate treatment (SAMHSA, n.d.-c). It is crucial, as many individuals do not believe they have a substance use problem (DHHS, 2016). There are various formalized assessments to use in screening for various substances among adults and adolescents. See Table 9.3 for a list of screening tool for both populations.

Following screening, the professional may use a brief intervention or brief treatment. Brief intervention includes one to five sessions that last 5 minutes to 1 hour and focuses on education and increasing motivation to reduce the concerning behavior (SAMHSA, 2011). Brief treatment typically includes 5–12 sessions and focuses on addressing more long-standing alcohol or drug problems, as well as helping individuals with high severity levels obtain long-term care (SAMHSA, 2011). If the screening process reveals the need for intensive treatment or brief intervention or brief treatment is not successful, the next step is referral to specialty treatment. While the SBIRT process was designed for substance-related concerns and disorders, a similar process may also be useful for behavioral addictions.

MOTIVATIONAL COUNSELING APPROACHES

Motivational counseling approaches include motivational interviewing (MI) and motivational enhancement therapy (MET). The FRAMES approach (Miller & Sanchez, 1994) involves six elements of motivational counseling that may be incorporated into the SBIRT process. FRAMES stands for Feedback about personal risk provided from population norms, Responsibility is with the client, Advice about how to change is provided by the counselor, Menu of treatment options is offered, Empathy is provided by the counselor, and Self-efficacy is emphasized in encouraging client change.

Motivational Interviewing. Motivational interviewing (MI) is a useful technique when a client may have ambivalence to change. The goal in MI is to help the client feel motivated and commit to changing their behavior (Miller & Rollnick, 2013). It is most helpful during the precontemplation and contemplation stages of change (SAMHSA, 2019). Four elements comprise the spirit of MI: Partnership, Acceptance, Compassion, and Evocation (PACE). The partnership relates to the counselor and client working together. Acceptance focuses on the counselor's respect for the client, including valuing the client's worth and offering empathy and affirmation. Compassion means focusing on what is in the best interest of the client. Evocation relates to exploring the client's strengths and resources (Miller & Rollnick, 2013; SAMHSA, 2019).

MI is offered within a person-centered counseling philosophy and involves four MI core skills: asking Open questions, Affirming, Reflective listening, and Summarizing (OARS; Miller & Rollnick, 2013). OARS is used throughout the four processes of MI: engaging, focusing, evoking, and planning (Miller & Rollnick, 2013). Engaging centers on developing a relationship with the client. Focusing relates to mutually agreeing on an area of focus/direction and identifying a target behavior. Evoking refers to eliciting the client's motivation for change, which is the core of MI. This involves multiple steps, such as gauging the client's value of changing, responding to sustain and change talk (sustain talk supports maintaining the current behavior, while change talk focuses on changing behavior), exploring discrepancies between the client's values and their behaviors, and supporting the client in developing hope and confidence to foster self-efficacy. Planning focuses on working with the client to develop an appropriate change plan (Miller & Rollnick, 2013; SAMHSA, 2019).

Motivational Enhancement Therapy. Motivational enhancement therapy (MET), like MI, is focused on helping address the client's ambivalence about change and engagement in treatment. The approach involves an initial assessment session and then two to four treatment sessions (National Institute on Drug Abuse [NIDA], 2018). The first treatment session focuses on the counselor reviewing the assessment results with the client and providing feedback, and then discussing the client's substance use (NIDA, 2018). The counselor integrates MI strategies within the treatment sessions to elicit client motivation and develop a change plan (NIDA, 2018).

Treatment

When considering treatment, it is concerning that only one in 10 people who need treatment receive it; this includes over 7 million women and over 1 million adolescents, as well as disparities for some racial and ethnic minority groups (SAMHSA, 2017). There are multiple types of treatment services. Additionally, several evidence-based practices are used for treatment.

TREATMENT SERVICES

There are four major levels of treatment: inpatient hospitalization, residential treatment, partial hospitalization, and outpatient services (DHHS, 2016). Inpatient hospitalization is usually required for individual needing withdrawal management or detoxification (DHHS, 2016). This is a process that usually involves medication. It is used to safely manage the physical and emotional side effects associated with stopping the use of a substance. The management of this process is necessary, as the withdrawal symptoms for quitting some substances may be severe, and life threatening in some cases, if not managed properly. Physical symptoms are usually associated with withdrawal from alcohol, sedatives, tranquilizers, and opioids, while withdrawal from caffeine, marijuana, and stimulants is usually associated with cognitive and emotional effects, and the withdrawal period usually lasts 3 to 5 days (DHHS, 2016). It is important to note that inpatient hospitalization is not needed for stopping all substances. Additionally, detoxification is not the entire treatment process, but instead is the first step in treatment.

Residential treatment involves an individual living in a facility and receiving a variety of services. The government started the first two residential treatment programs in Texas and Kentucky in the mid-1930s (Woody, 2014). Residential treatment is usually offered in a nonhospital setting. While inpatient hospitalization usually involves a short duration, residential treatment involves a longer stay, lasting from 3 to 6 weeks for short-term treatment and 6 to 12 months for long-term treatment. Residential treatment programs may use a therapeutic community model that views the entire community (staff, residents) as part of the treatment process (NIDA, 2018).

A step-down from residential treatment is partial hospitalization. In this setting, the person may spend several hours a day at the facility receiving various treatment services; however, they leave the facility daily instead of residing there and receiving 24-hour care. Thus, partial hospitalization is less restrictive than residential treatment. Outpatient services may be a step-down service from more intensive services (i.e., inpatient, partial hospitalization) or a starting point of services for an individual who has a mild or moderate concern or disorder. Outpatient services may range from an hour to a few hours of therapy once or multiple times a week. Treatment services may involve various counseling approaches.

EVIDENCE-BASED TREATMENT APPROACHES

There are many treatment approaches for people with addictions that have research supporting their effectiveness. Some evidence-based approaches include medication, cognitive behavioral therapy (CBT), contingency management, family therapy, and MET (discussed above). Treatment may involve individual, group, and family sessions.

Medication. Multiple medications are used to treat SUDs. There is controversy about this treatment approach, as some people view the use of medication as substituting one drug for another; however, there is research support for using medication to treat SUDs (NIDA, 2018). Medication is often used in combination with therapy. DHHS (2016) describes six medications the U.S. Food and Drug Administration (FDA) has approved for treating alcohol and opioid use disorders. Medications approved for alcohol use disorder include acamprosate, disulfiram, and naltrexone. Additionally, medications approved for opioid use disorder include buprenorphine-naloxone, buprenorphine hydrochloride, methadone, and naltrexone (DHHS, 2016). There are also nicotine replacement therapies (NRTs) to address tobacco use disorder. This includes the transdermal nicotine patch, spray, and gum. Other smoking cessation treatments include taking bupropion (Zyban) or varenicline (Chantix; NIDA, 2018; see Table 9.4).

Cognitive Behavioral Therapy. CBT is a structured counseling approach focused on addressing disturbing thought patterns and maladaptive behaviors and developing healthy coping skills. CBT techniques for substance-related concerns and disorders include exploring the consequences (positive and negative) of use, recognizing and monitoring cravings, and developing and implementing a plan to avoid situations in which an individual may be tempted to use, as well as coping strategies to address cravings (NIDA, 2018). Researchers have investigated the use of CBT to treat a variety of substance-related concerns and disorders and behavioral addictions, as well as use for treating other co-occurring mental health disorders.

Contingency Management. Contingency management (CM) is a positive reinforcement program that rewards positive behavior with tangible rewards (e.g., vouchers for food or activities, prizes). When using vouchers, the value starts small and increases the longer the individual maintains abstinence (NIDA, 2018; Rash et al., 2017). It is also used for attending counseling sessions or having a negative drug screening (DHHS, 2016; NIDA, 2018; Rash et al., 2017). The challenge of the voucher system is that it can become very expensive (Rash et al., 2017). The prize-based system involves drawing slips of paper from a fishbowl. Some of the slips contain prize values (e.g., money, prizes), while others may have words of encouragement or praise. With this system, the values may increase for success over time (e.g., maintaining continued abstinence over time), similar to the voucher system, or an individual may have the opportunity to draw more slips of paper for more chances to win (e.g., one slip for the first negative drug screen, two slips for the second one, etc.)

TABLE 9.4 MEDICATIONS USED IN SUBSTANCE USE DISORDER TREATMENT

MEDICATION	USED TO TREAT	EFFECTS OF MEDICATION
Acamprosate	Alcohol use disorder	Reduces cravings
Disulfiram	Alcohol use disorder	Deters alcohol consumption by causing physical effects (e.g., nausea, dizziness, headaches, heart palpitations)
Naltrexone	Alcohol use disorder	Inhibits pleasure obtained from drinking
Buprenorphine-naloxone and buprenorphine hydrochloride	Opioid use disorder	Schedule III drug (moderate to low potential for abuse), partial opioid agonist,activates receptors with less intensity (e.g., reduced euphoria and pain relief)
Methadone	Opioid use disorder	Schedule II drug (high potential for abuse), reduces cravings, prevents withdrawal symptoms, agonist, binds to receptors and produces similar effects
Naltrexone	Opioid use disorder	Antagonist,binds to receptors and stops them from having a desired response so that opioids have limited, if any, effects
Bupropion (Zyban)	Tobacco use disorder	Mild stimulant effects, reduces cravings
Varenicline (Chantix)	Tobacco use disorder	Partial agonist/antagonist, reduces cravings
Transdermal nicotine patch, nicotine spray, gum, and lozenges	Tobacco use disorder	Low levels of nicotine, prevents withdrawal symptoms

Source: Data from National Institute on Drug Abuse. (2018). *Principles of drug addiction treatment: A research-based guide* (3rd ed.). Author. https://nida.nih.gov/download/675/principles-drug-addiction-treatment-research-based-guide-third-edition.pdf?v=74dad603627bab-89b93193918330c223; U.S. Department of Health and Human Services, Office of the Surgeon General. (2016). *Facing addiction in America: The surgeon general's report on alcohol, drugs, and health.* Department of Health and Human Services.

(Rash et al., 2017). Programs may also use nonmonetary CM rewards, such as a free meal or a recreational activity (Rash et al., 2017).

Family Therapy Approaches. There are multiple family therapy approaches with research support for treating addictions. Family behavior therapy focuses on learning behavioral strategies to apply outside counseling sessions. The approach involves contingency management principles to reward positive behavior. It is used with couples, as well as with parents and their children (NIDA, 2018). There are also family therapy approaches that are specifically helpful in working with adolescents with substance-related concerns and disorders, including multisystemic therapy, multidimensional family therapy, brief strategic family therapy, and functional family therapy, which are explained more by the NIDA (2018).

Recovery Support Services

There are many definitions for recovery, but all of them extend beyond abstinence or remission to include personal change. It is a lifestyle change, not just an absence of the substance use or other addictive behavior (DHHS, 2016). Hope for overcoming challenges and resilience when experiencing relapse or setbacks is crucial for recovery. Family members must also be resilient when their loved one experiences setback (SAMHSA, n.d.-b). SAMHSA (n.d.-b) discusses four areas that support recovery: community, health, home, and purpose. Community relates to having healthy relationships with family members and friends characterized by support and love. Health relates to management of symptoms and a focus on both physical and emotional wellness. Having a safe home is also important. Finally, purpose relates to participating in meaningful activities and contributing to society.

Recovery support services are nonclinical services designed to support recovery and wellness (SAMHSA, 2010). There are many recovery support services that individuals may use in the recovery process, with some services provided by peers. Recovery support services include recovery coaching, recovery community centers, recovery housing, recovery management, recovery high schools, collegiate recovery programs, and mutual support groups (DHHS, 2016; Jason et al., 2021).

RECOVERY COACHES

Recovery coaches provide support for individuals entering and staying in recovery. This includes helping individuals connect with community resources, as well as providing strategies to help maintain abstinence (DHHS, 2016). Recovery coaches do not replace professional case managers, but provide an adjunct to the work of case managers. Some recovery coaches may be peer recovery coaches, meaning they are also in recovery, but not all recovery coaches are in recovery (DHHS, 2016).

RECOVERY COMMUNITY CENTERS

Recovery community centers (RCCs) provide a variety of services. These services may include 12-step meetings, recovery coaches, social activities, and employment services to name a few (Jason et al., 2021). They may also provide opportunities to engage in advocacy to address stigma and promote recovery support services in the community (DHHS, 2016). RCCs may be particularly helpful for individuals in recovery who have limited resources, with the provision of multiple services in one location (Jason et al., 2021).

RECOVERY HOUSING

Having a safe, drug-free living environment is important in the recovery process, as home is one of the four areas to support recovery identified by SAMHSA (2020). In recovery-supportive housing, individuals in recovery have a community-style living environment that is drug-free and includes support from peers who are also living in recovery residing in the home (DHHS, 2016; Mericle et al., 2022). There are multiple types of recovery housing that provide different levels and types of services, such as recovery homes, sober homes, and halfway houses. There are four levels of support: (a) Level I—self-run with no clinical staff, (b) Level II—a paid staff member oversees the house and coordinates groups and services, (c) Level III—employ clinical staff and administrators, and (d) Level IV—often licensed by the state and employ licensed clinical staff, and are sometimes known as residential therapeutic communities (Jason et al., 2021). Individuals residing in these homes have typically completed a treatment program or have been released from prison (Jason et al., 2021). In examining recovery housing availability, Mericle et al. (2022) identified 10,358 houses across the United States. They found recovery housing was available in all states, and while there was not a gap in providing housing in communities with a high percentage of people of color, they found a gap in low-income areas and rural areas. Thus, a need exists for advocating for recovery housing options in low-income areas and rural regions.

RECOVERY MANAGEMENT AND MONITORING

There are also multiple approaches to recovery management and monitoring that help support individuals in recovery, including recovery management checkups (RMCs) and telephone case monitoring (DHHS, 2016). The RMC model involves quarterly assessments for multiple years, feedback, and referral to treatment if an individual experiences signs of relapse (DHHS, 2016). Telephone case monitoring also provides ongoing monitoring, with the advantage of being provided via phone that eliminates transportation barriers.

RECOVERY HIGH SCHOOLS AND COLLEGIATE RECOVERY PROGRAMS

For young people in recovery, there are recovery high schools (RHSs) and collegiate recovery programs (CRPs). Jason et al. (2021) report that the first RHS started in the 1970s and now there are 35 RHSs in the United States. They typically have counselors to provide recovery support and require students to attend outside 12-step groups. Students graduate in some RHS programs, while students in others transition back to their traditional school (Jason et al., 2016). CRPs typically follow a 12-step model and may offer a variety of services (e.g., counseling, recreational activities, academic support) to help college students maintain their recovery (Jason et al., 2016). The first program was started in the 1970s, and as of 2020, there were 155 institutional members of the Association of Recovery in Higher Education (ARHE), which is the organization representing CRPs and collegiate recovery communities (CRCs; ARHE, 2020). Researchers have found promising results for the effectiveness of CRPs with both recovery and educational outcomes (Jason et al., 2021).

MUTUAL SUPPORT GROUPS

Mutual-aid support groups, based on the 12-step model, are designed to provide community support for individuals in recovery from various types of addictions. They are not designed to replace formal treatment approaches, but instead serve as an adjunct to treatment, as well as provide support to maintain abstinence over the long term. The 12 steps are spiritual principles that are practiced as a way of life (Alcoholics Anonymous, n.d.-c). There are also 12 traditions that focus on relationships between members, the group, and the organization and society (Alcoholics Anonymous, n.d.-b). See the Resources for links to both of these documents. Alcoholic Anonymous (AA), started in 1935, was the first 12-step self-help group (Alcoholics Anonymous, n.d.-a). Mutual-aid support groups for other prominent substance-related concerns and disorders include narcotics anonymous (NA) and cocaine anonymous (CA). There are also mutual-aid support groups for behavioral addictions, as mentioned earlier. Furthermore, there are mutual-aid support groups for people with family members who have an addiction, such as Al-Anon, also based on a 12-step model. Some mutual aid support groups are focused on specific populations, such as racial minority groups, women, young people, and LGBTQ populations (DHHS, 2016).

SMART Recovery is a mutual support group that was founded in 1994. SMART stands for Self-Management and Recovery Training. The approach is used with various substance-related concerns and disorders, as well as behavioral addictions. It is an educational and mental health program aimed to change behavior (SMART Recovery, n.d.). It focuses on using self-empowerment and incorporates evidence-based practices, including cognitive behavioral therapy and motivational interviewing (SMART Recovery, 2019). The program has a 4-point program: (1) build and maintain motivation; (2) cope with urges; (3) manage thoughts, feelings, and behaviors; and (4) lead a balanced life (SMART Recovery, 2019). Meeting are held in person and online and are led by facilitators that complete a 30-hour training program, or hosts that complete less training. Examples of SMART exercises include (a) cost-benefit analysis, which compares short-term benefits to long-term consequences, and (b) urge log, which is a daily log of things that trigger urges and cravings for the substance or compulsive behavior (SMART Recovery, 2019).

Harm Reduction

A final area to discuss regarding substance use care is harm reduction. It is an evidence-based individual and community level approach to reduce the negative personal and public health consequences of substance use (SAMHSA, n.d-a). Additionally, it is a social justice movement that involves acknowledging and respecting the rights of individuals who use drugs (National Harm Reduction Coalition, n.d.). Harm reduction includes strategies designed to reduce the negative consequences of drug use, including "safer use, managed use, abstinence, and meeting people who use drugs where they're at" (National Harm Reduction Coalition, n.d.). Harm reduction is grounded in eight principles. See the Resources for a link to these principles on the National Harm Reduction Coalition website. Some examples of harm reduction services include syringe service programs, sterile syringes, overdose education, fentanyl test strips to help prevent opioid overdose, and overdose reversal medications such as naloxone.

Caring for Diverse Populations

When working with diverse populations, it is important to be culturally responsive. It is crucial to consider culture because it influences a client's experience with treatment (SAMHSA, 2006). Therefore, not considering a client's culture may limit the effectiveness of treatment. In considering culture, it is important to remember that there are different groups within a particular racial or ethnic group, as these groups are heterogeneous. People also have multiple other identities that intersect with their racial and ethnic identities. When considering the worldview, it is important to remember that a client's view may differ from the Anglo-American culture of the United States. This may include embracing a holistic worldview, the importance of spirituality, a community focus (i.e., collective good) instead of a focus on the individual, role of family involvement in treatment that may include extended family, communication style, and multidimensional learning styles (e.g., beyond reading and teaching to include oral learning; SAMHSA, 2006).

It is important that professionals consider the unique cultural considerations of working with any individual. SAMSHA (2014) includes the aspects of cultural responsiveness using the mnemonic RESPECT (Respect, Explanatory model, Sociocultural context, Power, Empathy, Concerns and fears, and Trust/therapeutic alliance). Respect relates to learning how respect is demonstrated within the culture of a client and using those principles when interacting with a client. Explanatory model focuses on understanding the client's cultural beliefs related to substance use or other problematic behavior and how people change. Sociocultural context relates to considering how various personal characteristics (race, gender, ethnicity, SES, age) may affect treatment. Power focuses on recognizing the power differential in the counseling relationship. Empathy expression is crucial in the counseling relationship. Concerns and fears relate to understanding the clients' concerns about getting help and treatment. Trust/therapeutic alliance focuses on recognizing that the counselor must earn the client's trust and work to build the therapeutic alliance with the client (SAMSHA, 2014).

There are areas to consider in working with any client group. DHHS (2016) describes considerations related to working with racial and ethnic minority groups, LGBTQ+ individuals, veterans, and individuals involved with the criminal justice system. In regard to racial and ethnic minority groups, relevant factors may include ethnic pride; traditional, spiritual, and cultural beliefs;

discrimination; and mistrust of treatment professionals and treatment systems. For more information about treatment with various racial and ethnic minority groups, see SAMSHA (2014). Treatment for LGBTQ+ populations should include a focus on concerns particularly relevant for this population. A few of these areas include family issues, social support, and discrimination. Veterans also have unique considerations, including the possibility that they may also be experiencing posttraumatic stress disorder (PTSD). Finally, regarding individuals involved in the criminal justice system, initiating treatment during incarceration is important because addiction is the most significant factor for recidivism and rearrests (Nowotny, 2015). Individuals with criminal offenses may also be involved in drug courts, which includes a judge overseeing the provision of treatment services, as an alternative to being incarcerated. While only a few populations are briefly mentioned here, it is the author's intention that you become aware that each population will have specific considerations when working with individuals with substance-related concerns and disorders and behavioral addictions.

ADDRESSING STIGMA AND ADVOCACY

Stigma is "a set of negative and often unfair beliefs that a society or group of people have about something," (Merriam-Webster, n.d.) in this case, people with addictions. It is important to address stigma the public has about substance-related concerns and disorders and other behavioral addictions as well as stigma individuals with substance-related concerns and disorders or other behavioral addictions have about themselves. This is crucial as stigma may influence many aspects of addressing substance-related concerns and disorders and behavioral addictions, including funding for treatment, access to care, and someone's decision to seek treatment or stay in treatment. There are many stereotypes and myths related to problematic use and addictions. Some examples mentioned by Zwick et al. (2020) include the belief some people have that the concern/disorder is the person's fault and they just need willpower to stop, when research supports that the substance use or other problematic behavior affects the brain and is not simply a matter of willpower. Additionally, there is an assumption that using medication to help with an SUD is just replacing one drug with another one, when research supports the use of medication to help with substance-related concerns and disorders. These are just a few examples, and unfortunately, there are many others.

There are three overarching approaches that people can use to address stigma: (a) education approaches, (b) interactions with people in the stigmatized group, and (c) social activism or protest (Corrigan et al., 2012). Education related to substance-related concerns and disorders may include information provided for the general public, legislators, and professionals working with these individuals. This may involve presentations, as well as distributing information in various ways (e.g., posting information in public spaces, distributing information through social media). Advocacy may include activities at the local, state, and national level, such as supporting funding for treatment for people with substance-related concerns and disorders, addressing stigma related to this population, and developing and implementing programs to educate professionals and students in training programs to work with these populations. Counselors may also engage in personal advocacy, including sharing personal stories with legislators of individuals in their personal lives who have struggled with substance-related concerns and disorders or behavioral addictions, as well as voting for political leaders who will support legislation for funding treatment for substance-related concerns and disorders and behavioral addictions (Doyle, 2021).

Zwick et al. (2020) emphasize the importance of language in reducing stigma. This includes using people first language (e.g., a "person with an addiction" or "person with a substance use concern/SUD," instead of referring to the person as an "addict" or "abuser." Additionally, Zwick et al. (2020) caution about using the word "abuse" because it is an emotionally heavy word that translates to the person. When referring to someone with a "substance abuse disorder," a person may be viewed more negatively and punitively than if the reference is to a "substance use concern" or "SUD." Furthermore, Zwick et al. (2020) recommend not using the terms "clean" or "dirty" when discussing results from toxicology screenings. The Recovery Research Institute Addictionary (https://www .recoveryanswers.org/addiction-ary) provides definitions of terms related to addictions, and notes terms that may be stigmatizing.

CONCLUSION

Substance and behavioral addictions are not new in the United States; however, they remain prevalent among various populations and are continuously evolving. Therefore, ongoing research is crucial in learning more about the etiology of addictions and evidence-based practices to use with diverse groups. Additionally, it is necessary to address stigma and other barriers to treatment to promote and support quality care and recovery.

Summary

- Substance-related concerns and disorders, as well as behavioral addictions, affect many people in the United States.
- There are multiple evidence-based practices for treating addictions across the continuum of care.
- It is crucial to address stigma related to addictions.

Voices From the Field

Rosa West, PhD, Clinical Associate Professor, Counseling and Wellness Center, University of Florida

As a Black heterosexual Christian woman in the world and a new clinician working with substance use disorders, it was important to me to do all the right things to ensure my clients made the progress needed to sustain their recovery goals. I learned early in my training that successful recovery equated to "working the program." This is a traditional term used to describe 12-step programs, like Alcoholics Anonymous (AA) or Narcotics Anonymous (NA), which are intended to provide a framework for recovery that emphasizes adherence to key steps to sustain abstinence from alcohol and other drugs. It was stressed that the core ingredient for client progress was active engagement in abstinence-based treatment rooted in 12-step principles. I was fortunate to have immediate success in adopting this culture of care in working with substance use disorders. Clients made steady progress, they completed treatment having met therapeutic goals, and I grew more confident in my understanding of the recipe of recovery.

Then I met Angie. Angie was a 32-year-old Black heterosexual woman who was court-ordered for substance use treatment to regain custody of her children. She had a history of involvement with child welfare services due to abuse of alcohol/drugs and was returning for her third round of treatment. Initially, there was not anything inordinate about Angie's case to suggest that substance use counseling with her would be challenging. She was placed in the appropriate groups to learn about personal "triggers" to use, gain skills to maintain abstinence, develop a recovery plan, and strengthen her support system. She was assigned specific 12-step programs in the community to attend and was required to find a sponsor to support her in working the steps. Angie also met with me for individual counseling on a weekly basis to address the areas of concern outlined in her treatment plan. But there was no progress.

Each week I would show up to court to meet with the judge, representatives of child welfare, and Angie. We would discuss Angie's lack of progress, resistance to treatment, and defensiveness in working with providers. Angie would reaffirm her commitment to being with her children while I advocated for her to continue to be allowed to "work the program" so she could be with them. Fortunately, despite concerns that Angie would never be able to maintain a safe environment for her children because of her substance abuse, she was given one more opportunity to show progress before her parental rights would be terminated.

When Angie returned to treatment, I continued to receive reports that she was not actively participating in groups or completing assignments. She also continued to be guarded in individual counseling and shared that she had not been contacting her sponsor. Frustrated, I confronted Angie on her behavior and shared my disappointment that she was not showing her commitment to recovery despite my advocacy on her behalf to remain in the program. It was then that she looked at me directly and said, "Why would I trust the devil to help me?" I was thrown by this statement. I never imagined that Angie, or any client, would view my help as disingenuous. I quickly began to explain that I wanted to help Angie and that all my efforts had been to support her regaining custody. I questioned her assumption that she was not being supported, pointing out that she was extended the opportunity to receive the same type of treatment as other clients in similar situations. In response, Angie briefly stated, "You don't get it … this program's not for me … you're not for me."

It was in that moment that I clearly understood that I had not been helping Angie. I was helping a 32-year-old, diagnosed with multiple substance use disorders, with a history of treatment that included both inpatient and outpatient treatment. Remorseful, I apologized for failing to see Angie and not working to truly understand her unique recovery needs. I asked if she would be open to a "restart" because I wanted to support her in establishing a program that worked for her. Thankfully she was receptive, and I started by asking her to describe how the program was not helpful for her.

Angie began by sharing her distrust of me, the court, and the child welfare system. She acknowledged that substance abuse has been a problem for her for over 10 years, a problem she developed as a means to cope with childhood trauma, domestic violence, and financial/food insecurity. As an unemployed single mother of three children, Angie reported that she struggled to provide for her family and fell dependent on the minimal support offered by her abusive partner. She expressed frustration with the limited resources and services that were available for low-income families and the "system's" failure to respond to her repeated attempts to seek help for her addiction. While Black Americans have similar rates of obtaining treatment when compared to White Americans, they are more likely to be referred for treatment services through social service systems (e.g., criminal justice, child welfare; Evans-Polce et al., 2014). Angie acknowledged that she had not been able to afford the cost of available treatment programs in her community, and it was only through a court order that she was able to receive support through social services for substance abuse treatment.

Angie also voiced that the court system was unjust for preventing her from being with her children while the father, who also had a history of substance abuse, was permitted to meet freely with them. She expressed, "It's not right that we both have problems with drugs, but somehow it's worse for me because I'm supposed to be a good mother." Angie also believed that I was aligned with the child welfare system in its mission to "catch" her struggling so they could ultimately terminate her parental rights, rather than put Angie in a situation where she could be successful. This belief was reinforced for Angie each day that I failed to acknowledge the connection between her multiple identities and her substance use. In addition to completing substance use treatment, she was required to establish employment to demonstrate her ability to financially provide for her children. However, lack of transportation and an inability to find a job with hours that would enable her to care for her children were continuous barriers that were not considered by the court or child welfare when assessing Angie's "progress."

Programmatically, Angie shared that she did not like attending 12-step meetings. She did not feel a sense of community and support among a group comprising predominantly White men. Angie shared that she did not believe that those in attendance could relate to her struggles with addiction and, while she understood the purpose of such programs, she did not find it as meaningful as other sources of support like the church. Angie identified as Christian and reported that she was "raised in the Church." For Angie, it was misguided to seek help among a group of people who were also struggling with addiction. Outside of one's family, the church represented the only other space where one should receive spiritual guidance for "moral" failings, like substance abuse. Treatment groups were also ineffective for Angie. Again, she felt uncomfortable in homogeneous groups where there was little, if any, acknowledgment of the unique societal challenges Angie had to face each day to maintain her recovery.

To help Angie, we altered our treatment approach to focus on developing a recovery program that worked for her. It was important to engage in ongoing dialogue about barriers so treatment could be adjusted in response to each. For instance, unemployment was a significant stressor for Angie and increased her risk of relapse. We focused on connecting her to resources, like job training, to expand her employment opportunities and aid her in securing work that provided hours that fit her child-care needs. Another way treatment was tailored to Angie's needs was to incorporate religion and spirituality into her program to strengthen her resiliency. Angie was tasked with identifying a church "home" in her community and participating in services. She would provide proof of meeting with spiritual leaders, service attendance, and participation in community service activities provided through the church. The requirement of 12-step meeting attendance was dropped. Attendance at AA and NA meetings would now be optional for Angie.

In addition, individual counseling would be used as an opportunity for Angie to process and address historical experiences of trauma that contributed to her use of substances as a means of coping. We discussed instances of oppression and discrimination over time that she experienced as a Black woman, particularly related to injustices she experienced through the court and other social service systems. We unpacked feelings of guilt and shame she carried for failing to meet expectations of being a "mother." And, we incorporated culturally affirming interventions specific to Black culture.

It is important to work collaboratively with clients to establish a recovery program that works for them. Holistic approaches that acknowledge and respect the intersectionality of one's identities, and their relationship to substance use, is often necessary in meeting the needs of our clients. As new counselors working in substance use, I encourage you to be mindful that it is more important that clients are supported in "working a program" that aligns with their needs, than "working the program" that may ignore the significance of cultural identity.

A Call to Action

Identify a stereotype or myth that people may have about people with substance-related concerns and disorders or behavioral addictions. Develop and implement a strategy to address this stereotype/myth or stigma in general for this population. This may include engaging in one of the examples presented in the "Addressing Stigma and Advocacy" section of the text, such as creating a flyer or other educational materials about substance-related concerns and disorders or behavioral addictions and presenting it to others, educating others about stigma related to this population and ways to reduce stigma (e.g., language), interacting with someone with a substance-related concern or disorder or a behavioral addiction to change your own perceptions about the population, or participating in an advocacy activity (e.g., campaign for policy change or funding for services).

Case Study 9.1

Xavier is a 19-year-old African American male who is a sophomore in college. He had straight As his freshman year, but he is now failing four out of his five classes. He states that the classes are boring and stupid. He reports that he struggles with staying awake in his morning classes and so he rarely goes anymore. However, he had all morning classes as a freshman and had no problems with his classes. He admits to drinking several times a week with his friends and feeling hung over in the morning, but states that his drinking is not a problem, he only drinks to socialize, and he can quit at any time.

RESPONSE QUESTIONS

1. What stands out to you about the information presented about Xavier?
2. How might you approach working with Xavier?

Going Within

Due to the number of people experiencing substance-related concerns and disorders and behavioral addictions, you will likely have many clients throughout your career who have problematic use/an addiction, or have someone in their family that does, even if you do not specialize in working with this population. Therefore, it is important that you reflect on your thoughts and feelings related to this population and consider any work you need to do personally to be able to best serve your future clients. When you think about a person with a substance-related concern or disorder or a behavioral addiction, what thoughts, feelings, and biases come to mind? What have been your experiences interacting with people who have substance-related concerns and disorders or behavioral addictions? Do you have any views about this population that would make it challenging to work with them? How will you manage your views when you encounter a client struggling with a substance-related concern or disorder or behavioral addiction?

Group Process

In this chapter, we discussed substance-related concerns and disorders and behavioral addictions that some clients may struggle with. In small groups, select a substance-related concern or a problematic behavior that you want to know more about. Research key facts about the area, prevalence related to it, and treatment approaches. Share what you found in a 10-minute presentation to the class.

RESOURCES

Alcoholics Anonymous: https://www.aa.org

Association of Recovery in Higher Education (ARHE): https://collegiaterecovery.org

National Institute on Alcohol Abuse and Alcoholism (NIAAA): https://www.niaaa.nih.gov

National Institute on Drug Abuse (NIDA) DrugPubs Research Dissemination Center: https://drugpubs.drugabuse.gov

National Harm Reduction Coalition Principles of Harm Reduction: https://harmreduction.org/about-us/principles-of-harm-reduction

Recovery Research Institute Addictionary: https://www.recoveryanswers.org/addiction-ary

Substance Abuse and Mental Health Services Administration: https://www.samhsa.gov

The Twelve Steps: https://www.aa.org/the-twelve-steps

The Twelve Traditions: https://www.aa.org/the-twelve-traditions

Access this podcast at http://connect.springerpub.com/content/book/978-0-8261-6386-8/chapter/ch09.

KEY REFERENCES

Only key references appear in the print edition. The full reference list appears in the digital product found on https://connect.springerpub.com/content/book/978-0-8261-6386-8/chapter/ch09

Substance Abuse and Mental Health Services Administration. (2011). *Screening, brief intervention, and referral to treatment (SBRIT) in behavioral healthcare.* Author. https://www.samhsa.gov/sites/default/files/sbirtwhitepaper_0.pdf

Substance Abuse and Mental Health Services Administration. (2014). *Improving cultural competence.* Treatment Improvement Protocol (TIP) Series No. 59. https://store.samhsa.gov/product/TIP-59-Improving-Cultural-Competence/SMA15-4849

Substance Abuse and Mental Health Services Administration. (2019). *Enhancing motivation for change in substance use disorder treatment.* Treatment Improvement Protocol (TIP) Series No.35. SAMHSA Publication no.PEP19-02-01-003. https://www.ncbi.nlm.nih.gov/books/NBK571071/pdf/Bookshelf_NBK571071.pdf

Substance Abuse and Mental Health Services Administration. (n.d.-c.). *Screening, brief intervention, and referral to treatment.* Author. https://www.samhsa.gov/sbirt

U.S. Department of Health and Human Services, Office of the Surgeon General. (2016). *Facing addiction in America: The surgeon general's report on alcohol, drugs, and health.* U.S. Department of Health and Human Services. https://addiction.surgeongeneral.gov/sites/default/files/surgeon-generals-report.pdf

Zwick, J., Appleseth, H., & Arndt, S. (2020). Stigma: how it affects the substance use disorder patient. *Substance Abuse Treatment, Prevention, and Policy, 15*(1), 50. https://doi.org/10.1186/s13011-020-00288-0

CHAPTER 10

CRISIS COUNSELING

Derrick A. Paladino

Think about this...

In her discussion on trauma, Riethmayer (2004) stated that trauma (crisis), "tells the survivor that the world is no longer safe, kind, predictable, and trustworthy" (p. 219). Using yourself or creating a client, what type of crisis would introduce these beliefs into your life? What would it feel like for someone to question your perception?

LEARNING OBJECTIVES

After reading this chapter, you should be able to:

- Define and operationalize crisis
- Outline the difference between crisis counseling and traditional therapy
- Recognize the difference between types of crises
- Recognize how people in crisis react
- Summarize the role of assessment and intervention in crisis counseling

INTRODUCTION

Working with individuals in crisis is about empathy, relationship building, and believing perception. Believing a client's perception about their crisis experience is essential to developing a safe and brave therapeutic environment. This chapter specifically focuses on crisis counseling (trauma counseling is discussed in Chapter 11). The following sections include an overview of crisis and crisis counseling, crisis as experienced by individuals, crisis assessments and interventions, and crisis counseling skills.

As you become familiar with an overview of the profession, you are also learning the numerous ways helping professionals interact with individuals in need. Though both crisis counseling and longer-term therapy may use similar clinical and relational building skills, it is important to understand that they are quite different in practice. Jackson-Cherry and Erford (2014) describe this form of counseling as a "unique form of counseling, distinguished from other forms of counseling by its purpose setting, time, and intervention plan" (p. 18). Crisis counseling is a time-limited approach that assists clients in attaining a level of functioning. Unlike long-term therapy, where we might discover a behavioral etiology that forms overall current behavior, in crisis work, we are working with a specific emotional status that introduces disequilibrium. That is, we are working with a current "state" that impedes one's ability to function in ways that *keep them going* seminormally to normally. As crisis counselors, we assist the client in adding movement to their immobility. That movement can lead to a resolution of functioning or an assessment that a return to functioning, even temporarily, is not feasible. In all, crisis counseling is a time-limited approach (i.e., one sitting that can last 30 minutes to several hours) to restore a level of functioning that allows for further services. For example, when working with an individual assessed to hold suicidal ideation with high lethality, crisis counseling may include assisting the person to remain alive between the crisis session and ingress to longer-term counseling. When examining your role in crisis work, it is beneficial to frame this work as an intervention rather than a session.

Owen and Parsons (2018) further discuss the differences between crisis counseling (CC) and traditional counseling (TC). They break this down into seven main categories: focus, goal, client intent, strategy, nature and time, interventionist, and approaches. Within *focus*, CC resolves immediate concerns while developing interim coping skills while TC settles into longer-term client goals. The goal of CC is to "reduce immediate stress and incapacitation" (Owen & Parsons, 2018, p. 44) and in TC we see a process that provides for long-term resolution. From an individual perspective, CC views *client intent* as returning to normal, whereas TC focuses on pervasive changes in affect, behavior, and cognition. The *nature and time* of CC is short-term and directive versus TC's long-term and nondirective nature. It is important to note that TC can also be directive and brief in nature but does not hold the urgency that is attached to crisis. Regarding *interventionist* we may see several professionals assisting in CC. For example, after a natural disaster, you will typically find counselors, social workers, logistics specialists, and other community-based resources come together to reduce the immediate impact on individual and community functioning. Though both CC and TC *approaches* include creating a therapeutic alliance and treatment plan, the CC lens may shift more based on the specific crisis context and time parameters. Though empirically supported, crisis intervention is not grounded in personality and counseling theory.

DEFINITIONS

Caplan (1961), the father of modern crisis intervention, defines crisis as an "upset in the steady state of an individual" (p. 18). Since then, many scholars have introduced their unique take on this; however, sitting with the simplistic nature of Caplan's delineation offers a fundamental understanding of an individual's experience. In reviewing additional crisis definitions, several concepts and phrases are noted. As you read, think about what it would feel like to hold empathy in various situations and how you might assist the individual. These situations include an intolerable event, multiple obstacles, disorganization in functioning, significant life events, very intimate experience, a destabilizing experience, exhaustion of coping, acute and temporary, exceeding traditional and creative resources, deterioration in problem-solving, not a mental illness, critical turning point, and reduced functioning (Caplan, 1961; Cavaiola & Colford, 2018; Greenstone & Leviton, 2011; Hoff et al., 2009; Jackson-Cherry & Erford, 2014; Lillibridge & Klukken, 1978; Owen & Parsons, 2018; Roberts, 1991, 2000). The preceding should have provided you with a foundation of empathic understanding of someone in crisis. The following are some prominent definitions for crisis:

[C]risis refers to an acute emotional upset arising from situational, developmental, or sociocultural sources and resulting in a temporary inability to cope by means of one's usual problem-solving devices. (Hoff et al., 2009, p. 4)

Crisis is often an immediate, unpredictable event that occurs in people's lives—such as receiving a threatening medical diagnosis, experiencing a miscarriage, or undergoing a divorce—that can overwhelm the ways that they naturally cope ... crisis can also interfere with a person's ability to function in the world by negatively affecting several life domains, such as work, family, and social connections. (Duffy & Haberstroh, 2020)

A crisis occurs when unusual stress temporarily renders an individual unable to direct life effectively. (Greenstone & Leviton, 2011, p. 1)

Within these definitions is the idea of perception. The individual perception of a crisis is a critical aspect within defining and understanding the crisis. We all hold different thresholds for crisis dependent on personal culture, context, community, personal history, and support. In order to be a culturally competent counselor and attend to all aspects of an individual and their perceptions, it is critical for you to understand what the experience of crisis is for that person, leaving your own preconceptions aside. You are holding space for the person to unpack the experience with your assistance and make sense of what has happened and how it has affected them.

The initial question of "what is a crisis?" has an individual answer. As crisis counselors, we must fully believe and enter the personal lived perception for assessment and intervention to be successful. Areas such as suicide and homicidal ideation, sexual assault, death of a family member, natural disasters (e.g., hurricane, earthquake, blizzard), and terminal illness probably come to mind when thinking about what a crisis looks like. These perceptions may feel easier to enter because of society's view of their intensity and destabilizing nature. However, consider the example below.

Case Study 10.1: The Case of Marty

Marty (Venezuelan, cisgender, male) is a first-generation 20-year-old international college student in the spring semester of his sophomore year. He is studying prelaw at a large public institution. He can attend college by means of several academic scholarships and conditional grants. After learning that he earned a B- on his political science midterm he began to spiral. Typically, an "A-/A" student, Marty has stopped attending classes, believes his dreams are over, knows that he has let everyone down and that his life is an unrecoverable mess. He recently informed his roommates that he is thinking about killing himself by jumping off the student parking garage.

If we were to look solely at what initially occurred, we might conclude, "Well, it's only one B-. That's not really a crisis in the grand scheme of things." And for you, maybe not. For Marty, his perception of a B- raises a barrier to life that leads him to *know* that killing himself is the only answer. As you will learn in the assessment and treatment section, it is not our immediate job to logically assist clients in crisis. The instant a counselor moves to problem solve, Marty will know that you do not understand him and the gravity of his situation. As a result, the therapeutic relationship will be halted and the counselor will struggle to carry out further work. Perception would allow you to say, "Marty, it sounds like your midterm grade has ruined everything and that dying seems like your only way out." With that reflection, Marty will believe your empathy. Next we see how perception enters defining crisis.

Some scholars describe crisis as a three-part cycle or trilogy definition (Jackson-Cherry & Erford, 2014; Kanel, 2003; Owen & Parsons, 2018). This definition of crisis consists of three essential elements that, when present, characterize a situation as a crisis: (1) precipitating event, (2) perception of the precipitating event that leads to subjective distress (which can include increased vulnerability), and (3) a diminished functioning or failure to cope when the distress is not alleviated by customary coping resources. Let us explore this definition through the case of Marty. The first element is a precipitating event. Marty's precipitating event is earning a B- on his political science exam. Next, his perception of earning a B- has led him to believe that his life and dreams are over, he has let down important people in his life, and there is no way out of "this mess." Marty's perception of the event and his place in it will become a crisis when and if he has exhausted all coping mechanisms to keep him going (element 3). At that point, Marty enters a crisis state. When element 3 hits, so does the urgency to offer intervention for safety.

Finally, you will discover that many textbooks describe crisis as both a danger and an opportunity (Cavaiola & Colford, 2018; Hoff, 2014; James & Gilliland, 2017; Kanel, 2003). This is a popular metaphor based on the Japanese word for crisis, pronounced "kiki." Kiki is made up of two characters that when separated, mean "dangerous" and "opportunity." Opportunities are viewed as "learning, growth, and gaining strength to deal with future upsets" (Hoff, 2014, p. 1) as well as assisting the individual to discover and activate "inner strength"

(Cavaiola & Colford, 2018, p. 3). Though there is truth to hope and strength having survived any crisis, one must be mindful when using this concept while looking specifically at crisis counseling. The danger part, yes. The opportunity part, it depends. An individual in a crisis state will not perceive their experience as containing an opportunity. As a crisis counselor, you may discover hope that leads to the individual seeking additional and long-term assistance. From hope, opportunity will most likely develop through process and reflection in long-term counseling. As a crisis counselor, our role is to look for even the smallest atom of hope to work with to get clients to extended and consistent assistance.

TYPES OF CRISIS

Though crisis is a unique experience to an individual, the field does suggest several forms. Crisis impacts the individual as well as the larger group. Individual crisis can be seen through the case of Marty. However, if Marty does die by suicide, we will see a group and systemic impact that may lead to further crisis. For one, his family and friends will have a shared loss. In addition, the university he attended will have a community crisis to focus on. Examples of systems are "families, churches, businesses, neighborhoods, communities, large cities, geographical flood plains, and nations" (James & Gilliland, 2017, p. 10). These groups and systems can enter crisis states through economically based issues, family loss, and natural disasters (James & Gilliland, 2017). In addition, we see systemic crises develop through school shootings (Sandy Hook Elementary School, Parkland, Umpqua Community College), national and international threats (e.g., 9/11, Madrid train bombings, Orlando Pulse nightclub shootings), and most recently, public health crises such as the COVID-19 pandemic.

Crises are generally depicted as developmental, situational, or existential, with some scholars also introducing environmental, ecosystemic, transitional, and existential subtypes (Cavaiola & Colford, 2018; James & Gilliland, 2017; Kanel, 2003; Meyer, 2001). It is important to note that as a counselor supporting clients in crisis, you also have the opportunity to advocate for them while embracing the advocacy and multicultural and social justice competencies of our profession (see Ratts et al., 2016; Toporek & Daniels, 2018). Next we will briefly discuss developmental, situational, and existential crises.

Developmental Crisis

Developmental crises occur during normal events of human growth and transitional phrases or stages in one's life (James & Gilliland, 2017; Kanel, 2003). Such events may include childbirth, graduation, retirement, aging, menopause and other biological shifts with age, marriage, adoption, children moving out, and becoming or not becoming a grandparent. Examples are vast and one must consider the impact of culture, race, and target identities when exploring them. In addition, with many examples holding a Western lens and with society determining what should occur during stages of development, crisis counselors need to understand the power and influence of societal privilege. For instance, an individual from a low socioeconomic class may experience crisis differently from someone of middle- or upper-class status. The ability to access resources varies across socioeconomic statuses and those with fewer resources may perceive the crisis and its effects through a different lens. Counselors must take into account the client's multiple identities in order to provide effective, culturally responsive and competent support. Finally, it is of note that the level of significance placed on a developmental event as well as the potential for simultaneous events can impact the level of crisis reaction (Cavaiola & Colford, 2018; Meyer, 2001).

Situational Crisis

Situational crises are "those events that occur unexpectedly during the course of a person's life" (Meyer, 2001, p. 1). Unlike developmental crises, these events have a sudden onset and are unpredictable, shocking, and intense (Cavaiola & Colford, 2018; James & Gilliland, 2017; Meyer, 2001). James and Gilliland (2017) describe these crises as "uncommon and extraordinary events that an individual has no way of forecasting or controlling" (p.18). Some scholars also describe subsets of situational crises as "traumatic" (Cavaiola & Colford, 2018) or "ecosytematic" (natural or human-caused disaster; James & Gilliland, 2017). Examples of situational crises include vehicle accidents, fires, terrorist attacks, assaults, rape, natural disasters, job loss, illness, school shootings, homicide, violence, death, suicide, and relationship breakups. Finally, Meyer (2001) suggests that crisis intervention may be based upon whether the situational events were "premeditated and intentional or accidental" (p. 4).

Existential Crisis

An existential crisis is an internal struggle. James and Gilliland (2017) suggest that this internal conflict can fall in the areas of purpose, freedom, connectedness, responsibility, and independence. In essence, existentialism contains questions of *what is the meaning of life?* and more specifically, *what is the meaning of my life?* Because of the intimate struggle associated with existential crises they can be the most difficult to identify and be multilayered (Cavaiola & Colford, 2018). For example, turning a significant age can bring about a reflection on one's life's purpose and meaning. These can occur at a *normal* level of inquisition but also have the power to snowball. For some individuals, there are no classic coping mechanisms for existential query and when that happens, crisis can swiftly increase.

PEOPLE IN CRISIS

When preparing to work with individuals in crisis one must become familiar with potential crisis reactions as well as preventive factors. Regardless of crisis, individuals typically react in three main areas: affect, behavior, and cognition (Meyer, 2001). Meyer (2001) suggests that within affect is (1) anger/hostility, (2) anxiety/fear, and (3) sadness/melancholy (Meyer, 2001). Though these are normal feelings, as a crisis intensifies with a reduction of support and coping mechanisms, these reactions can feel unbearable. It is also of note that anger can often hold other feelings within it. Sometimes anger may be an easier way to express pain or sorrow. Behaviorally, an individual in crisis can act in avoidance, immobility, and approach. Like the fight, flight, and freeze concept when an individual comes across a personally threatening experience, their perception of the challenge, as connected with their affect and cognition, will impact their behavioral reaction. Within that perception is cognitive reactions based on time orientation where transgression (present), threat (future), and loss (past) further shape an individual's reaction and ability to cope with a developmental, situational, or existential crisis (Meyer, 2001). Taking a deeper dive into signs and symptoms of crisis reactions brings us to Table 10.1, which offers emotional (affective), behavioral, cognitive, and biophysical examples.

When individuals have strong protective factors and resources, there will be obstacles to a crisis state development. Essentially, these factors can either defend against or increase susceptibility to crisis. In addition, the amount and consistency of protective factors equate to individual and community response. Kanel (2003) suggests that these factors can typically be found in one's environment. Protective factors can fall into three main categories as follows:

■ Material resources—wealth, transportation, clothing, shelter, physical needs
■ Social resources—family, friends, coworkers, spiritual connections, colleagues, affinity groups, peers
■ Personal resources—maturity, perseverance, flexibility, optimism (Kanel, 2003; Owen & Parsons, 2018)

Defined, a protective factor is a characteristic that can reduce or balance out the impact of a potential crisis event. As seen earlier, the presence of a lasting and meaningful relationship or financial stability can be an additional layer of protection to negative events. For example, if someone lost their job but also has a partner who offers solid financial support, we would see a wall to financial crisis. However, there may still be the potential of an existential crisis regarding purpose. Due to this, it is important to note that protective factors are as good as their availability and direct connection to the perceived crisis event. In addition, the individual in crisis must have knowledge of and ability to employ these factors. On the other side of protective factors are risk factors. Some examples of risk factors that increase the probability of crisis are:

■ History of previously experienced crises that have not been effectively resolved
■ History of mental disorder(s) or severe emotional imbalance
■ Low self-esteem
■ Neglecting personal needs, safety, responsibility, or self-direction
■ Impulsive behavior
■ History of poor relationships
■ Excessive use of substances
■ Marginal income and lack of regular and fulfilling work
■ Unusual or frequent physical injuries
■ Frequent changes in or unsuitable residence
■ Legal issues (Greenstone & Leviton, 2011)

TABLE 10.1 COMMON CRISIS REACTIONS

DOMAINS	EXAMPLES
Emotional (affect)	Anxiety, guilt, grief, despair, outrage, inadequacy, helplessness, hopeless, worthless, angry, irritable, sadness, terrified, shock, fear, numb, worry, concern, distrust, denial, insecurity, panic, exhaustion, confusion, overwhelmed, melancholy, disbelief, trapped, stupid, crushed, bitter, disturbed, threatened, and dread
Behavioral	Tearfulness, avoidance of stimuli, hypervigilance, regressive behaviors, social withdrawal, isolation, jumpy, decrease in functioning (appetite and sleep disturbance), decreased motivation, work/school withdrawal, giving things away, substance use, noncompliance with medication, fight, flight, and freeze, and any change in behavior from prior to the crisis event
Cognitive	Denial and disbelief, reduced attention, impaired concentration, confusion, flashback/nightmares, preoccupation with death, delusional perception, rationalization, and self-blame
Biophysical	Nausea, vomiting, fatigue, gastrointestinal issues, fatigue, rapid heartbeat, pressured breathing, menstrual irregularity, sweating, rash, chest or abdominal pain, headache, pupils dilate, sexual disinterest. blood pressure increases, rash, digestion is inhibited, and adrenalin is secreted

Source: Adapted from Cavaiola, A. A., & Colford, J. E. (2018). *Crisis intervention: A practical guide.* Sage; Greenstone, J. L., & Leviton, S. C. (2011). *Elements of crisis intervention: Crises and how to respond to them* (3rd ed.). Brooks/Cole; Hoff, L. A. (2014). *Crisis: How to help yourself and others in distress or danger.* Oxford University Press; Kanel, K. (2003). *A guide to crisis intervention* (2nd ed.). Brooks/Cole; Owen, E., & Parsons, R. (2018). *Crisis and trauma counseling: Unique forms of helping.* Cognella Academic Publishing.

CRISIS COUNSELING SKILLS

Crisis can "aggravate existing emotional injuries" and further obstruct "a person's ability to respond to the incident" (Duffy & Haberstroh, 2020, pp.1–2).

Because of this, how we respond to an individual in crisis is paramount. With the time-limited nature of crisis counseling and how it differs from traditional approaches, clinicians need to pay particular attention to their approach. This includes strong clinical characteristics. James and Gilliland (2017) discuss eight characteristics of the effective crisis counselor. These are life experience, poise, creativity/flexibility, intellectual quickness, energy/resilience/optimism, multicultural competence, courage, and identifying client strengths. In addition, Cavaiola and Colford (2018) report the following necessary traits of a successful crisis counselor:

- Tolerance of ambiguity
- A calm, neutral demeanor
- Tenacity
- Optimism
- Adventuresomeness
- Capacity for empathy
- Flexibility
- Confidence
- Little need to rescue
- Capacity for listening
- Awareness of trauma indicators
- Openness to individual crisis reactions
- Capacity for information management (pp. 43–45)

Reviewing these characteristics can feel quite overwhelming as a new crisis counselor. Later in this chapter, the *Going Within* activity will allow you to assess your perception and awareness of what you already possess. Crisis counseling takes practice, but the fact that you are entering this field means that you naturally hold some of these characteristics.

Alongside characteristics are skills. Above all, the skills you employ must create a stable working environment that contains safety and bravery. Effective communication and rapport are the hallmarks of crisis work (Hoff et al., 2009). Regardless of what assessment or intervention model you use, your ability to create this consistent and intentional environment is vital. Paladino via Sanabria (2018) suggested seven characteristics for professionals that provide acute crisis care.

1. Have knowledge of crisis assessment and deescalation models as well as community resources.
2. Possess skills in creating a strong and trusting therapeutic bond and connection.
3. Understand that crisis escalates as coping mechanisms are exhausted and that this can leave the victim feeling hopeless and powerless.
4. Be able to identify and understand a victim's emotional, social, and logistical supports as well as the temporal nature of them to assist with resourcing.

5. Understand that victims may manifest symptoms in diverse and unique ways through their affective, cognitive, behavioral, and physiological domains.

6. Have an understanding that crisis is perception based, so honoring the victim's experience and allowing for ventilation is vital.

7. Know that crisis work is a first step toward healing, so what is acutely done can greatly affect future therapeutic work for the victim. (pp. 122–123)

Effective crisis skills allow the crisis worker to find a balance between the client's loss of power, the temporal urgency of the crisis, and an intentional, direct, yet compassionate approach. All skills should be used with intention down to the most concise refection of feeling. A crisis counselor should know where they are in the session and where they need to go in the most efficient way that still allows the client to feel understood and cared for. Within this approach are these necessary skills:

■ Attending behavior (physical and verbal)
■ Questioning (open-ended questions and closed-ended questions)
■ Paraphrasing (reflection of feeling/affect and reflection of content/context)
■ Summarization (write my own way)
■ Pacing (going with the client's ability to share with one's mind on potential urgency)
■ Advanced empathy
■ Tone (softer tones allow for richer communication)
■ Metacognition (maintain deep empathy while having knowledge of where the intervention must go)
■ Client personalized approach (using the client's name, asking and using the names of significant individuals and support, counselor communicating genuine care)
■ Use of silence to allow the client to reflect and process the above

Assessment

Assessment is a task within intervention. The several types of client assessment range from the fundamental affect, behavior, and cognitive approach to more specific assessments of lethality. Foundationally, assessment of orientation is one that all crisis counselors should employ several times during an intervention. There are four orientations to assess for a client.

■ Oriented to time (Do you know the time?)
■ Oriented to person (Do you know your name?)
■ Oriented to place (Do you know where you are?)
■ Oriented to circumstances (Do you know why you are here?)

A crisis counselor would reestablish orientation several times during an intervention. Depending on the topic, a client may slip in and out of certain knowledge due to either dissociation, substance use, or concentration.

As part of general assessment, it is also a search for protective factors, coping skills, and an ingrained support system. Coping skills can be positive (e.g., exercise, reading, connecting with friends, working, meditation, needlework) and negative (e.g., substance use, procrastination, self-harm, isolation, denial). Though we want to steer clients away from negative coping mechanisms, there are two points to understand: (1) their negative coping mechanisms may be the only thing keeping them alive and functional and (2) any coping mechanism is an indicator that the client wants to take care of themselves and they know themself. An effective crisis counselor will move the client toward healthy coping while honoring how the client has been able to function.

A more comprehensive assessment was first introduced by Lazarus (1976) and is called the BASIC ID. Though this was created as a part of his Multimodal Theory, the BASIC ID (i.e., Behavior, Affective Responses, Sensations, Images, Cognitions, Interpersonal, Relationships, and Drugs or Biological Influences) has several applications when working with clients in crisis. Paladino and Minton (2008) presented the BASIC ID tool as a method for conducting a suicide assessment. Using the BASIC ID over the ABC method provides a more comprehensive understanding of a client's current crisis state.

Certain crisis situations require a more specific type of assessment. We find this in the case of lethality. Lethality assessment is typically used with clients who report suicidal and homicidal ideation. This assessment goes beyond general modalities to include a client's plan to die or kill someone. Most assessments in this area can be used for suicidal and homicidal ideation and include both evaluation risk factors and level of lethality (i.e., the probability that a person will die by suicide or kill by homicide). There are many assessments (see Table 10.2), but they all contain a similar formula.

Four general areas of lethality assessment are (1) ideation, (2) lethality of method and determining means, (3) availability and proximity of means, and (4) plan specificity (Paladino, 2020). Table 10.3 provides lethality assessment examples.

TABLE 10.2 SUICIDE ASSESSMENTS

ASSESSMENT	AUTHOR
The Collaborative Assessment and Management of Suicidality (CAMS)	Jobes (2006)
Chronic Assessment of Suicide Events (CASE)	Shea (2002)
Suicide Assessment Five-Step Evaluation and Triage (SAFE-T)	Jacobs (2007)
Counseling on Access to Lethal Means (CALM)[a]	Suicide Prevention Resource Center (2009)

[a]Free online training available.

TABLE 10.3 SUICIDE LETHALITY ASSESSMENT

DOMAIN	QUESTIONS
Suicidal ideation	Are you thinking about killing yourself? How long have you held these thoughts of dying? When is the last time you thought about dying? Have you thought about killing yourself in the past? Have you attempted to kill yourself in the past?
Lethality of method and determining means	Have you thought about how you might kill yourself? Do you know what you were going to use to kill yourself? Do you know how to use the means? What is your perception of if these means will kill you?
Availability and proximity of means	Do you have these means? Where are the means? Do you have the ability to obtain these means?
Plan specificity	What is your plan for killing yourself? Do you know when you are going to kill yourself? Do you know under what circumstances you will kill yourself?

Source: Adapted from Paladino, D. A. (2020). Suicide prevention and intervention. In T. Duffy & S. Haberstroh (Eds.), *Crisis and trauma counseling: strategies for effective practice.* (pp. 137–163). American Counseling Association.

Intervention

To provide competent crisis intervention, one must be a technician as well as an artist. Some may call it a *dance* in which the counselor is moving with the client at their pace back and forth with their comfort level while trying to get across the dance floor. There are times when a crisis counselor can get to deeper emotion (which feels like progress) and then the client jumps back and puts up a wall due to the heaviness of the session. When this happens, an effective crisis counselor goes with them and reflects that moment over continuing without them fully engaged in the momentum. The goal of the crisis counselor is to prevent further dysfunction and to "diffuse a potentially disastrous situation before physical or emotional destruction occurs" (Greenstone & Leviton, 2011, p. 1). As with assessment, there are several different intervention models (see Table 10.4). Regardless of which model fits your style it is important to work with only one as you are learning the skill and art of intervention. Assessment and intervention should become muscle memory as you work within the uniqueness of a client's crisis with flexibility. To not overwhelm with models, we will focus on Cavaiola and Colford's (2018) L-A-P-C model.

The L-A-P-C model provides a simple and effective model and guide. A crisis counselor will follow four steps: (1) Listen, (2) Assess, (3) Plan, and (4)

TABLE 10.4 CRISIS INTERVENTION MODELS

INTERVENTION MODEL	STEPS OR TASKS
The Hybrid Model (James & Gilliland, 2017)	1. Predispositioning/engaging 2. Problem exploration 3. Providing support 4. Examining alternatives 5. Planning in order to reestablish control 6. Obtaining commitment 7. Follow-Up
The ABC Model (Kanel, 2003)	■ A. Developing and maintaining contact (attending behavior and basic counseling skills) ■ B. Identifying the problem and therapeutic interaction (precipitating event, cognitions, emotional distress, impairments in function, precrisis level of functioning, ethical issues, substance use, and use therapeutic interactions) ■ C. Coping (identify client's current coping mechanisms, encourage client to think of other coping strategies, present alternative coping ideas, and follow-up)
Roberts' Seven-Stage Model (1991)	1. Plan and conduct a crisis assessment (including lethality measures and immediate psychological needs) 2. Make psychological contact, establish rapport, and rapidly establish the relationship 3. Identify major problems 4. Deal with feelings and emotions 5. Generate and explore alternatives 6. Develop and formulate an action plan 7. Establish follow-up plan and agreement

(continued)

TABLE 10.4 CRISIS INTERVENTION MODELS *(CONTINUED)*

INTERVENTION MODEL	STEPS OR TASKS
Greenstone and Leviton (2011)	1. Immediacy (act immediately to control the emotional bleeding) 2. Control (reorder the chaos that exists in the sufferer's world) 3. Assessment (assess the situation) 4. Disposition (decide how to handle the situation after you have assessed it) 5. Referral (refer as needed) 6. Follow-up (follow up if possible or as agreed)
SAFE-R (Everly & Mitchell, 2000)	1. Stabilization 2. Acknowledgment 3. Facilitation of understanding 4. Encourage effective coping 5. Recovery or referral

Commit. In Step 1 (Listen) the crisis counselor focuses on active listening as a main skill. They will explore the client's story and understanding of the crisis event. In addition, it will be important to communicate safety, make sure the client knows who you are and your purpose, and communicate that the client is heard. The counselor will also have to balance between the need to take control and handing control to the client.

Step 2 (Assess) asks the counselor to "assess the client across several dimensions in order to understand the impact of the crisis event on the client" (Cavaiola & Colford, 2018, p. 57). Dimensions include emotions, behavior, thoughts, and support system. Assessing is also getting a read on the client's response to crisis including their personal strengths that may have assisted in the past (Cavaiola & Colford, 2018). In Step 3 (Plan) the crisis counselor works to "impart to the client a sense of hope and empowerment" (p. 57). This occurs through a co-creation of options that assist in bringing in support and process. Within the plan, it is important to make sure that they are obtainable and the client is onboard with them. Just because we would like the client to do something to protect themselves does not mean they have the desire or energy to do so. The hope is that there will be "a return to some state of equilibrium" (p. 57). The final step (Commit) either has the client connecting to the plan with agreement and action or has the counselor becoming directive due to the urgency and intensity of the crisis issue. For example, a client may need to be involuntarily hospitalized if they are assessed to have high lethality (i.e., suicidal ideation or homicidal ideation).

CONCLUSION

In this chapter, you explored what crisis assessment and intervention is, how it is employed, and the skills necessary to be effective. Crisis counseling can be intense due to the nature of the client's experience; however, with practice and an understanding of assessment and intervention models, this work can be extremely beneficial to all those who will sit across from you. Always remember, all one needs is one atom of hope to begin a return to functioning and thriving.

Summary

- Though crisis counseling uses similar skills to longer term counseling, the process is different and should be honed.
- Crisis grows out of a loss of predictability and a temporary inability to use coping skills.
- The therapeutic relationship is paramount in all crisis counseling work due to its short term and direct nature.
- Within the world of crisis counseling assessment and intervention are two important and distinct skill sets.
- Crises are developmental, situation, and/or existential.
- Crisis is always defined by the client's perception of the situation, not the counselor's bias or thoughts of the client's experience.

Voices From the Field

John Super, PhD, Clinical Operations Coordinator,
Community Counseling and Research Center and Couples and Family Clinical Director, University of Central Florida

Early morning on June 12, 2016, a shooter entered Pulse, an LGBTQ+ night club in Orlando, Florida, murdering 49 and injuring 53 patrons during the massacre. Within a few hours, counselors began a local response to help the community process the thoughts and emotions triggered by the event. During those first few weeks I helped create a crisis counseling response including organizing and supervising the hundreds of volunteer helpers as crisis counselors.

The Pulse massacre occurred at multiple cultural intersections. The shooter had strong ties to the Arabic community, the shootings happened on a Latin-themed night at Pulse, the media reported the shooter's religious beliefs motivated his attack, the religious and cultural beliefs of some victim's families affected their responses to learning their loved one died in an LGBTQ+ club, and the attack on the LGBTQ+ population challenged the public's social, religious, and moral beliefs on LGBTQ+ issues. The counselors responding to this collective crisis needed to integrate techniques used with marginalized populations into the crisis counseling. The counselors reported that working at these intersections created unique circumstances requiring the counselors to adapt as the intersectionality created dissonance for some and strong emotions for others. The counselors recognized each client conceptualization may need another multicultural lens and the client's treatment adapted to that lens.

In addition to the multicultural intersectionality, the counselor's personal connection to the local community was challenging as they were often processing their own thoughts and emotions while helping clients process their reaction to the massacre. This parallel process frequently occurred in those first few days. For example, while a client worried if a loved one would emerge as a victim, the counselor was also concerned a friend or family member would be identified. To lessen the parallel process, the counselors relied on bracketing their thoughts and emotions to effectively focus on counseling their clients.

When a crisis occurs, generally nationally organized professionals come to assist the community in the trauma, yet those national efforts may take several days to arrive, leaving the local counselors to be the first response. In a similar situation, a challenge a local counselor should recognize is the difficulty in holding empathy while being emotionally raw and facing beliefs or reactions they may disagree with when they are the only available counselors. For example, counselors strive to have an affirming stance, but during this time some counselors also found working with a client who was ashamed their loved one was a sexual minority or who struggled with integrating their grief and their disdain for the person's affectional orientation was difficult. These situations required the counselors to bracket their thoughts and emotions and caused them to seek peer supervision after the session.

The final lesson was reconceptualizing the counseling process for a community crisis response. After small numbers of clients sought grief counseling initially, we refocused our efforts to meet them where they were. In addition to the grief counseling sites, the counselors mingled with those waiting to donate blood, went into LGBTQ+ clubs and attended community vigils. The counselors watched for people experiencing extreme emotions (very emotional or the lack of any emotion) and asked a general question (e.g., "how do you think most people are feeling about the shooting?") to start a conversation, and if the person needed crisis counseling, they found a more private place to talk.

A Call to Action

Crisis impacts every population. Regardless of developmental level, age, race, religion, gender, sexual orientation, and culture crisis events have the power to disarm a person's ability to care for themselves and others. Many times, crises go unnoticed if they do not impact the individual. As an advocacy knowledge project, do a search of crises that impact target identities and marginalized and nonprivileged populations. After exploring these events, research what was provided to them in the aftermath of the crisis event. What was provided? What was missing? How might this event impact marginalized populations differently than privileged populations? What would have assisted to restore functioning to these individuals, population, or community? Finally, share your findings and reflection with a peer entering the counseling field.

Genevieve is a 19-year-old community college student living at home with her parents and 12-year-old sister. This past year Genevieve learned that she has terminal cancer. With only months left in her life (according to the oncologist), Genevieve has made peace with dying. You learn that Genevieve's parents are planning a trip overseas with no acknowledgment that she will not be alive for it. Genevieve displays very high emotion when she shares this information. She is tearful and angry.

RESPONSE QUESTIONS

Review your reading work with this case to determine the following:

1. Is this crisis developmental, situational, or existential? How do you know?
2. Putting yourself in Genevieve's shoes, what is she feeling? What beliefs does she hold about herself and the situation?
3. What does Genevieve wish?
4. What do you believe Genevieve needs?
5. What case factors impact your intervention?
6. Using Cavaiola and Colford's (2018) L-A-P-C model, take Genevieve through an intervention.

Going Within

You will find a crisis counselor skill self-assessment in Table 10.5. This was created off James and Gilliland's (2017) and Cavaiola and Colford's (2018) work in the area of what qualities make an effective crisis counselor. Please take the assessment below, evaluate, and reflect on your responses. Then answer the following questions:

- Looking at the total assessment, what comes up for you?
- What areas are you proud of?
- What areas need attention?
- What is your plan after seeing your competed assessment?

Group Process

Select a recent natural disaster (e.g., hurricane, tornado, tsunami, blizzard). In a group determine the following:

- What are the initial individual and community crises associated with this event?
- What is the potential approaching and future individual and community crises associated with this event?

TABLE 10.5 CRISIS COUNSELOR SKILL SELF-ASSESSMENT

CHARACTERISTICS AND SKILLS	PERSONAL EVALUATION			
	Highly Developed	Well Developed	Developing Skills	Lack of Skills
Multicultural competence				
Poise				
Calm under pressure				
Creativity				
Flexibility				
Intellectual quickness,				
Energy/resilience/optimism				
Life experience				
Courage				
Confidence				
Identifying client strengths				
Metacognition				
Tolerance of ambiguity				
Tenacity				
Capacity for empathy				

(continued)

TABLE 10.5 CRISIS COUNSELOR SKILL SELF-ASSESSMENT (*CONTINUED*)

CHARACTERISTICS AND SKILLS	PERSONAL EVALUATION		
Little need to rescue			
Capacity for listening			
Awareness of crisis reactions			

Source: Data from James, R. K., & Gilliland, B. E. (2017).. *Crisis intervention strategies* (8th ed.). Brooks/Cole;Cavaiola, A. A., & Colford, J. E. (2018).. *Crisis intervention: A practical guide.* Sage.

- How does this event leave individuals feeling, thinking, behaving?
- What are the acute needs for individuals and the community?
- What are the long-term needs for individuals and the community?
- What resources can assist with healing individuals and the community?
- What skills are needed to assist individuals and the community?
- What is your prediction on when full recovery will occur at the individual and community levels?

RESOURCES

American Association of Suicidology: https://suicidology.org

Aunt Bertha – Free and Reduced Cost Services: https://www.findhelp.org

CALM: Counseling on Access to Lethal Means Training: https://www.sprc.org/resources-programs/calm-counseling-access-lethal-means-0

Federal Emergency Management Agency (FEMA): https://www.fema.gov

Psychological First Aid (PFA) Training: https://www.nctsn.org

Red Cross: https://www.redcross.org

Veterans Crisis Line: 800-273-8255, press Option 1

Trans Lifeline: 877-565-8860 (U.S.) or 877-330-6366 (Canada); the Trans Lifeline's Hotline is a peer-support service for trans and questioning individuals in crisis. All operators are trans-identified.

Trevor Lifeline: 1-866-488-7386. The only national 24/7 crisis intervention and suicide prevention lifeline for LGBTQ young people under 25.

TrevorText: A free, confidential, secure service in which LGBTQ young people can text a trained Trevor counselor for support and crisis intervention, available Monday–Friday from 3–10 pm ET / Noon–7pm PT by texting START to 678678.

Crisis Text Line: A crisis-intervention hotline that conducts conversations exclusively by text message. Trained crisis counselors are available 24 hours a day. Text HOME to 741741 to connect with a Crisis Counselor (United States and Canada) https://www.crisistextline.org

 Access this podcast at http://connect.springerpub.com/content/book/978-0-8261-6386-8/chapter/ch10.

KEY REFERENCES

Only key references appear in the print edition. The full reference list appears in the digital product found on https://connect.springerpub.com/content/book/978-0-8261-6386-8/chapter/ch10

Cavaiola, A. A., & Colford, J. E. (2018). *Crisis intervention: A practical guide*. Sage. https://doi.org/10.4135/9781544327457

Duffy, T., & Haberstroh, S. (2020). Introduction to crisis and trauma counseling. In T. Duffy & S. Haberstroh (Eds.), *Crisis and trauma counseling: Strategies for effective practice* (pp. 1–23). American Counseling Association.

Greenstone, J. L., & Leviton, S. C. (2011). *Elements of crisis intervention: Crises and how to respond to them* (3rd ed.). Brooks/Cole.

Hoff, L. A. (2014). *Crisis: How to help yourself and others in distress or danger*. Oxford University Press.

James, R. K., & Gilliland, B. E. (2017). *Crisis intervention strategies* (8th ed.). Brooks/Cole.

Lazarus, A. A. (1976). *Multimodal behavior therapy*. Springer Publishing Company.

Meyer, R. A. (2001). *Assessment for crisis intervention: A triage assessment model*. Brooks/Cole.

Owen, E., & Parsons, R. (2018). *Crisis and trauma counseling: Unique forms of helping*. Cognella Academic Publishing.

Shea, S. (2002). *The practical art of suicide assessment: A guide for mental health professionals and substance abuse counselors*. Wiley.

CHAPTER 11

TRAUMA COUNSELING

Latoya Haynes-Thoby

Think about this...

What is trauma? What makes an event traumatic? How might we use counseling interventions to support individuals who have experienced or witnessed trauma? How might a counselor work to hold space for the possibility that a client's presenting symptoms are related to a trauma? How can counselors work to intentionally collaborate with clients who have experienced trauma?

LEARNING OBJECTIVES

After reading this chapter, you should be able to:

- Identify the prevalence and impact of trauma
- Describe the importance of assessing for trauma
- Recognize trauma symptoms and their presentation across settings
- Describe the basic tenets of trauma-informed counseling
- Summarize the importance of culturally responsive care
- Describe the benefits of trauma-informed counseling
- Explain the use of evidence-based treatments for trauma
- Recognize multicultural considerations in the presentation and treatment of trauma symptoms
- Identify factors that contribute to resilience and growth after trauma

INTRODUCTION

Counselors who work with clients across a variety of settings are likely to work with individuals, couples, families, and students who have experienced trauma (Perfect et al., 2016; Substance Abuse and Mental Health Services Administration [SAMHSA], 2014a, 2014b). Trauma is not determined by the severity of an event, but by the reaction that an individual has to an experience of adversity. Trauma is the result of an individual's reaction to an event or set of events that threatens imminent death or serious emotional or physical harm (SAMHSA, 2014a, 2014b; Van der Kolk, 2014). This means that an event that is experienced as a trauma can leave a person believing that they will not survive the event, or that they will surely experience serious harm as a result of the experience. Another person who has experienced the very same event may walk away unscathed. A traumatic event often leaves individuals feeling as if they are helpless or have very little control over the outcome of the event. As such, traumatic experiences often exceed an individual's current ability to cope (Van der Kolk, 2014), leaving a person to believe that they have lost control over their own well-being.

Experiencing the sense of loss of control over one's life can lead a person to question their own safety (Bloom, 2013). Traumatic events can have a lasting negative impression on an individual's sense of psychological, physical, social, moral, or spiritual safety in the world (Middleton et al., 2019). A disruption of safety across these dimensions can impact a client's sense of sanctity within their own mind or psychological well-being. A loss of psychological safety may necessitate support as a person works to get back to baseline after a trauma that has disrupted their ability to navigate affect, intrusive thoughts, sleep disturbances, or memories of the trauma. Trauma that impacts psychological safety can be related to a disruption of safety across physical, social, moral, or spiritual well-being disruptions after trauma. Losing agency to keep one's own body safe can directly impact psychological well-being, just as a loss of psychological safety can threaten physical well-being, such as when a person experiences emotional or physical abuse.

Safety within one's own body or physical safety can often leave a client feeling less clear about agency over their physical being after harm has been done. A client who is experiencing a diminished sense of physical safety may make compromises in an effort to increase a sense of control over what happens to their body after a trauma or repeated traumatic experiences (Perry & Szalavitz, 2017). In a bestselling text, Perry and Szalavitz (2017) describe the presentation of compromises that child trauma survivors might make after ongoing and unexpected assaults. This type of compromise is also common for victims of intimate partner violence. Decisions that a person makes as they work to regain some semblance of control after a trauma can impact their connection to others and themselves (Bloom, 1999; Covington, 2008). This challenge can heighten or contribute to isolation and a sense of helplessness for survivors of trauma. As such, after a traumatic experience, it is not uncommon for a person to struggle with navigating safety among others, or social safety.

Social safety can impact an individual's ability to feel safe around other people, and this dimension of safety can be compounded when the trauma represents a violation of interpersonal trust (Covington, 2008). Counselors who support clients who have experienced diminished social safety after a trauma work to remember that a violation of trust does not require an obvious breach of trust. This means that the client may not be aware that their trust has been violated, and counselors can work to support the client in exploring this in their work together. There are also times when a person may struggle with what Bloom (2013) describes as moral safety, or safety within oneself. Moral safety allows you to trust your own decision-making (Bloom, 2013). Challenges related to moral safety may make it much more difficult for a client to be able to make decisions for themselves without believing that their choices might not be sound. Moral safety diminishment is not uncommon for people who have experienced gaslighting, emotional abuse, or unexpected disruptions to what they might have held as a baseline of normalcy. Similarly, spiritual safety may be challenged after a trauma, as people work to make meaning of the event or set of events. A disruption of spiritual safety may leave a client wondering what this means for their future, who they are in the world, and their own value. Counselors may observe that all dimensions of safety are interconnected, and as one area of safety has been disrupted, one or more other areas of safety may also be challenged. Individuals who have experienced trauma may begin to question safety in the world, safety with others, and safety within themselves. Disruption of safety is evidenced for individuals across developmental processes, and can be especially challenging for vulnerable populations, such as children.

ADVERSE CHILDHOOD EXPERIENCES

Early experiences of adversity or trauma can disrupt a child's view of the world, their functioning, and their determinations about their own safety in the world. The 1998 Adverse Child Experiences Study (ACES) (Felitti et al., 2019) examined the adverse experiences of over 9,000 adults who had received medical care within the Kaiser Permanente Health System. Participants of the ACES responded to a 17-item survey that measured their exposure to adverse childhood experiences, such as psychological, physical, and sexual abuse, as well as household dysfunction (Felitti et al., 2019). The survey asked the participants about their experiences of being verbally abused, of being hit, and of childhood sexual assault, as well as the state of their household functioning in childhood, including the presence of substance abuse, mental illness, domestic violence, or criminal behaviors. Using this data, the researchers found that participants who reported higher experiences of childhood adversity were also more likely to demonstrate maladaptive coping, depression, anxious symptoms, suicidality, and smoking, and they had other serious physical health conditions, such as cancer, heart disease, a history of strokes, and obesity (Felitti et al., 2019). Felitti et al. (2019) suggested prevention measures and treatment strategies that would positively impact coping for individuals with experiences of adversity that were similar to the participants in their study. The ACES served as early evidence of the extending and long-term impact of trauma exposure on the lives of individuals, including those who have experienced adversity in early childhood. This study highlighted the need for counselors who serve children who have survived trauma to support both the prevention and early treatment related to trauma exposure. Since this study was published, researchers have explored the presence of adversity in childhood for communities across the world, and a variety of tools have been used to support the psychoeducation of individuals as they learn about their own childhood adversity. Screening for trauma and looking beyond common diagnoses for child and adolescent clients will allow for the integration of early prevention and supports that will aid in addressing the current and potential negative later life outcomes in the lives of children as they age.

TOXIC STRESS

Toxic stress is the result of ongoing and severe adversity experienced by an individual, family, or community, without the appropriate support or protections (Center for the Developing Child, 2014; Shonkoff et al., 2012). The psychological and physical reactions after trauma are often described as toxic stress. This type of stress can be experienced after exposure to ongoing abuse, neglect, adversity, poverty, or parental dysfunction. Individuals who are at greatest risk of trauma exposure are at greater risk for the development of toxic stress. Children, communities of color, immigrants, low-income populations, and people with disabilities are at greater risk of being impacted by factors that contribute to exposure to toxic stress due to systemic oppression and major barriers to wellness, such as adversity, poverty, and discrimination (Chetty et al., 2018; Goodman et al., 2011). Individuals outside these categories can also be at risk of trauma and toxic stress as well.

Toxic stress has been shown to impact both short-term and more lasting long-term changes to the brain, as well as overall mental and physical health (Shonkoff et al., 2012). Trauma can impact the health of individuals both shortly after trauma and years later, such as in the development of physical health challenges in later life. Assessments that include screenings for trauma aid in the identification of traumatic histories and toxic stress. Prevention and treatment have been shown to be effective for individuals impacted by toxic stress. Additionally, counseling that maintains considerations for the potential of trauma and toxic stress benefits clients who have and who have not experienced trauma (SAMHSA, 2014a, 2014b). In treating the needs of individuals, couples, and families that have been impacted by trauma, it will always be important to provide services that are culturally responsive (Petrosky et al., 2017) and to consider the specific needs of our clients in context.

TRAUMA COUNSELING

Clients who seek counseling for trauma are often seeking relief from the disruption, pain, loss, confusion, disconnection, or distress after a traumatic experience. Some clients will experience trauma symptoms shortly after a traumatic event, and others may not display many symptoms at all. An individual's reaction to a distressing event is what defines whether or not an event is traumatic, and those traumatic reactions are normal responses to distressing experiences. The *Diagnostic and Statistical Manual of Mental Disorders*, 5th Edition (*DSM-5*; American Psychiatric Association [APA], 2013) describes trauma as the direct experience of an event(s) that has threatened imminent death or serious injury of the individual, the learning or witnessing of a loved one's trauma, or repeated exposure to the details of trauma (such as for first responders). Many mental health professionals recognize that the sources of trauma are many and that not all traumatic experiences will result in a diagnosis such as posttraumatic stress disorder (PTSD; APA, 2013).

Following a traumatic experience, an individual may experience symptoms that can include emotional dysregulation; intrusive thoughts or memories of the event(s), or distressing dreams of the trauma; avoidance of reminders of the event; changes in mood or thoughts related to the trauma; changes in excitability; and anxious or depressive symptoms (APA, 2013). It will be important to remember that an individual may experience a trauma without developing a trauma-related disorder. An event that may result in the presence of trauma-related symptoms for one person may leave another person with no lingering negative effects. Additionally, while many trauma survivors may experience initial trauma reactions, this does not mean that all trauma survivors will go on to meet the criteria for PTSD. More than 64% of clients seeking counseling report trauma in their lifetimes (SAMHSA, 2014a, 2014b) and more than 80% of clients who enter counseling for substance use related treatment report a trauma history (Covington, 2008). In classrooms, 25%–33% of PK-12 children will have experienced a trauma before they reach adulthood (Perfect et al., 2016). Clients' reactions to these exposures will vary based on their coping, recurrence of the trauma, and available supports. Children, adolescents, adults, and whole families can be touched by trauma from a variety of sources, and counselors can often support clients to navigate those experiences.

Trauma can occur interpersonally, collectively (such as natural disasters, or mass violence), or intergenerationally, and can have cataclysmic effects, such as during a global pandemic. Interpersonal trauma includes intimate partner violence, child abuse, elder abuse, sexual assault, or stalking. Interpersonal trauma often occurs as a result of harm perpetrated by a trusted adult, friend, or loved one, such as dating violence. Interpersonal trauma can leave a person struggling to feel connected to others or to themselves as a result of a violation of trust (Covington, 2008). The breach of trust can extend to include the trust that a person has within themselves, as they may struggle to believe that they are safe in the world. Similarly, collective trauma can affect an entire society, and can disrupt safety on a larger scale. Collective traumas often go on to become a collective memory of an overwhelming societal event, such as a global pandemic, a large-scale natural disaster, or experiences such as the Great Depression. Collective traumatic events have been described as cataclysmic and can shape generational memory and the way that an entire generation orients to the world.

Trauma that is passed down across generations within families or communities is described as intergenerational trauma. Family members may or may not be aware of the source of the trauma, but intergenerational trauma can change the way that a family functions, or impact practiced traditions that may have originally begun as practices that maintained the family's survival during the actual trauma. Similarly, complex trauma is often the result of recurrent exposure to intrusive trauma, such as profound neglect or ongoing domestic abuse. Trauma can also include serious accidents, a traumatic loss, identity-based trauma (such as race-based trauma, anti-Asian hate, or trauma that occurs as a result of hate that is based on ability status, gender identity, or sexual orientation), child neglect, or child witnessing of a caregiver's abuse.

Trauma is widespread, as 67% to 80% of clients seeking counseling will have experienced a trauma in their lifetime (APA, 2013; Covington, 2008). This means that considerations for trauma should be a part of every counseling intake and assessment process, as it will be highly likely that clients will have experienced a trauma. When clients begin counseling, it may not be initially apparent that a presenting concern is related to a trauma. Allowing for the consideration that a client's challenges could be related to trauma will allow space for the consideration of trauma reactions that can often present similarly to other common mental health disorders, such as conduct disorders in children, mood-related disorders, or other presentations. Beginning our work with clients from a perspective that asks what might have happened to them versus what is wrong can allow for the healing of pain that could otherwise go unnoticed without a trauma lens.

Counselors who work with clients who have experienced a trauma are aware that each trauma-related treatment plan is not always for PTSD. While trauma exposure is not uncommon, a PTSD diagnosis is not as common. The APA (2013) reports that nearly 8.7% of individuals will experience PTSD in their lifetimes. Prevalence rates for trauma-related disorders range for attachment (~10%), adjustment (less than a 10%), or posttraumatic stress (8.7%), or acute stress disorders (10%–50%; APA, 2013). Clients may go on to develop symptoms that might meet the criteria of an acute stress-related disorder, but every client will not go on to develop prolonged (≥1 month) trauma symptoms that meet the full criteria for PTSD. Even without a trauma diagnosis, it will be paramount for counselors to ask about trauma exposure as a part of the intake, and ongoing, assessment process. Support and treatment of trauma-related symptoms can not only aid in symptom reduction, but can also support a client's well-being and functioning across life domains that their symptoms may have further challenged after a trauma.

Trauma symptoms such as emotional dysregulation or feelings of disconnectedness can impact a trauma survivor's interpersonal relationships, available supports, and academic/career well-being. A school-age child who experiences trauma symptoms may also be assumed to be inattentive, exhibit poor behavior, or have difficulty learning. Similarly, an adult with similar symptoms may experience challenges in their home lives, careers, or an educational setting as a result of a traumatic experience. As trauma disrupts connection, it can be difficult for a client to identify the new challenges to a recent or past trauma. Clients may not identify a trauma as the source of their current ailments, but the inclusion of trauma assessments can be beneficial in understanding our client's needs. Trauma is often missed as counselors work with clients who report presenting depression or anxiety symptoms. Including assessments for trauma is a best practice in counseling.

HISTORY OF TRAUMA TREATMENT

Early trauma treatment began after theorists such as Jean-Martin Charcot, Sigmund Freud, and Pierre Janet began to observe the psychological impact of trauma in the lives of their patients (Center for Substance Abuse Treatment, 2014; Herman, 1992). Freud's early understanding of trauma symptom presentations largely shaped how trauma was understood for a very long time. Freud's observations of hysteria in women trauma victims rooted trauma as an internal deficit that could be resolved within the victim of the trauma alone (Becker-Blease & Freyd, 2005; Herman, 1992). It was not until mental health professionals began to hear about the experiences of soldiers returning from World War I that the definition of trauma began to expand (Herman, 1992; Lasiuk & Hegadoren, 2006). Work with soldiers returning from the war allowed for clearer understandings of the long-term impact of trauma on the lives of individuals (Becker-Blease & Freyd, 2005; Herman, 1992; Lasiuk & Hegadoren, 2006). Many early soldiers experiencing trauma symptoms were often viewed through deficit framing that meant that they were described as having internal defects, and other trauma-related symptoms were assumed to be the result of nostalgia or homesickness (Lasiuk & Hegadoren, 2006). Initial trauma definitions did not consider the impact of a traumatic event, as the symptoms were viewed as evidence of a weakness within the impacted individual. While trauma has long affected individuals and systems, it was not recognized as such. It was not until the world began to hear reports of the pain experienced by returning veterans that attention to the experiences of trauma was reignited. Returning soldiers and the work to support them resulted in a new wave of heightened attention to the experience of trauma in the military.

It was not until 1978 that trauma-related stress reactions were included in the *International Classification of Diseases, Ninth Revision* (*ICD-9*), followed by its inclusion in the *DSM-III* in 1980 (Nicolas et al., 2015; SAMHSA, 2014a, SAMHSA, 2014b). It was through the knowledge gained from the returning Vietnam veterans that counselors began to identify similarities in their clients who were not veterans, but also showed evidence of ongoing traumatic responses (Herman, 1992). The first phases of treatment for trauma are often described as the "first generation" of trauma treatment, and included individual treatment of trauma symptoms, with the goal of integrating the trauma symptomatology into the individual's life in order to decrease distress (Center for Substance Abuse Treatment, 2014). By the 1970s the "second generation" of trauma treatment included individual treatment (Center for Substance Abuse Treatment, 2014), psychoeducation, group counseling, and empowerment counseling for victims of abuse (Herman, 1992). The "third generation" of trauma counseling has shifted to include a response that is evidence of a trauma-informed response, and this approach to trauma is now practiced across counseling settings.

TRAUMA-INFORMED COUNSELING

Trauma-informed care represented a paradigm shift, as it moved away from a deficit focus that queried the source of the defect within the client to an approach that acknowledged the impact of trauma on the individual (Bloom, 1997; SAMHSA, 2014a, 2014b; Trauma and Learning Policy Initiative [TLPI], 2013). After a person has survived a traumatic experience, questions about what was wrong with the client would represent an approach to care that was not trauma-informed, while trauma-informed counseling (TIC) questioned what happened to the client, removing the deficit from within the client. Counseling that is trauma-informed recognizes that a person's reaction to trauma is their work to survive after an experience that falls outside the range of what is considered normal. TIC is currently used within community counseling (Bemak & Chung, 2017; Goodman, 2015; SAMHSA, 2014a, 2014b), rehabilitation counseling (Koch et al., 2020; O'Sullivan et al., 2019), career counseling (Powers & Duys, 2020), school counseling (American School Counselor Association, 2016; Blitz et al., 2020; McIntyre et al., 2019), and a host of other counseling spaces (ACA, 2018). Trauma-informed counselors work from their knowledge of the prevalence of trauma, noting that it is widespread and common for children and adults. They operate from an understanding of the impact that trauma can have on human functioning, and they recognize the varied symptom presentation as they work to provide holistic care that begins with considering the possibility of trauma in the work with clients (SAMHSA, 2014a, 2014b). This means that trauma-informed counselors will work to consider the potential for trauma symptom presentation as they work to identify underlying concerns. This consideration aids in the reduction of misdiagnosis, especially for school-age children and adults. Trauma-informed counselors know that trauma impacts individuals' overall functioning and can present as psychological distress, later health conditions, or relational challenges. Trauma can impact the way that PK-12 students relate to each other, their schools, and their communities. Similarly, trauma can impact the way that individuals orient to their academic or career pursuits (Zeligman et al., 2020).

Trauma has been shown to increase individuals' risks for the development of mental health disorders, physical health disorders, and challenges in maintaining healthy relationships (Felitti et al., 2019; Shonkoff et al., 2012). Counseling can support clients as they work to rebuild healthy support systems and return to baseline. Simultaneously, TIC works to resist retraumatization and prioritizes six tenets, including client safety, transparency in the work with clients, inclusion of choice and empowerment, mutual support networks, and the use of shared power (Menschner & Maul, 2016). A trauma-informed approach is best utilized when it is integrated across a system and should begin with the reestablishment of safety for a client.

As counselors work to establish safety with clients, they support clients to navigate arousal system regulation after a trauma, and the development of skills in self-regulation that they are able to utilize independently. Bloom (1999) likens self-regulation as a means for clients to be able manage their emotional responses to everyday stimuli, in ways that are similar to adjusting the volume of a radio from zero to 10. Clients are supported to manage their reactions, and to feel good about responding in ways that do not leave them feeling depleted, or as if they reexperience a loss of control in their response to a stressor. As counselors work to support clients' self-regulation, they work to be sure that the client is able to facilitate this process safely and independently. Table 11.1

TABLE 11.1 CORE CONDITIONS NECESSARY TO BEGIN TRAUMA-INFORMED COUNSELING

- Begins with reestablishment of safety.
- Centers the counseling relationship and the building of rapport.
- Integrates tools for client empowerment.
- Supports the reestablishment of agency.
- Actively works to resist retraumatization in the work with clients.

provides an overview of the core conditions necessary to begin trauma-informed counseling.

Before beginning the process of exploring the trauma, a client should be in a safe and stable space with appropriate means to cope with the distress that trauma processing may bring to the surface. Counselors can work to support clients to develop appropriate coping and self-regulation through psychoeducation, distress reduction techniques, and practicing grounding techniques, as a means to support the client in identifying and managing their reactions to stimuli. Examples of techniques that counselors use to support healthy coping, grounding, and self-regulation can vary to include humanistic, behavioral, cognitive, and psychodynamic approaches to counseling. As treatment approaches are determined, clients should be a part of the collaborative decision-making process. Counselors can work with clients to support them as they make steps toward feeling empowered through psychoeducation about the trauma, specific approaches, and the potential benefits of a potential treatment. Empowerment can include assuring that a client understands how and why a treatment approach could be selected. The work of processing the trauma will not begin until a client has established safety and appropriate coping strategies. This will require rapport building, trust, and treatment that reflects the specific needs of the client receiving services. Table 11.2 provides an overview of the components of trauma counseling.

TABLE 11.2 COMPONENTS OF TRAUMA COUNSELING

1. Counselor operates with an awareness of the widespread prevalence of trauma.
2. Counselor understands the impact of trauma.
3. Counselor works to identify the signs and symptoms of trauma within their counseling setting.
4. Psychoeducation is a key component to support the development of healthy coping and empowerment building.
5. Integration of resources will support client empowerment, including culturally rooted tools.
6. The counselor supports the centering of the client in the collaborative work of treatment.
7. Counseling aids in the restoration or development of self-regulation.
8. Clients express their internal experience through healthy communication, as defined in collaboration with the client.
9. Counseling centers clients' needs and safety throughout the counseling process.

As counselors engage the work of integrating trauma-informed approaches into their work with clients, it will be important to note that TIC interventions differ across populations, communities, and settings in order to avoid a one-size-fits-all approach (Nicolas et al., 2015). The integration of the cultural values, context, and the specific needs of an individual, couple, or family will best facilitate effective treatment after a trauma. In order to understand a client's cultural values, their cultural understanding of the problem, and their needs, counselors work to intentionally incorporate counseling competencies, such as the multicultural and social justice counseling competencies (Ratts et al., 2015), the disability-related counseling competencies (Chapin et al., 2018), the ALGBTIC competencies for counseling LGBQIQA populations (Harper et al., 2009), and the competencies for addressing spiritual and religious issues into their work as counselors (Association for Spiritual, Ethical, and Religious Values in Counseling, 2009). In order to provide TIC that is culturally responsive, counselors will work to intentionally work toward cultural competence. Cultural competence is an ongoing endeavor, and the work is continuous for each counselor. As counselors work to provide culturally responsive counseling and TIC, they work to continually learn about the communities that they serve, and will seek consultation when appropriate in order to best meet the needs of their clients. Effective TIC must incorporate culturally rooted strengths that may contribute to resilience after adversity. Insights such as these cannot be ascertained without holding space to learn about the client's experience, independent work to learn more about the community that a counselor serves, and continued work to challenge any potential biases that may serve as barriers to clearly seeing our clients as whole and fully capable human beings.

TIC has been infused across a variety of settings, including school counseling (Blitz et al., 2020; McIntyre et al., 2019; TLPI, 2013), career counseling (Powers & Duys, 2020; Zeligman et al., 2020), rehabilitation counseling (Koch et al., 2020; O'Sullivan et al., 2019), and refugee counseling (Bemak & Chung, 2017). With nearly 67% of adults reporting having had experienced a trauma by the age of 17 (Perfect et al., 2016), counselors are very likely to work with clients who experienced trauma across settings. Knowledge about the prevalence, impact, and symptoms of trauma is a good starting place as counselors work to support clients as they navigate life after trauma. These building blocks coupled with a lens toward culturally responsive counseling can aid counselors as they continue training in their specialized areas in their work to meet the needs of clients who have been impacted by trauma.

EVIDENCE-BASED TRAUMA-INFORMED COUNSELING

When counselors use evidence-based practices, they select approaches that have strong research evidence in treating a specific concern, using interventions that they have received adequate training in and that are consistent with the values of their client (Blair, 2010; Institute of Medicine [IOM], 2009; Zalaquett & Haynes-Thoby, 2020). As counselors work to develop treatment plans with clients, it will be important to remember the basic tenets of TIC. Counselors work to integrate knowledge of the prevalence, impact, and symptoms of trauma (SAMHSA, 2014a, 2014b). Counselors who use trauma-informed approaches to counseling actively work to avoid retraumatizing clients, and the counseling relationship is built on intentional centering of client safety, transparency in the counseling relationship, client choice, employment of tools that will allow for client empowerment, and shared power (Menschner & Maul, 2016). Sharing power with clients means that counselors will work to use language that the client can also understand, goals and treatment plans are developed collaboratively, and power is intentionally addressed in the counseling relationship. As counselors work to consider appropriate treatments for clients, the clients' worldview, cultural factors, and contributors to both risk and resilience are a part of the selection process in determining appropriate treatment.

A few evidence-based TIC approaches that have been found to be effective are dialectical behavior therapy (DBT), cognitive behavioral therapies (CBT), and mindfulness-based interventions. These approaches support clients as they work to reconnect and to manage trauma symptoms. DBT was developed by Marsha Linehan (Linehan & Wilks, 2015), and it was initially used to treat clients with borderline personality disorder (BPD). While DBT continues to be used to effectively treat BPD, it has also been found to be effective in treating clients who are experiencing emotional dysregulation, some substance use disorders (Dimeff & Linehan, 2008), and PTSD (Bohus & Priebe, 2019). DBT broadens the counseling relationship beyond individual counseling sessions and includes opportunities for clients to learn from others such as in group counseling. DBT is a comprehensive treatment modality that consists of individual counseling, group counseling, and the use of counselor consultation in treatment.

CBT aims to improve client functioning by addressing patterns of thoughts, feelings, and behaviors. CBT has been used to effectively treat trauma symptoms and related disorders, but without considerations for an individual client's needs, CBT may not work for every counseling relationship (Hinton et al., 2012). Clinicians who have received training and possess expertise in CBT approaches have also worked to include cultural adaptations for both minoritized and refugee populations (Hinton et al., 2012). Trauma-focused CBT is another cognitive behavioral approach that has been shown to be effective in reducing trauma-related symptoms for children and adolescents (de Arellano et al., 2014). Trauma-focused CBT incorporates talk therapy to provide psychoeducation, exposure, emotional flexibility, empowerment, and cognitive coping and processing (de Arellano et al., 2014).

Many counselors also utilize mindfulness-based interventions. Mindfulness has been used for centuries and such approaches have been used in Buddhist and other non-Western practices for a very long time. Mindfulness practices focus on the body's sensations and awareness, and are used to support reconnection; decrease reactivity, distress, and depression; and to refocus on the here-and-now (Goodman et al., 2011). While the utility of mindfulness practices directly addresses many common short-term and long-term trauma symptoms, it will continue to be important to consider the current coping and safety of clients before implementing any practice. A person who has experienced a trauma may be reluctant or frightened by a myriad of factors related to a specific approach, including mindfulness practices. A trauma-informed approach to mindfulness counseling will include an invitation for clients to learn more about the practice, through psychoeducation, a choice to engage, and considerations for triggers (i.e., closing one's eye, proximity, or physical safety).

In addition, counselors use an array of counseling approaches to meet the needs of clients. Some advanced training techniques that have been used effectively with clients include eye movement desensitization and reprocessing (EMDR), and more recently, neurofeedback for trauma. EMDR uses bilateral stimulation to promote cognitive processing in an established safe environment. Counselors who use EMDR support clients to practice self-regulation Both approaches described here will require training beyond your counselor training program; counselors must be sure to work within the scope of their training and expertise (Blair, 2010; IOM, 2009). Neurofeedback in counseling can aid clients in learning to self-regulate, and counselors who are trained in the use of neurofeedback in counseling can utilize brainwave data to measure stress and to support clients to strengthen coping strategies. As with all trauma counseling, counselors work to support clients to be able to self-regulate, independently, before engaging in the work of processing trauma. In the work to support the needs of clients after trauma, factors that support the development of resilience have been identified.

RESILIENCE AND GROWTH AFTER TRAUMA

Counselors who work to support the needs of clients after trauma have borne witness to the ability of human beings to heal, to make meaning, to grow, and return to a place of baseline functioning after a trauma. Both resilience and growth can occur after a trauma, but it will be important for counselors to allow space for the grieving of losses related to the traumatic experience(s) (Bloom, 1999). Masten (2001) describes resilience as an individual's ability to return to baseline after adversity. Resilience does not require an individual to navigate the trauma completely unscathed or without reacting, but resilience is evidence of a process toward a return to baseline. Individual resilience requires both internal and external resources that a person is able to access, even unconsciously, that include a positive view of themselves, trust in themselves, healthy relationships, stress tolerance (Masten, 2001; Singh et al., 2012), and an orientation to spirituality that is affirming (Haynes-Thoby, 2019). Counselors have described the importance of shared experiences, traditions, understandings, and beliefs in facilitating resilience across family systems (Walsh, 2012). Identifying these tools and supporting resilience across the communities that counselors serve must include tools that may be culturally rooted that can support resilience and necessary resistance to adversity (Boyd-Franklin & Karger, 2012; Bell-Tolliver et al., 2009). As such, culturally relevant systems that facilitate resilience for PK-12 students should include families, schools, and communities that surround the families.

CONCLUSION

TIC has been shown to benefit all clients, including those who do not report a trauma history (SAMHSA, 2014a, 2014b). Given the prevalence of trauma, counselors will benefit from understanding how to operationalize trauma-informed care across treatment settings. As counselors work to support their clients, including family members that they have identified as important in their healing, community stakeholders, and treatment that is both culturally responsive and trauma-informed will be integral in effective treatment after trauma. Clients benefit when counselors work to learn about best practices, available resources within the communities that they serve, and an openness to bearing witness to the client's lived experience.

Counselors work to identify the signs and symptoms of trauma, with the knowledge that trauma exposure is common. The sources of trauma are many, including systemic barriers to well-being. In the work to facilitate client self-empowerment, counselors work to listen and collaborate in developing treatment plans with clients. Trauma-informed counselors understand the impact of trauma, including the ways that trauma can facilitate disconnection from support systems and ourselves. Counselors also work to support empowerment in light of the potential for diminished agency that clients may experience after a trauma. Through the offering of choice, psychoeducation, and strategies to facilitate coping skills, clients are empowered to utilize the tools as they continue through the work of processing their trauma.

Trauma-informed counselors also understand that trauma impacts individuals, families, schools, and whole communities. As counselors engage their work to support the needs of trauma survivors, it will also be important to remember that trauma-informed treatment plans and goals in counseling will not look exactly the same for each client. Trauma-informed counselors work to collaborate with clients to develop goals, formulate treatment plans, and to extend available supports.

Summary

- Trauma is prevalent and can have long-lasting impacts on the lives of individuals, families, and communities.
- Trauma symptom presentation can differ across counseling settings and individual clients.
- Assessment for trauma should be a part of every intake and assessment process.
- Trauma-informed counseling has been shown to be effective for all clients, including those who have not experienced a trauma.
- Counselors can work to support the facilitation of resilience and growth after trauma.
- A trauma response is a normal reaction to an abnormal situation.
- Culturally responsive care is an effective means to support the needs of clients and will require counselors to continue to challenge themselves to address any held biases that may hinder working with a client.

Voices From the Field

Ying Yang, PhD, Licensed Professional Clinical Counselor, Appletree Psychological Services, Fremont, CA

When I learned about advocacy in graduate school, I initially thought it was about protesting on behalf of clients and getting involved in large social movements. At the time, I often wondered, what does advocacy look like in practice, and how much can I do to advocate for my clients? I carried these concerns with me after graduation, hoping to find answers in my work as a mental health counselor at a local community counseling agency.

Most of my clients at the agency came from low-income backgrounds and had experienced multiple traumatic events. Many of them were homeless, unemployed, and self-medicated. Working with them, I often felt a sense of powerlessness. Sure, I could actively listen to their stories and be there for them; I could also reflect their feelings, challenge their distorted thinking, and even practice deep breathing with them. However, what could I do to take away the external factors contributing to their mental health symptoms? Soon, I realized that working with clients one-on-one in my counseling room was not enough. I needed to work as an agent of change in the environments where they lived.

To become an agent of change for my clients, I first had to connect them to the resources they needed. Luckily, I was able to collaborate with a group of knowledgeable counselors to provide the necessary support. With their assistance, I gradually developed an understanding of the resources available in the community, and when clients came in with various issues that were often related to their traumas, such as substance use, homelessness, or unemployment, I was able to connect them to local resources (e.g., support groups, shelters, employment assistance) by making phone calls, filling out forms for them, and providing them with info sheets.

In addition to working with a team of counselors, I connected with other professionals—psychiatrists, case managers, and translators—to support my clients. For example, because some of my clients did not speak English, I got their consent to work with translators so they could feel more fully heard and respected. Clients reported that conducting sessions in their native languages helped them to feel as if they could speak in their own voices and fully express themselves in therapy. Consulting with professionals from other fields has broadened my view of my work with clients and helped me provide or connect them to the care they needed.

As a community counselor who has worked with many trauma survivors, my advocacy does not stop at working with other professionals. It also involves helping marginalized groups be seen and heard. Many of my clients were new immigrants to the United States, and they often struggled to begin their lives in this new country. While system-level advocacy is crucial, advocacy for these populations must also occur at an agency level. It must include an understanding of the prevalence and impact of trauma, along with an incorporation of trauma-informed approaches to treatment. Advocacy can also involve simply letting your agency know that you have new immigrants on your caseload who need additional support to settle in, translating consent forms into clients' native languages, or helping clients to find local communities from their home countries.

Through my work with my clients, I have gradually come to realize that advocacy can begin with something as basic as considering that trauma might be a factor, or making a phone call or finding a local support line for clients. It closely aligns with the essence of counseling: helping people to be their best and fulfill their potential. I now recognize advocacy as the core of counseling. Without advocacy, talk therapy itself is not sufficient for clients.

A Call to Action

Select a treatment population that you will work with. Consider how you might communicate the importance of TIC in the setting that you will work in, based on the prevalence and impact of trauma, among other factors within this population. What resources might aid you in supporting your colleagues to learn more about this approach? Create a brochure or document that you will use to educate other counselors about the basic tenets of TIC and its prevalence in the client population that you will serve.

Case Study 11.1

Nikko is a seventh grade student at a new middle school. She attended schools within her previous school district since kindergarten, and up until this year Nikko lived at home with her parents, siblings, a favorite aunt, and an elderly grandfather. Nikko's family is very close and supportive. Nikko is the eldest child and has been described as really enjoying school since kindergarten. A few months ago, Nikko's family experienced a traumatic loss, resulting in the loss Nikko's favorite aunt. During the early months of the pandemic, Nikko relied on her aunt as a source of connection, fun, and academic support during the countywide shutdowns. Nikko's aunt died unexpectedly, and due to the global pandemic, Nikko's family was not able to have a funeral that would allow for the entire family to attend.

While Nikko was able to attend the funeral, the ceremony was much shorter than it would have been traditionally. Nikko's family has worked to navigate their grief, and to support each other as best as possible. Since the loss, Nikko has been immersed in schoolwork, and teachers described her as having become much more withdrawn than is typical.

Lately, Nikko has had difficulty sitting still in class, and the teacher reports that Nikko is easily startled. The teacher claims that this is unusual for Nikko, because she is generally much more "easy going," and "a generally happy kid." Nikko has become visibly upset during art, her favorite class, and has begun struggling with classwork that was previously mastered.

RESPONSE QUESTIONS

1. How might you approach your work with Nikko?
2. What might you need to know about Nikko in order to best support her?
3. What considerations might you make in your assessment of Nikko's presenting concerns?
4. How might you consider the potential for trauma to aid in your work with Nikko?
5. Where might you begin in your work with Nikko?
6. Who would you include as you work to develop a treatment plan?
7. What are some cultural considerations that might be important to consider in your work with Nikko and her family?

Going Within

Think about the various presentations of trauma symptoms. How might you work to support a client who has sought out your services to reduce ongoing distress related to trauma? What considerations might you make for elementary, middle school, or high school students? How about for college students or adult clients? How might your approach be different in your work with elderly clients, couples, or families? How might you work to facilitate authentic choice and empowerment in TIC?

Group Process

In small groups, discuss your thoughts about trauma symptoms that might resemble other mental health disorders. Explore the similarities and differences between these disorders, such as attention-deficit/hyperactivity disorder (ADHD) for children and trauma symptomology. How might counselors screen for trauma for clients who may not have realized the relationship between their current symptoms and a reported trauma?

RESOURCES

American Counseling Association. (2018). Resolution on trauma-focused mental health care and advocacy. https://www.counseling.org/docs/default-source/resolutions/trauma-focused-mental-health-care-and-advocacy-resolution---april-2018.pdf?sfvrsn=355f552c_2

American School Counselor Association. (2016). The school counselor and trauma-informed practice. https://www.schoolcounselor.org/Standards-Positions/Position-Statements/ASCA-Position-Statements/The-School-Counselor-and-Trauma-Informed-Practice.

American School Counselor Association. ASCA U pecialist. https://www.schoolcounselor.org/Events-Professional-Development/Professional-Development/ASCA-U-Specialist-Training/Trauma-Crisis-Specialist

Bryant-Davis, T. (2005). Thriving in the wake of trauma: A multicultural guide. Greenwood Publishing Group.

Curtois, C. A., & Ford, J. D. (2013). Treatment of complex trauma: A sequenced relationship-based approach. The Guilford Press.

Duffey, T., & Haberstroh, S. (2020). Introduction to crisis and trauma counseling. American Counseling Association.

Harris, N. B. (2015). How childhood trauma affects health across a lifetime [Video]. Ted Conferences. https://www.ted.com/talks/nadine_burke_harris_how_childhood_trauma_affects_health_across_a_lifetime

Love, B. L. (2019). We want to do more than survive: Abolitionist teaching and the pursuit of educational freedom. Beacon Press.

Menakem, R. (2017). My grandmother's hands: Racialized trauma and the pathway to mending our hearts and bodies. Central Recovery Press.

Nakazawa, D. J. (2015). Childhood disrupted: How your biography becomes your biology, and how you can heal. Atria Books.

National Child Traumatic Stress Network. https://www.nctsn.org

PCIT Web Course (Introductory Parent-Child Interaction Therapy web-based course): https://pcit.ucdavis.edu/pcit-web-course

Perry, B., & Szalavitz, M. (2017). The boy who was raised as a dog and other stories from a child psychiatrist's notebook: What traumatized children can teach us above loss, love and healing. Basic Books.

Ripley, A. (2009). The unthinkable: Who survives when disaster strikes—And why. Three Rivers Press.

Sanctuary Institute: https://www.thesanctuaryinstitute.org/about-us/the-sanctuary-model

Substance Abuse and Mental Health Services Administration. (2014). Improving cultural competence. Treatment Improvement Protocol (TIP) Series No. 59. Author. https://store.samhsa.gov/sites/default/files/d7/priv/sma14-4849.pdf

Substance Abuse and Mental Health Services Administration. (2014). Trauma-informed care in behavioral health services. Treatment Improvement Protocol (TIP) Series No. 57. HHS Publication No. (SMA) 13-4801. Author. https://www.ncbi.nlm.nih.gov/books/NBK207201

TF-CBT Web 2.0. https://tfcbt2.musc.edu An introductory training for trauma-focused cognitive behavioral therapy

Trauma and Learning Policy Initiative: https://traumasensitiveschools.org/tlpi-publications

Trauma and Learning Policy Initiative. (2005). Supportive school environments for children traumatized by family violence. https://traumasensitives chools.org/wp-content/uploads/2013/06/Helping-Traumatized-Children-Learn.pdf

Trauma and Learning Policy Initiative. (2013). Creating and advocating for trauma-sensitive schools. https://traumasensitiveschools.org/wp-content/uploads/2013/11/HTCL-Vol-2-Creating-and-Advocating-for-TSS.pdf

What ACEs/PCEs do you have? https://acestoohigh.com/got-your-ace-score

Yoshimura, C. G., & Campbell, K. B. (2016). Interpersonal violence and sexual assault: Trauma-informed communication approaches to university counseling centers. Journal of College Student Psychotherapy, 30(4), 300–312. http://dx.doi.org/10.1080/87568225.2016.1221720

Zimmerman, L., Darnell, D. A., Rhew, I. C., Lee, C. M., & Kaysen, D. (2015). Resilience in ommunity: A social ecological development model for young adult sexual minority women. American Journal of Community Psychology, 55(1–2), 179–190. https://doi.org/10.1007/s10464-015-9702-6

Access this podcast at http://connect.springerpub.com/content/book/978-0-8261-6386-8/chapter/ch11.

KEY REFERENCES

Only key references appear in the print edition. The full reference list appears in the digital product found on https://connect.springerpub.com/content/book/978-0-8261-6386-8/chapter/ch11

Bemak, F., & Chung, R. C. Y. (2017). Refugee trauma: Culturally responsive counseling interventions. *Journal of Counseling & Development*, *95*(3), 299–308. https://doi.org/10.1002/jcad.12144

Blitz, L. V., Yull, D., & Clauhs, M. (2020). Bringing sanctuary to school: Assessing school climate as a foundation for culturally responsive trauma-informed approaches for urban schools. *Urban Education, 55*(1), 95–124. https://doi.org/10.1177/0042085916651323

Goodman, R. D. (2015). A liberatory approach to trauma counseling: Decolonizing our trauma-informed practices. In R. D. Goodman & P. C. Gorski (Eds.), *Decolonizing "multicultural" counseling through social justice* (pp. 55–72). Springer. https://doi.org/10.1007/978-1-4939-1283-4

Perry, B., & Szalavitz, M. (2017). *The boy who was raised as a dog and other stories from a child psychiatrist's notebook: What traumatized children can teach us about loss, love and healing.* Basic Books.

Powers, J. J., & Duys, D. (2020). Toward trauma-informed career counseling. *The Career Development Quarterly, 68*(2), 173–185. https://doi.org/10.1002/cdq.12221

Trauma and Learning Policy Initiative. (2013). *Creating and advocating for trauma-sensitive schools.* https://traumasensitiveschools.org/wp-content/uploads/2013/11/HTCL-Vol-2-Creating-and-Advocating-for-TSS.pdf

Zeligman, M., Prescod, D. J., & Haynes-Thoby, L. (2020). The relationship between trauma symptoms, developmental work personality, and vocational identity. *The Journal of Counselor Preparation and Supervision, 13*(1). http://dx.doi.org/10.7729/131.1323

CHAPTER 12

CREATIVITY IN COUNSELING

Jacqueline M. Swank

Think about this...

In what ways do you use creativity for self-expression? What is your favorite creative method? What do you like about it? Are there any creative methods you do not like? What do you not like about them? How might you use creativity with your future clients?

LEARNING OBJECTIVES

After reading this chapter, you should be able to:

- Evaluate creativity as a mechanism for enhancing the counseling process
- Describe eight approaches to integrating creativity in counseling
- Analyze the research supporting the integration of creativity within counseling
- Discuss ethical considerations related to creative counseling approaches
- Recognize multicultural considerations for using creativity in counseling

INTRODUCTION

Creativity is a process of using one's imagination to act or think differently. It involves considering a topic or issue from a different perspective. Within the counseling process, a counselor may extend their work with a client beyond using talk therapy to encompass a variety of creative approaches. This can be beneficial in the counseling process because it allows clients to express themselves in ways that may be easier, more natural, or more congruent with them, or challenge them to view a concern or situation from a different perspective when they are stuck. Creative approaches can further stimulate the right hemisphere of the brain that focuses on creativity, instead of relying predominately on the left hemisphere that focuses on logic.

For centuries, humans have used creativity therapeutically in the form of the arts to promote healing and well-being, such as their use by traditional healers. The use of creativity in the counseling profession dates back to early theorists, such as Rogers (1959) in viewing the core conditions as fostering creativity, Jung (1972) in using visual arts, and Satir (1972) in using family sculpting. In 2004, the Association for Creativity in Counseling (ACC) became a division of the American Counseling Association, and in 2006, the division started the *Journal of Creativity in Mental Health*. The journal includes conceptual and research articles about the use of creativity in counseling with various populations experiencing mental health concerns, as well as the use of creativity in training counselors. Thus, counselors and counselor educators have a source to learn new ideas as well as share their ideas with others to promote further development of counselors and enhance the lives of clients. There are also many other publications that focus on specific creative approaches used in counseling (e.g., *Arts in Psychotherapy*).

To foster creativity, people can employ the SCAMPER model (Eberle, 1971). The acronym stands for seven techniques: substitute, combine, adapt/adopt, modify, put to other use, eliminate, and reverse/rearrange (see Table 12.1). Gladding (2016) described this approach related to counseling and the integration of use with creative arts.

In considering the basis for integrating creativity in counseling, Gladding also discussed eight reasons for using creative arts. One of these reasons includes client engagement in self-expression that is congruent with their identities, and provides an opportunity to learn about other cultures. This may help marginalized individuals feel heard and provide opportunities for healing. It can also foster greater awareness of privilege and provide opportunities for social justice and advocacy work. There is a further discussion of this related to the specific creative approaches. See a list of other reasons identified by Gladding (2016) in Table 12.2.

The following sections include an overview of eight creative approaches to integrate in counseling: (a) animals, (b) dance and movement, (c) drama, (d) literature and writing, (e) music, (f) nature, (g) play, and (h) visual arts. This includes describing each approach and its origin, identifying ways to use it in counseling, presenting research to support the use with different populations with various mental health concerns, and discussing multicultural and other considerations when using the approach in counseling. The final section of the chapter focuses on discussing ethical and other considerations when integrating creativity within counseling.

ANIMAL-ASSISTED INTERVENTIONS

Animal-assisted interventions (AAI) is the broad encompassing term that focuses on using animals as an intervention with humans for a variety of

TABLE 12.1 SCAMPER MODEL

TECHNIQUE	DEFINITION	COUNSELING EXAMPLE
Substitute	Replace a word or action with something else.	Instead of hurtful words, use other words to express self.
Combine	Integrate or bring together multiple things (e.g., approaches, verbal and nonverbal behavior).	Combine two types of dance to represent intersectionality of identities; use drama to involve verbal and nonverbal expression.
Adapt or adopt	Adapt—adjust Adopt—make something your own	Adapt—role-play how to respond differently to a situation. Adopt—use famous quote from a book or movie as personal mantra.
Modify	Includes magnify (make larger) and minify (make smaller)	Use different feeling words to express levels of feeling experienced (e.g., mad, irritated, enraged).
Put to other use	Use something for a different purpose.	Using energy related to worrying to take a walk, journal, create something out of clay.
Eliminate	Get rid of something.	Highlight concerning behavior to change by acting it out instead of talking about it.
Reverse or rearrange	Move things around or change order	Have clients move to be near different people in the room; have client change their routine or order of tasks to see if it has a different outcome.

Source: Data from Gladding, S. T. (2016). *The creative arts in counseling* (5th ed.). American Counseling Association.

TABLE 12.2 REASONS FOR USING CREATIVITY IN COUNSELING

Clients connect better with themselves and others.
Opportunities for clients to socialize and develop prosocial behavior.
Clients experience new or renewed energy and time to process their experiences.
Clients see things more clearly and develop new perspective about their life.
Being creative expands clients' views outwardly and inwardly.
Clients develop tangible strategies to use in real life.
Development of insight by the client, counselor, and the counseling profession.
Client engagement in self-expression congruent with their identities and learn about others' cultures.

Source: Data from Gladding, S. T. (2016). *The creative arts in counseling* (5th ed.). American Counseling Association.

purposes. Within AAI, animals and clients form a shared social connection that includes nurturing interactions (Chandler, 2017). This human-animal connection is supported by the biophilia hypothesis that postulates that humans have an innate need to connect with nonhuman nature, such as animals and plants (Wilson, 1984). Additionally, clients witness the animal-human bond between the animal and the animal handler or professional working with the animal.

Within the broad area of AAI, there are four categories: (a) animal-assisted activities (AAA), (b) animal-assisted therapy (AAT), (c) animal-assisted education (AAE), and (d) animal-assisted coaching/counseling (AAC). The International Association of Human-Animal Interaction Organization (IAHAIO, 2018) defines AAA as "a planned and goal-oriented informal interaction and visitation conducted by the human-animal team for motivational, educational, and recreational purposes," such as crisis and disaster responses and animal visitation programs in nursing homes (p. 5). AAT "is a goal oriented, planned and structured therapeutic intervention directed and/or delivered by health, education or human service professionals" (IAHAIO, 2018, p. 5). It focuses on various types of functioning, including behavioral, cognitive, emotional, physical, and social. AAE involves interventions delivered by educational and related personnel. Finally, AAC is interventions delivered by licensed coaches or counselors and focuses on enhanced social skills, personal growth, and social and emotional functioning (IAHAIO, 2018).

Humans have involved animals to help people for centuries. Chandler (2017) provided an overview of the historical roots of AAI. The first known use of animals for emotional therapy was in 1792 within the York Retreat, a facility developed as an alternative to asylums. People introduced therapy involving animal-human interaction, particularly dogs, in the United States in 1919 within Saint Elizabeth's Hospital to help socialize psychiatric patients. In the area of counseling, Freud had his dog present in sessions in the 1930s. However, Levinson, in the 1960s, was the first clinician to formalize the use of animals in sessions when he discovered his work with children was more effective when it involved his dog Jingles. AAT has grown tremendously in recent years, with increased use, training, and research, and in 2016, Stewart et al. (2016) developed the AAT counseling competencies. A variety of animals are now being used within the therapeutic process including dogs, cats, horses, various small animals (e.g., gerbils, rabbits, birds, fish), farm animals (e.g., pigs, cows, goats, chickens), and marine animals (e.g., dolphins).

AAT may involve a variety of interventions that range from observation of the animal to active engagement with the animal. Active engagement may include activities such as playing with the animal, caring for them (grooming, feeding), petting the animal, taking the animal on a walk, and talking with the animal. Children, especially, may want to tell the animal "secrets" they do not feel comfortable sharing with the counselor, but will tell them to the animal in the counselor's presence. The client may also role-play with the animal by talking to the animal to practice what they want to say to someone. Additionally, clients may have the animal sit near them or sit in their lap while they interact with the counselor. There are many benefits of using AAT for clients (e.g., calming presence of the animal, fun of playing with the animal, sensory stimulation, facilitation of rapport, and skill building; Chandler, 2017). Additionally, animals can interact with people without making assumptions or holding prejudices toward groups of people (i.e., race, socioeconomic status, sexual or affectional orientation). The animal and the counselor also benefit from AAT (e.g., animal receives stimulation and often is healthier; counselor gets to spend more time with animal, the animal assists with interventions, and the animal is good marketing for practice; Chandler, 2017).

Research support exists for the use of animals in counseling with clients with various concerns, including depression (Souter & Miller, 2007), behavioral and psychological symptoms of dementia (Hu et al., 2018; Klimova et al., 2019), communication and social skills (Chitic et al., 2012), and trauma (Germain et al., 2018). Researchers have also found positive results in using AAT with veterans with posttraumatic stress disorder (PTSD) and depression (Romaniuk et al., 2018), and with various groups of children including those with autism and who have experienced trauma (Hoagwood et al., 2017); PTSD, anger, anxiety, and disruptive behaviors (Jones et al., 2019); and youth at risk (Wilkie et al., 2016), among others. Furthermore, researchers have found positive outcomes in using dog-training programs with people in prison (Cooke & Farrington, 2016).

In considering the integration of animals within counseling, it is important to consider cultural and religious views regarding animals. For example, while some cultures view dogs as man's best friend, this is not universal. The Muslim culture views dogs as dirty and may be reluctant to touch them (Fine, 2015). Additionally, a client's religious views (e.g., animals not having a soul) may make them skeptical of the therapeutic value of AAT (Fine, 2015). Thus, it is crucial for the counselor to consider the cultural beliefs and values of the client; however, it is also important for the counselor to prioritize the health and well-being of the animal. For example, hitting an animal may be an acceptable practice in the client's culture; however, this does not mean that it is acceptable in the counseling setting and the counselor should discuss respect for the animal before integrating an animal within the therapeutic process with clients.

Fine (2015) described a culturally responsive framework for AAI that involves three components. The first area is cultural self-awareness, which involves exploring personal experiences and beliefs related to animals, and comfort level with discussing cultural practices and beliefs with clients. The second component is knowledge of the clients, and it involves understanding individual clients and their beliefs and values related to animals. The final area pertains to developing skills, which includes applying knowledge about clients in working with them through intercultural communication, collaborative work, and other techniques. Thus, counselors may employ this framework to provide culturally responsive counseling.

It is crucial for the counselor to have training in AAT and to have skill and experience in working with the animal. The counselor may also have an animal handler present in some cases. Additionally, the counselor should also ensure the animal is a good fit for AAT and properly trained, as well as having liability insurance that covers AAT. Finally, the counselor will want to screen clients before using AAT with them to ensure it is a good fit by exploring various considerations (e.g., allergies, fears, cultural practices and beliefs, experiences with animals, willing to have the animal present), as AAT may not be a good fit for all clients.

DANCE AND MOVEMENT

Dance is a powerful form of expression in many cultures (e.g., ceremonial dances of Indigenous people, voodoo dances, horah [Jewish celebratory dance]). People have used dance for celebrations, to pass down stories and traditions, for religious purposes, and for healing through connection of the mind, body, and spirit. Movement also communicates information nonverbally to others, influencing interactions and relationships.

The American Dance Therapy Association (ADTA) defines dance/movement therapy (DMT) as "the psychotherapeutic use of movement to promote emotional, social, cognitive, and physical integration of the individual for the purpose of improving health and well-being" (ADTA, 2020). DMT involves an individual sharing a connection with other people, while also moving to get their own needs met. This involves self-awareness and understanding about what an individual is experiencing in their body, and how they communicate this through movement. DMT is different from other therapies focusing on the body in that dance and movement is considered an art form with self-directed improvisations with symbolic meaning arising from the subconscious of the individual (Chaiklin, 2016). DMT originated in the 1930s when Marian Chace was curious why people attended her dance classes when they did not intend to dance professionally. She observed their movements and began tailoring instruction to the individual needs of her students. Then, she began working with psychiatric patients in Saint Elizabeth's Hospital in

1942 using dance and movement as a therapeutic intervention. Others followed her lead to develop the field of DMT. The ADTA was founded in 1966 (Chaiklin, 2016).

Counselors may integrate dance and movement within counseling in a variety of ways. This includes using it as an assessment technique, as well as a counseling intervention (ADTA, 2020). In working with a group, a counselor may have clients move in different ways and at different speeds to develop awareness of their bodies, how they move, and sharing of space with others. Additionally a counselor could play different types of music and have clients move to the music as they choose and then discuss what they noticed about their bodies, as well as thoughts and emotions that surfaced during the experience. Clients can also work in pairs or groups and practice mirroring the movements of others, and discuss how they experience this, as well as how their partner witnesses their movement through the mirrored movements. Furthermore, counselors can integrate traditional dances from clients' cultures within sessions to further explore their meaning for clients, while being careful not to presume meaning, as the intersectionality of identities may influence meaning for various clients. Researchers have examined the use of dance and movement with various populations and found promising results, such as individuals with depression (Pylvänäinen & Lappalainen, 2018), autism spectrum disorder (Koch et al., 2015), and cancer (Ho et al., 2016).

Hervey and Stuart (2012) outlined competencies for culturally competent dance and movement therapists. In having self-awareness, the counselor must be attuned and aware of how their movement is rooted in their own beliefs, values, and prejudices and historical factors that influence it. Chang (2016) discussed modifying Gresham's "The Dance of the Ancestors" to help clinicians become aware of their movement style and the unexplored areas of their ancestry. This may involve engaging in an ethnic dance, animating a photograph of an ancestor through movement, or creating movement to portray a memory of an elder in the family. Additionally, counselors are knowledgeable about how their clients' movements resemble their culture and worldview and their norms related to their nonverbal behavior and body. Finally, clinicians use culturally relevant and responsive dance and movement assessment practices and interventions. When working with minoritized clients, clinicians identified mirroring, somatic connecting, recognizing movement patterns, and awareness of whether congruence is present as important skills used within DMT (Golonka Carmichael, 2012).

Verbal and nonverbal microaggressions (i.e., verbal remarks or behaviors related to a person's identity that are insulting; Sue et al., 2007) reinforce stereotypes and oppression that affect the way people experience their bodies (Schultz, 2018). Counselors can use movement and dance to explore oppression and help clients experience healing of the mind, body, and spirit (Cantrick et al., 2018). Counselors can also engage in self-exploration, as well as help clients, to explore their privileged identities and how they are embodied, as well as communicated nonverbally, often unconsciously, in their interactions with others (Cantrick et al., 2018). Thus, counselors can engage in social justice practices through dance and movement.

DRAMA

The use of drama within counseling may encompass drama therapy or psychodrama. Drama is a user-friendly approach because (a) dramatic play is a natural part of child development, (b) acting involves presenting a believable, realistic performance, and (c) human interactions are dramatic (Orkibi, 2018). Drama therapy in the United States has roots in drama classes integrated within the educational curriculum, as well as experimental theater companies in the 1960s that worked toward promoting social change. The theater evolved to blend the real world with the created theatrical one and became a space shared between actors and the audience, laying the foundation for drama therapy (Petitti, 1992). Drama therapy involves metaphors and is fantasy-based, allowing the client to have more distance from the issue and work on it more indirectly. It "uses play, embodiment, projection, role, story, metaphor, empathy, distancing, witnessing, performance, and improvisation to help people make meaningful change" (NADTA, 2020). This approach allows clients to express feelings, tell stories, experience emotional release, and solve problems (NADTA, 2020). There are many techniques counselors use within drama therapy, including role-plays, improvisation, puppetry, masks, and storytelling.

Jacob L. Moreno is the father of psychodrama, an approach grounded in psychology, sociology, and theater (Cruz et al., 2018). Psychodrama differs from drama therapy in that it focuses more directly on client concerns. The process of psychodrama involves three phases: warmup, action, and sharing. Although typically occurring within a group, psychodrama focuses on the particularities of an individual with group members role-playing parts of the protagonist, their roles, and/or significant others in their life (Cruz et al., 2018). Some common psychodrama techniques include double, mirror, role reversal, scene setting/enactment, and soliloquy (see Table 12.3).

Researchers have found positive outcomes in using drama therapy to improve self-awareness, social skills, and empowerment among adults with mental health concerns (Bourne et al., 2018). Additionally, among older adults, researchers found greater self-acceptance and sense of meaning, and less depressive symptoms (Keisari & Palgi, 2017). Researchers also report promising results for using drama therapy to improve abstinence and quality of life for clients with substance use concerns (Leather & Kewley, 2019). Furthermore, clinicians have used drama with children and adolescents to address various concerns within a variety of capacities, such as using psychodrama to address behavioral concerns within family counseling (Maya et al., 2020), improvisational theater to reduce social anxiety within the school setting (Felsman et al., 2019), and musical theatre to address trauma among youth who are incarcerated (Palidofsky & Stolbach, 2012).

Regarding cultural considerations within the use of drama in counseling, the North American Drama Therapy Association has established guidelines (NADTA, 2015). These guidelines emphasize cultural response/ability in training, research, practice, supervision, advocacy, and organizational change. The counselor's self-awareness includes exploring their beliefs, values, and biases related to dramatic expression and their experiences with drama work. In the area of knowledge, counselors learn about the artistic traditions related to

TABLE 12.3 PSYCHODRAMA TECHNIQUES

TECHNIQUE	DEFINITION
Double	A person, positioned near the protagonist, serves as the auxiliary ego, expressing the thoughts and feelings of the protagonist that are unspoken.
Mirror	Auxiliary ego mirrors the expressions, behaviors, and words of the protagonist.
Role reversal	Protagonist puts self in others' shoes by reversing roles with others.
Scene setting/enactment	Group members act out a scene from the protagonist's life.
Soliloquy	Protagonist verbalizes thoughts, feelings, and intentions.

Source: Data from Cruz, A., Sales, C. M. D., Alves, P., & Moita, G. (2018). The core techniques of Morenian psychodrama: A systematic review of literature. *Frontiers in Psychology, 9,* 1263. https://doi.org/10.3389/fpsyg.2018.01263.

theatrical process of their clients. Finally, counselors use culturally sensitive techniques in using drama in their work with clients. Through the integration of drama within counseling marginalized populations, clients are empowered to explore and express hidden parts of themselves. They have a safe space to examine and challenge socially prescribed beliefs and behaviors associated with roles, and awaken potential within themselves to redefine their roles or embrace and practice new roles (Moller, 2013). Furthermore, through performances, others see and hear marginalized clients through the sharing of their personal stories and the narratives of their identity groups. This provides an opportunity to challenge dominant narratives, creating opportunities for change (Sajnani et al., 2017). Thus, drama is a powerful approach in counseling that can be therapeutic for clients as well as the community, and promote social justice and advocacy.

LITERATURE AND WRITING

Cultures across the world have used stories and poems to share information, entertain, and teach lessons. Elders have shared personal family stories with younger generations through spoken word and writings. Additionally, people have shared famous stories and tales not directly connected to one's family (e.g., Aesop's fables). The National Association for Poetry Therapy NAPT (n.d) reported the use of poetry by witch doctors and shamans for the well-being of tribes among early humans, as well as use in Egypt starting in the fourth millennium B.C.E., when patients digested a solution that had words written on papyrus dissolved in it. The first poetry therapist was Soranus, a Roman physician in the first century A.D. Poetry therapy is a type of bibliotherapy, which is a broader category that involves the use of reading materials to promote self-understanding and understanding of others, a term first used by Crothers (1916). Reading materials may include short stories, self-help books, biographies, poems, picture books, and fairy tales. Within counseling, clinicians may integrate existing literature within the therapeutic process (bibliotherapy), or have clients create their own writings. Counselors may also combine the two approaches. Mazza (2003) discusses these three forms within poetry therapy through outlining a three-part model: (a) receptive/prescriptive—reading poetry (bibliotherapy), (b) expressive/creative—writing poetry, and (c) symbolic/ceremonial—integrating poetry with other creative forms of expression, such as drama or dance and movement for a performance. Thus, counselors can use literature and writing as distinct processes or integrate them together.

Bibliotherapy

There are two types of bibliotherapy described by Allen et al. (2017): (a) developmental bibliotherapy that includes books focused on developmental adjustment problems (e.g., bullying, friendship), and (b) clinical bibliotherapy that focuses on mental health concerns (e.g., trauma, depression, anxiety). A variety of professionals may use reading materials for developmental bibliotherapy, while counselors may use developmental, as well as clinical bibliotherapy. It is important for counselors to read materials before they recommend them to a client to ensure the selected reading is appropriate for the particular client. A selected reading may have a great title and summary, but the counselor should not rely on this alone in making a decision about recommending it. For example, a book may have content that would trigger a particular client based on the client's personal experience. This could result in causing the client harm.

Halsted (2002) described four stages of bibliotherapy. Within the first stage, identification, the client is able to identify with a book character. This is sometimes easier when using a fictional book. The second stage, catharsis, involves following a character through a challenging situation that ends with a solution. This stage may evoke a variety of emotions. Stage three, insight, focuses on the client applying the character's experience in the story to their own life, which has the potential to create a positive change in thinking and behavior. The client may learn a new creative way to solve a problem they are experiencing or view it from a different perspective. Finally, in the fourth stage, universalization, the client develops an understanding that they are not alone in what they are experiencing, but others have experienced similar concerns.

In conducting a bibliotherapy session with children, Heath et al. (2005) described a three-step process. The first step, prereading, involves introducing the book with a goal of engaging the client by capturing their attention. The second step, guided reading, is the reading of the story, which may involve stopping at various points in the story for discussion. This may include discussing with the client possible courses of action for the character when experiencing a dilemma, which helps the client develop problem-solving skills. The third and final step is postreading, which involves further processing the story, the problems presented, and the outcome. This step may involve a variety of other creative interventions discussed in this chapter, including drama, writing, and visual arts. This additional processing may help the client internalize the story and experience.

The three-step process described by Heath et al. (2005) is ideal for children; however, bibliotherapy is appropriate for clients of all ages and may include a variety of approaches. With adolescents and adults, the counselor may have clients read a book or other reading materials on their own and then discuss them during a session, or read and discuss short selected readings in a session. Additionally, regarding children, clinicians may have parents read books to children on their own and provide opportunities for processing during a session. The counselor may have a library for clients to check out books. Within the school system, counselors can use bibliotherapy to promote mental health literacy (knowledge about mental health disorders). This may include working individually or with small groups of students, or integrating it within classroom lessons. Counselors may also advocate for school libraries to have books available on a variety of mental health topics for students to check out (Mumbauer & Kelchner, 2018). However, it is also important for students to have access to school counselors or other counselors to process the material. Bibliotherapy can be helpful for approaching a topic that a client may not want to talk about, as books can provide some personal distance from the issue and create openness to explore the topic through the book.

Researchers have found support in using bibliotherapy with various populations. For example, in a systematic review of the literature on using creative bibliotherapy (i.e., guided reading of poetry and fiction) with children and adolescents, Montgomery and Maunders (2015) found a small to medium effect for both internalizing and externalizing behaviors, and prosocial behavior. Additionally, regarding depression, researchers found support for using bibliotherapy in working with both adults (Gualano et al., 2017) and adolescents (Yuan et al., 2018). Furthermore, among individuals on probation, those involved in a bibliotherapy program had a decline in recidivism and offense severity (Schutt et al., 2013). Thus, bibliotherapy may be an effective invention for individuals across the lifespan with many different presenting concerns.

The reading materials (e.g., books, poems, stories) to choose from are vast and it is important for the clinician to consider the reading level and the interest of the client in selecting a book on a particular topic. It is also important to consider the client's identities and ability to relate to the character(s) in the reading materials. This includes characters representing the client's racial and ethnic group, culture, and family structure. It may not be feasible to identify a book that is congruent with all areas of the client's identities. However, striving for some representation is important in helping the client identify with the character, especially when materials are available. This communicates to the client that you recognize their identities and value them. Counselors may also use literature representing diverse cultures to help facilitate conversations about diversity and valuing differences, as well as facilitate empathy development (Gilmore & Howard, 2016).

Writing

People have used writing to express their thoughts and feelings since ancient times. The use of writing in counseling is scriptotherapy. Therapeutic writing encompasses journaling and writing in various forms, including stories, poems, and letters. It may also include individual writings, as well as writing collaboratively as a group. Mohammadian et al. (2011) described the use of poetry in three ways. The first involved reading and discussing poems, which is a bibliotherapy technique. The second approach involved clients receiving poems that had blanks for them to tailor the poems to express their thoughts and feelings. A final strategy involved clients receiving a few lines to start a poem and then being empowered to finish the poem. This is a scaffolding approach to help clients become more comfortable with the writing process, especially for clients without experience with therapeutic writing. Counselors can also have clients engage in writing in other forms, such as writing stories.

Therapeutic journaling may involve writing on one occasion or writing across time. Journaling across time provides an opportunity for reflection and self-awareness as the client is able to look back at what they have wrote to identify themes and change across time. Interactive journaling is a specific approach that involves specific writing topics, guided questions, and a focus on reframing thoughts through motivational interviewing (Canada et al., 2015). Therapeutic blogging is another form of journaling that involves a digital platform that has gained popularity with the increase in technology. In therapeutic letter writing, grounded in Michael White's work in narrative therapy, clients write letters that externalize their problems, identify positive exceptions, and then reauthor their stories with more positive narratives. Through this process, clients are able to view their lives separate from the problem, empowering them to create change (DeCino et al., 2018). In addition to the techniques already described, Gladding and Drake Wallace (2018) identified additional writing exercises that counselors can use to promote insight and wellness including stem sentences, word clusters or word clouds, autobiography, and reciprocal writing to name a few. Thus, there are numerous ways for counselors to integrate writing within the counseling process.

In examining the effectiveness of therapeutic writing within the counseling process, Mohammadian et al. (2011) found undergraduate students who engaged in poetry therapy had reduced signs of anxiety, depression, and stress. Additionally, Pinhasi-Vittorio (2018) discussed the use of writing, along with art, to help clients view their lives beyond their addictions, promoting healing and recovery. Canada et al. (2015) also found writing, specifically, journaling, to be helpful in fostering reflection and building communication skills among veterans involved in the criminal justice system. Furthermore, Ramsey-Wade et al. (2020) reported positive outcomes in using therapeutic writing to address disordered eating.

Therapeutic writing is powerful as it empowers clients to find their voices by examining and reflecting on their personal stories (Pinhasi-Vittorio, 2018). Through writings, marginalized clients put their voice on paper and have the opportunity to share it with others, breaking their silence. Expressing thoughts and feelings through writing is powerful for stigmatized populations that may feel pressure to conform to societal expectations, and therefore be prone to suppressing their feelings (Canada et al., 2015). Thus, counselors may use writing in a variety of forms to facilitate client expression of thoughts and emotions.

MUSIC

Music transcends cultures in a variety of forms, including diverse instruments, rhythms, and styles. Additionally, people may interact with music in different ways, including listening to music; playing an instrument; writing lyrics; or singing, humming, or chanting. The *Columbian Magazine* has the earliest reference to music therapy, appearing in 1789. In the 20th century, therapeutic use of music became well known following both world wars, when used with veterans within hospitals (AMTA, 2020). Today, counselors use music therapeutically in various forms with many different client populations.

In listening to music, counselors may have clients bring a song into session for the client and counselor to listen to together and discuss the client's emotions that arise when listening to the song, as well as the meaning of the lyrics. The client may also choose to sing along while playing the song. Additionally, the counselor may print out the lyrics to aid in examining and discussing them, as well as watch the music video with the client and discuss it. The counselor could also ask the client to bring in a song related to a specific topic. In session, the counselor may also play music in the background while clients talk or engage in other activities.

Counselors may provide opportunities to play instruments during sessions, such as play an instrument to represent how they are feeling. Drums, and the use of drum circles, are popular instruments used in counseling that focus on rhythm, patterns, and the beat. Clients may also write lyrics for an original song or rewrite lyrics for an existing song, which blends with the therapeutic writing technique. Piggyback songs, rewriting the lyrics to a popular tune, are common within educational settings for young children, such as during transitions, and counselors can use this technique in helping children develop skills (e.g., social skills, emotion regulation). Children can listen to the song, sing along, and practice doing what the song tells them. Furthermore, clients may also perform songs they have written within counseling sessions and then process them with the counselor.

People often have a connection to music; therefore, being open to a client sharing music in counseling that is meaningful to them can help facilitate rapport with the counselor, as well as with group members when used within group therapy. Music also provides an avenue for self-expression as the words or rhythm in a song may express what the client is experiencing, but is unable to articulate verbally. Researchers have found support for using music as a counseling intervention for various populations. Specifically, Castillo-Pérez et al. (2010) found a music therapy intervention was more effective than using psychotherapy in treating depression among adults, and Werner et al. (2017) found it was more effective in treating depression among the elderly in comparison to a recreational singing intervention. Additionally, in participating in drum circles, adolescents reported feeling better and that it helped them with lack of motivation, stress, anger, and self-confidence (Snow & D'Amico, 2010). Music therapy was also effective for improving social competence among children and adolescents (Gooding, 2011).

Counselors can be culturally responsive in using music within counseling by exploring music that resonates with the identities of their clients. For example, Elligan (2000) proposed a rap therapy model in working with Black men, reporting rap therapy is both culturally and developmentally appropriate for this population, as rap music depicts the life and struggles of Black youth and men. The model involves five steps: (a) assessment of whether rap therapy is a good fit for the counselor and the client and the client's connection with rap music, (b) therapeutic alliance developed through listening to rap music with the client as an example, (c) reframing and restructuring related to expanding the client's appreciation of rap music, (d) role-playing with reinforcement as a creative process that involves written exercises, and (e) action and maintenance, which involves applying what is written about in the previous step. Counselors may also engage in self-reflection about their own preferences for music, origins of these preferences, and biases related to music genres. Engaging in self-awareness will help prepare the counselor to be open to the music preferences and influences that resonate with clients. Thus, through engaging in self-exploration the counselor is prepared to use music therapeutically with clients in various forms.

NATURE

According to the biophilia hypothesis (Wilson, 1984) humans have a need to connect with nature. People may seek to fulfill this connection in many ways. This may include bringing nature inside within living and workspace, such as plants and other natural material and natural light. Within the outdoor environment, people can engage in activities within nature, such as sitting outside, taking a walk, or engaging in sports. Additionally, people can interact with nature such as gardening or building a sandcastle at the beach. Furthermore, with the emergence of technology, people are also using this format to engage in nature, including natural scenes on a computer or television screen and virtual trips to natural settings. Interactions with animals also fit within this area, but we will not focus on that here as we discussed it earlier in the chapter.

Ecotherapy is a broad term focusing on the integration of nature within counseling. Nature can serve as a partner or co-counselor in the therapeutic process. Nature can also serve as a powerful metaphor in counseling. There are many ways that counselors may integrate nature in counseling. Counselors may integrate nature within their counseling office to address challenges with offering counseling outside (e.g., lack of natural outdoor space, client or counselor allergies). Swank et al. (2020) discuss strategies for integrating nature within an indoor setting.

Regarding integration of the natural environment outside, counselors may sit and talk with clients outside or walk and talk. Additionally, adventure-based counseling (ABC) integrates adventure and experiential learning within counseling through a variety of activities, including problem-solving and communication tasks. Wilderness therapy also involves an adventure component that may include multiday wilderness trips. Another nature-based approach is horticultural therapy that involves working with plants and gardening. Swank and Swank (2013) discuss the integration of therapeutic gardening with children in a school setting. Integration of horticultural may include an outdoor garden, greenhouse, or a garden space within the counseling office, and counselors may use a variety of plants, such as succulents, flowers, herbs, and vegetable plants, as well as plant material (e.g., leaves, flower petals). Care farming is another therapeutic invention that may involve caring for livestock or plants on a farm. Counselors may also use virtual reality (VR) that simulates a natural environment. Finally, counselors may integrate nature within existing counseling approaches. For example, Swank and Shin (2015b) developed a model that integrates nature within child-centered play therapy (CCPT), called nature-based child-centered play therapy (NBCCPT), that focuses on creating a play space within nature that integrates natural, instead of human-made, materials and follows the child-centered approach of CCPT. Thus, counselors have numerous options when integrating nature therapeutically within counseling.

Attention restoration theory (Kaplan, 1995; Kaplan & Kaplan, 1989) supports the therapeutic value of nature, with the researchers postulating that spending time in nature requires effortless attention that increases focus and helps people concentrate better after exposure. Additionally, within the psychophysiological stress reduction theory, Ulrich (1983) proposes that nature exposure leads to reduced stress through triggering a response in the parasympathetic nervous system. Furthermore, Reese and Myers (2012) proposed ecowellness as a missing component of holistic wellness, defining ecowellness as "a sense of appreciation, respect for, and awe, of nature that results in feelings of connectedness with the natural environment and the enhancement of holistic wellness" (p. 400). Researchers have examined the integration of various forms of nature within counseling (Moeller et al., 2018) and found exposure to nature supports holistic health and wellness. Twohig-Bennett and Jones (2018) examined health outcomes in a systematic review of studies related to nature exposure and found a decrease in disease and health problems as well as mental health concerns. Researchers have also examined the effectiveness of nature-related interventions. In examining the mental health benefits within a systematic analysis, Clatworthy et al. (2013) found decreased anxiety and depression when using gardening as a therapeutic intervention. Additionally, researchers have found promising results related to using NBCCPT to address behavioral concerns (Swank et al., 2015, 2017; Swank & Smith-Adcock, 2018), as well as using therapeutic gardening with children to address self-esteem (Swank & Shin, 2015a).

When integrating nature within counseling, there are some important areas to consider, such as confidentiality and safety. It may be difficult to maintain confidentiality outside where there is a lack of an enclosed space (Greenleaf et al., 2014). It is important for the counselor to consider challenges with confidentiality and discuss it with clients in advance. Regarding safety, counselors will want to consider many factors, including temperature, weather, allergies, and creatures present when offering counseling outside. Counselors can be culturally responsive with integrating nature within counseling by integrating natural materials that represent a client's culture. Counselors should also explore their own beliefs and values and experiences with nature. It is also important to advocate for time and exposure to nature for holistic health and wellness. Louv (2005) discussed the concept of nature-deficit disorder, a term he coined to describe the decline in time spent outside and the potential health effects of the lack of nature exposure. Medical professionals have recognized the health benefits of nature, with some writing prescriptions for time in nature. Thus, the therapeutic use of nature may contribute to clients' holistic growth and wellness.

PLAY

People across the world of all ages engage in play in many forms. Counselors can use many of the techniques described in this chapter to integrate play in counseling with clients across the lifespan. However, play therapy is a specialized field within the helping professions and theorists have proposed theories and techniques for therapeutically integrating play within counseling. It is especially important to integrate play into counseling when working with young children, as play is the language of a child because developmentally they may not have the language to express themselves in words. For example, an adult who witnesses a car accident may call a friend to talk about what they witnessed, while a child may take two toy cars and run them into each other while making sound effects. Both the adult and the child are expressing what they have witnessed, but they are doing this in different ways based on their developmental levels.

In using play with children, a counselor may have a designated playroom, which may look different depending on the age of a child. Landreth (2012) identifies categories of therapeutic play materials, or therapeutic toys, that counselors should have available within the playroom to facilitate self-expression, development of sense of self, and skill development in multiple areas, including problem-solving and self-regulation, especially for younger children. Categories of toys and materials include expressive, nurturing, aggressive, scary, and pretend and fantasy (see Table 12.4). The appropriateness of this traditional playroom depends on the individual child. Some older children may be interested in this room, while sometimes a child in elementary school, such as an 8- or 9-year-old, may think the room is for babies. Therefore, a counselor may offer the room to a child, while also having an alternative space available.

A playroom for older children and adolescents may include beanbag chairs, board games, and more advanced art material, such as clay in addition to Play-Doh. Swank (2008) discussed how to use board games and other games in counseling, including modifying existing games, as well as using games designed for counseling. Counselors may also have a sandtray located in the counseling room. Sandtray or sandplay is a specialized area of play therapy that counselors can use with clients across the lifespan. When used with younger clients, counseling with the sandtray may involve playing in the sand using toys. In working with adolescents and adults, the counselor uses the sandtray and miniatures to allow the client to build their world in the sand. This is a powerful technique, as it brings up areas from the subconscious level. It is important that counselor have advanced training before using sandtray with clients.

TABLE 12.4 THERAPEUTIC TOYS FOR PLAY

TOY CATEGORY	PURPOSE	EXAMPLES
Expressive	Self-expression	Art materials
Nurturing	Relationship building, explore family interactions	Dolls, dollhouse, baby items
Aggressive	Express anger	Swords, military figures, bop bag, toy guns
Scary	Express and address fears	Dinosaurs, snakes, monsters
Pretend and fantasy	Role-play various roles, recreate events	Play kitchen, puppets, medical kit, blocks, phone, dress-up materials (e.g., clothes, hats, shoes, jewelry)

Source: Data from Landreth, G. L. (2012). *Play therapy: The art of the relationship* (3rd ed.). Routledge.

In examining the effectiveness of CCPT through a meta-analysis, Lin and Bratton (2015) found a moderate treatment effect size for externalizing behaviors, self-efficacy, and caregiver-child relationship stress. Additionally, in examining the effectiveness of CCPT within the school environment within a meta-analysis, Ray et al. (2015) found statistically significant effects for multiple outcomes variables, including self-efficacy, academics, internalizing behaviors, and externalizing behaviors. Researchers have also found effectiveness in using other play therapy approaches with children, such as the use of Adlerian play therapy to address children's behavioral problems (Meany-Walen et al., 2014). Furthermore, Roesler (2019) found positive outcomes in a review of studies using sandplay therapy with children and adults to address a variety of mental health concerns.

In using play with diverse populations, it is important that play materials are representative of clients' cultural groups. For example, within the playroom, the counselor should have dolls that have different skin colors and genders. Additionally, play food should be representative of different cultures, as well as dress-up clothing and hats. When using the sandtray, the counselor should also have miniatures that represent different cultures, including figures of people with different skin colors, as well as other cultural values, such as miniatures to represent different religious/spiritual groups. Thus, through the representation of materials from various cultures, clients are able to explore various concerns in a personal, relevant manner.

VISUAL ARTS

People have used visual arts for self-expression since ancient times. Techniques in this category have expanded across time with the evolution of technology. This broad encompassing category includes many techniques including drawing, painting, sculpting, crafts, photographs, and videos. Counselors use visual arts in counseling for assessment and interventions. While the discussion of visual arts techniques here is focused on engaging with the materials during the session, clients may also bring to session visual art products that they have created out of session and want to use in discussing their feelings and/or experiences.

Drawing is a common form of visual arts that a counselor employs using a variety of drawing materials, including pencils, colored pencils, pens, markers, crayons, and chalk, as well as materials to draw on (e.g., typing paper, drawing paper, construction paper). Having a variety of materials available is important because clients may have preferences for different materials. Clients may also be interested in using digital drawing programs on their electronic devices. Common drawing assessments include having the client draw a self-portrait, using the house-tree-person test (Buck, 1948), or having the client create a kinetic family drawing (Burns & Kaufman, 1970) in which the family is doing something or a kinetic school drawing (Thompson Prout & Phillips, 1974) involving the individual, the teacher, and one or more classmates. When used for assessment, counselors should use drawings as one of multiple methods, instead of using it as the sole assessment method. Additionally, counselors need training on interpreting drawings.

Drawings, and the use of other visual arts, can be helpful in expressing areas of one's life that an individual struggles with verbalizing. Additionally, aspects of the visual art process and product may reveal areas of the subconscious that the client was not previously aware of prior to the activity. The counselor may also use drawing or other visual arts to assess progress and counseling outcomes. Integrating drawing as an intervention within counseling may range from allowing the client to doodle or sketch during the session without a prompt while talking, to giving the client a directive prompt to focus the drawing on a specific topic or concern. An example of a drawing prompt is to draw three pictures to represent how you saw yourself in the past, how you see yourself now, and how you see yourself in the future. The counselor may also create a sketch during the session to discuss with the client (e.g., visual of patterns of family interactions discussed by the client).

There are various types of paint (e.g., tempera, watercolor, acrylic, and finger paint), brushes, and painting surfaces (e.g., paper, canvas, objects). Additionally, there are digital painting programs. The selection of the materials will depend on the client and the focus of the activity. However, the counselor should not make assumptions in selecting materials for various clients. For example, although finger painting is common for young children, older clients may also want to use this medium for self-expression when it is available and the client perceives the counselor as being nonjudgmental. Allowing an older client to choose materials generally associated with younger children may help them connect with their childhood, or let go of the pressure to be a good artist. For a parent, it may help them connect with their child. Clients may also use materials in different ways. For example, young children sometimes have difficulty with the concept of needing to add water to watercolor paint. Once they figure this out, they are sometimes more interested in changing the color of the water and playing in it than painting, which might be what the client needs in that session.

Sculpting involves shaping of materials (e.g., Play-Doh, clay, modeling clay) to create something in a three-dimensional form. This technique can involve a range of motion in the hands to manipulate the sculpting material (e.g., pound, squish). Clients may use the material to create things. For example, the counselor may ask the client to sculpt pieces into things that represent various parts of their self or members of their family. In contrast, clients may also manipulate the material without a goal of creating something. For example, the counselor may ask the client to think about what they are angry about and express their anger by pounding or squishing the clay, with a goal of experiencing emotional release during this activity.

Crafts is a large category that encompasses a broad range of materials (e.g., glitter, pipe cleaners, glue, tape, craft sticks, buttons, fabric, ribbon, yarn, feathers, magazines, cardboard, construction paper). Counselors may use craft materials in counseling in many ways. For example, clients may use craft sticks to build or pipe cleaners to create something. However, the benefit of using craft materials is that it can enhance the tactile experience for the client. Additionally, the client may feel less pressure and anxiety about needing to be an artist. Counselors can use magazines, in particular, to create collages, in addition to using music, as well as photos and videos. A collage is an art form that involves putting small pieces together to make the artwork. For example, the counselor may ask the client to create a collage about who they are, or their career goals. Clients may also use digital software or applications to create a digital collage.

Two final visual art mediums are photographs (phototherapy) and videos (videotherapy). With the evolution of technology, phones are readily available for children and adults, and many phones have the capacity to take photos. Therefore, photos and videos are feasible, accessible mediums to integrate in counseling. Additionally, the popularity of sharing photos and videos may facilitate greater openness among clients to use this creative medium. The therapeutic use of these mediums may include the process of taking photos or creating the videos, viewing photos or videos taken or created and discussing them, or viewing/watching photos or videos created by others and discussing them (similar to bibliotherapy). Videos provide an additional dimension to photos by allowing clients to add verbal context to images, which may include spoken word and music. Counselors may integrate photos and videos early in the counseling process to help develop rapport by having clients share personal examples representing themselves, family members, and other people important to them. As a counseling intervention, a counselor can have a client take photos or create a video to express their thoughts and feelings they experience during the week, or take photos to represent their experiences, thoughts, and feelings related to a specific topic. Clients can share photos or videos on their phones or other devices. Clients can also print photos to bring to sessions. Furthermore, counselors can have clients create a collage using photos or videos.

Researchers have found promising results in using visual art mediums with various client groups. Goldner and Scharf (2011) found support for using children's family drawings to assess attachment concerns and identify risk for adjustment concerns in school. Additionally, Woolford et al. (2015) found children shared more verbal information in a mental health assessment when also asked to draw about their presenting problem. Sandmire et al. (2016) also found decreased anxiety among college students following participation in mandala coloring, painting, and clay modeling sessions. Furthermore, Decker et al. (2019) found decreased PTSD and depression symptoms among veterans involved in an adjunctive art therapy intervention.

When using visual arts in counseling, there are various areas to consider. Specifically, it is important to consider the developmental level and skill level of the client when selecting materials. Older clients may appreciate more expensive, better quality art materials, while younger clients may not know how to use them. If the counselor is concerned about the care of the materials, this may negatively influence the session. For example, counselors should not be surprised if clients, especially young children, break crayons, mix different colors of Play-Doh together, or use an entire stack of paper or an entire container of paint if available. Therefore, the counselor may want to limit the type and amount of materials available. When integrating visual arts within the counseling process the counselor may take on a variety of roles (e.g., observe, create their own artwork, work with the client on artwork). The counselor's role will vary depending on the individual needs of the client and treatment goals. It is also important to remember that the process of creating the art is important, not only the final product. Furthermore, it is crucial for the counselor to allow sufficient time to discuss the art product and the process of developing it.

Some clients might be reluctant to engage in art, stating that they cannot draw, or they are not an artist. The counselor can be encouraging to clients who struggle with confidence in their ability by focusing on the process, not the product, and avoiding language that judges the quality of the artwork. Instead of using praise by saying, "That is pretty" or "I like your drawing," a counselor can use encouragement by stating, "You worked really hard on that" or "There is a lot of detail in it." A final consideration is what to do with the completed artwork. The client may choose to keep the artwork or want the counselor to keep it. At times, it might be important to keep the art as part of the client's file. If this is the case, and the client wants to keep the artwork, the counselor can request to make a copy of it for the file. The counselor should also refrain from displaying clients' artwork, unless a client asks the counselor to do so and it is appropriate to have visible for others to see. A counselor would not display a client's case note or share verbal content from a session with others, and similarly, it is important to keep artwork confidential. An exception would be if the client creates artwork specifically for the counselor to display.

In using visual arts with diverse populations, it is important to have materials that are representative of various groups, such as having drawing materials in various skin tone colors. Counselors can also use visual arts for social justice and advocacy, such as the use of photos in photovoice. Although a research methodology, photovoice can also benefit clients. Wang et al. (2000) identified three goals of photovoice: (a) document and reflect on one's community,

(b) facilitate discussion about critical issues in the community, and (c) share information with policy makers and other stakeholders to advocate for change. Through photovoice, marginalized populations can feel empowered to voice their concerns through photos and have stakeholders witness their experiences through the photo exhibit. Thus, counselors can use visual arts in a variety of ways within counseling.

ETHICAL USE OF CREATIVITY IN COUNSELING

In using creativity mediums ethically in counseling it is crucial for the counselor to receive training first in the specified area. However, the counselor does not need to complete the requirements to be recognized with the credentials or title (e.g., drama therapist, art therapist) to use the approach in counseling (e.g., counselor that uses drama within counseling, counselor that uses art in counseling), as long as they do not use the title without doing the requirements to earn the title. It is also important for the counselor to have experience exploring the medium themselves before using it with a client to ensure concerns do not come up for them that they first need to work through before using the medium with clients. Experiencing the approach in training will also help clinicians consider how they might use it with clients and obtain practice using it, instead of experiencing it in action for the first time with clients. Usually training will allow an opportunity to experience the medium.

Intentionality is another important consideration when using creative approaches within counseling. The counselor should have a purpose in using a medium, instead of using it because it would be cool to try, or to fill time during session. Additionally, it is important to focus on the process, instead of only on the product. A counselor who has a passion for a specific creativity medium may struggle with not focusing on the product or focusing on the client's process, instead of the quality of the work or the counselor's own process. When this arises, it is important for the counselor to work through these concerns before using the medium with clients. In focusing on the process, it is also important that the counselor allows sufficient time in the session to process with the client. The process of engaging in the creative approach is therapeutic, but processing further enhances the experience and creates greater therapeutic value. Although it is ideal to allow process time in the same session, there may be times when a therapeutic activity or processing of the activity extends across multiple sessions.

A final area to consider is the efficacy of the approach with the specified population. The author presents some research to support each creative approach within this chapter. However, it is not possible to explore the research based for every medium with every population or area of concern. The counselor should examine the efficacy of an approach before using it. Additionally, the counselor can advocate for research on using the medium with the specific client population, as well as engage in their own research, especially when there is limited research in the area. Shallcross (2012) reports the need for further research on creativity counseling approaches. This is crucial, as insurance companies may only want counselors to use evidence-based practices, and there may not be empirical support for the approach the counselor is using with the specific client population. Thus, the counselor can be an advocate for clients and the profession through collecting data from their clients regarding effectiveness, partnering with others to conduct research (i.e., counselor educators at a university), and advocating for research on the use of creativity in counseling.

CONCLUSION

Counselors have a vast array of creative mediums to consider integrating within counseling. Through careful planning, consideration of a client's identities, and intentional use, creativity may enhance the experience for clients and make counseling more meaningful. Thus, counselors are encouraged to engage in ethical use of creativity within counseling.

Summary

- Counselors may use creativity in a variety of ways within the counseling process.
- When integrating creativity in counseling, there are ethical considerations for the counselor to be aware of and address (e.g., training, self-awareness, intentionality).
- In using creativity, counselors need to provide materials that appeal to diverse groups.
- Creativity in counseling can help empower clients to have their voices heard.

Voices From the Field

Justina Wong
Founder of the Kwan-Chischilly Veterans Initiative

"So, where are you from?" As a BIPOC (Black, Indigenous, person of color) counselor who identifies as a Chinese American female, I cannot tell you how many times clients have asked me this question. After many inquiries by me to fully understand why they ask, it became clear that many of them held three beliefs. The first is that I do not belong in the counseling field because there are not many counselors who look like me. One client went as far as to tell me I should have pursued nursing, accounting, or the law. I have no interest in those three professions, and they are the three professions that my parents tried to persuade me to pursue. The second belief is that they believe I am a foreigner. I once worked with an older White male in his 90s, and he asked me if I have ever been to my home country. His question implied that the United States of America is not my home, even though I was born and raised in California. The last belief is that I cannot help them because we are from two different cultures. This last belief comes into my counseling sessions quite often. Many clients I have worked with believe that I cannot help them because I identify as Chinese. In my experience, clients who identify as BIPOC tend to be more open about the idea that I am their counselor. Approximately 85% of the clients I have worked with identify as White.

Through my fieldwork internship in graduate school, I learned that I must get creative when it comes to working with clients who do not want to work with a Chinese female. It is one of the first topics that I discuss with my current clients and limits of confidentiality and mandated reporting. When I was in fieldwork, I regularly used cinematherapy with my former clients. Cinematherapy was a hard sell because I worked with student veterans, and I do not identify as a veteran. Many of my clients at the time did not believe in counseling, therapy, or cinematherapy. Clients told me that cinematherapy is "stupid" because it differs from traditional talk therapy. It was particularly challenging working with combat veterans because they did not believe in my use of cinematherapy. I had a lot working against me. I identified as a Chinese female counselor-in-training who was not a veteran. I was not trustworthy in their eyes, and many of them believed that I did not know what I was doing. Some clients never came back to see me, and one client told me that I was "full of shit for thinking cinematherapy works." It was a hard pill to swallow because I am passionate about working with the veteran population, and my main goal was to support them to the best of my abilities. For a period throughout my fieldwork internship, I lost my confidence as a counselor-in-training and questioned whether I want to pursue the counseling profession at all. There were many times when I felt unworthy of being a counselor and criticized myself for my mistakes.

Although I felt unworthy of being a counselor, the BIPOC clients who I worked with convinced me that I was wrong. I worked with an Asian male veteran and a female dependent. Both were excited that I was their counselor because I was also Asian. I still struggled with the use of cinematherapy. The female client was more open to the idea of cinematherapy and enjoyed our work together. She did not realize that cinematherapy could be so effective in helping her process the trauma that she experienced. We used the Disney Pixar movie *Inside Out* many times throughout our work together. Cinematherapy helped her understand the importance of feeling all emotions and not only those that we deem positive. She realized that sadness played a key role in the main character's life and without sadness the main character would not have felt joy. The male client was highly resistant to the use of cinematherapy. He thought cinematherapy should be used for children and adolescents instead of adults. He reluctantly watched specific movie clips that I assigned as homework and eventually warmed up to the idea of cinematherapy as a therapeutic technique. He felt isolated from peers due to the pandemic restrictions and cinematherapy showed him that he was not alone. Watching the movie clips led him to make healthier life choices like setting boundaries in relationships with toxic family members.

As a female BIPOC counselor, it was hard work. I had to work through many obstacles to be the counselor that I am today. All the hard work was worth it in the end. My schooling, fieldwork internship, training, and mentors helped me understand that there is a reason I am the way that I am. This has helped me understand that my clients are the way that they are for a reason regardless of what the reason is. As a counselor, I hold a special kind of power and that power can change someone's life. I believe you must dedicate yourself to being a lifelong learner and working on yourself before trying to work on clients. It is the only way to persevere in this profession and avoid being a wounded healer.

A Call to Action

Although there is research to support using a variety of creative approaches in counseling, not everyone supports its use in the counseling process. How might you respond to colleagues who mainly rely on talk therapy and refer to creative approaches as "fluff" that are a waste of time and don't really help clients? How might you advocate for the use of creativity with a child client when a parent is skeptical? How might you justify your use of creativity to an insurance company for reimbursement?

It is time to advocate! Using creative approaches presented in this chapter, create a campaign to promote mental health awareness, dispel myths and stigma related to mental health, and advocate for counseling. This may include using visual art materials (e.g., drawing, painting, sculpting, and craft materials) to create artwork to post on the college campus, in the community, or on social media to support mental health awareness and promote the use of counseling services.

Case Study 12.1

Xavier is a 25-year-old Black male. He comes to counseling after friends express to him their concerns that he is withdrawn and appears depressed. During the first session, Xavier answers most of your questions with one- or two-word responses and often states, "I don't know." You ask about his strengths, and he smiles and states that he likes music and art. When you ask about significant, recent events, he reports experiencing discrimination and that hurt him deeply, but he provides minimal details. You finish gathering background information and state that you look forward to seeing him at the next session. In preparation for the next session, you feel stuck. You wonder if Xavier will come back, and if he does, how you might develop rapport with him.

RESPONSE QUESTIONS

1. What creative medium(s) may you consider using during your next session with intentionality to develop rapport and further explore Xavier's presenting concerns and recent experience of discrimination?
2. How do you propose using the medium(s) in session? Would you use them in a directive way through including a structured activity, or have creativity materials available for Xavier to explore and decide if and how he wants to use them?
3. What considerations should you think about before integrating the medium(s) you are proposing to use in session?

Going Within

After reading the chapter, what creative medium resonates with you the most? What are your personal and professional experiences with using the medium? Do you see yourself using the approach it in your future work as a counselor? Why or why not? If so, how will you ensure that you have the necessary training to use it appropriately? What will you need to consider in using the approach with diverse populations? Are their creative approaches that you would be uncomfortable with or reluctant to use in counseling? What are they? Explore why you might feel this way.

Group Process

Have students select creative approaches discussed in the chapter and use the approach to introduce themselves to their peers in small groups. Students have the flexibility to choose the approach and the way they use it. Some examples include creating and sharing a paper or music collage, performing a song or dance, and reading a story or poem. Process questions include: How did you decide which approach to use? What was it like to introduce yourself using the creative approach you selected? In what ways did the creativity approach help you to learn more about your peers? How might you use creativity with future clients to develop rapport?

RESOURCES

Association for Creativity in Counseling: https://www.creativecounselor.org
Association for Play Therapy: https://www.a4pt.org
Child and Nature Network: https://www.childrenandnature.org
International Expressive Arts Therapy Association: https://youtube.com/
    playlist?list=PLPpOopZoXeKMeoJUdyR7DV4km9dwZroe5
Professional Association of Therapeutic Horsemanship International: https://
    www.pathintl.org
Equine-Assisted Growth and Learning Association: https://www.eagala.org/
    index
Schoel, J., & Maizell, R. S. (2002). Exploring islands of healing: New perspectives on adventure based counseling. Project Adventure.
White, W. (2015). Stories from the field: A history of wilderness therapy. Wilderness Publishers.

Access this podcast at http://connect.springerpub.com/content/book/978-0-8261-6386-8/chapter/ch12

KEY REFERENCES

Only key references appear in the print edition. The full reference list appears in the digital product found on https://connect.springerpub.com/content/book/978-0-8261-6386-8/chapter/ch12

Cantrick, M., Anderson, T., Leighton, L. B., & Warning, M. (2018). Embodying activism: Reconciling injustice through dance/movement therapy. *American Journal of Dance Therapy, 40*(2), 191–201. https://doi.org/10.1007/s10465-018-9288-2
Chandler, C. K. (2017). *Animal-assisted therapy in counseling* (3rd ed.). Routledge. https://doi.org/10.4324/9781315673042
Gladding, S. T. (2016). *The creative arts in counseling* (5th ed.). American Counseling Association. https://doi.org/10.1002/9781119291961
Gladding, S. T., & Drake Wallace, M. J. (2018). Scriptotherapy: Eighteen writing exercises to promote insight and wellness. *Journal of Creativity in Mental Health, 13*(4), 380–391. https://doi.org/10.1080/15401383.2018.1486259
Halsted, J. W. (2002). *Some of my best friends are books* (2nd ed.). Great Potential Press.

Swank, J. M. (2008). The use of games: A therapeutic tool with children and families. *International Journal of Play Therapy, 17*(2), 154–167. https://doi.org/10.1037/1555-6824.17.2.154

Swank, J. M., & Shin, S. M. (2015b). Nature-based child-centered play therapy: An innovative counseling approach. *International Journal of Play Therapy, 24*(3), 151–161. https://doi.org/10.1037/a0039127

Wang, C. C., Cash, J. L., & Powers, L. S. (2000). Who knows the streets as well as the homeless? Promoting personal and community action through photovoice. *Health Promotion Practice, 1*(1), 81–89. https://doi.org/10.1177/152483990000100113

COMPLEMENTARY AND ALTERNATIVE APPROACHES TO COUNSELING

Ana Puig

Think about this...

What are the complementary and alternative therapies you may be familiar with? When you think about counseling clients of diverse backgrounds (race, ethnicity, gender identity, sexual orientation, cultural background), how can these nontraditional ways of healing be applied or considered to attend to their presenting issues? Have you ever experienced a complementary or alternative approach to wellness and healing? What do you need to know to be able to determine how to support clients who may wish to explore these approaches to therapy?

LEARNING OBJECTIVES

After reading this chapter, you should be able to:

- Define spiritual counseling and identify critical aspects of this approach to helping clients
- Discuss Indigenous healing practices, including drumming circles, and their applicability to diverse clients and issues
- Describe prevalent Eastern traditions to integrate in counseling practice and their applicability to diverse clients and presenting issues
- Identify the benefits of yoga for client mental health and wellness
- Describe applicability of mindfulness meditation to enhance client wellness and health
- Explain the major tenets of transpersonal counseling and its application in therapy
- Recognize the risks of cultural misappropriation and engage in multiculturally sensitive and competent practices

INTRODUCTION

Human beings have long sought help from their religious or spiritual leaders. The history of humankind tells us about people from myriad cultures seeking guidance, support, and healing from sages, shamans, priests, priestesses, or pastors in their communities. Indeed, one thing all cultures and races and ethnicities have in common across the world is this search for answers to vexing questions and situations. For many clients, a spiritual or religious leader is their first point of contact during a psychological, emotional, or other unexpected life crisis or event. Although psychotherapy and psychiatry have become the dominant paradigm in Western mental health service provision, Indigenous approaches to wellness are older and more established across the history of humankind.

In this chapter, we introduce you to salient alternative and complementary approaches to wellness and mental health. From spiritual and religious traditions to yoga and meditation practices, we hope exposure to these ways of health promotion and healing will expand the knowledge, awareness, and repertoire of interventions you can consider when you encounter clients who might benefit from a nontraditional approach to counseling, whether directly or as an adjunct to traditional therapy. As with any new approach, we ask you to keep an open mind and heart and a spirit of curiosity when you begin to explore these interventions. We also want to underscore the risk of cultural appropriation when it comes to adopting complementary therapies originating from Eastern traditions or Indigenous groups. Cultural appropriation is defined as the use of elements of a nondominant culture (e.g., hairstyle, tattoos, and makeup, religious or spiritual practices, dress) in a way that reinforces stereotypes or oppression of the minoritized culture (Cuncic, 2022). Some of the interventions you will learn about here have ancient, culturally anchored, religious and spiritual origins. If you are a member of a dominant cultural group not of Eastern or Indigenous background, you must approach these therapies in multiculturally competent and respectful ways and with careful attention to the spiritual and religious competencies set forth by our profession (see aservic .org/spiritual-and-religious-competencies for spiritual and religious competencies and Ratts et al. [2015], for the multicultural and social justice counseling competencies).

COMPLEMENTARY AND ALTERNATIVE THERAPIES

Complementary and alternative medicine (CAM) is used by practitioners to support client wellness and healing in holistic ways. Complementary therapies are adjuncts to standard treatment. Alternative therapy replaces traditional treatment. In the field of medicine, complementary therapies are often used to support patients during medical treatments for conditions like cancer, postoperative pain, and chronic illnesses, among others (National Cancer Institute, 2022). Similar to the CAM interventions in medicine, psychologists and counselors use complementary therapies or modalities in the course of serving their clients (Berger & Thompson, 2019). Berger and Thompson recommend that whenever possible, to provide ethical treatment, it is best if you secure certification or licensure, as applicable.

The National Cancer Institute (2022) states CAM therapies include the following types: mind–body therapies (e.g., biofeedback, creative outlets, hypnosis, imagery, meditation, tai chi, and yoga), biologically based practices (e.g., botanicals, dietary supplements, special foods or diets, and vitamins or supplements), manipulative and body-based practices (e.g., chiropractic therapy, massage, and reflexology), and energy healing (e.g., reiki and therapeutic touch). You can read more about these types of CAM modalities at www.cancer.gov/about-cancer/treatment/cam. Some of the Indigenous and Eastern traditions we will present here are also considered complementary therapies.

The National Institutes of Health (NIH), a federal government agency, is a steward of medical and behavioral health research and practice for the United States. One of its institutes is the National Center for Complementary and Integrative Health (NCCIH), which is the gold standard for research on complementary and alternative therapies and modalities. The NCCIH (2022) provides the following recommendations to clients interested in seeking complementary therapies:

1. If you need names of practitioners in your area, first check with your doctor or other healthcare provider. A nearby hospital or medical school, professional organizations, state regulatory agencies or licensing boards, or even your health insurance provider may be helpful. Unfortunately, the NCCIH cannot refer you to practitioners.

2. Find out as much as you can about any potential practitioner, including education, training, licensing, and certifications. The credentials required for complementary health practitioners vary tremendously from state to state and from discipline to discipline. (NCCIH, 2018)

Once you have found a possible practitioner, here are some tips about deciding whether they are right for you:

1. Find out whether the practitioner is willing to work together with your conventional healthcare providers. For safe, coordinated care, it's important for all of the professionals involved in your health to communicate and cooperate.

2. Explain all of your health conditions to the practitioner, and find out about the practitioner's training and experience in working with people who have your conditions. Choose a practitioner who understands how to work with people with your specific needs, even if general well-being is your goal. Remember that health conditions can affect the safety of complementary approaches. For example, if you have glaucoma, some yoga poses may not be safe for you.

3. Don't assume that your health insurance will cover the practitioner's services. Contact your health insurance provider and ask. Insurance plans differ greatly in what complementary health approaches they cover, and even if they cover a particular approach, restrictions may apply.

4. Tell all your healthcare providers about the complementary approaches you use and about all practitioners who are treating you. Keeping your healthcare providers informed helps you to stay in control and effectively manage your health. (NCCIH, 2022)

As you can see, securing credentials, certifications, or licensure is recommended, and working closely with the client's traditional medicine provider is also important. Additionally, it is worth noting that insurance companies may not provide coverage for some forms of complementary therapy. In the course of your practice, you may need to discuss alternative payments with your client if you plan to provide complementary therapy. Finally, we encourage you to stay abreast of developments in this rapidly growing field so that you can consider the best ways to integrate these approaches within your counseling practice.

We want to highlight the mind–body and manipulative body-based intervention, Emotional Freedom Technique (EFT). EFT is similar to acupuncture, except it uses tapping instead of needles to apply repetitive pressure on specific points in the body (meridians). EFT can be done by the client themselves, once they learn the technique, or by the counselor. EFT follows a prescribed set of steps, noted in the following list. Please be aware that learning this technique requires guidance by a trained professional and you should not attempt to do this without appropriate supervision:

■ Verbalize what is bothering you and score it from 0 to 10 with 10 being the highest possible level of distress or discomfort.
■ Verbalize a statement to set up the issue and follow it with a statement of self-acceptance.
■ Start the tapping sequence using two fingers (index and middle, usually), to tap the meridian specific point.
■ While tapping, repeat the statement of self-acceptance, focusing on the issue of concern. Do seven to nine taps on each meridian point.
■ The usual meridians are at the top of your head (upper forehead), under your arm, below the lips, the collarbone, just below the nose, and around the eyes.
■ At the end of tapping, rate the distress level.
■ You repeat the process until you reach the lowest level possible. (Anthony, 2018)

Brennan (2021) reported that studies exploring the efficacy of EFT tapping have shown improvement in patients struggling with depression, posttraumatic stress disorder (PTSD), and phobias.

Table 13.1 provides an overview of complementary therapy modalities, types, their effects, and required training.

SPIRITUAL AND RELIGIOUS COUNSELING

Early theorists provided conceptualizations about the spiritual aspect of self and its importance in holistic well-being (e.g., Carl Jung, Abraham Maslow;

TABLE 13.1 COMPLEMENTARY THERAPIES

COMPLEMENTARY THERAPY AND TYPE	DESCRIPTION AND EFFECTS	REQUIRED TRAINING
Acupuncture Manipulative and body-based Energy healing Eastern tradition	Traditional Chinese medicine technique aimed at balancing flow of energy or life force (chi) thought to flow through meridians in the body. Needles inserted into particular points along the meridians to rebalance energy flow.	Three years of training (master's equivalent) that includes practical experience. May earn a doctorate. Oversight by the National Certification Commission for Acupuncture and Oriental Medicine (NCCAOM; www.nccaom.org).
Aromatherapy Biologically based	Use of essential oils (extracts of natural botanicals) to improve emotional and physical health. Smells affect mind and body symptoms and sensations. Relieve stress and anxiety, and improve immune system, sleep, and energy.	Online certification, and may need knowledge of human anatomy and physiology. Oversight by the Alliance of International Aromatherapists (AIA; www. alliance-aromatherapists.org) or the National Association for Holistic Aromatherapy (NAHA; naha.org).
Biofeedback/ Neurofeedback Mind–body	Using special equipment, the practitioner teaches the client how to change physiological responses to pain, stress, and tension. It reduces negative symptoms and allows the client to self-regulate.	Certification and mentoring are required. Need a master's degree or PhD to qualify. Involves over 40 hours of training and 20 of mentoring/ supervision. Oversight by the Biofeedback Certification International Alliance (BCIA; www .bcia.org).

(continued)

TABLE 13.1 COMPLEMENTARY THERAPIES (*CONTINUED*)

COMPLEMENTARY THERAPY AND TYPE	DESCRIPTION AND EFFECTS	REQUIRED TRAINING
Holotropic breathwork Mind–body Energy healing	Breathing technique that helps regulate physical, mental, emotional, and spiritual health. Can be part of a meditation practice.	Requires an accredited program of study. Multiple trainings available (www.othership.us/resources/breathwork-training).
Chiropractic therapy Manipulative and body-based	Involves adjustments to the spine to treat neuromuscular disorders and pain. Malalignment of muscles and bones may cause physical distress and can be managed through these adjustments.	College degree plus chiropractic school and licensure (over 4,500 hours). Programs and license requirements vary by state. Oversight by the National Board of Chiropractic Examiners (NBCE; www.nbce.org/home).
Creative and expressive arts Mind–body	Art, music, and expressive therapists use creative and expressive modalities to enhance mental and emotional well-being of clients.	Requires a master's degree in the specific discipline. Some master's and PhD level counselors learn to use creative modalities through professional continuing education as adjunct therapy. Oversight by Art Therapy Credentials Board (ATCB; www.atcb.org), International Expressive Arts Therapy Association (www.ieata.org), and Certification Board for Music Therapists; www.cbmt.org).

Drumming/ Drumming circles Mind–body Indigenous tradition	Healing technique based on African, Australian, and Native American cultural and religious traditions and a form of sound and music therapy.	Drumming is an informal and fun way to create community. Drum circles can be carried out by people of all ages and backgrounds. You can access more information from Resources section and at www.drumcircle.com.
Emotional Freedom Techniques (EFT) Manipulative and body-based	Based on acupressure stimulation of specific points on the person to relieve stress, anxiety, depression, phobias, and posttraumatic stress disorder (PTSD). Similar to acupuncture, EFT focuses on pressure points in the body. This can be done by a practitioner or can be taught to the client to do themselves.	Multiple certification programs available. You can access more information at eftuniverse.com/certification/the-16-steps-to-becoming-an-eft-int-1-practitioner.

(continued)

TABLE 13.1 COMPLEMENTARY THERAPIES (*CONTINUED*)

COMPLEMENTARY THERAPY AND TYPE	DESCRIPTION AND EFFECTS	REQUIRED TRAINING
Forest bathing Mind–body Eastern tradition	Forest bathing and forest therapy (shinrin-yoku) means taking in, through all our senses, the forest (or natural) environment. It is an intentional and contemplative practice of immersion in smell, sounds, and sensations of the body while in nature. Developed in Japan in the 1980s. Health benefits have been recorded by researchers in Japan and South Korea (globalwellnessinstitute.org/wellnessevidence/forest-bathing).	Counselors can learn how to conduct sessions via the Forest Therapy Hub (foresttherapyhub.com/forest-bathing-guide-training). To find a therapy guide and learn more at /www.natureandforesttherapy.earth.
Guided imagery Mind–body	Involves focused meditation by having the person concentrate on an object, sound, or narrated story to decrease anxiety, stress, and improve relaxation and well-being. Also used to decrease pain and improve sleep. May include background music or sounds.	Accessible to anyone and frequently done via recordings a person can listen to independently, or a live guided narration by a practitioner. To find examples, search YouTube for "guided imagery" and see www.healthjourneys.com.

CHAPTER 13: COMPLEMENTARY AND ALTERNATIVE APPROACHES ■ 349

Homeopathy Biologically-based	Involves use of natural remedies to ameliorate health and wellness. Homeopathic doctors treat emotional, mental, and physical well-being without focusing on illness or disease. This tradition believes the body is self-healing, and remedies given will assist with that natural process.	Some states require a medical degree. A 4-year professional practice degree is the minimum requirement. You can enroll in an institution accredited by the Accreditation Commission of Homeopathic Education (ACHENA; achena.org/refresh). You have to pass the National Certification with the Council for Homeopathy Certification (CHC) exam to practice.
Hypnosis Mind–body	Involves having the person enter a state of focused relaxation to promote pain relief, stress relief, or changes in unhealthy habits. May be used at bedside for patients undergoing medical or dental procedures.	Requires between 40 and 100 hours of hypnotherapy training workshops, 20 hours of supervised individual training, and 2–5 years of practical experience. No federal regulations exist. The International Board of Hypnotherapy (IBH) provides certification (internationalboardofhypnotherapy.com).

(continued)

TABLE 13.1 COMPLEMENTARY THERAPIES (CONTINUED)

COMPLEMENTARY THERAPY AND TYPE	DESCRIPTION AND EFFECTS	REQUIRED TRAINING
Massage therapy Manipulative and body-based	Used to increase relaxation, and reduce pain, stress, and tension. Requires hands-on manipulation of body muscles using pressure, movement, and other techniques.	There are multiple types of massage therapies and licensure is regulated by states. Therapists can become members of the American Massage Therapy Association (www.amtamassage.org).
Meditation or mindfulness Mind-body Eastern tradition	Involves focused breathing or use of mantras (repetitive phrases or words) to induce a relaxed state of consciousness. Multiple religious faiths have meditative or contemplative practices and Western approaches are secularized for nonbelievers (e.g., Mindfulness Based Stress Reduction, Kabat-Zinn).	There are myriad training sources for mindfulness and meditation practice. Here are a few: Insight Meditation Society: www.dharma.org/teachers/teacher-training-program Mindfulness Based Stress Reduction: mbsrtraining.com Mindfulness Meditation Teacher Certification Program: mmtcp.soundstrue.com
Reflexology Manipulative and body-based	Involves applying pressure to areas of the feet (and hand) thought to correspond with organs in the body. The pressure provides relaxation and healing to the area of the body associated with the spot.	Training lasts 6–12 months and 150–300 hours of study and practice. Oversight by American Reflexology Certification Board (arcb.net). There are multiple schools dedicated to reflexology education.

Reiki Mind–body Energy healing Eastern tradition	Energy healing method originated in Japan in the 1920s. It can help clients release blocked energy in the body and experience relaxation and stress and pain relief.	Usually involves three levels of training by certified instructors. Levels 1 and 2 take about a year. Level 3 prepares you to become a reiki teacher or master. It is not nationally regulated. You can learn more through the International Center for Reiki Training (www.reiki.org).
Somatic therapy (somatic experiencing)	Created by Peter Levine, therapy focuses on physical body sensations of stress, tension, and trauma. Once sensations are identified, they are processed through mind–body exercises (e.g., grounding, dancing, breathing, therapeutic touch, mediation).	Somatic experiencing training may be obtained through Somatic Experiencing International (traumahealing.org).
Tai chi (a form of qigong) Mind–body Energy healing Eastern tradition	This ancient Chinese martial art alleviates physical pain and reenergizes practitioners. It improves balance and well-being and is considered a meditative movement practice. It balances ying and yang energies in the body and involves slow and controlled movements.	You can learn more about tai chi practice at www.taichifoundation.org and qigong practice at www.nccih.nih.gov/health/qigong-what-you-need-to-know. There are multiple offerings for classes online via YouTube channels.

(continued)

TABLE 13.1 COMPLEMENTARY THERAPIES (*CONTINUED*)

COMPLEMENTARY THERAPY AND TYPE	DESCRIPTION AND EFFECTS	REQUIRED TRAINING
Yoga Mind–body Eastern tradition	Yoga is an ancient tradition attending to body-mind alignment and is associated with Hinduism. Yoga blends meditation, deep breath work, and body postures aimed at wellness and health. Yoga reduces stress, depression, and anxiety, strengthens muscles, increases flexibility, and enhances quality of life.	Yoga training is available via yoga studios across the United States and training is extensive and rigorous. Yoga can be integrated into clinical practice individually and in groups by certified yoga instructors.

Note: For additional information on complementary therapies, consult the sources listed under Resources at the end of this chapter.

Archer & McCarthy, 2007). More specifically, Clark (n.d) describes Jung's analytic therapy as deeply concerned with the individual's spiritual longings and hunger for answers about the meaning of life. Similarly, Maslow's theory of human development highlighted the individual's ultimate need for transcendence and spiritual pursuits to achieve their full potential (Archer & McCarthy, 2007). The integration of spirituality and religion (SR) and attention to spiritual and religious concerns in counseling are not new; however, mental health professions have traditionally been reluctant to address these areas with clients (Cashwell & Young, 2020). According to Rollins (2019) counselors may feel unprepared or be concerned about broaching anything related to SR issues to avoid appearing biased or for fear of imposing their own beliefs or values on the client. Some clients you will encounter will invariably bring up spiritual or religious issues to the session and you need to be prepared to address them. In order to provide effective and ethical treatment related to spiritual and religious issues in counseling, the Association for Spiritual, Ethical, and Religious Values in Counseling (ASERVIC; aservic.org), a division of the American Counseling Association (www.counseling.org), developed a set of competencies that counselors should have (see Association for Spiritual, Ethical and Religious Values in Counseling, 2009). The competencies highlight the need for counselors to have foundational knowledge and awareness about clients' cultural backgrounds and worldviews, and keen self-awareness of their own beliefs, values, and limitations about their ability to address spiritual or religious issues with clients. Counselors should also have knowledge of human and spiritual development models and be able to communicate effectively with clients about SR topics. Finally, counselors must have a clear foundation on the assessment, diagnosis, and treatment of clients struggling with SR issues. Addressing all of these areas is beyond the scope of this chapter; however, the Resources section provides recommendations for you to learn more about how to address SR issues with clients.

A recent large-scale research study by counselor educators, the Spiritual and Religious Competencies Project, funded by the Templeton Foundation, aims to address the limited training that counselors receive in attending to this aspect of clients' lives. The research team proposes to do this by enhancing graduate education training in clinical and research competencies, exploring the current status of graduate training and identifying gaps, and delivering competencies training on a large scale through subgroups of faculty researchers. For more information about this effort, you can visit www.spiritualandreligiouscompetenciesproject.com/about/purpose.

By the year 2040, the United States will be composed of a majority minority landscape and counselors will be encountering clients from myriad cultures and varied races, ethnicities, religions, and spiritualities (Kight, 2019). It is timely and extremely important that the type of research described here is taking place. As a developing counselor, you will need to develop competencies and be comfortable addressing SR issues and serving clients of multiple intersectional identities. Multicultural and social justice counseling competencies are also critical and must be part of your counselor skill set (Ratts et al., 2015).

TABLE 13.2 INDIGENOUS VERSUS WESTERN WORLDVIEWS

INDIGENOUS VIEW	WESTERN VIEW
Spiritually oriented	Scientifically oriented
There are many truths based on each human experience.	There is one truth based on science or the law.
We are all connected. Society is relational.	We are all individuals. Society is compartmentalized.
Our land is sacred and given by a Supreme Being and should be respected and honored.	The land is a resource to be owned and exploited for human benefit.
Time is not linear. Time is cyclical. Time is here and now.	Time is linear and future oriented.
Comfort is based on the quality of our relationships.	Comfort is based on your ability to succeed and achieve goals.
Humans are not the most important part of nature. All beings are important, including the land.	Humans are the most important thing in the world and sit at the top of all living things.
Amassing wealth is done for the good of the tribe.	Amassing wealth is for personal gain.

Note: Adapted from Indigenous Corporate Training. (2016, January 26). *Indigenous peoples worldviews vs. western worldviews.* https://www.ictinc.ca/blog/indigenous-peoples-world-views-vs-western-worldviews

INDIGENOUS HEALING PRACTICES

Indigenous or shamanic practices precede modern counseling and psychological frameworks that inform our work as professionals. Humans have long sought guidance and support from community or tribal elders, shamans, and sages (Fukuyama & Sevig, 2012). Indigenous peoples across the world are not a monolithic group, nor do they all hold the same worldviews. However, many share a history of genocide, discrimination, oppression, violence, and trauma at the hands of colonizers who invaded their lands and attempted to force integration and acculturation into Western ways of being in the world (Fukuyama & Sevig, 2012; Narvaez, 2019). Narvaez (2019) highlights the intergenerational trauma experienced by Indigenous communities by colonizers over hundreds of years and outlines the ways in which modern counseling practitioners can enhance their understanding of Indigenous ways of healing (e.g., sweat lodge purification rituals, and ayahuasca [South America] or peyote [North America] rituals). Narvaez summarizes work developed by Rupert Ross, a Canadian attorney, who spent multiple hours working with Indigenous tribes and learning about their traditional ways of healing. It is important that you understand the differences between Indigenous and Western worldviews. Table 13.2 provides an overview, with the caveat that these may not all apply to all Indigenous peoples in the world (Indigenous Corporate Training, 2016).

Some of the most salient Indigenous healing practices are reflections of the worldviews described in Table 13.2. Narvaez (2019) outlines the important aspects of Indigenous peoples' worldview as follows: (1) strong spiritual focus (humans have been given spiritual gifts that make us stronger; health and healing can only occur through our spirits and through our relationships with every living being on Earth); (2) definition of health (health is attained through a strong relationship with nature and all living beings, and it requires us to be humble, respectful, and open; interdependence is valued and autonomy is not); (3) group healing is valued more than individual work (healing happens in community); (4) individual health is contingent on social health; (5) emotions are central to healing (tuning into the heart, each other, and spirit is the way to heal); (6) ceremonies and catharsis are healing practices (healing happens through sacred rituals, such as sweat lodges); (7) First Nations Healers (healers are elders who understand the individual's experience that can only be known by the person themselves; healing is not hierarchical and must integrate knowledge of the community the person inhabits); (8) every person has worth (all living beings are worthy and born good, sacred, and kind); (9) talking is not important (emotions and relationships are the mediums of healing); (10) the land is central to healing (we cannot defy nature; we must accept the power of nature to help heal and connect all of us). As you can see, Indigenous peoples' approach to healing and wellness runs counter to many of the tenets of traditional psychotherapy. We must be mindful of this whenever we encounter a native, Indigenous, or aboriginal client, and strive to learn as much as we can from them before we decide how to best serve them.

We want to highlight the Indigenous practice of drumming and drum circles. Muller (2015) describes the heart as a drum machine and drumming as a powerful healing practice. He provides an overview of drumming as a healing technique based on African, Australian, and Native American cultural and religious traditions, and a form of sound and music therapy. Some counselors use this technique in combination with other traditional counseling practices to work with clients who suffer from depression or anxiety or who are survivors of trauma. Although this practice has been secularized, Muller asserts that the ritual and communal aspect of drumming can enhance connection and community among clients in group settings.

Drum circles can be structured or free flowing. Drumming can take place individually or in groups, with the latter serving as a way of creating community and shared expression. Drumming circles align well with the collectivistic values of clients from minoritized groups (Ho et al., 2011). Studies have documented the benefits of drumming for adults (e.g., Ascenso et al., 2018; Dunbar et al., 2012) and children (e.g., Ho et al., 2011). Ascenso and colleagues (2018) conducted research on the impacts of drumming circles on adult participants and reported beneficial effects including positive emotions and a pleasant physical experience, improved sense of control and accomplishment, and increased self-awareness and sense of community connectedness. Dunbar et al. (2012) were able to document that engagement in actual music creation (rather than passive listening), including drumming, releases endorphins in the brain that leads to positive affect. Ho et al., 2011 conducted an intervention study with a control group to explore the impacts of school counselor–led drumming groups on socioemotional behaviors of low-income children. The focus was on providing support, psychoeducation, and drumming activities to kids without the stigma associated with therapy. Researchers reported significant improvements in the children's social and emotional behaviors, including focusing and listening skills. Thus, drumming circles show evidence of positive outcomes for clients at various developmental stages. Some examples of drumming exercises are provided next:

Say My Name

Drumming can be a great ice breaker and a chance to teach cooperation. Choose one participant to start a drumming rhythm. Once the rhythm is established, have the participant say the name of another person in the group. That person starts drumming. Continue this process to include others in the group. Add a new dimension by having the participant tell one person to stop while selecting another to play. This can create endless variations on how your participants contribute.

Pieces of Eight

In the circle, invite players to mentally choose a number between 1 and 8 (or 1 to 4 to make it simpler). Tell them you will count from one to eight and each player hits their drum when you say the number they picked. Start counting slowly as each participant gets familiar with the activity. Once they get the hang of it, increase the tempo or change the order of the numbers. Gradually fade your voice and invite the group to play on their own.

Pass the Pattern

Start out by playing a simple beat. Have the group do their best to echo the beat. Then have each person play their solo version of the beat. Depending on your participants' abilities, you could have sections of the group do different beats.

Emotion Drum

This is a good activity for higher functioning participants. Before drumming, have your participants write down a single word describing their mood then collect the papers. Give one of the "mood" papers to a participant and have them interpret the emotion on the drum. Let the others in the group guess what emotion the person is trying to convey. Then have the group try to express the mood together. Repeat the process.

Drumming "Hot or Cold"

Remember the "hot or cold" game you played as a kid? Someone hid an object in the room. As you walked around, they would say you were getting warmer while getting close and colder if you were walking away from the object. Once you got really close, others in the group would exclaim "Hot!" or "Boiling!"

You could try a version of this game during your drum circle. Have a participant leave the room while the group decides where to hide an object like a stuffed animal. Once the person reenters the room, the drum circle will play louder and/or faster as he or she gets closer to the object. The game has the potential for a lot of noise and laughs (Gruzewski, 2018).

Drumming and drumming circles are considered recreation or music therapy activities that benefit clients of all ages and are easy to implement. See the Resources section for more ideas about this therapeutic practice.

EASTERN TRADITION

In counseling practice, you may come across clients who have a racial or ethnic background rooted in Eastern traditions. It is important that you learn how to attend to the needs of these clients in competent ways that integrate their race, ethnicity, religion, and/or spirituality. Here again, we point you to the multicultural and social justice counseling competencies and the spiritual and religious competencies previously mentioned and included in the Resources section. The Eastern part of the world refers to Asian and Middle Eastern countries and cultures, and pertains to their races, ethnicities, and religions. Accordingly, we are referring to the religions of Buddhism, Hinduism, Islam, Jainism, Shenism, and Taoism (Michelini, 2021). Huang (2010) offers guidance about Eastern spiritual and religious practices and considerations for implementation in counseling. Cohen (2021) provides an overview of the ways in which Western psychology has secularized and integrated religious and spiritual practices from the East and explores the history behind this phenomenon. These approaches include yoga, meditation (e.g., mindfulness meditation), qigong, tai chi (a form of qigong), reiki, and forest bathing. We direct you to Table 13.1 for details about these therapies. Two of the most popular therapies in this category, yoga and meditation, are described next.

Yoga

Yoga is an ancient spiritual practice based on Hindu and Buddhist religious principles and has become a popular form of self-care in the United States. There are six branches of yoga: bhakti, hatha, jñāna, karma, raja, and tantra (Carrico, 2007) and types of yoga traditions include ashtanga, bikram, hatha, iyengar, kundalini, vinyasa, and yin (Shacknai, 2020). Shacknai (2020) discussed the different types of yoga in greater detail.

Researchers have found positive outcomes of using this Eastern tradition, including improved mental health (e.g., see Adams & Puig, 2008), social connection (e.g., see Thompson et al., 2017), physical and muscular strength and flexibility, and reduced anxiety and stress (Novotney, 2009).

Additional benefits include reduced inflammation and burnout and improved quality of life, immunity, balance, heart health, self-esteem, and sleep (Ezrin, 2021).

TABLE 13.3 MEDITATION TYPES AND DESCRIPTION

MEDITATION TYPE	DESCRIPTION
Spiritual	Based on Eastern spiritual traditions of Buddhism, Hinduism, JudeoChristian contemplative practices, and Taoism. May include silence or praying. Focus on self-awareness, reflection, loving-kindness, and compassion.
Mindfulness	Became popular after Kabat-Zinn secularized it as mindfulness based stress reduction. Based on Buddhist principles. Includes still awareness of the body, sensations and thoughts, watching the breath and returning to it repeatedly, and having complete acceptance of the present moment just as it is. Combines concentration with awareness.
Movement	Includes mindful movement, such as walking or other forms of controlled movement, such as tai chi and qigong. Beneficial for people who have difficulty sitting.
Focused	Involves complete and undivided attention to the task at hand. Could be eating, sipping tea, or making art. The idea is to stop the tendency to multitask. Requires concentration and returning to the task, regardless of where the mind goes.
Visualization	Involves engaging the creative mind to focus on a vision or image to concentrate on that brings stillness and peace in the present moment. For the religious practitioners it may be a deity; for secular practice, it could be a nature scene.
Chanting	Involves a repeated mantra and generates alert attention and peacefulness in the present moment. It could be the mantras "Om" or "Shalom."

Note: Adapted from Mindworks Team. (n.d.). *What are the different types of meditation?* https://mindworks.org/blog/different-types-meditation-technique

Mindfulness Meditation

Meditation practice is thought to be over 5,000 years old and has roots in Egypt, China, Hinduism, Buddhism, and Judaism (Ross, 2016). Meditation involves sitting or lying down, focusing on the breath, and bringing attention repeatedly to the present moment. The study of meditation dates back to the 1960s and its benefits have been well documented (Ross, 2016). There are multiple types of meditation practice, with the most common ones including spiritual, mindfulness, movement, focused, visual, and chanting. They are described in Table 13.3.

Mindfulness-Based Stress Reduction

Mindfulness-based stress reduction (MBSR) is a popular meditation practice secularized by Jon Kabat-Zinn in the late 1970s. Kabat-Zinn adapted this Eastern tradition to deliver to patients struggling with diseases such as cancer, immune disorders, and other chronic conditions (e.g., hypertension and diabetes; Niazi & Niazi, 2011). Niazi and Niazi conducted a systematic review of MBSR research and concluded that it is an effective intervention to reduce stress and improve patient symptoms overall. Multiple clinicians from diverse disciplines have trained in MBSR principles and practices over the past 40 years, and over 700 medical centers offer the MBSR training in the United States and worldwide (mbsrcollaborative.com). MBSR training includes the following:

- Eight weeks of classes either in person or live online, each 2.5 hours in length
- One day-long retreat after the final class session
- Daily homework consisting of guided audio practices and a variety of exercises completed individually outside the structured group class
- Approximately 10 to 40 participants per session, sometimes all experiencing the same challenge (e.g., anxiety), and other times involving a mix of problems
- Education in mindfulness, meditation, and the nature of difficulties
- Group discussions
- Yoga and other gentle stretching and mindful movement exercises. (Peterson, 2021)

MBSR is a strong evidence-based intervention that benefits practitioners and providers alike. If you are interested in MBSR training, you can find providers at https://mbsrtraining.com.

TRANSPERSONAL COUNSELING

Transpersonal psychology is based on the works of Carl Jung and Viktor Frankl, among others. It is focused on the spiritual and transcendental aspects of the human experience, and is concerned with the mind and psychology, but not necessarily religion (Cherry, 2021). See Grof (2008) for a historical overview of transpersonal psychology. Friedman (2014) discusses various ways to conduct therapy, including the assessment process. Therapy includes the use of guided imagery, meditation, hypnosis, prayer, and neurofeedback. These interventions can facilitate the exploration of altered states of consciousness with clients. Additionally, Friedman outlines the following approaches: biochemical (use of psychedelics, e.g., psilocybin, which is becoming increasingly researched and in some states legal to use), depth psychological (involves creative or expressive arts), existential (exploration of meaning; meaning-making), and somatic (holotropic breathwork or other somatic experiencing). Transpersonal therapy is a holistic approach and involves attending to the clients' mental, emotional, physical, social, intellectual, and spiritual well-being. It is effective in treating multiple mental health concerns, including depression, anxiety, and phobias (www.psychologytoday.com/us/therapy-types/transpersonal-therapy). The Association for Transpersonal Psychology offers additional information and resources about this type of therapy (www.atpweb.org/default.aspx).

CONCLUSION

Complementary and alternative approaches in individual and group counseling have been shown to have beneficial effects for client emotional and mental health. There are myriad specialized trainings, interventions, and techniques you can use in the course of your work as adjuncts to traditional therapy. As an emerging counselor, you should become familiar with the spiritual and religious counseling competencies because it is highly likely that you will encounter clients struggling with these issues.

Summary

- Complementary and alternative approaches are useful adjuncts to traditional counseling and may benefit diverse groups of clients.
- Multiple trainings are available for counselors to expand their repertoire of interventions and techniques about these approaches.
- The integration of spirituality and religion in counseling is an important skill for counselors given the number of clients who may want to discuss this aspect of themselves and their lives.
- Knowledge and awareness of Eastern and Indigenous traditions is important for counselors to competently serve clients who may align with these practices.
- Yoga and meditation are useful interventions for clients' holistic wellness and healing.

Voices From the Field

Emi Lenes-Cortez, PhD, LMFT, LMHC
Assistant Clinical Professor, Counseling and Wellness Center (CWC), University of Florida

Inner states of expansiveness and depth are made visible in the landscapes of nature. Nature gives us stimuli that can remind us of a widened perspective and can be especially helpful when we feel contracted, myopic, or chaotic inside. The medicinal quality of a breath of fresh air is immeasurable.

At Home

After years of loneliness, in a time of excruciating grief, I paid a phenomenal local artist, Jerald Davis, to create a large painting, as a vision board of what I was looking for in a partner. Within the artwork (see Figure 13.1) was a depiction of metaphors of partnered animals in nature, including the vulnerability and slow forward movement of turtles peeking out from their shells; the big picture awareness of two eagles' perspectives in the large sky; zooming into a closeup of the details of ladybugs; the playfulness of kittens simultaneously on the ground and reaching upward; the strength of horses being close together even when seeing different points of view; the grace of two deer being hydrated from the same stream; deep roots of trees beside two unique waterfalls that each have their own spaciousness as they flow into a river of togetherness.

On a grand scale, many people's experiences of loneliness and grief skyrocketed when COVID-19 arrived in our shared world. We were abruptly quarantined (some enclosed in small living areas), and much of our typical daily lives got unexpectedly canceled and rearranged. Some people got to virtually connect with loved ones, and some were more alone than ever before. Although there has been a widespread impact of the pandemic across humanity, I am

FIGURE 13.1 Illustration of relationship metaphors.

Source: Reprinted with permission from Jerald Davis.

being continually educated about the vastly different circumstances that people are in. Suffering is enormously compounded for those who are simultaneously dealing with war, domestic violence, being unhoused, being immunocompromised, food insecurity, mental health crises, or an endless number of other possibilities. The reverberations of the pandemic vary significantly based on physical and social location. I am sometimes unconscious about how my life has been influenced by the differential societal privileges given to those of us who are White, cisgender, heterosexual passing, middle class, able-bodied, U.S. citizens, etc. While there are some universal implications of the pandemic, varied individualized life experiences and sociopolitical context can significantly influence health and safety.

In 2020, there was a viral recognition across social media of the egregious murders of Breonna Taylor, Ahmaud Arbery, Tony McDade, and George Floyd, among many other irreplaceable human beings. This sparked an exponential response about the brutality that has been inflicted upon Black people throughout the centuries. People have been joining together outdoors in protest, with an outpouring of creative uprising. Consciousness of the staggering trauma happening continuously throughout people's bodies, families, communities, and nations can wreak havoc on our nervous systems. There are times that I tap into a glimpse of the enormity of the global sorrow, violence, and fear. To help ground myself, I often visit a sparsely populated forest. The isolated wilderness allows me ample room to expel animal noises of rage. I have wailed to the

FIGURE 13.2 Photograph of a majestic tree in the woods that could symbolize reaching in and reaching out.

Source: Reprinted with permission from Emilie Lenes.

trees, who are distanced enough to hold spaciousness for difficult emotionality, including my White tears about racism (Liebow & Glazer, 2019; Figure 13.2).

At Work

My direct supervisor, the UF CWC Outreach Director, Dr. Rosa West, invited the creativity of our team, and she provided a template of structure and a timeline for us to offer mental health support during these times. Among many other workshops, we provided a "Zooming into Nature" online healing space that was open to community members, as well as university students, faculty, and staff. As many of us engage in gut wrenching and exhausting work related to addressing trauma, these moments in nature can be restorative and re-source some of our depleted energy. After much adventurous trial and error with figuring out how to move from in-person to online, Lisa Buning (LMHC and Couples Counseling Coordinator), Dr. Ana Cikara, and I learned the importance of quality wifi, and having a still computer, rather than a moving cell phone, when trying to transmit a natural scene through an online space. We visited horses and were reminded of the power of equine therapy. In our glorious springtime, we zoomed into emerging green leaves, sprouting plant life with their colorful flowers, and the ebb and flow of the waves at the beach.

Studies have indicated that time in nature may help with well-being, physical and psychological health, anxiety, depression, rumination, complex memory tasks, life satisfaction, cognitive performance, and social or spiritual connectedness (Bratman et al., 2015; Keniger et al., 2013; Rather, 2019). When addressing the potential benevolent influences that nature can have on health, we would be remiss if we did not acknowledge that many lower income areas have less access to nature or have been subject to devastation of the surrounding natural environment. Environmental racism has been embedded within policy making and regulation enforcement where toxic waste facilities are located (Pellow, 2005). In some places there is irreversible pollution and poison that is contaminating the drinking water and has been correlated with higher rates of cancer (Castellon, 2021). There are disproportionate impacts (e.g., rates of asthma, vulnerability to flooding) of climate change in communities with minoritized races and ethnicities (Mays et al., 2021). Aid and support after natural disasters has been differential based on race and socioeconomic status (Keithly & Rombough, 2007). Furthermore, it is of profound importance to recognize and respect the enduring relationship that exists between Indigenous Peoples and their traditional territories. There are no words that could suffice to recognize the intergenerational traumatic impact on those native to the land we are currently inhabiting, considering the genocide and forced removal from one's home (Dunbar-Ortiz, 2014), along with the continued horrific displacement of sacred grounds (e.g., irreparable harm on Standing Rock ancestral lands; Estes, 2019).

Time in nature somehow gives me more energy to reengage with local, national, and international opportunities to help. Considering our historical and present-day realities, it is vital to consider what possibilities are within our realm of power and influence. For example, the following action steps have helped me to feel less helpless when facing colossal situations:

- Listen to and uplift representative voices of those with embodied wisdom on the topic (e.g., www.standingrock.org).
- Commit to learning (e.g., counseling.ufl.edu/healing-rt).
- Practice cultural humility (Tervalon & Murray-García, 1998), share insights with family, friends, colleagues.
- Speak out (e.g., When I hear a microaggression, I give voice to how it feels in my body, and acknowledge how the impact can often be different than the intention).
- Look within at our own social conditioning, and be accountable in our words and actions.
- Support BIPOC-led organizations and businesses.
- Sign petitions.
- Tell lawmakers to take action (e.g., www.aclufl.org/en/take-action-0).
- Vote if able.
- Promote, create, or attend fundraisers or protests.
- Recruit a group of people to make a task force or action research team.
- Donate money and/or time.
- Work at a place that is aligned with your values.

Prepandemic, having worked for over 12 years at an alternative middle and high school that provides holistic services for undersupported adolescents, there were innumerable ways that nature was transformative. In Alachua County, the majority of students enrolled are Black and African American teenagers who have endured various individualized, institutional, and intergenerational traumas. When something particularly distressing happened, the students and I would take walks around the heart-shaped lake, and they would find symbolism, such as the new bud growing through what had looked like a dead plant, green algae on top of the water, hiding all that's happening beneath the surface, and a fence that reminded them of how trapped they feel at times. A piece of trash on the ground reminded some of them of feeling out of place and a lack of belonging. Alternatively, another student saw that same item in nature and was reminded that there are always opportunities to help make the world a bit better. She picked up that broken cup to help clean up the area, one piece at a time.

Also, there were such enhancements to self-esteem, as we would go outside in the beautiful scenes and take pictures of the students expressing various emotions such as joy, heart-broken, afraid, closed, open, gratitude, and worthiness, among others. These photographs in nature provided a container for those sometimes quite intense human emotions to be experienced and honored. One student who had been born with a congenital upper arm difference took a picture next to a tree with a limb cut off, and in the picture, she saw a glimpse of how beautiful and intact she truly is.

These adolescents shared themes of perseverance, teamwork, confidence, strength, facing fears, goal achievement, community support, and trust building as we debriefed the life lessons learned from the outdoor Challenges Ropes courses. When we went on a field trip to advocate with legislators at the capitol, I remember students referencing the life-changing benefits they received from these therapeutic adventures. Furthermore, when interacting with sandtray miniatures designed for self-expression, these teenagers described receiving hope and empowerment from insights they gained, problem-solving benefits, and coping skills (Swank & Lenes, 2013).

Although this list is certainly not exhaustive, additional illustrations of therapeutic nature-related approaches include the following.

Counseling Considerations

We can use our power as mental health professionals to help with the process of clients receiving access to an animal companion. If this is an advocacy avenue you might like to take as a clinician, there are important differences to understand between emotional support and service animals (Owenby, 2022).

Plants in counseling offices can create a calming atmosphere that can be grounding for clients to focus on.

Dr. Sara Nash has demonstrated how writing and remembering song lyrics with nature analogies (e.g., "watching trees, dropping leaves, trying to let go" and "Green fruit don't fall ripe from the vine") can help cultivate patience, acceptance, and liberation.

Nature metaphors can bring forth clarity, new possibilities, and expansiveness. For example, Figure 13.3 is a photograph of a picture that was drawn by a dear friend (who is also a counselor) Kristen Shader, LPC, LMHC. She drew

FIGURE 13.3 Illustration with markers on construction paper of the imaginative pilgrimage of a kayak arriving to help a person feeling alone and lost in the middle of an overwhelming sea, full of resources and a map to a nearby island.

Source: Reproduced with permission from Kristen Shader.

this after listening to me describe feeling like I was metaphorically struggling to swim forward in the middle of a journey across a dissertation ocean.

Workshops

Nature Reminds Us has been offered with Dr. Nic Williams at the UF CWC in collaboration with UF Mindfulness. This is the description: Pausing. Feeling the breeze and ground beneath us is so powerful. There are so many therapeutic metaphors in what we see, hear, feel, smell, and taste in nature! Together, we can practice breathing.

LGBTQ+ Celebrating in Nature was co-created with Lisa Buning and Corrine Buchanan. This workshop is designed for people with LGBTQ+ identities to celebrate connection to nature and shared humanity. This space is for reflection, perspective taking, nature-based experiential activities, and community. Activities involve participants interacting with our immediate natural environment (plants, rocks, trees, flowers, pine cones, the sky, etc.).

Take a Hike: A CWC Walk-shop invites college students to walk together throughout nature paths on campus. To get a glimpse of that, the video at this link describes that weekly experience: www.youtube.com/watch?v= DXTujWsMcJE.

Experiencing the Sunset can be offered in many different venues, especially when you have access to bodies of water, mountains, hills, or spacious fields. Through this workshop, participants often receive an inner shift, as they see the ever-evolving shifting of clouds and light in the sky, the glimmering moon yet to rise.

Groups (Online or In-Person)

Calming Anxiety with Nature (CAN) includes nature-based meditations, emotional expression, expanded perspectives, interpersonal feedback, and support for challenging life circumstances. We meet outside and sit in camping chairs in a circle. We provide various anxiety-relieving strategies, as well as space for members to connect with themselves, one another, and the environment.

Understanding Self and Others through Nature (USON) is designed to help members to develop newfound comprehension, release emotions, learn about interpersonal feelings, and build trust while engaging with nature metaphors. We engage with poetry, imagery, photographs, and meaning making with natural items or scenes.

Community Organizations

Bike & Build entails being able to travel and visit different landscapes, while actively raising money and enduring physical laboring to assist with home construction. Someone who rode her bike across the country, in an effort for the affordable housing cause, shared that the perspective of a bike seat lent a deeper understanding into the communities who exist in these places and how to help them (M. Shuman, personal communication, February 22, 2022). More info is at this link: bikeandbuild.org.

Native Women's Wilderness honors and educates about ancestral lands and the voices of native women. For more information visit www.nativewomens wilderness.org.

Venture Project serves LGBTQIA + community members through outdoor activities to promote community building, leadership skills, and confidence. For more information visit www.ventureoutproject.com.

Wilderness Torah provides holiday retreats and opportunities for youth to experience spiritual teachings and traditions become alive amidst the elements. For more information, visit wildernesstorah.org/programs/youth-programs.

Outdoor Journal Tour was founded by two BIPOC women who invite hiking and healing through journaling. At this website, they offer a card deck of nature meditations: www.outdoorjournaltour.com/nature-meditations-deck.

Research

Therapeutic gardening can be a counseling approach for those experiencing bereavement related to suicide (Machado & Swank, 2019).

Latinx family-based nature activities can reinforce family relationships and cultural heritage (Izenstark et al., 2021).

The practice of Zulu, and expanding consciousness of balance, harmony, context, and interrelatedness can be vital for mental and spiritual healing of people of Afrikan descent (Washington, 2010).

Projects in urban areas involving human-nature relations, land-making, and wellness among Indigenous youth can promote feelings of belongingness and thriving (Hatala et al., 2019).

In Eastern and Western contexts, therapeutic landscapes, green public spaces, gardens strategically placed in healthcare facilities can have meaningful benefits (e.g., pressure relief, space for contemplation, communication, well-being; Jiang, 2014).

People with disabilities can travel to national parks for enrichment, escape and adventure (Chikuta et al., 2017).

Photo-elicitation can provide opportunities for people across the lifetime to explore, play, and find beauty in their lives (Swank et al., 2017).

Higher Education

In a *Multicultural Mindfulness* course, graduate and undergraduate students were invited to have portions of class sessions outdoors, where we created a stretching circle, inhaled and exhaled with one another, and connected across the differences.

For our campfire ritual in Dr. Mary Rockwood Lane's *Creativity and Spirituality in Healthcare* class, students threw in something that felt ready to be let go of. Students burned their raw dissertation notes, a bra from an ex-romantic partner, greeting cards, photographs, journals, etc. The dancing orange flames transformed and released stagnant energy, so that there was room for newfound spaciousness.

A Call to Action

For this call to action, we invite you to experience a complementary therapy that is new to you. Attend a yoga, meditation, or tai chi class or go to a local drumming circle in your community. Write a reflection paper about your experiences observing, engaging with, practicing, or sharing time and space doing something you have never done before. Describe the event or experience; who was there and what happened? How did you feel while engaging in the activity? What are your takeaways about what you learned and how you will integrate this learning into your counseling practice? How can you advocate for your clients gaining access to these potentially beneficial interventions?

Case Study 13.1

Imagine that you are doing a practicum at the university counseling center. Pavlo is a 20-year-old international college student. His family is in Lviv, Ukraine where the Russian invasion and atrocities of took place starting in the year 2022 and following the annexation of Crimea. Pavlo had just learned that one of his best friends who volunteered to fight in the war was killed in battle and he presented to you for help. He was clearly in crisis. He is angry, anxious, and depressed. He is also having difficulty sleeping and focusing in school work. He tells you that all his life he has been a devout Orthodox Christian and he feels God has abandoned the Ukranian people. He does not know what to believe anymore. He is holding back tears and is visibly shaken.

RESPONSE QUESTIONS

1. How would you approach Pavlo during the intake process?
2. Whom would you engage in your counseling center for guidance about next steps?
3. What do you think are the most important issues to address with Pavlo so you can best support him?
4. What types of interventions can you consider using to help Pavlo cope with his emotions and cognitions? What types of complementary therapies do you think he would benefit from? What resources would you consider using to help Pavlo with his presenting problems?
5. What else would you want to explore with him during the first session? During subsequent sessions?

Going Within: Spirituality Genograms

Counselors, teachers, and supervisors need to be comfortable with religious and spiritual matters, and gain clarity about their personal spiritual beliefs to effectively include a spiritual focus in their work (Haug, 1998). The purpose of constructing a personal spiritual genogram is threefold: to explore (1) one's personal history of spirituality and religiosity, (2) one's current understanding of spirituality and religiosity, and (3) the interaction between one's personal spirituality/religiosity and professional functioning.

Step 1: Constructing a Genogram

A genogram provides a structure for collecting and "storing" family information. It is similar to a family tree. The first step is to design your family genogram. If this is a new process to you, use the following guidelines and example. There is no "right" way to construct a genogram. Therefore, each person's genogram will be unique. Before you build your genogram, read stanfield.pbworks.com/f/explaining_genograms.pdf.

Now that you reviewed the genogram chart, start to build your own family genogram. In the course of drawing your genogram, identify individuals in the various generations (as many as you are able to) and their known religious or spiritual affiliations. List the religious or spiritual affiliation next to the icon for each person.

Step 2: Exploring and Collecting Historical Information

Step 2 entails gathering family information and "filling in" your genogram. Use the following questions as a guide to enhance historical knowledge concerning religion and spirituality within your multigenerational system. Remember, you are looking for facts and patterns related to spirituality and religiosity. You are a detective.

1. How important was religious practice or affiliation? What religious affiliations exist within your family?

2. What was the importance of religion in the extended family? How did it influence family members' beliefs (about human nature, life's meanings, etc.), feelings (such as hopelessness, caring, fear, guilt, etc.), their behaviors (in relationships inside or outside the family, religious practices, etc.)?

3. How have religious/spiritual beliefs influenced self-esteem, marriage, parenting, sexuality, and familial responsibilities and loyalties?

4. How has/does your family system celebrate rituals of connection: family meals, rising and retiring, coming and going, going out and going away, couple rituals, etc.?

5. How has/does the family system observe rituals of celebration and community: special-person rituals (birthdays, Mother's Day, Father's Day), Thanksgiving, Christmas, community and religious rituals, rituals of passage (weddings and funerals), etc.?

6. What do you see as the core spiritual, empowering messages embedded in your family's religious beliefs and practices?

7. Who in your extended family was particularly spiritual and how did it show in their way of life (cognitively, affectively, behaviorally) and through the life cycle?

8. In what ways was spirituality or religion ever a source of strength and/or a cause of conflict in the family? Explain.

9. What about the family's or specific family members' spirituality or religion did you personally experience as empowering or constraining?

10. What positive or negative messages did you get publicly or implicitly about other spiritual or religious beliefs and practices?

11. What are the unique features of the religious/spiritual orientation of your family?

Step 3: Clarifying Your Personal Spirituality or Religiosity

While Step 2 focused more on the past, Step 3 focuses on the present. Now is the time to ask yourself a series of questions about your own spirituality/religiosity. Remember to make abbreviated notes on your genogram, as your genogram probably includes a lot of information now. Use your discretion on what you add. Here are a few guiding questions:

1. Do you maintain a particular religious affiliation? If yes, how actively involved are you, and how does this translate into daily practice and lifestyle choices?

2. What does spirituality mean to you? Write a few keywords next to your name on your genogram.

3. How has your family's spiritual or religious heritage influenced your personal philosophy (about human nature, right action, wrong doing and forgiveness, life's meaning, etc.), your feeling (hopelessness, guilt, confidence, etc.), and your behavior?

4. How and through what experiences have these understandings changed through the years, particularly, how have they changed as a result of professional training? Have you seriously considered alternative beliefs and their consequences for your life? Explain.

5. What, if anything, about your spirituality or religion do you experience as confining or tyrannical? What do you experience as life enhancing or liberating?
6. How free are you to challenge unhelpful beliefs and choose more empowering alternatives? Explain.
7. How willing are you to act on your beliefs? Give examples.
8. What language (terms) are you comfortable using to convey spiritual beliefs?
9. How willing and comfortable are you in sharing your spiritual beliefs with clients? When do you think this might be appropriate?

Step 4: Linking Your Personal Spirituality with Professional Functioning

Step 4 entails reflecting upon your family history (Steps 1 and 2) and your personal understandings (Step 3) and exploring their influence/impact on your professional functioning. The following questions should get you started:

1. How do your spiritual beliefs inform your conceptualizations, attitudes, and behaviors within the counseling context—the way you constitute yourself in relation to clients, your view of human nature, relationships, and change, etc.?
2. How might your spirituality or religion help or hinder your effectiveness as a therapist, or make it difficult for you to work with particular clients?
3. How comfortable are you with other forms of spirituality or religion, including their language, rituals, and metaphors?
4. What, if any, religious/spiritual issues might clients raise that might make you uncomfortable?
5. How will you respond to clients whose beliefs or behaviors violate your personal spiritual beliefs?
6. Given your spiritual beliefs, what is your preferred model of counseling?

The following sources were used in the development of this exercise: Haug (1998), DeMaria et al. (1999), and Miller (1999).

Group Process

Engage in a small group follow-up discussion based on your spiritual genogram. You are encouraged to bring your genogram with you to share with the class. You may use these guiding questions:

1. What was most salient in the genogram?
2. What did you learn about your family system and your spiritual or religious upbringing?
3. What surprised you about the process?
4. How have you evolved in your own spiritual or religious beliefs and practices? How have you remained the same?

5. How does this exercise inform your approach to supporting clients in a discussion about their family and individual or personal values related to spirituality and/or religion?

RESOURCES

Adams, C. M., Puig, A., Baggs, A., & Wolf, C. P. (2015). Integrating religion and spirituality into counselor education: Barriers and strategies. Counselor Education and Supervision, 54, 44–56. doi: 10.1002/j.1556-6978.2015.00069.x

Association for Spiritual, Ethical, and Religious Values in Counseling Competencies: https://aservic.org/spiritual-and-religious-competencies

Duran, E. (2019). Healing the soul wound: Trauma-informed counseling for indigenous communities (2nd ed.). Teachers College Press.

Fukuyama, M. A., & Puig, A. (2016). Religion, spirituality and culture-oriented counseling. In P. B. Pedersen, W. J. Lonner, J. G. Draguns, J. E. Trimble, & M. R. Scharrón del Río (Eds.), Counseling across cultures: Toward inclusive cultural empathy (7th ed., pp. 477–498). Sage.

Fukuyama, M. A., Puig, A., Baggs, A., & Pence-Wolf, C. (2014). Exploring the intersections of religion and spirituality with race-ethnicity & gender in counseling. In M. L. Miville, & A. D. Ferguson (Eds.), Handbook of race-ethnicity and gender in psychology (pp. 23–44). Springer.

Fukuyama, M. A., Puig, A., Pence-Wolf, C., & Baggs, A. (2014). Religion and spirituality. In F. T. L. Leong, L. Comas-Diaz, G. Nagayama Hall, V. McLoyd, & J. Trimble (Eds.), The APA handbook of multicultural psychology, Vol. 1: Theory and research (pp. 519–534). American Psychological Association. https://doi.org/10.1037/14189-000

Goodwin, L. K., Lee, S. M., Puig, A., & Sherrard, P. A. D. (2005). Guided imagery and relaxation for women with early stage breast cancer. Journal of Creativity in Mental Health, 1(2), 53–66. https://doi.org/10.1300/J456v01n02_06

Hull, A. (n.d.). The unwritten rules of drum circle etiquette. DRUM! https://drummagazine.com/the-unwritten-rules-of-drum-circle-etiquette

Hull, A. (2022). Different types of drum circles. Village Music Circles. https://villagemusiccircles.com/different-types-of-drum-circles

Inclusive Genogram Symbols: https://stanfield.pbworks.com/f/explaining_genograms.pdf

Johnson, R. (2013). Spirituality in counseling and psychotherapy: An integrative approach that empowers clients. Wiley.

Jung, Carl: https://jungiancenter.org

Jung, C.G. (1955). Modern man in search of a soul. Harcourt Brace.

Jung, C.G. (2006). The undiscovered self: The dilemma of the individual in modern society. Penguin.

Jung, C. G., Read, H., Fordham, M., & Adler, G. (Eds.). (1953). The collected works of C.G. Jung. Pantheon Books.

Kabat-Zinn, J. (1991). Full catastrophe living: Using the wisdom of your body and mind to face stress, pain, and illness. Delta Trade Paperbacks.

Kabat-Zinn, J. (1994). Mindfulness meditation for everyday life. Piatkus Books.

Kabat-Zinn, J. (1994). Wherever you go, there you are: Mindfulness meditation in everyday life. Hyperion Books.

Kabat-Zinn, M., & J. (1997). Everyday blessings: The inner work of mindful parenting. Hyperion Books.

Kabat-Zinn, J. (2006). Coming to our senses: Healing ourselves and the world through mindfulness. (2006). Hyperion Books.

Kabat-Zinn, J. (2008). Arriving at your own door. Piatkus Books.

Kabat-Zinn, J. (2009). Letting everything become your teacher: 100 lessons in mindfulness. Dell Publishing Company.

Kabat-Zinn, J. (2012). Mindfulness for beginners: Reclaiming the present moment—And your life. Sounds True.

MacDonald, D. A. (2009). Identity and spirituality: Conventional and transpersonal perspectives. International Journal of Transpersonal Studies, 28(1), 86–106. https://doi.org/10.24972/ijts.2009.28.1.86

O'Connor, M. (2022, March 30). The best 7 instruments for drum circles. Electronic Drum Advisor. https://www.electronicdrumadvisor.com/drum-circles

Puig, A., & Adams, C. M. (2007). Introducing spirituality into multicultural counseling. In W. M. Parker & M. A. Fukuyama. Consciousness raising: A primer for multicultural counseling (3rd ed., pp. 181–203). Charles C Thomas Publisher.

Puig, A., Baggs, A., Mixon, K., Park, Y. M., Kim, B. Y., & Lee, S. M. (2012). Relationship between job burnout and personal wellness in mental health professionals. Journal of Employment Counseling, 49, 98–109. https://doi.org/10.1002/j.2161-1920.2012.00010.x

Puig, A., & Fukuyama, M. (2008). A qualitative investigation of multicultural expression of spirituality: Preliminary findings. Counseling and Spirituality, 27(2), 11–37.

Ratts, M. J., Singh, A. A., Nassar-McMillan, S., Butler, S. K., & McCullough, J. R. (2015). Multicultural and social justice counseling competencies. https://www.counseling.org/docs/default-source/competencies/multicultural-and-social-justice-counseling-competencies.pdf?sfvrsn=14

Rodriguez-Díaz, C. E., & Lewellen-Williams, C. (2020). Race and racism as structural determinants for emergency and recovery response in the aftermath of hurricanes Irma and Maria in Puerto Rico. Health Equity, 4(1), 232–238. https://doi.org/10.1089/heq.2019.0103

Rosmarin, D., & Koenig, H. (Eds). (2020). Handbook of spirituality, religion, and mental health. Academic Press.

Taylor, G. T., Bylund, C. L., Kastrinos, A., Alpert, J., Puig, A., Krajewski, J., Sharma, B., & Fisher, C. L. (2022). Practicing mindfulness through mobile applications: Emerging adults' health-enhancing and inhibiting experiences. International Journal of Environmental Research and Public Health, 19(5), 2619. https://doi.org/10.3390/ijerph19052619

Transpersonal Psychology. (n.d.). Types of transpersonal therapy. https://www.psychologytoday.com/us/therapy-types/transpersonal-therapy

Tristan, J., Nguyen-Hong-Nhiem, L., & Tristan, J. T. (1989). Horticultural therapy and Asian refugee resettlement. Journal of Therapeutic Horticulture, 4, 15–20.

Access this podcast at http://connect.springerpub.com/content/book/978-0-8261-6386-8/chapter/ch13.

KEY REFERENCES

Only key references appear in the print edition. The full reference list appears in the digital product found on https://connect.springerpub.com/content/book/978-0-8261-6386-8/chapter/ch13

Association for Spiritual, Ethical and Religious Values in Counseling. (2009). *Spiritual competencies: Competencies for addressing spiritual and religious issues in counseling.* http://www.aservic.org/spiritual-and-religious-competencies

Cashwell, C. S., & Young, J. S. (2020). *Integrating spirituality and religion into counseling: A guide to competent practice.* American Counseling Association.

DeMaria, R., Weeks, G., & Hof, L. (1999). *Intergenerational assessment of individuals, couples, and families: Focused genograms.* Brunner/Mazel.

Friedman, H. (2014). Finding meaning through transpersonal approaches in clinical psychology: Assessments and psychotherapies. *International Journal of Existential Psychology and Psychotherapy, 5*(1), 45–49.

Fukuyama, M. A., & Sevig, T. D. (2012). *Integrating spirituality into multicultural counseling.* Sage.

Grof, S. (2008). Brief history of transpersonal psychology. *International Journal of Transpersonal Studies, 27*(1), 46–54. https://doi.org/10.24972/ijts.2008.27.1.46

Huang, J. (2010). Counseling persons from Eastern religions and spiritualities. In J. G. Ponterotto, J. M. Casas, L. A. Suzuki, & C. M. Alexander (Eds.), *Handbook of multicultural counseling* (3rd ed., pp. 491–501). Sage.

Niazi, A. K., & Niazi, S. K. (2011). Mindfulness-based stress reduction: a non-pharmacological approach for chronic illnesses. *North American Journal of Medical Sciences, 3*(1), 20–23. https://doi.org/10.4297/najms.2011.320

Ratts, M. J., Singh, A. A., Nassar-McMillan, S., Butler, S. K., & McCullough, J. R. (2015). *Multicultural and social justice counseling competencies.* https://www.counseling.org/docs/default-source/competencies/multicultural-and-social-justice-counseling-competencies.pdf?sfvrsn=14

CHAPTER 14

CURRENT TRENDS IN COUNSELING AND THE FUTURE OF COUNSELING

Jacqueline M. Swank and Ana Puig

Think about this...

What are current trends that are influencing counseling now and how might counseling continue to evolve in the future? How might you apply the concepts of advocacy, social justice, and intersectionality to clients impacted by these emerging trends?

LEARNING OBJECTIVES

After reading this chapter, you should be able to:

- Outline neurocounseling practice and its influence on the mental health field

- Recognize telemental health as a format to providing counseling, especially post-COVID-19 pandemic

- Discuss the effects of an aging population on counseling services and needs for clients and their caregivers

- Evaluate the influence of social media on counseling

- Discuss climate change as a growing mental health and counseling concern

- Analyze the effect of internationalization of mental health awareness and client needs

- Discuss emerging novel psychopharmacological therapies and client populations that may benefit from this emerging trend

INTRODUCTION

The chapter highlights important emerging trends and areas of focus in the counseling profession. We see these as issues informing counseling practice now and in the future. From the increased understanding of brain functioning and how it can inform our perception of mental and emotional health and illness to the more recent exploration of novel psychedelic therapies to address depression and anxiety, and enhance recovery from trauma, we expect these developments to increase in popularity and become integrated more in counseling practice and research. In the sections that follow, we discuss the following trends: (a) neuro-informed counseling, (b) telemental health, (c) counseling the aging population and their caregivers, (d) social media's influence in counseling, (e) addressing climate change in counseling, (f) international counseling, and (g) novel psychopharmacological therapies.

NEURO-INFORMED COUNSELING

Neuroscience focuses on the study of the nervous system, and research in this area has enhanced understanding of emotions, behaviors, and cognitions (Beeson & Field, 2017). Neurocounseling or neuro-informed (neuroscience-informed) counseling involves

integrating neuroscience principles related to the nervous system and physiological processes underlying all human functioning into the practice of counseling for the purpose of enhancing clinical effectiveness in the screening and diagnosis of physiological functioning and mental disorders, treatment planning and delivery, evaluation of outcomes, and wellness promotion. (Beeson & Field, 2017, p. 74)

In learning about neurocounseling, it is important to understand some basic concepts of neurobiology, including the structure of the brain (understood through the hand metaphor described by Siegel, 2012), neuroplasticity (brain is shaped by experiences), which occurs across the lifespan, and neurogenesis (brain's ability to develop cells called neurons and neural networks; Lorelle & Michel, 2017). It is also important to understand the brain's role in attachment, as well as the effect trauma has on the brain (Lorelle & Michel, 2017). Social justice issues (e.g., racism, poverty, oppression, discrimination) create stress and can result in trauma that affects brain development (Ivey & Zalaquett, 2011). Therefore, neurocounseling is important to consider in working with marginalized groups.

Neurocounseling encompasses multiple forms, including conducting neuroscience research, using neuroscience research to understand counseling processes and client concerns (translational neuroscience), and the use of brain-based techniques, such as neurofeedback (Beeson & Field, 2017). Neurofeedback is a type of biofeedback that helps people develop healthy brain functioning by reinforcing positive brain activity through positive feedback and providing negative feedback for negative brain activity in response to the measurement of brain waves (Marzbani et al., 2016). While researchers have found support for the use of neurofeedback, it is not a brief treatment, as it may require

20–60 sessions to reach the desired outcome long-term (Myers & Young, 2012). Counselors can also use neuroeducation, which involves educating clients about the nervous system and the brain (information on neuroplasticity, brain functions and structures, and memory) to help reduce distress and improve client outcomes by fostering empathy for oneself, instilling hope that change is possible, and understanding setbacks are part of the counseling process (Miller, 2016). Furthermore, clinicians can use a metaphor-based approach, described by Luke (2019), which involves using metaphors to understand the functioning of the brain and life experiences.

Some counseling researchers have examined neurocounseling outcomes. Specifically, Field et al. (2016) found clients who participated in neuroscience-informed cognitive behavioral therapy had reduced symptoms of anxiety and depression. Additionally, Russell-Chapin et al. (2013) found support for the use of neurofeedback with children diagnosed and receiving medication for attention deficit hyperactivity disorder (ADHD). Dreis et al. (2015) also found improvements in clients' perceived well-being in using neurofeedback. Interest in neurocounseling is also apparent in the development of interest networks focused on neurocounseling within counseling organizations, including the American Counseling Association (ACA), the American Mental Health Counselors Association (AMHCA), and the Association for Counselor Education and Supervision (ACES). Furthermore, the (AMHCA, 2020) has a section on the biological bases of behavior (BBB) within the AMHCA Standards for the Practice of Clinical Mental Health Counseling. Thus, while there are efforts to advance neurocounseling, more research and training are needed in this area.

As with any treatment approach, there are cautions and considerations to be aware of when using neurocounseling with clients. Luke et al. (2020) identified a variety of concerns and ethical considerations. Specifically, clients may want only psychotropic medication without counseling if they believe their mental health concerns are solely biologically based. Counselors may also have biases when using neurocounseling by relying too much on biology, without valuing the client's experience. It is important for counselors to view biological aspects as one area of consideration, not the only area, as it is crucial to view clients holistically. Training is also essential before implementing neurocounseling with clients, which emphasizes the need for consistent training standards, and identifying the scope of practice for counselors regarding neuroscience. Counselors should stay abreast on the research related to neurocounseling and ensure that they are not stretching the interpretation of findings. Furthermore, there is a need for counseling research on neuroscience to expand understanding of its efficacy in counseling practice and to inform training.

TELEMENTAL HEALTH

Telemental health (TMH) is the use of technology to facilitate mental health services without the provider and client being in the same physical location. This may involve various communication mechanisms (e.g., video conferencing, phone calls, text messages, email). Other terms used for TMH include online counseling, e-counseling, teletherapy, virtual counseling, and internet-based counseling, to name a few.

In the 1950s, TMH emerged with mental health providers, such as Van Lear Johnson using closed circuit television at the Nebraska Psychiatric Institute to facilitate group therapy and consultation (Adams et al., 2018). Despite being beneficial, especially for rural areas where care was not easily accessible, TMH was expensive and cost prohibitive in the early years for many providers. As technology became more advanced in the last few decades, it also became less expensive and more accessible (Adams et al., 2018). This created more interest in TMH among mental health providers. In 1997, the National Board for Certified Counselors (NBCC) adopted the first set of standards regarding TMH for mental health providers (*Standards for the Ethical Practice of WebCounseling*). As TMH evolved, NBCC revised the standards and created *The Practice of Internet Counseling*, which they retitled in 2016 as the *NBCC Policy Regarding the Provision of Distance Professional Services* (NBCC, 2016). NBCC also has a credential titled *Board Certified-TeleMental Health Provider* (BC-TMH).

To promote the ethical use of TMH and other forms of technology in counseling, the American Counseling Association (ACA) included a new section in the 2014 version of the *ACA Code of Ethics* entitled Section H: Distance Counseling, Technology, and Social Media. This was a crucial step in providing quality care through TMH. Although TMH is not a treatment approach, but instead a format to provide treatment, there are important ethical and legal areas to consider. For example, counselors need to be familiar with licensure parameters when providing TMH with clients in another state. Counselors need to also consider confidentiality, and security and privacy concerns. In additional to ensuring the counselor is in a private space, the counselor should also discuss with the client the identification of a private time and space in their home where they will not be interrupted or overheard during sessions. It is also important for the counselor to engage in the informed consent process with the client, which will include areas specific to TMH (e.g., facilitation of sessions, procedures for technological difficulties, emergency procedures, risks and benefits of format) (ACA, 2014, Standard H.2.a).

Although TMH was gaining in popularity, many practitioners still chose not to use TMH, until the COVID-19 pandemic changed everything in 2020. The pandemic increased the need for mental health services, while presenting challenges for offering face-to-face services due to social distancing requirements. Clinicians who had limited, if any, experience and interest in providing TMH needed to quickly educate themselves on providing counseling in this format to be able to continue serving their existing clients and help meet the increasing demand for mental health services. Fortunately, many practitioners and clients had access to technology that made TMH an option for them during the pandemic. However, TMH is unfortunately not realistic for all current and potential clients due to existing barriers, such as financial constraints limiting access. Additionally, some remote rural areas continue to have limited cell phone and internet access. Thus, although TMH has increased accessibility for mental health services, underserved and marginalized populations may struggle with obtaining TMH services.

In considering the use of TMH, it is important to examine the effectiveness of this approach in comparison to in-person mental health services. In a review of published studies, Hilty et al. (2013) found TMH was effective for assessment and diagnosis with multiple populations, including children and adults, encompassing the elderly as well. It was also effective in multiple settings and was comparable to in-person services. Hilty et al. (2013) found TMH increased access to care and clients reported satisfaction with TMH. Additionally, Simpson and Reid (2014) conducted a review of 23 TMH studies, specifically focusing on the therapeutic alliance within videoconferencing sessions. They found clients rated presence and bond as strongly in TMH sessions as during in-person sessions. Clients reported personal space and more control contributed to the therapeutic alliance. Clinicians also reported a moderate to strong therapeutic alliance with clients during TMH. Thus, research supports the use of TMH.

Clinicians' views about TMH may influence their use of it; therefore, it is important to explore clinicians' attitudes with using this treatment format. Connolly et al. (2020) reviewed 38 studies on clinicians' attitudes about TMH, specifically the use of videoconferencing, and found they rated the format positive overall. Additionally, clinicians' views about TMH improved with continued use, despite some still preferring in-person services. Furthermore, clients viewed TMH more positively than clinicians did. The researchers identified four constructs that encompassed both positive and negative aspects identified by clinicians: (a) performance expectancy, (b) effort expectancy, (c) social influence, and (d) facilitating conditions. See Table 14.1 to examine the positive and negative aspects of the four constructs.

In considering the use of TMH, it is crucial that clinicians attend training to facilitate ethical and effective implementation of this treatment format. Additionally, counselors should ensure they have the technology and technological support to implement and sustain TMH counseling. Furthermore, it is crucial to help clients prepare for and use this treatment format, as well as acknowledge that clients will have varying levels of comfort with engaging in TMH. Thus, while there are benefits to using TMH, there are also negative aspects, and some clients may still prefer in-person counseling when possible. Furthermore, as stated earlier, some clients may not have the necessary resources to engage in remote sessions using TMH and therefore need in-person services.

COUNSELING AN AGING POPULATION AND THEIR CAREGIVERS

The U.S. population of people age 65 and older in 2019 was 54.1 million (30 million women and 24.1 million men), representing 16% of the total U.S. population (ACL, 2021). As the older adult population increases, the need for caregiving also increases for this population. In 2020, the National Alliance for Caregiving and AARP published a report regarding caregiving of people 50 years old and older in the United States. They found 41.8 million people (16.8% of the U.S. population) reported being caregivers for someone age 50 or older. Caregivers reported the needs of those they are providing care for have increased, along with the number of conditions the care recipients are

TABLE 14.1 CLINICIANS' VIEWS OF POSITIVE AND NEGATIVE ASPECTS OF VIDEOCONFERENCING IN TELEMENTAL HEALTH

CONSTRUCT	POSITIVE ASPECTS	NEGATIVE ASPECTS
Performance expectancy	Cost and time efficiency	Impersonal
	Increased access	Legal and safety issues
	Increased effectiveness	Confidentiality and security issues
	Client satisfaction	Concern that clients would not like it
	New opportunities	Concerns about conducting an in-depth assessment
	Greater flexibility	Thinking it was inappropriate for some clients
Effort expectancy	Usability	Technology problems
Social influence	Organizational support	Lack of support and communication from leadership
Facilitating conditions	Technical support	Limited equipment, funding, space, training, and technical support

Source: Data from Connolly, S. L., Miller, C. J., Lindsay, J. A., & Bauer, M. S. (2020). A systematic review of providers' attitudes toward telemental health via videoconferencing. *Clinical Psychology Science and Practice, 27*(2) 12311. https://doi.org/10.1111/cpsp.12311

experiencing. As the number of caregivers has increased, the well-being of caregivers has decreased with 20% reporting their health is fair to poor, 40% reporting caregiving as highly emotionally stressful, and another 28% reporting it as being moderately emotionally stressful. However, 51% reported that caregiving provided them with meaning in life and a sense of purpose. Worse health is reported by caregivers of marginalized groups (e.g., racial and ethnic minorities, lower household income, lower level of education; National Alliance for Caregiving & AARP, 2020). See Table 14.2 for additional statistics about older adults and their caregivers.

The increasing number of older adults and the comorbidity of conditions among them, as well as the increase in caregivers and their reported levels of stress and overall health concerns underscore the need for counseling services for older adults and their caregivers. However, trends in counseling do not support this increasing need. This includes a lack of emphasis on both research and training. Regarding research, Fullen et al. (2019) found that only 1.68% of articles

TABLE 14.2 STATISTICS ABOUT OLDER ADULTS AND THEIR CAREGIVERS

OLDER ADULTS
25% were members of a racial or ethnic minority group
4.9 million lived below the poverty line and 2.6 million identified as "near poor"
9.8 million were working or seeking work
1.1 million were raising a grandchild
CAREGIVERS
89% were caring for a relative
4 years was the average length of care
22 hours was average length of care per week
Caregivers of color more often reported that they cared for someone who resided with them
Number of individuals requiring care increased by 7.6 million in the last 5 years

Source: Adapted from the Administration for Community Living. (2021). *2020 profile of older Americans.* Author. https://acl.gov/sites/default/files/Aging%20and%20Disability%20in%20America/2020ProfileOlderAmericans.Final_.pdf; National Alliance for Caregiving, & AARP. (2020). *Caregiving in the U.S. 2020: A focused look at family caregivers of adults age 50+.* Author. https://doi.org/10.26419/ppi.00103.022

across a 26-year span focused on gerontological counseling. Additionally, the Council for Accreditation for Counseling and Related Educational Programs (CACREP) dropped the gerontological counseling track from the 2009 Standards due to only two programs having the specialization area since introducing the standards in 1992 (Bobby, 2013). Not only does this create concern regarding lack of counselor preparation in working with older adults, it also ignores the need for advocacy to address ageism (stigma toward older adults; Fullen, 2018) and other issues affecting older adults such as Medicare reimbursement (Fullen et al., 2019). Thus, a need exists for advocacy for training standards, more research, and further education about the need for counseling for older adults and their caregivers.

Older adults may experience physical, cognitive, mental health (e.g., depression, anxiety, grief and loss, suicidality, substance abuse), sexuality and sexual expression, and financial concerns. They may also struggle with making decisions about retirement, living arrangements, and end-of-life decisions. An additional strain some older adults experience relates to serving as a caregiver for their spouse or other caregiving responsibilities, such as raising their grandchildren. Marginalized groups may experience additional concerns (e.g., LGBT elders may fear discrimination, have strained family relationships, and have lack of support and access to resources (Kimmel, 2014). Therefore, older adults need support to help navigate the complexity of concerns they may experience in life.

Researchers have examined the effectiveness of various types of counseling with older adults. In a review of animal-assisted interventions with older adults, Bernabei et al. (2013) found a reduction in agitation and improved social interactions among those with dementia, as well as improved communication and coping skills. They also found promising results in the use of a pet robot. Additionally, Virués-Ortega et al. (2012) found support for animal-assisted therapy with improving social interactions and reducing depression among those with psychiatric conditions, and reducing behavioral disturbances among those with dementia. Branson et al. (2019) also found older adults identified having strong, secure relationships with family members, such as adult children and grandchildren, as being a significant factor in successfully navigating living transitions. This emphasizes the importance of family counseling inventions (e.g., systemic counseling) that focus on strengthening family relationships. In a review of suicide prevention strategies, Okolie et al. (2017) found support for primary care interventions due to frequent contact older adults generally have with physicians. Additional interventions included screening for depression, referrals for counseling, counseling (including telehealth via phone), pharmacotherapy, community-based programs, and group interventions (Okolie et al., 2017). Researchers have also found support for interventions focused on memories, gratitude, and forgiveness in decreasing anxiety and depression, and improving life satisfaction and happiness (Ramírez et al., 2014).

When considering the older adult population, it is also crucial to bear in mind the needs of caregivers. Caregivers may experience a myriad of challenges, including role transition and role strain, depression, isolation, financial concerns, anxiety (Jenkins, 2019), decreased personal time, additional stress, and lack of social and emotional support (Collins & Hawkins, 2016). However, some caregivers also report satisfaction from being a caregiver (Jenkins, 2019). Among caregivers, more African American women are caregivers than White women, with elders held in high esteem in the African American culture, and kinship bond and collective responsibility valued by their culture (Jenkins, 2019). In discussing the caregiving challenges of African American families in particular, Collins and Hawkins (2016) reported that African American families often rely on informal support systems (e.g., friends, church), instead of formal support services (e.g., professionals), because they do not trust professional service providers, believe formal systems may be biased, or think these systems will not recognize the importance of their cultural experiences. The church can help address this concern by partnering with service providers or hiring professionals as members of the church staff to work with families, including offering space to facilitate caregiver support groups (Collins & Hawkins, 2016).

Counselors can help support caregivers by providing psychoeducation on caring for the elderly, connecting them with resources, and helping them develop coping skills and self-care practices to help avoid feeling overwhelmed, isolated, and burnout, and identifying resources for them (Jenkins, 2019; Thorson-Olesen & Eckert, 2014). Using a strength-based approach, as well as humor, may also be beneficial in working with caregivers (Thorson-Olesen & Eckert, 2014). Jenkins (2019) also described multiple models that counselors

TABLE 14.3 SOCIAL MEDIA PLATFORM USAGE OF ADULTS AND ADOLESCENTS

PLATFORM	ADULT USAGE	ADOLESCENT USAGE
YouTube	73%	85%
Facebook	69%	51%
Instagram	37%	72%
Pinterest	28%	
LinkedIn	27%	
Snapchat	24%	69%
Twitter	22%	32%
WhatsApp	20%	
Reddit	11%	7%
Tumblr		9%

Note: Blank cells indicate data was not reported for this area.
Source: Adapted from Anderson, M., & Jiang, J. (2018). *Teens, social media, and technology.* Pew Research Center. https://www.pewresearch.org/internet/2018/05/31/teens-social-media-tech-nology-2018; Perrin, A., & Anderson, M. (2019). *Share of U.S. adults using social media, including Facebook, is mostly unchanged since 2018.* Pew Research Center. https://www.pewresearch.org/fact-tank/2019/04/10/share-of-u-s-adults-using-social-media-including-facebook-is-mostly-un-changed-since-2018

may consider using with caregivers, including the Relational-Cultural Model of Development, Finding a Balance Point Model, Cognitive Stress and Coping Model, Empowerment Practice Group Model, and wellness approaches. Furthermore, in a review of internet-based supportive intervention for caregivers of individuals with dementia, Boots et al. (2014) found some support for these interventions improving caregiver well-being, including increasing self-efficacy and confidence and decreasing depression. They also found caregivers may benefit from communication with other caregivers and coaches. Thus, a need exists for advocacy regarding the training of counselors to work with older clients and their caregivers as well as promoting research in this area.

SOCIAL MEDIA'S INFLUENCE ON COUNSELING

Social media involves using various forms of electronic communication to share information and interact with others in online communities (Merriam-Webster, n.d.). There are numerous social media platforms that adults and adolescents report using in their lives; however, platform preferences of adults and youth differ (see Table 14.3). Additionally, regarding adults users, approximately 75% of Facebook users, and over 50% of users on Instagram, Snapchat, and YouTube also reported using the sites at least daily (Perrin & Anderson, 2019). Among youth, 95% reported having access to a smartphone, and 45% reported being online almost constantly. Thus, social media use is common among adolescents and adults; however, specific platform and app preference differs by age group.

With the abundance of social media use among youth and adults, it is important to consider how it may influence counseling, as well as the integration within counseling. Counselors have various options related to social media use and its use within their counseling practice. Crtalic et al. (2015) reported that counselors might ignore social media completely, have personal accounts but not integrate it within their professional work, use it professionally only, or use it personally and professionally. Although there are many areas to consider, Crtalic et al. (2015) remarked that it is unlikely that counselors can just avoid social media to prevent ethical dilemmas due to the prevalence of use among youth and adults. Therefore, it is important to be proactive in considering use of social media personally and professionally and how counselors may address ethical concerns related to use.

Before using social media in counseling, it is important for counselors to engage in training to develop competency in using this technology in counseling (Jordan et al., 2014). Communication through social media is different from in-person communication and there are important ethical considerations to think about regarding its use in counseling. Jordan et al. (2014) reported counselors might be engaging in a dual relationship with clients when they interact with them through social media (e.g., friending a client on Facebook, responding to online posts). Counselors should use caution to avoid blurring boundaries with clients. This includes separating personal and professional social media accounts and staying informed on privacy setting to restrict access to information shared on personal accounts (Johnson, 2011). Additionally, clinicians should also avoid accessing clients' personal information on social media, unless there is a therapeutic purpose for doing so within the counseling relationship (Jordan et al., 2014). Moreover, counselors should never post any information about clients on social media, even if the information does not identify a specific client (Johnson, 2011). It is also important for counselors to be aware that clients may discover personal information about them through the counselor's accidental disclosure of information through social media, even if the account is personal and the client does not have access to it. This is important as clients' awareness of this information may affect the therapeutic relationship (Knox et al., 2019). Thus, counselors may consider what they post on social media and what their reaction might be if a client discovered this information intentionally or unintentionally.

Regardless of whether counselors use social media in counseling, the prevalence of use among youth and adults will likely result in counselors needing to address it to some degree with their clients. Knox et al. (2019) reported that counselors should be prepared to address friend requests from clients. This involves reflecting on their thoughts and feelings related to potential requests and how they may respond to them. Addressing social media before it becomes an issue helps prevent negative client outcomes, such as the client feeling unwanted, ashamed, embarrassed, or rejected when the counselor does not respond to their social media requests, denies their friend request, or unfriends the client (Knox et al., 2019). To be proactive in addressing social media, counselors may consider developing a social media policy within their informed consent document that addresses multiple areas of social media use (e.g., friend requests, communication through social media sites). Dr. Keely Kolmes' social media policy is available online as an example that counselors may consider in developing their own policy (www.drkkolmes.com/docs/socmed.pdf).

Perspectives about social media may differ among individuals who grew up with it (social media natives) compared with individuals who have witnessed the emergence of social media during their lifetime and integrated it into their adult lives (social media immigrants) (Prensky, 2001). This is important to consider as these groups may view ethics related to social media differently (Crtalic et al., 2015). The unique ethical dilemmas presented by social media has prompted mental health organizations to integrate ethical standards regarding social media within their ethical codes (e.g., ACA [2014] *Code of Ethics*). Crtalic et al. (2015) emphasizes the importance of understanding the unique privacy settings and features of each social media platform and/or app the counselor is considering using in counseling. It is also important for the counselor to have information about social media practices used by the client, even if the counselor will not be using it within the counseling process. This is important because social media may be a significant influence (positive or negative) in the client's life that is worth discussing in counseling.

Crtalic et al. (2015) describe a variety of benefits and challenges of integrating social media within counseling. Similarly to using TMH, social media provides clients an opportunity to access services that may be difficult to access in person due to distance to travel for counseling, especially in rural areas. Additionally, an individual who is comfortable with social media may feel more comfortable engaging in counseling services using it, and it may help reduce stigma associated with attending counseling in-person. Therefore, clients who would otherwise not pursue counseling may be open to exploring it. It also allows clients to access services outside the traditional office hours' timeframe. Clients may also network with others outside their geographical area who are experiencing similar concerns for peer support, as well as connect with counselors with specialty areas outside their region. Moreover, counselors can use social media to help market their practice, as well as connect with other counselors across the world. Counselors may consider blogging, which can help establish themselves as experts, using this format to share research and recommendations regarding mental health. However, when blogging, it is crucial to monitor comments, or disengage this feature (Johnson, 2011). Counselors and clients can also use social media to educate others about mental health concerns to raise awareness and advocate for mental health services (Crtalic et al., 2015). Thus, there are many benefits of integrating social media within counseling.

Although it can be advantageous to use social media in various ways within counseling, Crtalic et al. (2015) also discuss challenges with using it. Similar to TMH, issues may arise related to privacy and confidentiality. When communicating without seeing the client, the counselor should establish a practice for how they know the person they are interacting with is actually their client and not someone else pretending to be their client. Lack of nonverbal communication may also present a challenge in social media communication, as clients and counselors can misinterpret written messages. Finally, there is always a chance of technological difficulties when communicating through internet-based platforms. Thus, counselors work to minimize challenges associated with social media use to support clients who want to integrate social media at varying levels within the counseling process.

ADDRESSING CLIMATE CHANGE IN COUNSELING

Climate change refers to significant modifications in weather patterns resulting in gradual environmental changes across time (e.g., increased temperatures, rising sea levels), as well as increased intensity and frequency of severe weather, such as heat waves, droughts, floods, wildfires, and hurricanes (NASA.gov, n.d.). Climate change is a significant issue for counselors, as researchers report that up to 54% of adults and 45% of children experience depression following a natural disaster (APHA, n.d.). Berry et al. (2010) reported that natural disasters resulting from climate change may affect mental health directly or indirectly. It may have direct effects through exposure to trauma, as well as increased prevalence of anxiety that may lead to more chronic, long-term mental health concerns. Indirect mental health effects may include (a) physical injury and health problems that result in mental health concerns and (b) damage to the natural environment that affects the social environment and community well-being.

Clayton et al. (2017) discussed physical and mental health concerns, as well as community effects that result from the devastating consequences of severe weather, including loss of life, property damage, displacement, strained relationship and loss of support systems, loss of autonomy, loss of personal and occupational identity, and violence. Physical health concerns include various injuries, heat-related illness, heart attacks, allergies, obesity resulting from a change in fitness routine due to temperature changes, and other illnesses. Mental health concerns include anxiety, depression, stress, shock, trauma, posttraumatic stress disorder (PTSD), complicated grief, substance use, and suicidality. However, people may also experience posttraumatic growth (positive psychological change) following a natural disaster (Clayton et al., 2017). Finally, community effects include loss of cohesion and belonging and increased crime (Clayton et al., 2017).

Although climate change affects everyone, it does not affect everyone equally. Clayton et al. (2017) discussed populations that are more vulnerable to the psychological effects of climate change. This includes people who rely on the natural environment for their livelihood (e.g., farmers). Additionally, marginalized groups and disadvantaged communities may lack sufficient physical, financial, and mental health resources. Indigenous people are also at high risk related to losing their cultural heritage. Moreover, climate change may affect the growth and development of children. Individuals with chronic physical and mental health concerns, as well as the elderly and women, are also at greater risk (Clayton et al., 2017).

Hilert (2021) proposed that counselors embrace the role of environmental justice advocates by applying the Multicultural and Social Justice Counseling Competencies (MCSJCC; Ratts et al., 2016). As we have already outlined herein, Hilert also highlights that climate change effects worsen social inequities, adding that these inequities coupled with extant systemic racism affect the most vulnerable among us; namely marginalized, disenfranchised, poor communities. Hilert (2021) proposed integration of the MCSJCC and environmental justice also highlights the role on intersectionality. He explains issues of environmental racism were central to environmental justice; however, the understanding of this concept has more recently been influenced by other theories (e.g., critical race, Indigenous, ecofeminism, among others; see Sarathy, 2018 for an in-depth discussion). Additionally, both the MCSJCC and the environmental justice tenets emphasize a socioecological perspective and expand our understanding of contextual factors that influence the emotional and mental well-being of people exposed to climate change. Hilert also contends that we must also acknowledge "climate change is an international crisis that will exacerbate social inequality on a global scale" (p. 182). Furthermore, Hilert's article offers an array of examples about the various ways counselors can become ready to apply the MCSJCC to their environmental justice work (see Table 14.4).

It is crucial for counselors to consider their role in addressing the mental health effects of climate change. In a survey of 382 helping professionals (counselors, psychologists, and social workers), Reese et al. (n.d) found approximately 45% of participants felt incompetent to address climate change within counseling. Only 5% of the helping professionals reported having training in addressing climate change within counseling, and less than 10% reported access to resources related to climate change, with the most desired resources being fact sheets focused on climate change and mental health and research on the mental health effects of climate change. Thus, it is crucial for counseling preparation programs to consider integrating content in the curriculum about the effects of climate change on mental health, as well as organizations such as ACA developing resources on climate change to help counselors in addressing this issue with clients.

ACA issued a statement on climate change in 2018 acknowledging the effects it has on mental health and wellness, and the role counselors have in promoting advocacy, education, and research about climate change (ACA, 2018). The organization also developed a task force to develop resources for counselors related to climate change, with the committee still working on developing these resources. Clayton et al. (2017) emphasize the role of mental health professionals related to climate change. This includes learning about climate change and the effects it has on mental health and reflecting on one's own beliefs about climate change and how it is affecting one's physical and mental health. Additionally, counselors can engage in conversations with other counselors and mental health professionals about climate change, as well as conduct workshops and presentations on the topic to create a more informed profession. Counselors can also be leaders in their communities to educate others about the effects climate change has on mental health and to advocate for climate solutions. Furthermore, counselors can support national and international initiatives regarding climate change, which may include educating a broader audience about the mental health effects of climate change to influence public policy.

Clayton et al. (2017) also provide strategies to support individuals in becoming resilient, including (a) foster a belief in personal resilience, (b) promote optimism, (c) develop healthy coping skills, (d) connect to a source of personal

TABLE 14.4 APPLYING MCSJCC TO ENHANCE ENVIRONMENTAL JUSTICE

MCSJCC DOMAINS	COUNSELOR ACTIVITIES
Counselor self-awareness	Explore and reflect on your identities, attitudes, beliefs, and the influence of your privilege and/or oppression upon these. Examine the role you play in climate change via inaction or engagement in unsustainable behaviors. Embrace antiracism and humility as part of your counselor identity. Immerse yourself in nature and mindfulness practice to develop appreciation for the Earth.
Client worldview	Develop understanding of diverse cultures, worldviews, and their social group status. Develop awareness of systemic racism issues in your community, the nation, and the world. Adopt a strength-based approach to client care, highlighting resilience and inherent assets of their social group membership and facilitating exploration of grief, loss, and trauma.
Counseling relationships	Understand how your privilege as counselor influences your relationship to your clients. Learn to recognize and process issues of power, privilege, and oppression with your clients. Learn about climate change and injustices in your area and advocate for clients, as needed, via active community engagement and outreach. Utilize a culturally responsive and trauma-informed approach to clients, including tapping into their spiritual and social support systems, as applicable.

(continued)

TABLE 14.4 APPLYING MCSJCC TO ENHANCE ENVIRONMENTAL JUSTICE (*CONTINUED*)

MCSJCC DOMAINS	COUNSELOR ACTIVITIES
Counseling interventions and advocacy	Broach discussions of multicultural concerns and use interventions that align with your client's worldview. Learn about ways to promote psychological and climate resilience to help clients actively cope with their losses and preempt future ones. Advocate for green spaces in urban communities, as applicable to your clients and contexts, including public policy at the local, regional, national, and global levels.

MCSJCC, Multicultural and Social Justice Counseling Competencies
Source: Data from Hilert, A. J. (2021). Counseling in the Anthropocene: Addressing social justice amid climate change. *Journal of Multicultural Counseling and Development, 49*(3), 175–191. https://doi.org/10.1002/jmcd.12223

meaning, (e) encourage preparedness (e.g., emergency plan, emergency kit), (f) promote social support and connectedness, (g) remain connected to a physical place that has meaning to avoid solastalgia (feeling of losing a physical place [e.g., natural landscape] that is important to an individual, resulting in being forced to migrate), and (h) stay connected to one's culture. Furthermore, researchers provide strategies for supporting communities to prepare for and address mental health concerns related to natural disasters, as well as gradual effects of climate change. Some of these strategies include strengthening community mental health services including reducing disparities by improving access and funding (Clayton et al., 2017; Hayes et al., 2018), fostering community cohesion and engagement, keeping the community informed, creating a postdisaster plan (Clayton et al., 2017), monitoring ED visits and other health-related data following natural disasters and other climate change events (e.g., heat waves), providing training for first responders and other health providers (e.g., psychological first aid), and creating resiliency plans (Hayes et al., 2018). Thus, counselors may address climate change and its effects on mental health by discussing it with clients, networking with other mental health professionals to share resources and educate other mental health professionals, and engaging in climate change education and advocacy efforts at the local, national, and international levels.

INTERNATIONAL COUNSELING

Mental illness affects people worldwide, and the vast majority of people who need mental health services do not have access to them. Several factors contribute to the global mental health treatment gap, such as stigma related to mental illness, lack of mental health providers, separating mental health treatment from physical healthcare, and lack of research (Wainberg et al., 2017). Mental health providers, advocates, and leaders have sought to further the development of counseling worldwide to address the global mental health treatment gap. Counseling professionals in the United States have been involved in these efforts; however, Western views do not translate well to countries across the globe. Therefore, care is needed in developing the counseling profession worldwide to be culturally sensitive to the people of each country and their needs, without simply integrating counseling models and approaches from the United States and Europe (Alvarez & Lee, 2012). Additionally, educational requirements and training standards are vastly different among countries (Alvarez & Lee, 2012), with some countries having limited, if any, standards for practicing counseling. Furthermore, there is limited, if any, recognition of counseling as a profession in some countries. Thus, a need exists to expand global mental health services.

Efforts to promote counseling throughout the world include the development of the International Association for Counselling (IAC) that was started as a roundtable with its first international seminar in 1966 in Switzerland. The vision of IAC is "a world where counselling is available to all" (IAC, n.d.). Nearly 100 countries have been represented at the IAC conferences. The organization also has a journal: *International Journal for the Advancement of Counselling*. IAC has a world mapping of the counseling profession on their website that provides information about counseling in countries across the globe, including counseling organizations, training for counselors, the background of counseling, regulatory status, practice settings, challenges and trends, and references for various countries. Additionally, the National Board for Certified Counselor (NBCC) has initiatives to promote international counseling, including international institutes, international counseling certifications, and their mental health facilitators program that trains laypeople in basic helping skills. There is also a European Branch of the American Counseling Association (EB-ACA), as well as counseling associations in several countries across the globe. Furthermore, to promote education and training standards for counselors worldwide, the Council for Accreditation of Counseling and Related Educational Programs (CACREP) developed the International Registry of Counsellor Education Programs (IRCEP).

Many factors affect the development of counseling globally, including the economic, political, social, and cultural contexts of individual countries (Montgomery et al., 2018). The starting point for the development of counseling in many countries is school counseling, with school counselors providing mental health services and advocating for the further development of counseling in their countries (Alvarez & Lee, 2012). In addition to addressing mental health concerns, there is also a need for career counseling globally, which may include career exploration and development for youth within the school system, as well

TABLE 14.5 STEPS FOR PROFESSIONALIZATION OF COUNSELING

STEPS FOR PROFESSIONALIZATION
Engage stakeholders, including practitioners, law makers, clients.
Develop a professional identity.
Educate others (e.g., public, education/training providers, health professionals) about their identity.
Standardize education/licensure requirements, conferences, and portability across regions of the country.
Conduct research within the country, while also consuming research from other countries.
Establish the viability of counseling (e.g., market).
Prioritize client welfare in decision-making processes.

Source: Data from Montgomery, M. L. T., Shepard, B., Mokgolodi, H., Qian, M., & Tang, M. (2018). Professionalization of counseling: Perspectives from different international regions. *International Journal for the Advancement of Counselling, 40*(4), 343–364. https://doi.org/10.1007/s10447-018-9330-6

as career services for adults. In a review of three Asian countries (Korea, Japan, and Taiwan), scholars reported an increased focus on career counseling, while experiencing continued challenges in this area, including counselor competency, evidence-based career interventions, and culturally sensitive individualized services (Gong et al., 2013). Thus, a need exists for addressing mental health concerns, as well as providing career counseling globally.

In reviewing counselors' perspectives from three different countries (Canada, China, and Botswana), Montgomery et al. (2018) found all participants valued and prioritized client welfare, as well as professionalization of counseling due to the need to distinguish counseling from other mental health fields, create counseling jobs, develop training standards, emphasize client well-being, and address the demand for treatment options. Montgomery et al. (2018) identified seven steps to facilitate the professionalization process (see Table 14.5). Through continued advocacy, professionalization efforts, and collaboration of leaders across the globe, it is the hope that counseling will continue to grow internationally to meet the mental health needs of individuals across the world.

NOVEL PSYCHOPHARMACOLOGICAL THERAPIES

Indigenous peoples and cultures across the world have used naturally occurring herbal and psychoactive plants for ritualistic and medicinal use (Heinrich & Casselman, 2018; Thomford et al., 2015). Hallucinogenic and mind-altering compounds (e.g., ayahuasca, ketamine, lysergic acid diethylamide [LSD], methylenedioxy-methamphetamine [MDMA], psilocybin) have garnered increased attention in the pharmacological and clinical research community related to the development of psychedelic assisted therapies.

In a historical review of the use and application of psychedelic drugs, Hall (2022) reported that initial interest and research in novel psychopharmacological therapies was hampered in part by Nixon's "War on Drugs" (p. 26) and the ensuing regulatory tightening and lack of interest by the pharmaceutical industry. The use of psychedelic drugs was criminalized and recreational use went underground from the 1950s through the 2000s. Aday et al. (2020) reported that 2019 was a year of explosive growth in the psychedelic world of therapeutic development and exploration, including industry, science, and regulatory bodies. Additionally, psychedelics have been increasingly decriminalized across the United States and the world resulting in burgeoning interest and shifting attitudes on their use (Aday et al., 2020). It should be noted that decriminalization does not imply legalization (Quality Spores, n.d.). The use of psilocybin-assisted therapy has not been widely approved. However, psychotherapists like Rick Doblin have been active in legitimizing their use. In his TED Talk, Doblin (2021) discussed the steps he has followed to secure permission from the federal government to train psychotherapists in the responsible and ethical use of novel pharmacological assisted therapies with clients who may benefit from this intervention (see www.npr.org/2021/03/19/978814555/rick-doblin-how-can-we-use-psychedelic-assisted-therapy-to-treat-trauma). Doblin founded the Multidisciplinary Association for Psychedelic Studies (MAPS) where research is conducted and psychotherapists are trained in this evidence-based treatment (see maps.org). Their research focus is on MDMA, cannabis, LSD, and ayahuasca, among others (maps.org/our-research).

The integration of these novel psychotherapies into psychiatric and psychological treatments is a growing area of inquiry for multiple physical and mental health conditions. Researchers have reported beneficial effects of psilocybin-assisted psychotherapy for cancer-related distress (Swift et al., 2017), treatment-resistant depression (Watts et al., 2017), PTSD (Grant-Howard & Steele, 2018), trauma-based psychopathology (Bird et al., 2021), older long-term AIDS survivors (Hendricks, 2020), various mental and substance use disorders (Rootman et al., 2021; Smith & Sisti, 2020), and group therapy–based interventions (Agin-Liebes et al., 2021; Hendricks, 2020; Stauffer et al., 2021). Researchers have also found beneficial effects for major depressive disorder, smoking cessation, and alcohol use reduction or abstinence (Aday et al., 2020). In 2021, the National Institutes of Health (NIH) granted the first large study in 50 years toward further exploration of the use of psilocybin to assist with tobacco addiction.

For over two decades, ketamine psychedelic therapy has been studied as a treatment for depression, with Krupitsky and Grinenko (1997) reporting beneficial outcomes for alcoholism and Krystal et al. (2019) adding remarkable evidence for use with treatment-resistant depression. Cherry (2021) provides a survey of psychedelic therapies currently used and discusses the known benefits, efficacy, and potential applications. She states that since there is not a standardized protocol for the implementation of these psychoactive agents with clients in therapy, counselors have developed their own procedures. She adds that these generally include several common elements: (a) the substance dosage is usually small or moderate, (b) an experienced professional is present during the session (it is imperative that neophyte counselors receive training in the use and application of psychedelic therapies, being mindful of whether the substances are decriminalized where they are being used), and (c) doses may be reapplied at the discretion of the practitioner (usually 1–2 weeks between sessions). It should be noted that ketamine and MDMA or ecstasy are different compounds and produce distinct experiences in users (see Brown [2021] for an overview).

Counselors using novel pharmacotherapies, such as psychedelics, spend time preparing the client, the setting, and themselves for the process. Most of these sessions are facilitated during carefully controlled clinical trials supervised by physicians. The goal of the session is integration of the experience, and steps must be taken to maximize benefits and reduce potential harm. A strong and trusting client-therapist relationship and client readiness are crucial. The client must not have any active or recent substance use before the session, and usually a 7-day period of detoxification precedes the experience. The integration process is about processing and making meaning of everything that transpired in the session. These sessions may be repeated over time, as needed. Cherry (2021) underscores that more research is needed to ascertain the long-term effects of these types of novel pharmacotherapies. An overview of psychedelic therapies, conditions treated, potential benefits, and potential negative reactions is outlined in Table 14.6.

There is a current resurgence in the research to examine the effects of these novel therapies. The Johns Hopkins Psychedelics Therapies and Psilocybin Research lab (n.d.) is dedicated to such pursuits. The research lab is funded by private donors and federal grants and aims to explore the efficacy of treatments for specific mental health and substance use disorders, as well as examining the effects with healthy volunteers to better support human flourishing (see www.hopkinsmedicine.org/psychiatry/research/psychedelics-research .html).

Hall (2022) cautions against unbridled use of psychedelics in clinical practice. Trained psychiatric and clinical professionals should carry out application of novel pharmacotherapies under careful supervision, to lessen the risk of misuse or psychological injury to patients. Hall adds that use of these psychoactive drugs in spiritual or religious ritual may also present problems to practitioners if not done in ethical ways. The use of psilocybin and other hallucinogenic compounds in religious ritual by organized groups is considered legal. In 2006, the U.S. Supreme Court unanimously ruled that these groups are protected under the 1993 Religious Freedom Restoration Act (Pew Research Center, 2006). Given the current trend toward decriminalization of these novel pharmacological compounds, we expect that interest in the research and application of these therapy-assisted modalities will continue to rise. You must always be mindful of the legal and ethical issues associated with choosing to engage in these practices and make sure you receive appropriate training before doing so. A number of training programs are available to psychotherapists who are interested in practicing these modalities with their clients (see Resources section for details).

TABLE 14.6 TYPES OF PSYCHEDELICS, CONDITIONS TREATED, AND TREATMENT EFFECTS

PSYCHEDELIC	CONDITIONS TREATED	POTENTIAL BENEFITS	POTENTIAL NEGATIVE REACTIONS
Ayahuasca	Addiction	Reduction in anxiety and depression	Serotonin syndrome
Psilocybin	Anxiety Substance use	Reduction in substance and alcohol use and cravings	Medication interactions
LSD	Addiction Anxiety	Reduction in substance use and cravings	Altered sense of time and space
MDMA and ketamine	Addiction Depression PTSD	Increased feelings of relaxation, well-being, social connection, introspection, and spiritual engagement Reduction in PTSD symptoms	Reality distortion Negative psychological or emotional reactions Intense or overwhelming emotions Paranoia Hallucinations

LSD, lysergic acid diethylamide; MDMA, methylenedioxy-methamphetamine; PTSD, posttraumatic stress disorder.
Source: Data from Brown, E. (2021). *How is ketamine different from MDMA?* https://www .mindbloom.com/blog/how-is-ketamine-different-mdma; Cherry, K. (2021). *What is psychedelic therapy?* https://www.verywellmind.com/psychedelic -therapy-how-does-it-work-5079161

CONCLUSION

The counseling profession is continuously evolving to integrate advancements in technology and new treatment approaches to meet the ever-changing societal trends and needs of individuals, families, and communities. This involves rigorous research and continued education and training. Through this advancement of practice, counselors strive to continue providing quality care and promoting client welfare.

Summary

- Neuro-informed counseling may enhance counseling practice and promote client outcomes through education about the brain and the use of brain-based techniques.

- The growing number of older adults creates a need for more training and research in providing counseling to this population and their caregivers.

- Counseling is evolving to integrate more technology, including telemental health and social media.

- Integration of technology in counseling involves new ethical considerations.

- Climate change affects mental health, and counselors have a responsibility to be informed about and prepared to work with clients regarding this issue.

- It is crucial to advance the counseling profession across the world to address global mental health needs and treatment gaps.

- The research and application of novel psychopharmacological therapies are gaining attention in the counseling community.

Voices From the Field

LoriAnn S. Stretch, PhD, LPC (VA), LCMHC-S (NC), NCC, ACS, BC-TMH
Clinical Associate Professor in Counselor Education, William & Mary

I began working in telehealth in the mid-1990s well before there was any official guidance on how to engage in telehealth. Fortunately, we now have ethical and legal guidance to help us protect our clients as we engage in telehealth. In fact, the COVID-19 pandemic has firmly established telehealth as an acceptable modality for behavioral health treatment.

I started providing telehealth out of necessity. I had clients who were struggling with child care, work/life balance, and transportation. Telehealth provided a means for continuity of care when in-person services simply were not feasible. As a clinician, telehealth allowed me to reach and assist individuals who might not otherwise have access to care.

One such client was John (pseudonym). John was 76 years old and lived in rural North Carolina. His wife of 25 years had suddenly left him and had filed for divorce. While this life transition would be startling for anyone, for John it was debilitating, because John was unable to read due to a severe learning disability. Our initial consultation was via the telephone. Initially, John was hesitant because he was unsure of the counseling process and what to expect. I spent a significant portion of initial consultation educating John about counseling and providing open space for him to share his story. As he talked, I gained insight into how debilitating his illiteracy was for him on a day-to-day basis.

John was struggling to pay bills, take his medication as prescribed, and communicate his needs effectively. As a telehealth provider, I understood how long silences were necessary due to the lack of visual cues in our phone exchanges and the silence provided time for John to process and respond. This additional space in telephone sessions is often uncomfortable for new therapists who feel an urgency to fill the space. However, this extra time was essential for John, who needed unconditional positive regard to talk about his shame and difficulties.

Another benefit of using telehealth in John's case was access to his support system, who lived a distance away from John but cared deeply about him. John was very close to his daughter. I was able to conference call her into a session with John's permission. During our family session, I was able to provide resources to John and his daughter about four reader applications that had been developed for individuals with visual impairments. These reader applications would read products, medication labels, bills, mail, etc. for John and he would now be able to "read" on his own. They were on board but there was one more issue, John did not have a cell phone.

John needed a cell phone to be able to use the application he and his daughter selected. As a telehealth provider, I need to know the community resources available to clients. I did a little research and discovered that John qualified for Lifeline, a federal program that is funded through the Universal Service Fund fee that appears on most cellular bills. John's daughter was relieved to learn of the plan and with her help, John was able to secure a phone within 2 weeks and the app they had selected. John's daughter visited one weekend to help John set up the cell phone and the app. John was ecstatic to be able to "read" on his own without assistance.

John and I continued to work together for 6 more weeks. Now that his basic needs were met, he was able to be more self-sufficient. Consequently, his depression and anxiety dropped significantly, and we were able to begin processing the grief and loss of his divorce. Thanks to telehealth, I was available to John, who later reported that he would have never sought help in-person due to being embarrassed. I was able to advocate for John and empower him and his support system, which resulted in wellness and autonomy for my client.

A Call to Action

Research current literature about novel pharmacological therapies used in conjunction with psychotherapy. Outline the benefits and potential drawbacks of such treatments. Would you choose to advocate for the legalization of these practices? Why or why not? Summarize your findings and present them to the class. Discuss the legal and ethical implications for counseling practice.

Case Study 14.1

David is a 32-year-old veteran with a history of PTSD and alcohol abuse. He was mandated to inpatient treatment at the Veterans Administration hospital where you work, after an arrest for assault at a local bar he frequented. David tells you he feels lost, hopeless, and helpless. He has tried everything since returning home from the war in

(continued)

Case Study 14.1 (continued)

Afghanistan. During a group therapy session, David casually mentions that he read an article about the use of ketamine, MDMA, and magic mushrooms to treat depression and PTSD. He wants to know what you think about these therapies and how he can access this type of treatment.

RESPONSE QUESTIONS

1. How do you respond to David in the session? Do you provide your opinion about these types of treatment?
2. What would you do regarding this request during and after your session with David?

Going Within

What are your thoughts about the integration of technology (e.g., telemental health, social media) within counseling? Do you see yourself integrating technology within your future work with clients? Why or why not? What interests and challenges you about considering this integration? Has this chapter caused you to think differently about your personal use of technology (e.g., social media)? If so, in what ways?

Group Process

As a group, discuss your current social media practices. What applications do you currently use (e.g., Facebook, Instagram, Twitter, others)? As a beginning counselor, what is your stance about social media use? What would you do if one of your clients finds your profile and sends you a friend request or starts following you? Would you make any changes based on what we have discussed in this chapter? Why or why not?

RESOURCES

ACA Statement of Climate Change: https://www.counseling.org/docs/default-source/resolutions/climate-change-statement--november-2018.pdf?sfvrsn=a65c552c_2

California Institute of Integral Studies (n.d.). About the certificate in psychedelic-assisted therapies and research. https://www.ciis.edu/research-centers/center-for-psychedelic-therapies-and-research/about-the-certificate-in-psychedelic-assisted-therapies-and-research

Effective remote counseling: https://www.counseling.org/knowledge-center/mental-health-resources/trauma-disaster/telehealth-information-and-counselors-in-health-care/remote-counseling

Icahn School of Medicine at Mount Sinai (n.d.). The Center for Psychedelic Psychotherapy & Trauma Research. https://icahn.mssm.edu/research/center-psychedelic-psychotherapy-trauma-research/training-education

International Association for Counseling: https://www.iac-irtac.org

Johns Hopkins Psychedelics Research and Psilocybin Therapies: https://www.hopkinsmedicine.org/psychiatry/research/psychedelics-research.html

Kolmes, K. (n.d.). Social media policy. https://www.drkkolmes.com/docs/socmed.pdf

Multidisciplinary Association for Psychedelic Studies (n.d.). Information for people seeking training in psychedelic-assisted therapy. https://archive.maps.org/news/posts/9583-information-for-people-seeking-training-in-psychedelic-assisted-therapy

Naropa University (n.d.). Psychedelic-assisted therapies certificate. https://www.naropa.edu/academics/extended-campus/psychedelic-assisted-therapies-certificate

Ratts, M. J., Singh, A. A., Nassar-McMillan, S., Butler, S. K., & McCullough, J. R. (2016).. Multicultural and Social Justice Counseling Competencies: Guidelines for the counseling profession. Journal of Multicultural Counseling and Development, 44(1), 28–48. https://doi.org/10.1002/jmcd.12035

Rick Doblin: https://www.npr.org/2021/03/19/978814555/rick-doblin-how-can-we-use-psychedelic-assisted-therapy-to-treat-trauma

Salt City Psychedelic Therapies and Research (n.d.). Psychedelic therapy training program. https://www.scptr.org/psychedelic-therapy-training-program

Access this podcast at http://connect.springerpub.com/content/book/978-0-8261-6386-8/chapter/ch14.

KEY REFERENCES

Only key references appear in the print edition. The full reference list appears in the digital product found on https://connect.springerpub.com/content/book/978-0-8261-6386-8/chapter/ch14

Adams, S. M., Rice, M. J., Jones, S. L., Herzog, E., Mackenzie, L. J., & Oleck, L. G. (2018). Telemental health: Standards, reimbursement, and interstate practice. Journal of American Psychiatric Nurses Association, 24(4), 295–305. https://doi.org/doi:10.1177/1078390318763963.

Administration for Community Living. (2021). 2020 profile of older Americans. Author. https://acl.gov/sites/default/files/Aging%20and%20Disability%20in%20America/2020ProfileOlderAmericans.Final_.pdf

Alvarez, C. M., & Lee, S. (2012). An international perspective on professional counselor identity. Journal of Professional Counseling, 39(1), 42–54. https://doi.org/10.1080/15566382.2012.12033881

Berry, H. L., Bowen, K., & Kjellstrom, T. (2010). Climate change and mental health: A causal pathways framework. International Journal of Public Health, 55(2), 123–132. https://doi.org/10.1007/s00038-009-0112-0

Clayton, S., Manning, C. M., Krygsman, K., & Speiser, M. (2017). Mental health and our changing climate: Impacts, implications, and guidance. American Psychological Association, ecoAmerica. https://www.apa.org/news/press/releases/2017/03/mental-health-climate.pdf

Crtalic, A. K., Gibbs, R. L., Sprong, M. E., & Dell, T. F. (2015). Boundaries with social media: Ethical considerations for rehabilitation professionals. *Journal of Applied Rehabilitation Counseling, 46*(3), 44–50. https://doi.org/10.1891/0047-2220.46.3.44

Fullen, M. C. (2018). Ageism and the counseling profession: Causes, consequences, and methods for counteraction. *The Professional Counselor, 8*(2), 104–114. https://doi.org/10.15241/mcf.8.2.104

Hayes, K., Blashki, G., Wiseman, J., Burke, S., & Reifels, L. (2018). Climate change and mental health: Risks, impacts and priority actions. *International Journal of Mental Health Systems, 12,* 28. https://doi.org/10.1186/s13033-018-0210-6

Hilty, D. M., Ferrer, D. C., Parish, M. B., Johnston, B., Callahan, E. J., & Yellowlees, P. M. (2013). The effectiveness of telemental health: A 2013 review. *Telemedicine Journal and E-Health, 19*(6), 444–454. https://doi.org/10.1089/tmj.2013.0075

Ivey, A. E., & Zalaquett, C. P. (2011). Neuroscience and counseling: Central issue for social justice leaders. *Journal for Social Action in Counseling & Psychology, 3*(1), 103–116. https://doi.org/10.33043/JSACP.3.1.103-116

Jenkins, Y. (2019). Caregivers for the elderly: Clinical issues and intervention. *Women & Therapy, 42*(3–4), 447–468. https://doi.org/10.1080/02703149.2019.1622905

Johnson, L. (2011). Clients, connections, and social media. *Annals of Psychotherapy and Integrative Health, 14*(1), 10–11.

Luke, C. (2019). *Neuroscience for counselors and therapists: Integrating the sciences of mind and brain* (2nd ed.). Sage.

Siegel, D. J. (2012). *The developing mind: How relationships and the brain interact to shape who we are* (2nd ed.). Guilford Press.

Index

Professional Quality of Life Scale (ProQOL), 79, 82
professional self-care, 83
project implicit, 54
psilocybin-assisted therapy, 392
psychiatry profession, 6
psychoanalytic theory, 32, 34
psychoanalytic therapy, 148–149
  countertransference, 148
  multicultural considerations, 149
  transference, 148
psychodrama, 320, 321
psychodynamic theories
  assumptions, 147
  existential-humanistic theories, 149–151
  gestalt therapy, 152–153
  issues and root causes, 148
  logotherapy, 152
  object relations theory, 147–148
  person-centered therapy, 153–154
  pros and cons, 145–147
  psychoanalytic therapy, 148–149
  psychodynamics, 142
psychological domain, self-care, 84
psychological model, addiction, 244–245
psychological safety loss, 294
psychopharmacological therapies
  hallucinogenic and mind-altering compounds, 391
  psychedelic drugs, 392–394
psychotherapy
  integrative, 167
  meta-analytic research, 167
Public Offender Counselor Association (POCA), 190

quantitative critical analysis (QuantCrit), 232–233
questions, 131–132

Racial Cultural Identity Development Model (R/CID), 41
Racial Identity Development Theories
  American Indian Identity Development model, 42–43
  Asian American Identity Development Model, 41
  Biracial Identity Development Model, 42
  Cross's Black development, 40–41
  Latino Identity Orientations, 42
  Minority Identity Development Model (MID), 41

Racial Cultural Identity Development Model (R/CID), 41
  timeline, 43
  White Racial Identity Development (WRID) Model, 42
rational emotive behavior therapy (REBT), 155–157
rational therapy (RT), 155
reciprocal determinism, 33
recovery community centers (RCCs), 258–259
recovery high schools (RHSs), 259
recovery management checkup (RMC) model, 259
recovery support services, substance use
  collegiate recovery programs (CRPs), 259–260
  housing, 259
  management and monitoring, 259
  mutual support groups, 260
  recovery coaches, 258
  recovery community centers (RCCs), 258–259
  recovery high schools (RHSs), 259
reflections
  conciseness, 128
  content, 129
  feeling reflection, 128–129
  feeling word categories, 127–128
  immediacy, 130
  minimizing phrases, 128
  summarization, 130–131
rehabilitation facilities, 200
relational-cultural theory (RCT), 166
relational domain, self-care, 84
relationality, 79
religious institutions, 198–199
research and program evaluation
  consumer, 213–216
  outcome evaluation, 213
  process evaluation, 213
  social justice and advocacy, 217–218
residential treatment, 187
Roberts' Seven-Stage, crisis model, 283
rural counseling settings, 204–205

SAMHSA. See Substance Abuse and Mental Health Services Administration
SCAMPER model, 314, 315
school-based mental health counselors, 6
school counselors
  action strategies, 204
  elementary school counseling, 202